The Great Composers

John Farleigh's wood engraving
for Shaw's short story,
'Don Giovanni Explains'
1934

The
Great
Composers

REVIEWS
AND
BOMBARDMENTS
BY
BERNARD SHAW

———

Edited with
an introduction by
Louis Crompton

University of California Press
Berkeley, Los Angeles, London

University of California Press
Berkeley and Los Angeles, California

University of California Press, Ltd.
London, England

Library of Congress Catalog
Card Number: 76-14311

Printed in the United States of America

Contents

PART THREE: The Opera House

PART FOUR: English Music

Editor's Introduction

People who are quite familiar with Shaw as a playwright and social reformer are often amazed to learn that he was also a music critic. Yet music was his first and longest love. His published writings on the subject range over a remarkable seventy-five years, from his youth till his death in 1950. He had grown up in a thoroughly musical environment in Dublin. His mother was a singer in opera and oratorio, and an Irish impresario, George John Vandaleur Lee, was for several years a member of the Shaw household and rehearsed his performances there. If Shaw had had a good voice he might well have become an operatic baritone, and the English stage might have lost its second greatest dramatist. As it happened, he had a nondescript voice and no special talent for playing the piano, the one instrument he tried to master. But his early fascination with dramatic music stimulated him to accumulate a considerable knowledge of theory through reading, and to become enough of a pianist to be able to play scores at home, a necessity for any serious music lover in the days before recordings.

This background proved useful when he abandoned Dublin and arrived in London in 1876 as an impecunious young man of twenty. For two years he "ghosted" for Lee (who had also removed himself to the metropolis) as a music critic for *The Hornet*. Seven years later he began writing on music for a number of publications, among them *The Dramatic Review, Art Corner,* the *Magazine of Music,* and the *Pall Mall Gazette.* In 1888 he became the second-string reviewer for the *Star,* and the next year its major reviewer under the pseudonym of Corno di Bassetto, a performance that brought him his first real public fame as a journalist. Finally, he served as music critic for *The World* for four years, till 1894.†

In these reviews Shaw wrote what is perhaps the most lively and brilliant musical journalism ever penned. He once boasted that he could make a deaf stockbroker read his two pages on music in *The World.* No reputation was too sacred for Shaw to demolish, no public

---

†The reader will find a good account of these journalistic stints in the preface to Dan H. Laurence's *How to Become a Musical Critic,* 1961.

idol was safe from his quizzical probing. Shaw became a master of humorous and satirical English prose not as a would-be novelist—the novels he wrote during these years are all failures—but as a critic of concerts. Fortunately, his knowledge never congealed into pedantry. Pedantry, of course, is a special temptation to music critics, for obvious reasons. Music is the most technical of the arts and critics are naturally inclined to establish their credentials by one-upmanship on points of technique. Shaw once had occasion to review a book called *Form and Design in Music* by Heathcote Statham, which had analyzed a Mozart symphony in this fashion: "The principal subject, hitherto heard in the treble, is transferred to the bass (Ex. 28), the violins playing a new counterpoint to it instead of the original mere accompaniment figure of the first part. Then the parts are reversed, the violins taking the subject and the basses the counterpoint figure, and so on till we come to a close on the dominant of D minor, a nearly related key (commencement of Ex. 29), and then comes the passage by which we return to the first subject in its original form and key."

Shaw commented impishly, "How succulent that is: and how full of Mesopotamian words." He parodied such musical "parsing" by analyzing Hamlet's soliloquy in the same style: "Shakespear, dispensing with the customary exordium, announces his subject at once in the infinitive, in which mood it is presently repeated after a short connecting passage in which, brief as it is, we recognize the alternate and negative forms on which so much of the significance of repetition depends"!

But engaging as Shaw's fun is, he is not just a trenchant musical journalist with a literary flair. He is also among the most serious and profound critics of the art in the English language. This is because he possesses the one thing any philosophic critic must have: a clearly defined set of values. Behind the sparkle is a consistent point of view, and each of the composers he writes about is judged by it. This is a quality musical journalism and even musical scholarship too often lacks, and it is the quality that makes Shaw not just a good critic but a great one.

But if Shaw is a writer on music *par excellence*, why has his achievement been so little appreciated? The main reason is its inaccessibility and Shaw's own poor editing. Shaw had published *The Perfect Wagnerite* in 1898, and later revised it through four editions, down to 1922. But most of his reviews lay buried in nineteenth-century magazines and newspapers. In 1932, when Shaw made up the collected edition of his works, he simply reprinted, without headings or comment, the longest unbroken series of his writings on music—the weekly columns in the *World* from May 28, 1890, to August 8, 1894. The result is an uncharted miscellany, with profundities and ephemera jumbled together, and so clotted with the names of extinct performers that only an enthusiast or a scholar is tempted to persevere. Shaw's overly modest introductory paragraph recommends the three volumes only to those who like to read about "dead prima donnas." Three years later, when his wife pressed him into reprinting his *Star* criticisms, Shaw left the editorial chore to her with the result that even the chronology is misleading, the book being published as *London Music in 1888–89*, though the last hundred pages belong to 1890.

What popular reputation Shaw now has as a writer on music he owes to his later editors. In 1955 Eric Bentley put together a good paperback anthology—now long out of print—of miscellaneous reviews from these four volumes. But the major credit must go to Dan H. Laurence. Six years later Mr. Laurence, who is an indefatigable Shaw bibliographer, edited a collection of unreprinted articles and reviews called *How to Become a Musical Critic* which, in effect, did the crucial job Shaw had been disinclined to tackle. For, besides making available for the first time important reviews of Bach, Mozart, Beethoven, and Berlioz, Laurence also tracked down a number of substantial critical essays on Handel, Mozart, Rossini, Liszt, Wagner, Strauss, and Elgar that Shaw had written not as occasional pieces inspired by performances, but as considered judgments of these composers *sub specie aeternitatis.* These latter essays, which Shaw had never reprinted, are naturally on a significantly higher plane than the day-by-day or week-by-week commentaries, fine as many of them are. Laurence's plan, however, led him to include in his collection all of Shaw's unreprinted writings on music apart from some juvenilia in *The Hornet,* and this intention, admirable enough, of completing the scholarly record, naturally involved the inclusion of a good deal of skim milk with the new cream.

What I have tried to do is to make a collection that comes closer, so to speak, to pure cream than any heretofore. It aims at presenting the heart and soul of what Shaw thought about music over his long lifetime. It does this by presenting, in Part One, his broad views on the social function of music and on musical history. In the two next sections I have placed together, under the names of individual composers and their compositions, all the significant judgments I have found, whether in the form of essays, reviews of performances, or paragraphs written by the way when Shaw was dealing with other matters. In the last section, I have collected his major thoughts on a subject that much exercised him—the failure of the British in the nineteenth century to rival the Germans or come up to the earlier level of Purcell, a question that led Shaw to wrestle energetically with the problem of contemporary musical history. This volume does not reprint all the significant writings by Shaw on music. For instance, it touches only incidentally on some subjects he dealt with repeatedly—the art of singing, the stage management of opera, the economic side of concerts, standards of musical journalism, etc. But it does contain just about everything he had to say about the art of composition as it is reflected in the works of the great composers. The essential Shaw is here. What the reader has before him is, in effect, the book on musical history that Shaw could have written, and should have written, but never did write. It selects from the three or four thousand paragraphs Shaw wrote on music the one thousand most important.

In this welter of judgments, is there a central point of view? By calling Shaw a "philosophical" critic I have, in effect, implied that there is. In attempting to understand Shaw, however, it is necessary to grasp that, for him, aesthetic and social judgments are inextricably connected. Shaw's philosophy of music is not reducible to a simple formula, it is in its very essence a dialectical philosophy, but it was also self-consciously partisan. Shaw never posed as an impartial judge meting out abstract "justice" in his music columns. He frankly compared his journalism with his efforts in political campaigns— with "electioneering." He even apologized to hapless artists who might, in this critical warfare, find themselves unexpectedly raked by the crossfire of what he called "the conflict of art movements." We cannot, he wrote, "get away from the critic's tempers, his impatiences, his sorenesses, his friendships, his spite, his enthusiasms (amatory and other), nay, his very politics and religion if they are touched by what he criticizes." No doubt Shaw, if pressed, would have admitted that we must finally discount the critic's private crochets and personal susceptibilities. He would, however, have defended the introduction of serious political and religious concerns into the critic's judgment of the art of composition. The reader will note that one section of Part One is headed "Music and Revolution" and another "Music and Religion."

But if Shaw, like Plato, conceived music as a political and moral activity, where does he stand? Was he a radical, a conservative, or a revolutionary? To readers who have taken him at his word and placed him unequivocally in the revolutionary camp the question may seem absurd. But consider, for instance, his analysis of the situation in Europe after the death of Beethoven. As he saw it, three different schools had aspired to follow in Beethoven's path—the first group Shaw dubbed the "Titanists," the second were the academics (or Mendelssohnians), and the third the Wagnerites. In his brilliant centenary broadcast in 1927, Shaw hailed Beethoven as "a giant wave in that storm of the human spirit that produced the French Revolution," and his sympathy both for Beethoven and the Revolution is what we would expect from a Fabian, a democrat, and an ardent egalitarian. He enthusiastically approved Beethoven's willingness to trample on the formal patterns of the eighteenth century when they stood in the way of his own "giant moods." What could be more revolutionary? Compared to Beethoven the rebellious sansculotte, Mozart is depicted by Shaw as a lackey in livery.

Yet Shaw definitely ranked Mozart above Beethoven, even as a symphonist, that is, in exactly the form in which Beethoven is greatest. This conservatism comes out even more strongly in Shaw's judgment of the generation that tried to exploit the sensational new style Beethoven had created. His term for this trend in nineteenth-century music was "Titanism." Writing in 1889, a hundred years after the French Revolution, Shaw contemplated the neurotic and grandiose music that had followed in its wake and heartily decried "its effort, its hurry, its excitement, its aspiration without purpose, its forced and invariably disappointing climaxes, its exhaustion and decay." Whom did he have in mind? His estimates of Rossini, Liszt, Meyerbeer, Tchaikowsky, and even Berlioz indicate that he saw all of them as exploiting Beethoven's nervous energy without his control or high purpose. And it is significant that Shaw turns to Mozart when he judges these composers: "In the ardent regions where all the rest are excited and vehement, Mozart alone is completely self-possessed: where they are clutching their bars with a grip of iron and forging them with Cyclopean blows, his gentleness of touch never deserts him: he is considerate, economical, practical under the same pressure of inspiration that throws your Titan into convulsions."

All this might appear to put Shaw squarely among those Victorians who looked backward musically. Yet in his centenary essay on Mozart, Shaw argues that Mozart's formal training was beside the

point and that he would have been as great a composer, on the basis
of his innate expressiveness, if he had written in the free forms of
Liszt! More dramatically, Shaw's anti-conservatism appears in his
war on the Mendelssohn-Schumann-Brahms tradition. Against its
earnest respectability and scholarly scruples Shaw never ceased to
inveigh with the vehemence of the born rebel. He especially objected
to the English over-estimation of Mendelssohn. "For the musical
critic in England," Shaw wrote in response to an irate reader who
had taken exception to his views on *St. Paul*, "Mendelssohn is The
Enemy." Shaw scoffed at "the Sunday-school profundities" of the
Italian Symphony, and complained that the Scotch Symphony
"would be great if it were not so confoundedly genteel." He thought
Mendelssohn's extremely popular oratorios were parasitic on
Handel the way Victorian blank verse tragedy was parasitic on
Shakespeare. Like Wagner, he was firmly convinced that "the modern Mendelssohnian 'culture,' with all its refinement, its elegance, its
reticence, and its 'chastity'" was "far too negative to equip a conductor for a struggle with Bach or Beethoven."

Anyone reading Shaw today may be startled by the passion of his
anti-Mendelssohnism. But Victorian Mendelssohn-worship was carried to a point we may now find it difficult to imagine. The musical
"establishment" set up Mendelssohn's music as *the* norm to which
young men should aspire, and new musicians were judged by the
success with which they met this standard. Perhaps the most telling
evidence of the Mendelssohn-mania is the fact that the first edition
of Grove's great *Dictionary* devoted sixty pages to Mendelssohn and
only thirty to Wagner. But Shaw's final objection to Mendelssohn
was religious. "Art has never been great," he later wrote in the preface to *Back to Methuselah*, "when it was not producing an iconog-
raphy for a live religion." Shaw admired the poetry of the Bible, the
paintings of Giotto and Michelangelo, Handel's Messiah, and Bach's
B Minor Mass as pinnacles of western art, which were at the same
time the greatest expressions of the faith of their times. But like
Goethe and Carlyle, Shaw believed that the religious inspiration of
Europe after the Enlightenment had to take a form different from
dogma or biblicism. Mozart, Beethoven, and Wagner in writing
The Magic Flute, the Ninth Symphony, the *Ring*, and *Parsifal* had
crowned their lives with works which Shaw thought genuinely re-
ligious in the new dispensation of revolutionary humanitarianism.
Popular religious music like Mendelssohn's oratorios, on the other

hand, catered to those Puritans who shunned the theater but revelled in the melodrama of hellfire and damnation. It was the blood-sacrifice theology of *St. Paul* and *Elijah* that convinced Shaw that Mendelssohn had sinned against the light. "When I am asked to spend an afternoon," he wrote, "listening to oratorios that must stand and fall, not by the grace and tenderness of their prettiest strains, but by the depth and moral dignity of their conception, then Mendelssohn gets roughly handled."

Shaw found this "depth and dignity" in, of all places, the opera house. Opera was the form of art that Shaw knew first as a boy and the one he wrote most about. But he held it in very mixed esteem. He derided it, tolerated it benevolently, inveighed against its sillinesses, and rhapsodized about it. Throughout all this he also showed one very marked bias. While the taste of the public in England ran heavily in favor of Italian and French opera, Shaw rarely praised an opera composer who was not German. He had a very un-English enthusiasm for Gluck: his review of *Orfeo* is perhaps the closest he ever comes to a rave. Shaw placed Mozart at the very summit of operatic art, both for his unique ability to characterize men and women dramatically and for the power of the finales of *The Marriage of Figaro* and *Don Giovanni*. Indeed, Shaw called *Don Giovanni* the greatest of all operas and boasted that his early acquaintance with it in his mother's house was the most important part of his artistic education. He also wrote more about it than any other piece of music. This anthology reprints Shaw's essay of 1887 on the hundredth anniversary of its premiere, his defense of the opera against Ruskin's moral strictures, and a final evaluation in 1918. But *Don Giovanni* worked as strongly on Shaw's imagination as it did on his critical powers. In 1887 he wrote not only his review but also a short story called "Don Giovanni Explains," in which he projected himself into Mozart's hero and retold his adventures from a Shavian point of view. When he reprinted this tale in 1934, he commissioned the English artist John Farleigh to do a woodcut of the final scene, which we have reproduced as the frontispiece to this collection. Then, in *Man and Superman*, he made Mozart's opera the imaginative basis for his most brilliant literary production, the Don Juan in Hell dialogue.

Shaw thought *Fidelio* was a great opera foolishly neglected by opera managements. But he has mainly contempt for composers like Meyerbeer and Rossini who used the new effects Beethoven had created in an empty, mechanical way. The operas of Donizetti and

Bellini he dismissed as worn-out war-horses, not foreseeing their resurrection in the twentieth century as vehicles for spectacular voices. He acknowledges Verdi's greatness and immediately recognized Puccini as his successor, but the praise for both men comes grudgingly from someone who cannot take Italian composers quite seriously. To Shaw the philosopher-critic, their operas are small beer compared to the real masterpieces of the nineteenth-century musical stage—the first three parts of *The Ring, Tristan, The Mastersingers,* and *Parsifal.* It was Wagner and Wagner alone who stood on a double pinnacle—as the successor of Beethoven in the great tradition of German music, and as a poet who redeemed the opera from triviality by introducing serious social themes and dramatic integrity. Shaw also hailed Wagner's essays as important contributions to aesthetic theory and to social thought. Naturally their socialist bias appealed to him, and their anti-semitism struck him as only a silly bee in Wagner's bonnet, which could be ignored. On this latter point, Shaw was lacking in prescience: strongly anti-racist himself, he failed to guess what a virulent form racism would take in twentieth-century Germany.

In making his claims for Wagner, Shaw persistently represents himself as a crusading pioneer. But this view has been challenged recently by informed critics on the ground that the battle for Wagner's music had been fought and won before Shaw entered the lists. True, the English had failed to appreciate Wagner when he had served as a conductor in London in 1855 and the first translations of his prose in the *Musical World* had been notoriously bad. But Edward Dannreuther and Ashton Ellis had produced much better ones, and Francis Hueffer had also ably espoused Wagner's cause in his position as critic for *The Times.* Shaw himself went so far as to admit that the one way a conductor could assure himself of a full house was to announce a Wagner evening. How could he, then, in 1935, represent himself as having fought for a "coming man" who was not an accepted classic?

The answer was that though London concert-goers delighted in Wagner, the opera public did not. Hueffer had complained that the English liked serious music and liked the stage, but they did not care for serious music on the stage. When Shaw began writing for the *Star* only the early operas, up to *Lohengrin,* were regularly sung in England. None of the half dozen music-dramas that formed the summit of Wagner's work had been produced by an English company, and during the next seven years only one—*The Mastersingers*—was put into production under an English management at Covent Garden. To hear the others it was necessary to travel to Bayreuth or depend on rare performances by imported German companies, such as the production of *The Ring* that Mahler brought to London in 1892.

In 1898, four years after he had given up his last post as a music critic, Shaw published *The Perfect Wagnerite*, the only book he ever wrote on a musical subject. The interesting fact, however, is that less than a quarter of the book is on music. His main aim is to show how *The Ring* reflects the socialist and anarchist ideals of the German revolutionary movement of 1848–49, in which Wagner was deeply involved. Shaw gives a lengthy analysis of *The Rhinegold* as a "poetic vision of unregulated industrial capitalism as it was made known in Germany in the middle of the nineteenth century by Engels's Condition of the Laboring Classes in England." His case for this interpretation is convincing, and has been endorsed by a writer as different in temperament as Thomas Mann. In Siegfried, Shaw found a vital and spontaneous anarchist hero, who challenged all the bourgeois codes, rather after the fashion of the New Left of our own day. But it is his interpretation of Wagner's Wotan that is most interesting and suggestive. For Shaw, Wotan is everything we now call "The Establishment." That is to say, he represents civil authority in its executive and judicial roles, well-intentioned, but fatally compromised in its exercise of power. What adds poignant interest to this conception is that Wotan is well aware of the dilemma his repressive role has forced upon him and secretly hopeful that he will be superseded by a freer and more humane order.

Wagner's influence on Shaw as a music critic was enormous and all-embracing. Both exalt Mozart and Gluck, deprecate Meyerbeer and Mendelssohn, decry fashionable virtuosity, and prefer music drama to conventional opera. Yet it is arguable that Shaw would have been a "Wagnerite" if Wagner had never been born. Everything in his make-up impelled him in this direction—his contempt for academic art (whether literary, plastic, or musical), his political radicalism with its anti-aristocratic and anti-bourgeois slant, his humanitarian free-thinking and his vitalist approach to religion and morals—even his vegetarianism, anti-vivisectionism and teetotallism. The fact is that Shaw and Wagner shared a complex of ideas common to the radical left in nineteenth-century Europe.

Shaw's most significant summing-up of his views appears in his essay, "The Religion of the Pianoforte," written just at the end of his career as a professional music critic, early in 1894. This is his clearest general statement on the nature of music. For Shaw, music is powerful because it appeals directly to the senses and creates immediate and intense pleasure. Shaw is enough of an anti-Puritan to think that human life should be pleasurable and not painful, and enough of a Puritan to decry the cruder pleasures of drugs, sex, and blood sports. Music is the answer to this dilemma, since it allows us to become "skilled voluptuaries" without being self-destructive or cruel. Moreover, through this positive education of the senses, we can experience in music an intensity of emotion far beyond what other arts, such as literature, provide. Shaw contrasts the feeling a schoolboy might have on reading a description of a duel by Scott or Dumas with the far more vivid experience of playing the fight scene from *Les Huguenots* on the piano. One notes the connection of music with drama in this analysis. "I searched all the music I came across for the sake of its poetic or dramatic content," Shaw admitted, "and played the pages in which I found drama or poetry over and over again, whilst I never returned to those in which the music was trying to exist ornamentally for its own sake and had no real content at all." Thus, he tells us, "when I came across the consciously perfect art work in the music dramas of Wagner, I ran no risk of hopelessly misunderstanding it as the academic musicians did."

Where Shaw thought drama was incomplete without music, Wagner thought music was incomplete without a verbal text. In *The Art Work of the Future* Wagner shows the great German symphonic tradition of Haydn, Mozart, and Beethoven culminating in the setting of Schiller's Ode in the finale of the Ninth Symphony. In this movement, music, hitherto only able to express moods and feelings, can now show them evolving logically out of each other at the command of the "Moral Will." Shaw is also interested in music's moral effect. Indeed, he thinks any educator who begins with facts and logic is putting the cart before the horse. The aesthetic is the key to the intellectual. "High thinking" can only evolve out of "high feeling." This in turn will influence us as social beings. As he puts it elsewhere, the advantage of a sonata over a syllogism is that the sonata can inspire courage, awe, and devotion. Consequently, music is both the root and crown of knowledge.

However you may despise romantic novels, however loftily you may be absorbed in the future destiny of what is highest in humanity, so that for mere light literature you turn from Dante to Goethe, or from Schopenhauer to Comte, or from Ruskin to Ibsen—still, if you do not know Die Zauberflöte, if you have never soared into the heaven where they sing the choral ending of the Ninth Symphony, if Der Ring des Nibelungen is nothing to you but a newspaper phrase, then you are an ignoramus, however eagerly you may pore in your darkened library over the printed labels of those wonders that can only be communicated by the transubstantiation of pure feeling [into] pure tone. The greatest of the great among poets, from Æschylus to Wagner, have been poet-musicians: how then can any man disdain music or pretend to have completed his culture without it?

The late-Victorian musical world was sharply divided into two camps—the more traditional and academic critics favored Brahms, the radicals Wagner. Anti-Brahmsianism was therefore almost a part of the Wagnerian religion. This accounts for what in this collection will probably startle the modern reader most—Shaw's violent depreciation of Brahms. Shaw ridiculed Brahms as the "Leviathan Maunderer," and never tired of lambasting the German Requiem with impish irreverence—"I do not deny that the Requiem is a solid piece of music manufacture. You feel at once that it could only have come from the establishment of a first-class undertaker." Shaw decried Brahms' formalism—"Euphuism, which is the beginning and end of Brahms' big works, is no more to my taste in music than in literature," and denied that he had any serious constructive capacity in his symphonies, which he dismissed as "really a string of incomplete dance and ballad tunes." He admitted Brahms' "extraordinary faculty of harmonic worksmanship" and his real charm in less pretentious works like the vocal quartets. Rereading his 1888 *World* estimate of a Brahms concerto in 1936, Shaw was a bit shocked at his own attacks, which he now deprecated as "hasty" and "silly." But he was unrepentant as late as 1920, when, in an enthusiastic essay on Elgar, he wrote that "Brahms, with a facility as convenient as Elgar's, was a musical sensualist with intellectual affectations, and succeeded only as an incoherent voluptuary, too fundamentally addleheaded to make anything great out of the delicious musical luxuries he wallowed in." Since this was written twenty-five years after his other anti-Brahms statements, when the partisan war between the Brahmsians and Wagnerites had long ended, and Shaw's prejudice against absolute music had vanished, it perhaps deserves as much weight as the better-known 1936 "apology."

Walter Pater had declared in *The Renaissance* that all art should aspire to the condition of music. By this, Pater meant that painting and poetry were to become, like music, absolute, formal, and devoid of didacticism. The arabesque was to prevail over the story or sermon. Shaw took exactly the opposite view, and held that music itself was greatest when it approached literature, i.e. was least absolute. This is clearly the premise behind "The Religion of the Pianoforte." But in the long run Shaw did not find this position on absolute music a tenable one. History was against him. Where Shaw's musical creed looked back to Beethoven and Wagner, it was Pater whose aesthetic forecast the direction of the twentieth century, that is, the art of Eliot, Joyce, Picasso, and Stravinsky. Though the first world war is the watershed that most clearly marks the line between the Age of Revolt and the Age of Formalism, the tide was running strongly in the formalist direction by the mid-nineties, as Shaw himself became more and more aware. It is one of the ironies of Shaw's career as a music critic that two months after he published "The Religion of the Pianoforte," the definitive statement of his beliefs, he should have published a review announcing that they were superannuated.

The occasion was a performance of Charles Villiers Stanford's music for Tennyson's *Becket* in April, 1894. There is a prevision of the way Shaw's mind was moving in his review of Parry's *Art of Music*, published the week before. There, Shaw had argued that the true line of development in the nineteenth century had been from absolute to program music. But Shaw admitted that even before Wagner's death, absolute music "was reviving in the hands of men who were musicians alone, and not wits, dramatists, poets, or romancers." Then, in the *Becket* review, Shaw wrote, almost with alarm, "Something is happening to my attitude towards absolute music. Perhaps I am fossilizing, perhaps I am merely beginning to acquire at last some elementary knowledge of my business as a critic." He had previously assumed that a number of disastrous efforts by English composers to wed texts and formal musical patterns had proved the folly of formalism. Now he has decided it was the texts and not the forms which wreaked havoc in these experiments: the English should follow Brahms, and their own national genius, and return to the writing of absolute music. Shaw thinks he mis-read the Zeitgeist. Wagner's *Art Work of the Future* has become the art work of the past: the route for modern musicians is towards music for music's sake.

Nothing could highlight more clearly the paradox of Shaw. During his career as a journalist and playwright Shaw had won—and deserved—a reputation as a revolutionist in politics, economics, morals, and religion. In his plays and prefaces, the spirit of the French Revolution reached maturity and the mood of the Russian Revolution is adumbrated. But his aesthetic looked back to Wordsworth, Shelley, Carlyle, and Ruskin. It was prophetic and humanitarian, and subordinated form to meaning. So, while the revolutionary content of his work on the social and moral side still challenges us with a deep suggestiveness, his aesthetic has been out of key with the twentieth century in western Europe. Whether this will continue is hard to say. The giants of 1916 are dead, a kind of artistic twilight has set in, when the new courses are not clear. Perhaps it is the moment to reconsider the nineteenth-century critical tradition.

Shaw is unique among the masters of English literature in having plied the trade of music critic. Sidney, Dryden, Johnson, Wordsworth, Coleridge, and Eliot sit in judgment only on poets, playwrights, and essayists. Ruskin and Pater are critics of literature who are also critics of the visual arts. Only Shaw chose music as his second field, and gave us a body of writing on the subject that is of permanent interest. It was his experience as a writer on music that formed Bernard Shaw the drama critic and then Bernard Shaw the dramatist. In reading these pages, the reader may do well to ponder Shaw's oft-reiterated claim that it was Mozart who influenced him as a comic playwright rather than any English dramatist. Mozart's gaiety blends with Mozart's seriousness in *Man and Superman,* that most quintessentially Shavian of all Shaw's plays. The perceptive reader will also note how Shaw's 1894 reminiscence of a "superhuman" Wagner at a London concert in 1877 foreshadows his Caesar in *Caesar and Cleopatra.* Indeed a very strong flavor of Wagnerism pervades that play and *Back to Methuselah,* which was Shaw's *Ring.* And would Shaw's heroine manifest her defiant spirit in the way she does in the trial scene of *Saint Joan* if Beethoven had not written *Fidelio,* with its passionate hatred of political prisons? It is hard to think so.

Does Shaw's music criticism merit our attention today? Clearly, it does. For one thing, it is remarkable how much of the music he wrote about is still the staple of our concert and opera seasons. Apart from Shakespeare and four or five dramas by Wilde and Ibsen, nearly all the plays Shaw reviews in his drama criticism have vanished from the boards. But the music he listened to is still very much with us, for good or bad. The composers he celebrates most enthusiastically—Bach, Handel, Mozart, Beethoven, and Wagner —are still the giants to whom we go to recreate our souls. And we are still called upon to evaluate Liszt and Berlioz, Schubert and Gluck, Tchaikowsky and Grieg and Richard Strauss, not to mention Rossini and Verdi and Gounod and Puccini. Shaw's insights into the merits or failings of these composers must still strike the modern music lover as pertinent. Finally, Shaw raises the most important critical question of all: what is musical greatness? In reading Shaw, over and over, one is challenged to distinguish between the truly great and the merely beguiling, sensational, or pretentious. Whether or not you agree with Shaw, no one can fail to be challenged and stimulated by judgments expressed in prose that is itself a feast of art and intellect, wit and humanity.

Note on
the Selections

Shaw's music criticism presents real difficulties for any an-
thologist. To begin with there is its bulk—six sizable volumes. There
is also its original journalistic topicality, which is now its datedness. I
have tried to present Shaw the critic of "great" music, but Shaw was
primarily a reviewer of performances on a day-to-day basis. Shaw's
judgments of musicians like Bach and Bizet have had to be extracted
from columns where the newsworthy question was how the singers
or instrumentalists performed. This has raised several problems.
There were masterpieces Shaw admired and never reviewed, like
The Magic Flute. There were masterpieces he admired and reviewed,
like *Fidelio,* but where he devoted his review to some extraneous
question—in this case the audience's bad manners. I have tried to
concentrate on reviews which give some significant judgment of the
work itself. But I must confess not quite all the pieces I have included
meet this rigorous test. The excerpts on *Carmen* and *Aïda* deal mainly
with the performers, as one might expect. And the essay on the
Eroica is an example of Shaw's impish personality wantonly disport-
ing itself. But generally, literary brilliance has not been a criterion.
Many scintillating columns have been omitted as well as serious and
substantial ones on voice production, staging, etc. In some cases
where Shaw has set out to review one work he makes remarks on
another which seem to me even more significant. Thus I have boldly
transferred a review of Gounod's *Redemption* into the opera section
because of its comments on *Faust,* a work that is alive today as the
Redemption is not.

The central theme of this collection is Shaw's view of musical
greatness. The first section consists of essays on musical history,
musical forms and the social import of music. These give us Shaw's
values and the framework in which he made his judgments. The
second and third sections bring together Shaw's writings on the
great symphonists and opera composers. Here I should perhaps
explain that I am using the word "great" in both its strict and looser

senses. For Shaw, only five men—Bach, Handel, Mozart, Beethoven, and Wagner—qualified as "great composers" when measured by the highest standards. But in the broader, more popular sense we may also apply the term to anyone whose works are still given a place of honor in a serious symphony program or produced by a leading opera house. In Shaw's columns these lesser lights set off the greater. Thus, for Shaw, Puccini's stature is best appreciated by setting him beside Mascagni, and his limitations appear clearest when he is compared to the German symphonists. The final section in this anthology, on English music, defines greatness largely negatively. Shaw ranked Purcell highly and greeted Elgar's appearance with enthusiasm, but his articles on forgotten lights like Parry and Stanford seemed worth including because they prompted Shaw to serious thoughts on the plight of English music in the years between.

One vexing problem in preparing this edition has been where to cut. Given the decision to concentrate on important composers and their works, cutting became an inevitable necessity, since Shaw often deals with several performances in one review, some important and some not. But even where the review sticks to one work it often begins with significant judgments and descends to lesser particulars about the performance or production. Naturally, decisions about cutting in many cases have been arbitrary. I feel less compunction about tailoring Shaw's writings in these cases than elsewhere because it appears that Shaw, perhaps after some unhappy experiences, deliberately wrote his reviews in a diminuendo style so they might be cut at the end if space required. I have hence indicated when cuts occur in the body of an article but not at the beginning or end. I have, however, provided references so that readers who desire can trace the review back to its full original form.

The most difficult decision, however, was whether my aim committed me to include *The Perfect Wagnerite*. At first I was inclined to omit it as the most readily available of Shaw's writings on music, and in order not to overbalance this collection on the Wagnerian side. But this would have left the reader relatively unenlightened about Shaw's views on what he thought to be the greatest achievement of nineteenth-century music, Wagner's *Ring*. My final solution, admittedly imperfect, was to perform drastic surgery, cutting the prefaces to the first three editions, the chapters on Bayreuth, and Shaw's remarks on Wagner's later politics. Other parts of the book I have boldly transferred to the section on musical history, where I believe they provide a unique illumination. But the heart of *The Perfect Wagnerite* I have reprinted in the section on Wagner, where it completes my scheme of giving Shaw's views of the major operas. I have, however, reluctantly omitted Shaw's very detailed analytical synopses of the plots of *The Rhinegold, The Valkyrie,* and *Siegfried,* as out of keeping with the format of the rest of this book. Readers seriously interested in the subject should certainly look these up in Shaw's original treatise. The analysis of *Die Götterdämmerung* has, however, been included, because in this case Shaw, contrary to his previous practice, put his judgment of the opera (a very mixed one) into the midst of his synopsis, from which it cannot be intelligibly separated.

The selections in this anthology are reprinted from the Constable Standard Edition of Shaw's plays and prose, prepared by Shaw in the 1930's. For this edition, Shaw "Shavianized" his original periodical pieces to accord with his own highly idiosyncratic spelling (*shew, wernt,* etc.) and typography (quotation marks avoided, open spacing for italics, etc.). Selections from *How to Become a Musical Critic* follow Dan H. Laurence's editing, which took the Constable edition as its norm. For consistency's sake, I have myself adopted some of Shaw's rather out-of-date usages, for instance, "Tchaikowsky" for "Tchaikovsky."

KEY TO REFERENCES

*—   Dan H. Laurence (ed.), *How to Become a Musical Critic* (New York: Hill and Wang, 1961)

C—   *London Music in 1888–89 as Heard by Corno di Bassetto* (London: Constable, 1937)

I, II, III— Volumes in the series, *Music in London,* 1890–94 (London: Constable, 1932)

Other sources are identified in notes to the selections.

PART ONE

Overviews

———

The Religion of
the Pianoforte

The Fortnightly Review, February 1894

The other day somebody went to Rubinstein and said, "Is the pianoforte a musical instrument?" That is just the sort of question people put nowadays. You call on the Prince of Wales to ask, "Is England a republic?" or on the Lord Mayor with, "Is London a city?" or on Madame Calvé to take her opinion, as an expert, on "Is Cavalleria Rusticana an opera?" In treating such questions as open ones you have already achieved a paradox; and even if the Prince of Wales should have the presence of mind to simply say No, and the Lord Mayor and Madame Calvé, Yes, and have you immediately shewn out, still you are in a position to fill the contents bill of one of our weekly scrap papers with, "Is England a republic?—What the Prince of Wales says"; and so sell off an edition to people who cannot bring themselves to think that the plain explanation of the mystery is that you are a foolish person.

Yet it will not do to reply to "Is the pianoforte a musical instrument?" by a simple Yes. That would be an understatement of a quite extraordinary case. The pianoforte is the most important of all musical instruments: its invention was to music what the invention of printing was to poetry. Just consider the analogy for a moment. What is it that keeps Shakespear alive among us? Is it the stage, the great actors, the occasional revivals with new music and scenery, and agreeably mendacious accounts of the proceedings in the newspapers after the first night? Not a bit of it. Those who know their Shakespear at all know him before they are twentyfive: after that there is no time—one has to live instead of to read; and how many Shakespearean revivals, pray, has an Englishman the chance of seeing before he is twentyfive, even if he lives in a city and not in the untheatred country, or in a family which regards the pit of the theatre as the antechamber to that pit which has no bottom? I myself, born of profane stock, and with a quarter-century of play-going, juvenile and manly, behind me, have not seen as many as a full half of Shakespear's plays acted; and if my impressions of his genius were based solely on these representations I should be in darkness indeed. For what is it that I have seen on such occasions? Take the solitary play of Shakespear's which is revived more than twice in a generation! Well, I have seen Mr Barry Sullivan's Hamlet, Mr Daniel Bandmann's Hamlet, Miss Marriott's Hamlet, Mr Irving's Hamlet, Signor Salvini's Hamlet, Mr Wilson Barrett's Hamlet, Mr Benson's Hamlet, Mr Beerbohm Tree's Hamlet, and perhaps others which I forget. But to none of these artists do I owe my acquaintance with Shakespear's play of Hamlet. In proof whereof, let me announce that, for all my Hamlet-going, were I to perish this day, I should go to my account without having seen Fortinbras, save in my mind's eye, or watched the ghostly twilight march (as I conceive it) of those soldiers who went to their graves like beds to dispute with him a territory that was not tomb enough and continent to hide the slain. When first I saw Hamlet I innocently expected Fortinbras to dash in, as in Sir John Gilbert's picture, with shield and helmet, like a medieval Charles XII, and, by right of his sword and his will, take the throne which the fencing foil and the speculative intellect had let slip, thereby pointing the play's most characteristically English moral. But what was my first Hamlet to my first Romeo and Juliet, in which Romeo, instead of dying forthwith when he took the poison, was interrupted by Juliet, who sat up and made him carry her down to the footlights, where she complained of being very cold, and had to be warmed by a love scene, in the middle of which Romeo, who had forgotten all about poison, was taken ill and died? Or my first Richard III, which turned out to be a wild *potpourri* of all the historical plays, with a studied debasement of all the best word music in the lines, and an original domestic scene in which Richard, after feebly bullying his wife, observed, "If this don't kill her, she's immortal"? Cibber's Richard III was, to my youthful judgment, superior to Shakespear's play on one point only, and that was the omission of the stage direction, "Exeunt fighting," whereby Richmond and the tyrant were enabled to have it out to the bitter end full in my view. Need I add that it was not through this sort of thing, with five out of every six parts pitiably ill acted and ill uttered, that I came to know Shakespear? Later on, when it was no longer Mr Blank's Hamlet and Miss Dash's Juliet that was in question, but "the Lyceum revival," the stage brought me but little nearer to the drama. For the terrible cutting involved by modern hours of performance; the foredoomed futility of the attempt to take a work originally conceived mainly as a long story told on the stage, with plenty of casual adventures and unlimited changes of scene, and to tight-lace it into something like a modern play consisting of a single situation in three acts; and the commercial relations which led the salaried players to make the most abject artistic sacrifices to their professional consciousness that the performance is the actor-manager's "show," and by no means their own or Shakespear's: all these and many other violently anti-artistic conditions of modern theatrical enterprise still stood inexorably between the stage and the real Shakespear.

The case of Shakespear is not, of course, the whole case against the theatre: it is, indeed, the weakest part of it, because the stage certainly does more for Shakespear than for any other dramatic poet. The English drama, from Marlowe to Browning, would practically not exist if it were not printed. To extend the argument to literature in general it is only necessary to imagine the nation depending for its knowledge of poetry and romance on the recitations of elocutionists and the readings with which some of our sects replace the "lessons" of the Church of England. Such a conception dies of its own absurdity. Clearly, the literature which the private student cannot buy or borrow to take home and puzzle out by himself may be regarded as, at best, in a state of suspended animation.

But what has all this to do with the pianoforte? Well, can anything be more obvious? I decline to insult the intelligence of the public by explaining.

Let me, however, do an unsolicited service to thousands of fellow creatures who are huddling round the fire trying to kill time with such sensations as they can extract from novels, not suspecting a far more potent instrument stands dumb by the wall, unthought of save as one of those expensive and useless pieces of show furniture without which no gentleman's drawing room is complete. Take a case by way of illustration. You are a youth, let us suppose, poring over The Three Musketeers, or some romance of Scott's. Now, in the name of all that is real, how much satisfaction do you get out of mere *descriptions* of duels, and escapes, and defiances, and raptures of passion? A good deal, you think (being young); but how if you could find a sort of book that would give you not merely a description of these thrilling sensations, but the sensations themselves—the stirring of the blood, the bristling of the fibres, the transcendent, fearless fury which makes romance so delightful, and realizes that ideal which Mr Gilbert has aptly summed up in the phrase, "heroism without risk"? Such a book is within your reach. Pitch your Three Musketeers into the waste-paper basket, and get a vocal score of Meyerbeer's Huguenots. Then to the piano, and pound away. In the music you will find the body and reality of that feeling which the mere novelist could only describe to you; there will come home to your senses something in which you can actually experience the candor and gallant impulse of the hero, the grace and trouble of the heroine, and the extracted emotional quintessence of their love. As to duels, what wretched printed list of the thrusts in *carte* and *tierce* delivered by D'Artagnan or Bussy d' Amboise can interest the man who knows Don Giovanni's duel in the dark with the Commandant, or Romeo's annihilation of Tybalt (not Shakespear's, but Gounod's Romeo), or Raoul's explosion of courage on the brink of the fight in the *Pré aux Clercs*. And mark, it is only at the piano that that *Pré aux Clercs* fight is really fought out—that Maurevert comes out of the darkness with his assassins to back San Bris, and that Marcel, in extremity, thunders his *Eine feste Burg* at the door of the inn, and brings all the Huguenot soldiers tumbling out to the rescue with their rataplan. Go to the theatre for that scene, and there is no sense in what passes: Maurevert is cut; Marcel is cut; everything that makes the scene grow and live is cut, because the opera is so long that even with the fourth act omitted it is impossible to present it unmutilated without an ungentlemanly curtailment of the waits between the acts. Besides, it is a curious circumstance that operatic stage managers never read operas, perhaps because, since they never conceive cause and effect as operating in the normal way, the composer's instructions would only lead them astray. At all events, we have Meyerbeer at the same disadvantage on the stage as Shakespear.

Here I can conceive our Musketeer-loving youth interrupting me with some impatience to explain that he cannot play the piano. No doubt he cannot: what of that? Berlioz could not play the piano; Wagner could not play the piano; nay, I myself, a musical critic of European reputation, *I* cannot play. But is any man prevented from reading Othello by the fact that he cannot act or recite? You need not be able to play your Huguenots: if you can read the notes and bungle over them, that is sufficient. This only leads our youth to put his difficulty more precisely: he cannot even read the notes. Of course not; but why? Because he has never discovered that they are worth learning. Pianism has been presented to him as a polite accomplishment, the object of which is to give pleasure to others—an object which has not been attained, he has observed, in the case of his sisters. To him, therefore, I seem to propose that he shall, in pure and probably unsuccessful altruism, spend so many hours a day for a year over Czerny's, Plaidy's, or Cramer's exercises in order that he may be able to play Beethoven's Pathetic Sonata slowly and awkwardly, but note-accurately, to the manifest discomfort and disturbance of all within earshot. Now, he does not care two straws about the Pathetic Sonata, and would not spend twelve hours, much less twelve months, over Czerny to save all Beethoven's works from destruction, much less to oblige me. Therefore, though he will learn to smoke, to skate, to play billiards, to ride, to shoot, to do half-a-dozen things much more difficult than reading music, he will no more learn his notes than a sailor will learn ploughing. Why should he, since no pleasure can come of it for himself? As to giving pleasure to others, even sisterless youths know, first, that there are not ten men in Europe among the most gifted and arduously-trained professionals whose playing gives pleasure to enough people to fill St James's Hall; and second, that the effect of ordinary amateur playing on other people is to drive them almost mad. I learnt my notes at the age of sixteen or thereabouts; and since that time I have inflicted untold suffering on my neighbors without having on a single occasion given the smallest pleasure to any human being except myself. Then, it will be asked, Why did I begin? Well, the motive arose from my previous knowledge of music. I had been accustomed all my life to hear it in sufficing quantities; and the melodies I heard I could at least sing; so that I neither had nor desired any technical knowledge. But it happened one day that my circumstances changed, so that I heard no more music. It was in vain now to sing: my native woodnotes wild— just then breaking frightfully—could not satisfy my intense craving for the harmony which is the emotional substance of music, and for the rhythmic figures of accompaniment which are its action and movement. I had only a single splintering voice; and I wanted an orchestra. This musical starvation it was that drove me to disregard the rights of my fellow lodgers and go to the piano. I learnt the alphabet of musical notation from a primer, and the keyboard from a diagram. Then, without troubling Czerny or Plaidy, I opened Don Giovanni and began. It took ten minutes to get my fingers arranged on the chord of D minor with which the overture commences; but when it sounded right at last, it was worth all the trouble it cost. At the end of some months I had acquired a technique of my own, as a

sample of which I may offer my fingering of the scale of C major.
Instead of shifting my hand by turning the thumb under and finger-
   C D E F G A B C
ing 1 2 3 1 2 3 4 5, I passed my fourth finger over my fifth and
   C D E F G A B C
played 1 2 3 4 5 4 5 4. This method had the advantage of being
applicable to all scales, diatonic or chromatic; and to this day I often
fall back on it. Liszt and Chopin hit on it too; but they never used it to
the extent that I did. I soon acquired a terrible power of stumbling
through pianoforte arrangements and vocal scores; and my reward
was that I gained penetrating experiences of Victor Hugo and Schiller from Donizetti, Verdi, and Beethoven; of the Bible from Handel;
of Goethe from Schumann; of Beaumarchais and Molière from
Mozart; and of Mérimée from Bizet, besides finding in Berlioz an
unconscious interpreter of Edgar Allan Poe. When I was in the
schoolboy-adventure vein, I could range from Vincent Wallace to
Meyerbeer; and if I felt piously and genteelly sentimental, I, who
could not stand the pictures of Ary Scheffer or the genteel suburban
sentiment of Tennyson and Longfellow, could become quite maudlin over Mendelssohn and Gounod. And, as I searched all the music I
came across for the sake of its poetic or dramatic content, and played
the pages in which I found drama or poetry over and over again,
whilst I never returned to those in which the music was trying to exist
ornamentally for its own sake and had no real content at all, it followed that when I came across the consciously perfect art work in the
music dramas of Wagner, I ran no risk of hopelessly misunderstanding it as the academic musicians did. Indeed, I soon found that they
equally misunderstood Mozart and Beethoven, though, having
come to like their tunes and harmonies, and to understand their
mere carpentry, they pointed out what they supposed to be their
merits with an erroneousness far more fatal to their unfortunate
pupils than the volley of half-bricks with which they greeted Wagner
(who, it must be confessed, retaliated with a volley of whole ones
fearfully well aimed).

Now, in this fragment of autobiography, what is it that stands as
the one indispensable external condition of my musical culture?
Obviously, the pianoforte. Without it, no harmony, no interweaving
of rhythms and motives, no musical structure, and consequently no
opera or music drama. But on the other hand, with it nothing else
was needed, except the printed score and a foreknowledge of the

power of music to bring romance and poetry to an enchanting intimacy of realization. Let a man once taste of the fruit that brings that knowledge, and no want of technical instruction will prevent him from doing what I did, if only he can get access to a piano and ten shillings' worth of cheap editions of operas and oratorios. I had not the key to the instrument, but I picked the lock by passing my ring finger over my little finger, driven as I was to that burglarious process by my craving for the booty within. It was easier than learning to read French; and how many of us learn to read French merely to satisfy our craving for a less reticent sort of novel than England produces! It is worth anyone's while to do likewise for the sake of Meyerbeer, Gounod, and Verdi alone—nay, for the sake of Offenbach and the Savoy operas. For one must not affright people of moderate capacity by promising them communion with the greatest men, whom they are apt to find dry. On the other hand, let me not lead those older and abler souls to whom the heroics of Verdi, the seraphic philanderings of Gounod, and the pseudo-historical effect-mongering of Meyerbeer are but children's entertainments, to suppose that there is no music at their level. Music is not always serenading Jessica and Lorenzo: it has higher business than that. As one of those swaggering bronzes from the furniture-shops—two cavaliers drawing their swords at one another from opposite ends of the mantelpiece—is to a statue by Praxiteles, so is an opera by Meyerbeer to one by Mozart. However you may despise romantic novels, however loftily you may be absorbed in the future destiny of what is highest in humanity, so that for mere light literature you turn from Dante to Goethe, or from Schopenhauer to Comte, or from Ruskin to Ibsen—still, if you do not know Die Zauberflöte, if you have never soared into the heaven where they sing the choral ending of the Ninth Symphony, if Der Ring des Nibelungen is nothing to you but a newspaper phrase, then you are an ignoramus, however eagerly you may pore in your darkened library over the mere printed labels of those wonders that can only be communicated by the transubstantiation of pure feeling [into] musical tone. The greatest of the great among poets, from Æschylus to Wagner, have been poet-musicians: how then can any man disdain music or pretend to have completed his culture without it?

Thus to the whole range of imaginative letters, from the Bab Ballads to Prometheus Unbound, you have a parallel range of music from Trial by Jury to Tristan und Isoldè, conveying to your very senses what the other could only suggest to your imagination. Only, to travel along this higher range rather than along the lesser one, you must use your piano. This is the mission of the pianoforte, to assert which adequately is such an answer to "Is the pianoforte a musical instrument?" as will send the questioner away an abashed idiot.

Now let us consider the drawbacks to culture by pianoforte as opposed to culture by ordinary reading. To begin with, people do not read aloud; consequently half-a-dozen persons can sit in the same room and enjoy six different books by the light of the same lamp. Imagine these people going to six pianos and simultaneously striking up The Mikado, Dinorah, Faust, Aïda, Fidelio, and Götterdämmerung. Nay, imagine them doing it, not in the same room, but even in the same house, or in the same square, with the windows open in summer! In German towns they have a music curfew, and will not let you play after a stated hour in the evening. When Liszt was teaching at Weimar, playing the pianoforte with the window open was a public misdemeanor punishable by fine. The only wonder is that the piano is permitted at all except in lighthouses and other detached residences. At present unmusical people get used to the noise of a piano just as they get used to the noise of cabs clattering past; but in the end the pianos will make most people musical; and then there will be an end of the present anarchic toleration. For just in proportion as you like bungling on a piano yourself does the bungling of others offend and disturb you. In truth, just as the face a man sees when he looks in the glass is not his face as his neighbor sees it, so the music we hear when we play is not what our neighbors hear. I know no way out of this difficulty just at present. We cannot go back to the clavichord unless we listen to it through a microphone; for though you can play Bach fugues on a clavichord, you cannot play *Suoni la tromba*, or *Di quella pira*, or the Rákóczy March, or the Ride of the Valkyries—at least, not to your heart's content. Even good playing and good pianos are eternally impossible. For the laws of nature forbid good playing with our keyboard, which defies the human hand and only gives us the run of the twelve keys on condition that they are all perceptibly out of tune. And the laws of nature equally seem, so far, to decree that the pianoforte string which gives the most beautiful tone and the pianoforte action which gives the most perfect touch will not last; so that if you get an ideal piano at a cost of some hundreds of pounds, in five years you will want a new one. But you are far more likely, as the income-tax returns prove, to be compelled to put up with a twentyfive pound piano on the three years' system; and though excellent French pianets (considering) are to be had at that price, the ordinary British householder prefers a full-sized walnut piano of the sort that justifies the use of dynamite. Thus we appear to be driven to this lamentable alternative: either to give up the best part of our culture or else make it a curse to the people downstairs or next door. We seem hardly to have the right to hesitate; for now that the moral basis of pianism as a means of giving pleasure to others is exploded, and shewn to correspond to the exact opposite of the facts of the case, it appears to be our plain duty to forbid amateur music altogether, and to insist on romance and poetry being restricted to their silent, incomplete, merely literary expression.

But this, I submit, we dare not do. Without music we shall surely perish of drink, morphia, and all sorts of artificial exaggerations of the cruder delights of the senses. Asceticism will not save us, for the conclusive reason that we are not ascetics. Man, as he develops, seeks constantly a keener pleasure, in the pursuit of which he either destroys himself or develops new faculties of enjoyment. He either strives to intensify the satisfaction of resting, eating, and drinking, the excitement and exercise of hunting, and the ardor of courtship, by "refining" them into idleness, gluttony, dipsomania, hideous cruelty, and ridiculous vice, or else he develops his feeling until it becomes poetic feeling, and sets him thinking with pleasure of nobler things. Observe, if you please, the order of development here: it is all-important, as I shall shew, even at the cost of a digression. It is feeling that sets a man thinking, and not thought that sets him feeling. The secret of the absurd failure of our universities and academic institutions in general to produce any real change in the students who are constantly passing through them is that their method is invariably to attempt to lead their pupils to feeling by way of thought. For example, a musical student is expected to gradually acquire a sense of the poetry of the Ninth Symphony by accumulating information as to the date of Beethoven's birth, the compass of the *contra fagotto*, the number of sharps in the key of D major, and so on, exactly analogous processes being applied in order to produce an appreciation of painting, Greek poetry, or what not. Result: the average sensual boy comes out the average sensual man, with his tastes in no discoverable way different from those of the young gentleman who has preferred an articled clerkship in a solicitor's office to Oxford or Cambridge. All education, as distinct from technical instruction, must be education of the feeling; and such education must consist in the appeal of actual experiences to the senses, without which literary descriptions addressed to the imagination cannot be rightly interpreted. Marriage, for instance, is admittedly an indispensable factor in the education of the complete man or woman. But in educational institutions appeals to the senses can only take the form of performances of works of art; and the bringing of such performances to the highest perfection is the true business of our universities.

This statement will surprise nobody but a university man. Fortunately there is no such thing as an absolutely pure specimen of that order. If it were possible to shut off from a boy all the influence of home, and to confine him absolutely to public-school life and university life, the resultant pure product of what we call "education" would be such a barbarous cub or insufferable prig as we can only conceive by carefully observing the approaches to these types which are occasionally produced at present. But such a complete specialization is not possible. You cannot wholly shut art out now, even with the assistance of modern architects. Though my name is to be found on the books of no Oxford college, I have enjoyed all the real education which the university has to offer by simply walking through the university and looking at its beautiful old quadrangles. I know fairly-educated Oxford men—though, to be sure, they are all truants and smugglers, connoisseurs of the London theatres and galleries, with pictures, pianofortes, and beautiful things of one kind or another in their rooms, and shelves upon shelves of books that are never used as textbooks. I remember conversing once with the late Master of Balliol, an amiable gentleman, stupendously ignorant probably, but with a certain flirtatious, old-maidish frivolity about him that had, and was meant to have, the charm of a condescension from so learned a man. In Oxford he was regarded as a master educator. I would ask what right he had to that distinction in a country where Hallé had made, and was conducting, the Manchester band; where August Manns, with Sir George Grove, had created the Crystal Palace orchestra; and where Richter was teaching us what Wagner taught him? Sir Frederick Burton, as master of the National Gallery, Sir Augustus Harris, as master of the Royal Italian Opera, were and are worth to England, educationally, forty thousand Masters of Balliol. Which is the greater educator, pray— your tutor when he coaches you for the Ireland scholarship or Miss

Janet Achurch when she plays Nora for you? You cannot witness A Doll's House without *feeling*, and as an inevitable consequence, thinking; but it is evident that the Ireland scholarship would break up Oxford unless it could be won without either feeling or thinking. I might give a thousand illustrations, if space permitted, or if criticism of the university system were my main purpose instead of my digression.

Taking it, then, as established that life is a curse to us unless it operates as pleasurable activity, and that as it becomes more intense with the upward evolution of the race it requires a degree of pleasure which cannot be extracted from the alimentary, predatory, and amatory instincts without ruinous perversions of them; seeing, also, that the alternative of "high thinking" is impossible until it is started by "high feeling," to which we can only come through the education of the senses—are we to deliberately reverse our Puritan traditions and aim at becoming a nation of skilled voluptuaries? Certainly. It may require some reflection to see that high feeling brings high thinking; but we already know, without reflection, that high thinking brings what is called plain living. In this century the world has produced two men—Shelley and Wagner—in whom intense poetic feeling was the permanent state of their consciousness, and who were certainly not restrained by any religious, conventional, or prudential considerations from indulging themselves to the utmost of their opportunities. Far from being gluttonous, drunken, cruel, or debauched, they were apostles of vegetarianism and waterdrinking; had an utter horror of violence and "sport"; were notable champions of the independence of women; and were, in short, driven into open revolution against the social evils which the average sensual man finds extremely suitable to him. So much is this the case that the practical doctrine of these two arch-voluptuaries always presents itself to ordinary persons as a saint-like asceticism.

If, now, relieved of all apprehensions as to the social safety of allowing the world to make itself happy, we come to consider which of the arts is the most potent to this end, we must concede that eminence to music, because it alone requires for its enjoyment an artistic act on the part of its reader, which act, in its perfection, becomes such an act of re-creation as Wagner found in Liszt's playing of Beethoven's sonatas. There is no need in this account to set up the musician above the painter, the masterbuilder, or the sculptor. There are points at which all rivalry between the arts vanishes. When you are looking at the Turner water-colors in the National Gallery, the poetic feeling which they so exquisitely and sufficingly express completely delivers you from that plane on which mere hero-worshipers squabble as to whether the painter or the composer of music is the better man. None the less, in the National Gallery the feeling is expressed by the painter and not by you, although your feeling, too, struggles for expression, sometimes almost painfully. You stand dumb, or at best you turn to your neighbor and say, "Pretty, aint it?" of which remark most art criticism is but an elaboration.

Now suppose the feeling were aroused, not by a picture, but by a song! At once your tongue is loosed: you sing the song, and thereby relieve one of your deepest needs—strange as that may sound to people who sing songs solely to gain the applause of others. Further, you gain by practice the power of expressing feeling, and with that power the courage to express it, for want of which power and courage we all go miserably about today, shrinking and pretending, misunderstanding and misunderstood, making remarks on the weather to people whose most nourishing sympathy or most salutary opposition we might enjoy if only we and they could become fully known to each other by a complete self-expression. Music, then, is the most fecund of the arts, propagating itself by its power of forcing those whom it influences to express it and themselves by a method which is the easiest and most universal of all art methods, because it is the art form of that communication by speech which is common to all the race.

This music wisdom has been urged on the world in set terms by Plato, by Goethe, by Schopenhauer, by Wagner, and by myself. As a rule, when, in order to obtain concreteness, I couple my teachings with the name of any individual who enjoys opportunities of carrying out my ideas, he threatens me with legal proceedings, on the ground that I have taken him seriously. And indeed the common-sense of the country under present circumstances feels that to take music as seriously as religion, morals, or politics is clear evidence of malicious insanity, unless the music belongs to an oratorio. The causes of this darkness are economic. What is the matter with us is that the mass of the people cannot afford to go to good concerts or to the opera. Therefore they remain ignorant of the very existence of a dramatic or poetic content in what they call "classical" or "good" music, which they always conceive as a web of learnedly and heavily decorative sound patterns, and never as containing a delicious kernel of feeling, like their favorite Annie Laurie. Consequently they do not crave for pianos; and if they did they could not afford to buy them, and would perforce fall back on the poor man's piano—the German concertina or accordion. At the same time, our most gifted singers, instead of getting ten or fifteen pounds a week and a pension, have to be paid more than Cabinet Ministers, whose work turns them prematurely grey, or officers in the field, or musical critics. All this must be altered before any serious advance in culture can be effected. The necessity for change in the social structure is so pressing that it drives the musician into the political arena in spite of his own nature. You have Wagner going out in '48 with the revolutionists because the State declined to reform the theatre, just as I am compelled, by a similar obtuseness on the part of our own Governments, to join the Fabian Society, and wildly masquerade as a politician so that I may agitate for a better distribution of piano-purchasing power.

If I were now to string all these points in their logical order on the thread of a complete argument, to prove that the future of humanity depends at present on the pianoforte, I should render my case repugnant to the British mind, which sensibly objects to be bothered with logic. But let me, in allowing the British mind to jump at its conclusion, plead for a large construction for the word pianoforte. An organ, an harmonium, a vocalion, an æolion, an orchestrion, or any instrument upon which the full polyphony of an opera or symphony can be given, may obviously replace the pianoforte; and so far as the playing can be done, wholly or partly, by perforated cards, barrels, or other mechanical means of execution, by all means let it be so done. A fingering mechanism so contrived as to be well under the *artistic* control of the operator would be an unspeakable boon. Supply me with such a thing and I will make an end of Paderewski.

Finally, let no one suppose that because private readings and performances are better than nothing, they are therefore an efficient substitute for complete dramatic and orchestral representations. Far from it; they are makeshifts, and very miserable makeshifts too. In Italy, when you go from the picture gallery to the photograph shop, you are revolted by the inadequacy of the "reproductions" which turn Carpaccio's golden glow into sooty grime. At Bayreuth when, on your way back of an evening from the Festival Playhouse, you hear someone strumming a pianoforte arrangement of the overture to Die Meistersinger, you wonder how the wretch can bear to listen to himself. Yet, after a few months in England, when you pull out your photograph, or sit down to the pianoforte score of Die Meistersinger, you are very pleasantly and vividly reminded of Carpaccio or Wagner. Also, however diligently you may read your Shakespear or your Ibsen, you must date your full acquaintance with any work of theirs from the time when you see it fully performed on the stage as they meant you to. The day will come when every citizen will find within his reach and means adequate artistic representations to recreate him whenever he feels disposed for them. Until then the pianoforte will be the savior of society. But when that golden age comes, everybody will see at last what an execrable, jangling, banging, mistuned nuisance our domestic music machine is, and the maddening sound of it will thenceforth be no more heard in our streets.

Music
and Revolution

Radio Times, 18 March 1927†

A hundred years ago a crusty old bachelor of fifty-seven, so deaf that he could not hear his own music played by a full orchestra, yet still able to hear thunder, shook his fist at the roaring heavens for the last time, and died as he had lived, challenging God and defying the universe. He was Defiance Incarnate: he could not even meet a Grand Duke and his court in the street without jamming his hat tight down on his head and striding through the very middle of them. He had the manners of a disobliging steamroller (most steamrollers are abjectly obliging and conciliatory); and he was rather less particular about his dress than a scarecrow: in fact he was once arrested as a tramp because the police refused to believe that such a tatterdemalion could be a famous composer, much less a temple of the most turbulent spirit that ever found expression in pure sound. It was indeed a mighty spirit; but if I had written the mightiest, which would mean mightier than the spirit of Handel, Beethoven himself would have rebuked me; and what mortal man could pretend to a spirit mightier than Bach's? But that Beethoven's spirit was the most turbulent is beyond all question. The impetuous fury of his strength, which he could quite easily contain and control, but often would not, and the uproariousness of his fun, go beyond anything of the kind to be found in the works of other composers. Greenhorns write of syncopation now as if it were a new way of giving the utmost impetus to a musical measure; but the rowdiest jazz sounds like The Maiden's Prayer after Beethoven's third Leonora overture; and certainly no negro corobbery that I ever heard could inspire the blackest dancer

†*Pen Portraits and Reviews.*

17

with such *diable au corps* as the last movement of the Seventh Symphony. And no other composer has ever melted his hearers into complete sentimentality by the tender beauty of his music, and then suddenly turned on them and mocked them with derisive trumpet blasts for being such fools. Nobody but Beethoven could govern Beethoven; and when, as happened when the fit was on him, he deliberately refused to govern himself, he was ungovernable.

It was this turbulence, this deliberate disorder, this mockery, this reckless and triumphant disregard of conventional manners, that set Beethoven apart from the musical geniuses of the ceremonious seventeenth and eighteenth centuries. He was a giant wave in that storm of the human spirit which produced the French Revolution. He called no man master. Mozart, his greatest predecessor in his own department, had from his childhood been washed, combed, splendidly dressed, and beautifully behaved in the presence of royal personages and peers. His childish outburst at the Pompadour, "Who is this woman who does not kiss me? The Queen kisses me," would be incredible of Beethoven, who was still an unlicked cub even when he had grown into a very grizzly bear. Mozart had the refinement of convention and society as well as the refinement of nature and of the solitudes of the soul. Mozart and Gluck are refined as the court of Louis XIV was refined: Haydn is refined as the most cultivated country gentlemen of his day were refined: compared to them socially Beethoven was an obstreperous Bohemian: a man of the people. Haydn, so superior to envy that he declared his junior, Mozart, to be the greatest composer that ever lived, could not stand Beethoven: Mozart, more farseeing, listened to his playing, and said "You will hear of him some day"; but the two would never have hit it off together had Mozart lived long enough to try. Beethoven had a moral horror of Mozart, who in Don Giovanni had thrown a halo of enchantment round an aristocratic blackguard, and then, with the unscrupulous moral versatility of a born dramatist, turned round to cast a halo of divinity round Sarastro, setting his words to the only music yet written that would not sound out of place in the mouth of God.

Beethoven was no dramatist: moral versatility was to him revolting cynicism. Mozart was still to him the master of masters (this is not an empty eulogistic superlative: it means literally that Mozart is a composer's composer much more than he has ever been a really popular composer); but he was a court flunkey in breeches whilst Beethoven was a Sansculotte; and Haydn also was a flunkey in the old livery: the Revolution stood between them as it stood between the eighteenth and nineteenth centuries. But to Beethoven Mozart was worse than Haydn because he trifled with morality by setting vice to music as magically as virtue. The Puritan who is in every true Sansculotte rose up against him in Beethoven, though Mozart had shewn him all the possibilities of nineteenth-century music. So Beethoven cast back for a hero to Handel, another crusty old bachelor of his own kidney, who despised Mozart's hero Gluck, though the pastoral symphony in The Messiah is the nearest thing in music to the scenes in which Gluck, in his Orfeo, opened to us the plains of Heaven.

Thanks to broadcasting, millions of musical novices will hear the music of Beethoven this anniversary year for the first time with their expectations raised to an extraordinary pitch by hundreds of newspaper articles piling up all the conventional eulogies that are applied indiscriminately to all the great composers. And like his contemporaries they will be puzzled by getting from him not merely a music that they did not expect, but often an orchestral hurlyburly that they may not recognize as what they call music at all, though they can appreciate Gluck and Haydn and Mozart quite well. The explanation is simple enough. The music of the eighteenth century is all dance music. A dance is a symmetrical pattern of steps that are pleasant to move to; and its music is a symmetrical pattern of sound that is pleasant to listen to even when you are not dancing to it. Consequently the sound patterns, though they begin by being as simple as chessboards, get lengthened and elaborated and enriched with harmonies until they are more like Persian carpets; and the composers who design these patterns no longer expect people to dance to them. Only a whirling Dervish could dance a Mozart symphony: indeed, I have reduced two young and practised dancers to exhaustion by making them dance a Mozart overture. The very names of the dances are dropped: instead of suites consisting of sarabands, pavanes, gavottes, and jigs, the designs are presented as sonatas and symphonies consisting of sections called simply movements, and labelled according to their speed (in Italian) as allegros, adagios, scherzos, and prestos. But all the time, from Bach's preludes to Mozart's Jupiter Symphony, the music makes a symmetrical sound pattern, and gives us the dancer's pleasure always as the form and foundation of the piece.

Music, however, can do more than make beautiful sound patterns. It can express emotion. You can look at a Persian carpet and listen to a Bach prelude with a delicious admiration that goes no further than itself; but you cannot listen to the overture to Don Giovanni without being thrown into a complicated mood which prepares you for a tragedy of some terrible doom overshadowing an exquisite but Satanic gaiety. If you listen to the last movement of Mozart's Jupiter Symphony, you hear that it is as much a riotous corobbery as the last movement of Beethoven's Seventh Symphony: it is an orgy of ranting drumming tow-row-row, made poignant by an opening strain of strange and painful beauty which is woven through the pattern all through. And yet the movement is a masterpiece of pattern designing all the time.

Now what Beethoven did, and what made some of his greatest contemporaries give him up as a madman with lucid intervals of clowning and bad taste, was that he used music altogether as a means of expressing moods, and completely threw over pattern designing as an end in itself. It is true that he used the old patterns all his life with dogged conservatism (another Sansculotte characteristic, by the way); but he imposed on them such an overwhelming charge of human energy and passion, including that highest passion which accompanies thought, and reduces the passion of the physical appetites to mere animalism, that he not only played Old Harry with their symmetry but often made it impossible to notice that there was any pattern at all beneath the storm of emotion. The Eroica Symphony begins by a pattern (borrowed from an overture which Mozart wrote when he was a boy), followed by a couple more very pretty patterns; but they are tremendously energized, and in the middle of the movement the patterns are torn up savagely; and Beethoven, from the point of view of the mere pattern musician, goes raving mad hurling out terrible chords in which all the notes of the scale are sounded simultaneously, just because he feels like that, and wants you to feel like it.

And there you have the whole secret of Beethoven. He could design patterns with the best of them; he could write music whose beauty will last you all your life; he could take the driest sticks of themes and work them up so interestingly that you find something new in them at the hundredth hearing: in short, you can say of him all that you can say of the greatest pattern composers; but his diagnostic, the thing that marks him out from all the others, is his disturbing quality, his power of unsettling us and imposing his giant moods on us. Berlioz was very angry with an old French composer who expressed the discomfort Beethoven gave him by saying "*J'aime la musique qui me berce,*" "I like music that lulls me." Beethoven's is music that wakes you up; and the one mood in which you shrink from it is the mood in which you want to be let alone.

When you understand this you will advance beyond the eighteenth century and the old-fashioned dance band (jazz, by the way, is the old dance band Beethovenized), and understand not only Beethoven's music, but what is deepest in post-Beethoven music as well.

· SEVENTEEN EIGHTY-NINE ·

13 May 1889 (C)

This week seems to be devoted to celebrating the French Revolution of 1789 which produced such an effect on music that it has never been the same since. I can bring the connection down to this very week; for the first musical product of the Revolution was the Eroica Symphony, utterly unlike anything that had ever been heard in the world before. That very symphony, though nobody feels particularly excited about it now, was performed at the first Richter concert the other day. This would be an excellent opportunity to introduce a criticism of the concert; but unluckily I was not there— though that, of course, need not prevent me from writing a notice of it. I had gone down to Surrey to inspect the newest fashions in spring green; and when the concert began I was communing perplexedly with Nature as to the probability of catching the last train but one from Dorking.

Between ten and eleven, as I sat at Redhill Junction awaiting the arrival of the ten minutes to ten train, I meditated on the Revolution music—on its grandioseness, splendioseness, neuroseness, and sensationaloseness; on its effort, its hurry, its excitement, its aspiration without purpose, its forced and invariably disappointing climaxes, its exhaustion and decay, until in our own day everything that was most strenuously characteristic of it seems old-fashioned, platitudinous, puerile, forcible-feeble, anything but romantic and original. Just think of the mental condition of the enthusiastic musicians who believed that the operas of Meyerbeer were a higher development of those of Mozart, that Berlioz was the heir and successor of Beethoven, Schubert an immortal tone poet as yet only half come to light, Rossini such another as Handel, and Wagner a cacophonous idiot! It is not twenty years since this was quite an advanced program.

If, however, we are to have a Revolution, do not let us sing the Marseillaise. The incurable vulgarity of that air is a disgrace to the red flag. It corresponds so exactly in rhythmic structure with the Irish tune called The Red Fox, or, as Moore set it, Let Erin Remember the Days of Old, that the two airs can be harmonized, though not in what Cherubini would have considered strict two-part counterpoint. But compare the mechanical tramp and ignobly self-assertive accent of Rouget de Lisle's composition with the sensitiveness of the Irish melody and the passion that is in all its moods. My own belief is that the men of Marseilles were horribly frightened when they went to the front, as any sensible person would be; and Rouget de Lisle's tune enabled them to face it out, exactly as "Ta-ran-ta-ra" encouraged the policemen in The Pirates of Penzance.

· FITZGERALD ON ROMANTICISM† ·

9 August 1889 (C)

The Musical Times has had the happy idea of extracting from Edward Fitzgerald's letters his notes upon music. On the whole, Fitz was a sound critic; by which you will please understand not that his likings and dislikings in music were the same as yours, but that he knew one sort of music from another, and was incapable of speaking of the overtures to Mozart's Zauberflöte, Beethoven's Leonora, and Rossini's William Tell as if they were merely three pieces cut off the same roll of stuff by three different tailors. His walking out of the house after the first act of Les Huguenots because it was "noisy and ugly" was rash but perfectly consistent with his remark on the C minor symphony "I like Mozart better: Beethoven is gloomy." The two criticisms bring to light the whole secret of the extraordinary sensation made by such men as Byron, Beethoven, and Meyerbeer in the first half of the century. Beethoven was the first to write gloomy music for its own sake. Meyerbeer was the first opera composer who had the courage to write persistently lugubrious music for its own sake. This was quite a different thing from writing a funeral

†Edward Fitzgerald (1809–93) had published his English version of the *Rubáiyát* in 1859.

march because Saul was dead, tromboning a terrible invocation to the *divinités du Styx* because a heroine had to descend into the shades, or in any of the old tragic ways purifying the soul with pity or terror. Mozart's Don Giovanni was the first Byronic hero in music; but the shadows cast by him were so full of strange reflections and beautiful colors that such lovers of beauty as Fitz were not alarmed. But when Beethoven came, the shadows were black and gigantic; the forms were rough and bold; the Mozartian enchantment was gone. Instead of it there came a sense of deep import in the music—of, as Fitzgerald says, "a Holy of Holies far withdrawn; conceived in the depth of a mind, and only to be received into the depth of ours after much attention." The translator of Omar Khayyàm did not like the black shadows; and though he recognized that Beethoven had "a depth not to be reached all at once," and was "original, majestic, and profound," yet he liked the no less deep and more luminous Mozart better. As to Meyerbeer, who had the lugubriosity of the new school without its profundity, Fitz simply walked out of the house at the end of the first act, and thereby missed the discovery that the arch trifler could rise magnificently to the occasion when his librettist offered it to him.

His worst shot at the music of later days is his description of Carmen as "an opera on the Wagner plan," a description which shews that his notion of "the Wagner plan" was entirely superficial. But his dismissal of Bizet's opera as containing "excellent instrumentation, but not one new or melodious idea through the whole," though it seems absurdly severe, is the natural deliverance of a man who speaks from that zone of Parnassus in which Handel has his place. Fitz appears to have lived on Handel; and Carmen is the very smallest of small beer to a palate accustomed to even Acis and Galatea, much more Samson, Messiah, Israel in Egypt, or Jephtha.

· MOZART AND TITANISM ·

19 April 1893 (II)

Last week an unexpected event occurred—nothing less than a concert. I had been for a long time wishing to hear a little music; so I went off to Prince's Hall and found Miss Dora Bright wasting a very good program on a very bad audience, with the help of Messrs Willy Hess, Kreuz, and Whitehouse. They began with Mozart's pianoforte quartet in G minor, to my delight, as all my musical self-respect is based on my keen appreciation of Mozart's works. It is still as true as it was before the Eroica symphony existed, that there is nothing better in art than Mozart's best. We have had Beethoven, Schubert, Mendelssohn, Schumann, Götz, and Brahms since his time: we have even had Dr Parry, Professor Stanford, Mr Cowen, Dr Mackenzie, and Sir Arthur Sullivan; but the more they have left the Mozart quartet or quintet behind, the further it comes out ahead in its perfection of temper and refinement of consciousness.

In the ardent regions where all the rest are excited and vehement, Mozart alone is completely self-possessed: where they are clutching their bars with a grip of iron and forging them with Cyclopean blows, his gentleness of touch never deserts him: he is considerate, economical, practical under the same pressure of inspiration that throws your Titan into convulsions. This is the secret of his unpopularity with Titan fanciers. We all in our native barbarism have a relish for the strenuous: your tenor whose B flat is like the bursting of a boiler always brings down the house, even when the note brutally effaces the song; and the composer who can artistically express in music a transport of vigor and passion of the more muscular kind, such as the finale to the seventh symphony, the Walkürenritt, or the Hailstone chorus, not to mention the orgies of Raff, Liszt, and Berlioz, is always a hero with the intemperate in music, who are so numerous nowadays that we may confidently expect to see some day a British Minister of the Fine Arts introducing a local Option Bill applied to concert rooms.

With Mozart you are safe from inebriety. Hurry, excitement, eagerness, loss of consideration, are to him purely comic or vicious states of mind: he gives us Monostatos and the Queen of Night on the stage, but not in his chamber music. Now it happens that I have, deep in my nature, which is quite as deep as the average rainfall in England, a frightful contempt for your Queens of Night and Titans and their like. The true Parnassian air acts on these people like oxygen on a mouse: it first excites them, and then kills them. Give me the artist who breathes it like a native, and goes about his work in it as quietly as a common man goes about his ordinary business. Mozart did so; and that is why I like him. Even if I did not, I should pretend to; for a taste for his music is a mark of caste among musicians, and should be worn, like a tall hat, by the amateur who wishes to pass for a true Brahmin.

Music
and Religion

· FROM BACH TO GOUNOD ·

Art Corner, December 1885 (*)

Mors et Vita, the sacred trilogy composed by M. Gounod for the last Birmingham Festival, and received there with something short of enthusiasm, was performed for the first time in London at the Albert Hall by Mr Barnby's choir on the 4th of November. M. Gounod is no Voltairean: he is the romantically pious Frenchman whose adoration of the Virgin Mother is chivalrous, whose obedience to the Pope is filial, and whose homage to his God is that of a devoted royalist to his king. It follows that he is not a deep thinker. But his exquisite taste, his fastidious workmanship, and an earnestness that never fails him even in his most childish enterprises, make him the most enchanting of modern musicians within the limits of his domain of emotion and picturesque superstition. Religious music is not now the serious work it used to be. One hundred and fifty years ago it was still possible for a first-rate intellect to believe that in writing for the Church its highest powers were enjoying their worthiest use. A Mass and a series of religious Cantatas embody the greatest achievements of John Sebastian Bach, the greatest composer of his age (which implies much more than that he was merely the greatest musician). Mozart, the immediate inheritor of Bach's supremacy, was so orthodox a man in his nonage that he exulted when, as he phrased it, Voltaire "died like a dog." Yet religion got no grip of his mature power. His reputation as a moralist and philosopher rests, not on his Masses, but on his two great operas, and on his allegorical music-play Die Zauberflöte, which might have been composed by a modern Positivist or Agnostic Socialist.

Beethoven's masterpiece, the Choral symphony, culminates in a setting of Schiller's Ode to Joy, a poem that might almost have been written by Shelley. After Beethoven, composers who, like Schumann, were thinkers as well as musicians, unconsciously dropped the Bible and the liturgy, and devoted themselves to secular poetry and to such works as the second part of Goethe's Faust. Berlioz was no exception: the Requiem Mass was to him only a peg to hang his tremendous music on; to a genuinely religious man the introduction of elaborate sensational instrumental effects into acts of worship would have seemed blasphemous. Mendelssohn was, like M. Gounod, no very profound thinker. The decay of what is called orthodoxy appeared quite as strikingly in its failure to call into action the highest faculties of philosophic composers who were not consciously heterodox, as in its overt repudiation by many commonplace persons at and about the revolutionary epoch. And so nowadays religious music means either a legend from scripture, melodramatically treated exactly as a legend from Hoffman or an opera libretto would be, or else a Mass in which the sensuous ecstasies of devotion and adoration, the hypnotic trances and triumphs which make religion a luxury, are excited in a refined fashion by all the resources of the accomplished musician, just as they are in a cruder way by the tambourines and cornets of the Salvation Army. Mors et Vita, like Rossini's Stabat Mater and Verdi's Requiem, belongs to this class; but in it there is also some of the descriptive melodrama of the modern oratorio.

Just as the introduction to the last act of M. Gounod's Roméo et Juliette is descriptive of the sleep of Juliet, so the introduction to the second part of his new sacred trilogy is entitled Somnus Mortuorum. The resurrection at the sound of the trumpets is then musically set precisely as if it were a scene in a ballet. A curious effect is produced by sharpening the fifth of the chord figured by the fanfares of the trumpets, which thus play the intervals of the augmented triad as if it were a conmon chord. As may be supposed, the resolution of the discord is somewhat urgently demanded by normal ears long before the dead are fairly awake. This central episode in the work is preceded by a requiem, and followed by scenes descriptive of the judgment and the new Jerusalem. Long before it is all over—it lasts three hours—one feels that a more vigorous composer would have made shorter work of it. At bottom, M. Gounod's piety is inane, and so, at bottom, his music is tedious. The charms of beauty and natural refinement without brains may be undeniable; but they pall. M. Gounod's religious music is beautiful; it is refined; it is negatively virtuous in the highest degree yet attained; the instrumentation is continuously delightful; the whole would realize a poetic child's conception of the music of angels. But men grapple with the problems of life and death in the nineteenth century in another fashion. Feeling that the consummate musician is a puerile thinker, we are compelled to deny that he is a great composer whilst admiring the loveliness of his music.

· MODERN HUMANITARIANISM ·

13 April 1889 (C)

The [Popular Musical] Union has given two imposing concerts lately. At the last one Gounod's Redemption was performed in the People's Palace. I did not go, because I cannot stand listening to a band and chorus practising the chromatic scale in slow time for nearly three hours even when it is harmonized by Gounod. Progression by semitones is too gradual for my ardent nature. I understand that various members of the industrial classes of Mile End pretended to enjoy it, which shews how the hyprocrisy of culture, like other cast-off fashions finds its last asylum among the poor. Now, in my opinion, the East-enders ought to be ashamed to have anything to do with the affectations of their parasites in the West. If the East listens patiently for a while, and never condescends to pretend to like what bores it, it will save itself from much tedium and consequent prejudice against pseudo-sacred music. Roughly, the novices of the East End may take it that the only Scriptural oratorios worth listening to are those of Bach, Handel, and Haydn. After Mozart struck the modern secular humanitarian note in The Magic Flute, and Beethoven took it up in his setting of Schiller's Ode to Joy, oratorio degenerated into mere sentiment and claptrap. With the exception of a few cantatas by Mendelssohn, all the Biblical music of this century might be burnt without leaving the world any the poorer. If the Musical Union is wise, it will train its audiences to nineteenth century vocal music by means of opera recitals.

· ORATORIOS ·

25 June 1890 (I)

I have been getting my mind improved at the Crystal Palace. Naturally that was not what I went for. My sole object in submitting to the unspeakable boredom of listening to St. Paul on Saturday afternoon was to gain an opening for an assault on the waste of our artistic resources—slender enough, in all conscience, even with the strictest economy—caused in England every year by the performance and publication of sham religious works called oratorios. In so far as these are not dull imitations of Handel, they are unstaged operettas on scriptural themes, written in a style in which solemnity and triviality are blended in the right proportions for boring an atheist out of his senses or shocking a sincerely religious person into utter repudiation of any possible union between art and religion. However, there is an intermediate class in England which keeps up the demand in the oratorio market. This class holds that the devil is not respectable (a most unsophisticated idea); but it deals with him in a spirit of extraordinary liberality in dividing with him the kingdom of the fine arts. Thus in literature it gives him all the novels, and is content to keep nothing but the tracts. In music it gives him everything that is played in a theatre, reserving the vapidities of the drawing room and the solemnities of the cathedral for itself. It asks no more in graphic art than a set of illustrations to its family Bible, cheerfully devoting all other subjects to the fiend. But people who make a bad bargain never stick to it. These ascetics smuggle fiction under the covers of the Society for the dissemination of their own particular sort of knowledge; drama in the guise of "entertainments"; opera in scores labelled "cantata" or "oratorio"; and Venus and Apollo catalogued as Eve and Adam. They will not open a novel of Boisgobey's, because novels are sinful; but they will read with zest and gloating how The Converted Collier used to beat his mother in the days when he was an unregenerate limb of Satan. They console themselves for Coquelin by Corney Grain; and, since they may not go to Macbeth at the Lyceum, they induce Mr Irving to dress the Thane in a frock-coat and trousers, and transport him, Sullivan, Miss Terry, and all, to St James's Hall. It is just the same with music. It is wrong to hear the Covent Garden orchestra play Le Sommeil de Juliette; but if Gounod writes just such another interlude, and calls it The Sleep of the Saints before the Last Judgment, then nothing can be more proper than to listen to it in the Albert Hall. Not that Gounod is first favorite with the Puritans. If they went to the theatre they would prefer a melodramatic opera with plenty of blood in it. That being out of the question, they substitute an oratorio with plenty of damnation. The Count di Luna, grinding his teeth and longing to "centuplicar la morte" of his rival with "mille atroci spasimi," is a comparatively tame creature until he takes off his tunic and tights, hies to a "festival," and, in respectable evening-dress, shouts that "the Lord is angry with the wicked every day," and that "if the wicked [meaning the people who go to the Opera] turn not, the Lord will whet His sword and bend His bow." What a day Sunday must be for the children of the oratorio public! It was prime, no doubt, at the Crystal Palace on Saturday, to hear the three thousand young ladies and gentlemen of the choir, in their Sunday best, all shouting "Stone him to death: stone him to death"; and one could almost hear the satisfied sigh of Mr Chadband as St Paul's "God shall surely destroy them" was followed in due time by the piously fugal "See what love hath the Father bestowed on us." But to me, constitutional scoffer that I am, the prostitution of Mendelssohn's great genius to this lust for threatening and vengeance, doom and wrath, upon which he should have turned his back with detestation, is the most painful incident in the art-history of the century. When he saw Fra Diavolo, he was deeply scandalized at the spectacle of Zerlina undressing herself before the looking-glass on her wedding eve, singing "Oui, c'est demain," with the three brigands peeping at her through the curtains. "I could not set such things to music," he said; and undoubtedly the theme was none too dignified. But was it half so ignoble and mischievous as the grovelling and snivelling of Stiggins, or the raging and threatening of Mrs Clennam, which he glorified in St Paul and Elijah? I do not know how it is possible to listen to these works without indignation, especially under circumstances implying a parallel between them and the genuine epic stuff of Handel, from which, in spite of their elegance, they differ as much as Booth does from Bunyan. The worst of it is that Mendelssohn's business is still a going concern, though his genius has been withdrawn from it. Every year at the provincial festivals some dreary doctor of music wreaks his counterpoint on a string of execrable balderdash with Mesopotamia or some other blessed word for a title. The author is usually a critic, who rolls his own log in his paper whilst his friendly colleagues roll it elsewhere. His oratorio, thus recommended, is published in the familiar buff cover, and played off on small choral societies throughout the country by simple-minded organists, who display their knowledge by analysing the fugues and pointing out the little bits of chorus in six real parts. In spite of the flagrant pedantry, imposture, corruption, boredom, and waste of musical funds which the oratorio system involves, I should not let the cat out of the bag in this fashion if I thought it could be kept in much longer; for who knows but that some day I might get into business myself as a librettist, and go down to posterity as the author of St Nicholas Without and St Walker Within, a sacred oratorio, founded on a legend alluded to by Charles Dickens, and favorably noticed in the columns of The World and other organs of metropolitan opinion? But I fear I was born too late for this. The game is up; and I may as well turn Queen's evidence whilst there is some credit to be got by it.

· THE MASS ·

25 January 1893 (II)

To Miss E. M. Smyth, the composer of the Mass performed for the first time at the Albert Hall last Wednesday, I owe at least one hearty acknowledgment. Her Mass was not a Requiem. True, it was carefully announced as "a Solemn Mass"; but when it came to the point it was not so very solemn: in fact, the Gloria, which was taken out of its proper place and sung at the end by way of a finish, began exactly like the opening choruses which are now *de rigueur* in comic operas. Indeed, the whole work, though externally highly decorous, has an underlying profanity that makes the audience's work easy.

If you take an average mundane young lady, and ask her what service to religion she most enjoys rendering, she will probably, if she is a reasonably truthful person, instance the decoration of a church at Christmas. And, beyond question, a girl of taste in that direction will often set forth in a very attractive and becoming way texts of the deepest and most moving significance, which, nevertheless, mean no more to her than the Chinese alphabet. Now I will not go so far as to say that Miss Smyth's musical decoration of the Mass is an exactly analogous case; for there are several passages in which her sense of what is pretty and becoming deepens into sentimental fervor, just as it also slips back occasionally into a very unmistakeable reminiscence of the enjoyment of the ballroom; but I must at least declare that the decorative instinct is decidedly in front of the religious instinct all through, and that the religion is not of the widest and most satisfying sort.

There are great passages in the Mass, such as "I look for the life of the world to come," which stir all men who have any faith or hope left in them, whether the life they look for is to be lived in London streets and squares, or in another world, and which stand out in adequate modern settings of religious services from among the outworn, dead matter with which creeds inevitably become clogged in the course of centuries. Every critic who goes to hear a setting of words written hundreds of years ago knows that some of them will have lost their sincerity, if not their very meaning, to the composer of today; and at such points he looks for a display of pure musicianship to fill the void; whilst he waits with intense interest and hope for the live bits.

Miss Smyth, however, makes no distinctions. She writes undiscriminatingly, with the faith of a child and the orthodoxy of a lady. She has not even those strong preferences which appear in the early religious works of Mozart and Raphael. Consequently, her Mass belongs to the light literature of Church music, though it is not frivolous and vulgar, as so much Church music unfortunately is. It repeatedly spurts ahead in the briskest fashion; so that one or two of the drum flourishes reminded me, not of anything so vulgar as the Salvation Army, but of a crack cavalry band.

There is, too, an oddly pagan but entirely pleasant association in Miss Smyth's mind of the heavenly with the pastoral: the curious trillings and pipings, with violin obbligato, which came into the Creed at the descent from heaven; the Et vitam venturi, on the model of the trio of the Ninth Symphony; and the multitudinous warblings, as of all the finches of the grove, at the end of the Gloria, conveyed to me just such an imagination of the plains of heaven as was painted by John Martin. Much of the orchestral decoration is very pretty, and shews a genuine feeling for the instruments. The passage in the Hosanna for the long trumpet which Mr Morrow mastered for the use of the Bach Choir, fairly brought down the house.

I have often tried to induce composers to avail themselves of this instrument; and now that Miss Smyth has set the example, with immediate results in the way of applause both for herself and the player, I do not see what there is to prevent a triumphant renovation of the treble section of the brass, especially now that Mr Wyatt's application of the double slide to the trumpet has at last made the slide-trumpet as practicable as the incurably vulgar but hitherto unavoidable cornet. Miss Smyth's powers of expression do not go beyond what the orchestra can do for her. None of the vocal solos in the Mass have that peculiar variety and eloquence which are distinctively human: the contralto solo, in which the voice is treated merely as a pretty organ-stop, and the setting of the Agnus Dei for the tenor, which is frank violin music, conclusively prove her limitations, which, let us hope, are only due to want of experience of what can be done with really expressive singers.

The work, as a whole, is fragmentary, with too many pretentious *fugato* beginnings which presently come to nothing, and with some appallingly commonplace preparatory passages before the sections of the continuous numbers; but it is very far from being utterly tedious and mechanical like Dvořák's Requiem, or heavy, sententious, and mock-profound like—well, no matter. Above all, it is interesting as the beginning of what I have so often prophesied—the conquest of popular music by woman. Whenever I hear the dictum, "Women cannot compose," uttered by some male musician whose whole endowment, intellectual and artistic, might be generously estimated as equivalent to that of the little finger of Miss Braddon or Miss Broughton, I always chuckle and say to myself, "Wait a bit, my lad, until they find out how much easier it is than literature, and how little the public shares your objection to hidden consecutives, descending leading notes, ascending sevenths, false relations, and all the other items in your *index expurgatorius!*"

What musician that has ever read a novel of Ouida's has not exclaimed sometimes, "If she would only lay on this sort of thing with an orchestra, how concerts would begin to pay!" Since women have succeeded conspicuously in Victor Hugo's profession, I cannot see why they should not succeed equally in Liszt's if they turned their attention to it.

Form
versus Feeling

·FUGUES·

Magazine of Music, November 1885 (*)

To the average Briton the fugue is still an acute phase of a disease of dulness which occasionally breaks out in drawing rooms, and is known there as classical music. It has no pleasant tune in four strains to add to such stores of memory as Grandfather's Clock and Wait till the clouds roll by. Its style vaguely suggests organ music or church music. Its polyphonous development defies the amateur who picks up things by ear: not that Dutchman himself, who astonished the Philharmonic Society by playing chords on the flute when Sterndale Bennett was conductor, could have whistled a fugue. Those who are, comparatively speaking, connoisseurs, guess the piece to be "something by Handel." Outsiders, who have often wondered what a fugue may be, cease talking and listen curiously, generally with growing disappointment culminating in a relapse into whispered conversation. This is a relief to the player, who, conscious of having taken a desperate step in venturing on a fugue in a drawing room, becomes more and more diffident as the hush indicates that the company have adopted the unusual course of listening to the pianoforte. Many a player, under stress of too much attention, has lost heart; paused on the first dominant seventh that presented itself; and glided off into a waltz, which never fails to set all tongues going again except perhaps those of a few sentimental young people who have overpowering recollections of the last partner with whom they danced that very waltz. The classicists who rail at dance music should never forget the cluster of associations, rich with the bloom of youth and the taste of love, which the lounger, without the slightest previous knowledge of music, can gather from a waltz by Waldteufel.

Professional pianists, and those hardy amateurs who are not to be put out by any concentration of diffusion of the attention of their audience, usually confine themselves to their own compositions in the drawing room. They do not play fugues because they cannot write them. The standard precept runs:—"Learn thoroughly how to compose a fugue, and then *dont*"; and on the second clause of this they act perforce, since they have neglected the first for lack of the economic pressure which is needed to make the average man take serious pains with any subject. It does not pay an ordinary professor of music to learn double counterpoint any more than it pays a journalist to write Latin verses. Fugues are unsaleable: of the considerable number written every year by students, candidates for degrees, and organists, hardly one comes into the market, and for that one there is seldom a purchaser. As to the value of the practice in double counterpoint gained by fugal composition, all that can be said from a commercial point of view is that a musician can make as much money without it as with it. And even from an artistic point of view there are some plausible nothings to be said against the weary climb up Fux's Gradus ad Parnassum. If Beethoven had not worried himself as he did over counterpoint, we might have been spared such aberrations of his genius as the Mass in D. Cherubini's music might have been more interesting if he had not been stopped short by satisfaction with the scientific smoothness and finish which his technical resources enabled him to attain. Besides, one can pick up the art of fugue at any time if occasion should arise. Spohr never wrote a fugue until he had to furnish an oratorio with an overture. Then he procured a copy of Marpurg, looked at the rules, and wrote a respectable fugue without further preparation. Mozart tried his hand successfully at all sorts of contrapuntal curiosities the moment he came across examples of them. It may be true that the best contrapuntists were also the most skilful composers; but their good counterpoint was the result of their skill, and not their skill the result of their counterpoint. To study fugue, not for immediate use in composition, but for its own sake, eventually leads to writing it for its own sake, which means writing dry and detestable music. Such are the excuses at hand for the student who has privately made up his mind that life is not long enough for a thorough course of counterpoint.

Since even the most urgent advocates of such a course falter when the question is no longer one of learning how to write fugues, but of actually writing and publishing them, even the student whose aims are purely artistic finds himself at last debating whether fugue is not obsolete. Many have answered the question in the affirmative.

The old-fashioned deliberate form no longer seems to express anything that modern composers are moved to utter. It is not the power
to write fugues that is lost, it is the will. The St Paul proves that
Mendelssohn could write elaborate fugues and embroider them
with florid orchestral accompaniments; but the Elijah suggests that
in his mature judgment these features of his earlier oratorio were
but scholarly vanities. Meyerbeer and Donizetti were academic
adepts; and Meyerbeer at least was never lazy, perfunctory, or hurried; yet neither of them made any considerable direct use of their
knowledge: many comparatively unschooled composers, who only
got up Marpurg as Spohr did, to write an Amen chorus or an
oratorio prelude (just as a barrister gets up a scientific point when it
happens to be the pivot of a case in which he holds a brief), have left
more fugal counterpoint on record than either of them. Wagner
wove musical tissues of extraordinary complication; but the device
of imitation had no place in his method. The history of fugue as
employed by the great composers during the last hundred and thirty-
five years, is one of corruption, decline, and extinction. Sebastian
Bach could express in fugue or canon all the emotions that have ever
been worthily expressed in music. Some of his fugues will be prized
for their tenderness and pathos when many a melting sonata and
poignant symphonic poem will be shelved for ever. Lamentation,
jubilee, coquetry, pomposity, mirth, hope, fear, suspense, satisfaction, devotion, adoration—fugue came amiss to none of these in his
hands. The old vocal counterpoint reached its zenith then, as the
five-act tragedy in blank verse did in the hands of Shakespear. The
decadence was equally rapid in both instances. Within half a century
after Bach's death, Mozart was not only expressing emotions by
means of music, but expressing them in the manner of a first-rate
dramatist, as they are modified by the characters of the individuals
affected by them. Like Bach, he was not merely an extraordinary
man—Offenbach, strictly speaking, was that—but an extraordinary
genius. And yet he made no use in his greatest work of the form
which was as natural to Bach as the German language. The customary omission of the brisk little *fugato* at the end of Don Giovanni
does not obscure the superlative excellence of that opera. In the
Figaro there is not even a *fugato*. In the Zauberflöte the chorale sung
by the two armed men is accompanied by some fugal writing of impressive beauty, which, with the Recordare of the Requiem, shews
what Mozart could have done with the imitative forms had he prefer-

red them. But this only gives significance to the fact that he did without them. In the last movement of the Jupiter symphony, and in the Zauberflöte overture, the fugue and sonata forms are combined. But the overture is distinctly a *tour de force*, a voluntary reversion to an old form, undertaken by Mozart partly from his rare sympathy with what was noble and beautiful in the old school; partly because, in the overture to Don Giovanni, he had already produced a model for the modern opera overture which he could not himself surpass, and which remains unique to this day. The Jupiter *finale* is historically more important. It is the first notable instance of the nineteenth-century tendency to regard fugue, not as a vehicle of expression, but as a direct expression in itself of energy, excitement, and bustle. This view seized Beethoven, who took a great deal of trouble to acquire skill in double counterpoint and canon, in order to use it for certain *tours de force* which were much less successful than Mozart's. But in his natural characteristic works he used it only to produce a sort of spurious fugue or *fugato*, consisting of a vigorous subject treated with a fast and furious *stretto*, and then thrown aside. He had no command of the form: on the contrary, it commanded him. A particular effect to which it lent itself had caught his fancy, that was all. His *fugato* was invariably an ebullition of animal spirits. In it the parts had no vocal fitness: the accents of human emotion which occur in every bar of Bach's subjects and countersubjects are absent in Beethoven's fugal compositions. He brutalized the fugue as completely as he humanized the sonata. After his spurious fugue came Meyerbeer's spurious *fugato*, in which the subject, instead of being continued as countersubject to the answer, drops its individuality by merging in the harmony. In the prelude to Les Huguenots all the fugal effects which Meyerbeer cared for were produced in a striking way without the trouble of writing a bar of double counterpoint. Handel's fugal setting of the words He trusted in God that He would deliver Him. Let Him deliver Him, if He delight in Him! is a masterly expression of the hatred, mockery, and turbulence of an angry and fanatic mob. Meyerbeer, in the third act of his famous opera, obtained an effect of the same kind, sufficient for his purpose, by means of a sham fugue. This was his deliberate choice: he was perfectly competent to write a genuine fugue, and would undoubtedly have done so had not the counterfeit suited the conditions of his work better.

Little mock fugal explosions are not uncommon now in opera. There is a ludicrous example in the overture to Vincent Wallace's

Maritana. Verdi has occasionally threatened the theatre-goer with a display of fugal science, but the pretense has never been carried very far. Similar symptoms, also speedily suppressed, appear in the third act of Boïto's Mefistofele. Gounod often gives us a few pretty bars in canon, or a theme, with a bold skip or two at the beginning, introduced and answered in the rococo "dux and comes" style. There is a charming *fughetta* in the first act of Bizet's Carmen. But all these examples are either whims, pursued for a few measures and then abandoned, or exciting pantomime music to what is called by stage managers and prizefighters a rally. Wagner and Goetz, the only men of our time who have been, like Handel and Bach, great both as harmonists or chord writers and as countrapuntists or part writers, have not dealt in fugue. They have associated themes with definite ideas, and practiced all the combinations which their logic led them to in consequence. It has not led them to the device of imitation, which has been therefore left to men who, like the late Frederic Kiel of Berlin, have possessed great talent and industry without originality or genius. Imitation is often very pretty, and it always, by giving the part writing a definite and obvious aim, produces an air of intelligibility in the composition which is very welcome to the many people who are apt to get befogged when they endeavor to follow music of any complexity. But nowadays the life has gone out of it: we practice it principally for its own sake now and then, but never for the purpose of expressing subjective ideas.

· SONATA FORM ·

21 March 1890 (C)

The Star printers are getting so musical that I can no longer depend on having my plain and studiously untechnical language set up faithfully. The other day I wrote about "a couple of moments" during a performance; and it came out "a couple of movements." What I wanted to say about the Popular Concert was, that it introduced to us a pianoforte quintet by Giovanni Sgambati, a Roman composer who is pretty well known here. My objection to him is that though he is at Rome he does not do as the Romans do, but writes academic music in sonata form, as the Germans and the English, in spite of my remonstrances, persist in doing.

The fact is, that musicians fail to see the real difficulties of the sonata form through allowing their teachers to engross their attention with a horrible conceit of its technical difficulties, which any fool can master. There is no more to prevent you or I from turning out a string of bars in the form of a sonata than to prevent us from turning out a string of lines in the form of a sonnet or a tragedy in five acts and in blank verse. It is not the form that baulks us of a Shakespearean immortality, but the inordinate quantity of first-class stuffing that is required to make these forms, long, severe, and tedious as they are in themselves, interesting, or even endurable, to any but the performers or the author. You really must have something very important to say to a man, if you expect him to allow you to buttonhole him and claim his undivided attention for even twenty minutes at a stretch, much more (as in the case of a tragedy) for a whole evening.

Sgambati had matter enough in hand to amuse an audience for eight or nine minutes. But in trying to make a whole quintet with it, he had so to wire-draw it and to pad it with desperate commonplaces, culminating in that last resource of musical bankruptcy, a *fugato*, that he failed to amuse us at all. Madame Backer-Gröndahl managed to scatter a handful of pearls here and there over the dull fabric; but the general feeling (I always speak of my own private sensations as the general feeling) was that of Christopher Sly at The Taming of the Shrew: "Would 'twere done!"

· REQUIEMS ·

9 November 1892 (II)

To Dvořák's Requiem, which was performed last Wednesday at the Albert Hall, I could not be made to listen again, since the penalty of default did not exceed death; and I had made, first at Birmingham, and then at Kensington Gore, to sit it out. It is hard to understand the frame of mind of an artist who at this time of day sits down to write a Requiem *à propos de bottes*. One can fancy an undertaker doing it readily enough: he would know as a matter of business that in music, as in joiners' work, you can take the poorest materials and set the public gaping at them by simply covering them with black cloth and coffin-nails. But why should a musician condescend to speculate thus in sensationalism and superstition?

When I hear Dvořák's weird chords on muted cornets (patent Margate Pier echo attachment), finishing up with a gruesome ding on the tam-tam, I feel exactly as I should if he held up a skull with a lighted candle inside to awe me. When in the Dies Iræ, he proceeds, as who should say, "Now you shall see what I can do in the way of stage-thunder," to turn on organ pedal and drum to make a huge mechanical modern version of the Rossini crescendo, I pointedly and publicly turn up my nose, and stare frigidly. But the public, in spite of Charles Dickens, loves everything connected with a funeral.

Those who are too respectable to stand watching the black flag after an execution, take a creepy sort of pleasure in Requiems. If Sir Joseph Barnby were to conduct with a black brass-tipped bâton; if the bandsmen wore black gloves and crape scarves; if the attendants were professional mutes (*sordini*), and the tickets edged with a half-inch jet border, I believe the enjoyment of the audience would be immensely enhanced. Dvořák seems to have felt this. Mozart's Requiem leads you away from the point: you find yourself listening to the music as music, or reflecting, or otherwise getting up to the higher planes of existence. Brahms' Requiem has not the true funeral relish: it aims at the technical traditions of requiem composition rather than the sensational, and is so execrably and ponderously dull that the very flattest of funerals would seem like a ballet, or at least a *danse macabre*, after it.

Dvořák alone, mechanically solemn and trivially genteel, very careful and elaborate in detail, and beyond belief uninspired, has hit the mean. One almost admires the perseverance with which he has cut all those dead strips of notes into lengths, nailed and glued them into a single structure, and titivated it for the melancholy occasion with the latest mortuary orchestral decorations. And then, the gravity with which it is received and criticized as a work of first-rate importance, as if it brought the air of a cathedral close with it, and were highly connected! Whereas, if the same music had been called "Ode to Revolution," or "The Apotheosis of Ibsen," or "Dirge for the Victims of Vaccination," it would have been found out for what it is before the end of the first ten bars, as I found it out at the Birmingham Festival.

Wagnerism

· WAGNERISM† ·

Again, my duties as a musical critic compelled me to ascertain very carefully the exact bearings of the controversy which has raged round Wagner's music-dramas since the middle of the century. When you and I last met, we were basking in the sun between the acts of Parsifal at Bayreuth; but experience has taught me that an American‡ may appear at Bayreuth without being necessarily fonder than most men of a technical discussion on music. Let me therefore put the case to you in a mercifully intelligible way. Music is like drawing, in that it can be purely decorative, or purely dramatic, or anything between the two. A draughtsman may be a pattern-designer like William Morris, or he may be a delineator of life and character, like Ford Madox Brown. Or he may come between these two extremes, and treat scenes of life and character in a decorative way, like Walter Crane or Burne-Jones: both of them consummate pattern-designers, whose subject-pictures and illustrations are also fundamentally figure-patterns, prettier than Madox Brown's, but much less convincingly alive. Do you realize that in music we have these same alternative applications of the art to drama and decoration? You can compose a graceful, symmetrical sound-pattern that exists solely for the sake of its own grace and symmetry. Or you can compose music to heighten the expression of human emotion; and such music will be intensely affecting in the presence of that emotion, and utter nonsense apart from it. For examples of pure pattern-designing in music I should have to go back to the old music of the thirteenth, fourteenth, and fifteenth centuries, before the operatic movement gained the upper hand; but I am afraid my assertions that much of this music is very beautiful, and hugely superior to the stuff our music publishers turn out today, would not be believed in America; for when I hinted at something of the kind lately in the American Musical Courier, and pointed out also the beauty of the

---

†From *The Sanity of Art*, 1895
‡I.e. Benjamin Tucker, for whose magazine, *Liberty*, Shaw wrote his essay.

instruments for which this old music was written (viols, virginals, and so on), one of your leading musical critics rebuked me with an expatiation on the superiority (meaning apparently the greater loudness) of the modern concert grand pianoforte, and contemptuously ordered the Middle Ages out from the majestic presence of the nineteenth century.[1] You must take my word for it that in England alone a long line of composers, from Henry VIII to Lawes and Purcell, have left us quantities of instrumental music which was neither dramatic music nor descriptive music, but was designed to affect the hearer solely by its beauty of sound and grace and ingenuity of pattern. This is the art which Wagner called absolute music. It is represented today by the formal sonata and symphony; and we are coming back to it in something like its old integrity by a post-Wagnerian reaction led by that greatly gifted absolute musician and hopelessly commonplace and tedious homilist, Johannes Brahms.

To understand the present muddle, you must know that modern dramatic music did not appear as an independent branch of musical art, but as an adulteration of decorative music. The first modern dramatic composers accepted as binding on them the rules of good pattern-designing in sound; and this absurdity was made to appear practicable by the fact that Mozart had such an extraordinary command of his art that his operas contain numbers which, though they seem to follow the dramatic play of emotion and character without reference to any other consideration whatever, are seen, on examining them from the point of view of the absolute musician, to be symmetrical sound-patterns. But these *tours de force* were no real justification for imposing the laws of pattern-designing on other dramatic musicians; and even Mozart himself broke away from them in all directions, and was violently attacked by his contemporaries for doing so, the accusations levelled at him (absence of melody, illegitimate and discordant harmonic progressions, and monstrous abuse of the orchestra) being exactly those with which the opponents of Wagner so often pester ourselves. Wagner, whose leading lay characteristic was his enormous common-sense, completed the emancipation of the dramatic musician from these laws of pattern-designing; and we now have operas, and very good ones too, written by composers like Bruneau, who are not musicians in the old sense at

---

[1] Perhaps by this time, however, Mr Arnold Dolmetsch has educated America in this matter, as he educated London and educated me. [Shaw's note.]

all: that is, they are not pattern-designers; they do not compose music apart from drama; and when they have to furnish their operas with dances, instrumental intermezzos or the like, they either take themes from the dramatic part of their operas and rhapsodize on them, or else they turn out some perfectly simple song or dance tune, at the cheapness of which Haydn would have laughed, and give it an air of momentousness by orchestral and harmonic fineries.

If I add now that music in the academic, professorial, Conservative, respectable sense always means decorative music, and that students are taught that the laws of pattern-designing are binding on all musicians, and that violations of them are absolutely "wrong"; and if I mention incidentally that these laws are themselves confused by the survivals from a still older tradition based on the Church art, technically very highly specialized, of writing perfectly smooth and beautiful vocal harmony for unaccompanied voices, worthy to be sung by angelic doctors round the throne of God (this was Palestrina's art), you will understand why all the professional musicians who could not see beyond the routine they were taught, and all the men and women (and there are many of them) who have little or no sense of drama, but a very keen sense of beauty of sound and prettiness of pattern in music, regarded Wagner as a madman who was reducing music to chaos, perversely introducing ugly and brutal sounds into a region where beauty and grace had reigned alone, and substituting an incoherent, aimless, formless, endless meandering for the old familiar symmetrical tunes like Pop Goes the Weazel, in which the second and third lines repeat, or nearly repeat, the pattern of the first and second; so that anyone can remember and treasure them like nursery rhymes. It was the unprofessional, "unmusical" public which caught the dramatic clue, and saw order and power, strength and sanity, in the supposed Wagner chaos; and now, his battle being won and overwon, the professors, to avert the ridicule of their pupils, are compelled to explain (quite truly) that Wagner's technical procedure in music is almost pedantically logical and grammatical; that the Lohengrin and Tristan preludes are masterpieces of the form proper to their aim; and that his disregard of "false relations," and his free use of the most extreme discords without "preparation," are straight and sensible instances of that natural development of harmony which has proceeded continuously from the days when common six-four chords were considered "wrong," and such free use of unprepared dominant sevenths and minor ninths as had become common in Mozart's time would have seemed the maddest cacophony.

The dramatic development also touched purely instrumental music. Liszt tried hard to extricate himself from pianoforte arabesques, and become a tone poet like his friend Wagner. He wanted his symphonic poems to express emotions and their development. And he defined the emotion by connecting it with some known story, poem, or even picture: Mazeppa, Victor Hugo's Les Préludes, Kaulbach's Die Hunnenschlacht, or the like. But the moment you try to make an instrumental composition follow a story, you are forced to abandon the decorative pattern forms, since all patterns consist of some form which is repeated over and over again, and which generally consists in itself of a repetition of two similar halves. For example, if you take a playing-card (say the five of diamonds) as a simple example of a pattern, you find not only that the diamond figure is repeated five times, but that each side of each pip is a reversed duplicate of the other. Now, the established form for a symphony is essentially a pattern form involving just such symmetrical repetitions; and, since a story does not repeat itself, but pursues a continuous chain of fresh incident and correspondingly varied emotions, Liszt had either to find a new musical form for his musical poems, or else face the intolerable anomalies and absurdities which spoil the many attempts made by Mendelssohn, Raff, and others, to handcuff the old form to the new matter. Consequently he invented the symphonic poem, a perfectly simple and fitting commonsense form for his purpose, and one which makes Les Préludes much plainer sailing for the ordinary hearer than Mendelssohn's Mesuline overture or Raff's Lenore or Im Walde symphonies, in both of which the formal repetitions would stamp Raff as a madman if we did not know that they were mere superstitions, which he had not the strength of mind to shake off as Liszt did. But still, to the people who would not read Liszt's explanations and cared nothing for his purpose, who had no taste for symphonic poetry, and consequently insisted on judging the symphonic poems as sound-patterns, Liszt must needs appear, like Wagner, a perverse egotist with something fundamentally disordered in his intellect: in short, a lunatic.

The sequel was the same as in the Impressionist movement. Wagner, Berlioz, and Liszt, in securing tolerance for their own works, secured it for what sounded to many people absurd; and this tolerance necessarily extended to a great deal of stuff which was

really absurd, but which the secretly-bewildered critics dared not
denounce, lest it, too, should turn out to be great, like the music of
Wagner, over which they had made the most ludicrous exhibition of
their incompetence. Even at such stupidly conservative concerts as
those of the London Philharmonic Society I have seen ultra-modern
composers, supposed to be representatives of the Wagnerian movement, conducting pretentious rubbish in no essential superior to
Jullien's British Army Quadrilles. And then, of course, there are
the young imitators, who are corrupted by the desire to make their
harmonies sound like those of the masters whose purposes and prin-
ciples of work they are too young to understand, and who fall between the old forms and the new into simple incoherence.

Here, again, you see, you have a progressive, intelligent, whole-
some, and thoroughly sane movement in art, producing plenty of
evidence to prove the case of any clever man who does not understand music, but who has a theory which involves the proposition
that all the leaders of the art movements of our time are degenerate
and, consequently, retrogressive lunatics.

· WAGNER'S *OPERA AND DRAMA* ·

1 November 1893 (III)

Another book which is in evidence just now is Wagner's famous
Opera and Drama. Mr Ashton Ellis has doubled the pace of his
translation of Wagner's prose works, which is now coming out in
sixty-four-page two-shilling parts, so as to complete a volume every
year. The last few parts have been occupied with the translation of
the book which did more than any other writing of Wagner's to
change people's minds on the subject of opera.

Like all the books which have this mind-changing property—
Buckle's History of Civilization, Marx's Capital, and Ruskin's Modern Painters are the first instances that occur to me—it professes to
be an extraordinarily erudite criticism of contemporary institutions,
and is really a work of pure imagination, in which a great mass of
facts is so arranged as to reflect vividly the historical and philosophical generalizations of the author, the said generalizations being nothing more than an eminently thinkable arrangement of his own way
of looking at things, having no objective validity at all, and owing its
subjective validity and apparent persuasiveness to the fact that the
rest of the world is coming round by mere natural growth to the

author's feeling, and therefore wants "proof," historical, philosophical, moral, and so on, that it is "right" in its new view. People
who are still in a state of perfect satisfaction with Faust and Les
Huguenots, and perfectly bored by Tristan and puzzled by Parsifal,
will never be persuaded by Opera and Drama that opera is a flimsy
sham, standing as an inevitable refuse product at the end of a historic evolution in which the rise of Christianity is but an incident.

Wagner's *aperçus* of the whole history of human thought and
aspiration, culminating in the double world-catastrophe of Meyerbeer being mistaken for a great composer and Mendelssohn for a
model conductor of Beethoven's symphonies, are enormously
suggestive to me, clearing my perception of the whole situation as
regards modern music, and entertaining me beyond measure by the
author's display of transcendent inventiveness and intellectual
power. But I can shift my point of view back to that of the elderly
gentlemen who still ask for nothing better than another Mario to
sing Spirto gentil or Di pescator for them, or a quartet of Italian
singers capable of doing justice to A te O cara. To recommend them
to join the ranks of Mr Ashton Ellis's subscribers would be to mock
them.

I can remember when I was a boy being introduced to Wagner's
music for the first time by hearing a second-rate military band play
an arrangement of the Tannhäuser march. And do you suppose that
it was a revelation to me? Not a bit of it: I thought it a rather commonplace plagiarism from the famous theme in Der Freischütz; and
this boyish impression was exactly the same as that recorded by the
mature Berlioz, who was to me then the merest shadow of a name
which I had read once or twice. At the time I was in a continual state
of disappointment because the operatic music which had so delighted and stirred me as a child seemed no longer to inspire singers.

I will hardly be believed now when I say that Donizetti's Lucrezia
was once really tragic and romantic, and the Inflammatus in Rossini's Stabat Mater really grand; but it was so. What is now known
only as the spavined *cheval de bataille* of obsolete Italian prima donnas
and *parvenu* Italian tenors was formerly a true Pegasus, which carried fine artists aloft as Gounod's music carries Jean de Reszke—or
did until it was superseded in his worship by the music of Wagner (I
see by the latest interviews that Jean now declares that Siegfried is his
favorite part. I have hardly recovered my breath since).

I have no doubt that if Rossini had had Wagner's brains, he too
would have produced magnificent generalizations and proved his

William Tell the heir of all the ages; but as he would also in that case have written much better music, I, for one, should not have objected. He would have been quoted with the utmost reverence in the days when people could not hear any melody in Die Meistersinger, and when the Philharmonic Society used to think Spohr's Power of Sound, as it was called, one of the greatest of instrumental masterpieces. Nowadays everybody under forty sees that all the composers that have lived since Beethoven would not, if rolled into one, make a single Wagner; and I am obliged to conceal the fact that I know every bar of Lucrezia as well as I know Pop Goes the Weasel, lest I should be stripped of my critical authority as a hopeless old fogey.

· WAGNER'S REFORM OF OPERA ·

17 January 1894 (III)

It is not often that one comes across a reasonable book about music, much less an entertaining one. Still, I confess to having held out with satisfaction to the end of M. Georges Noufflard's Richard Wagner d'après lui-même (Paris, Fischbacher, 2 vols., at 3.50 fr. apiece). Noufflard is so exceedingly French a Frenchman that he writes a preface to explain that though he admires Wagner, still Alsace and Lorraine must be given back; and when he records an experiment of his hero's in teetotalism, he naïvely adds, "What is still more surprising is that this unnatural régime, instead of making Wagner ill, operated exactly as he had expected." More Parisian than this an author can hardly be; and yet Noufflard always understands the Prussian composer's position, and generally agrees with him, though, being racially out of sympathy with him, he never entirely comprehends him. He is remarkably free from the stock vulgarities of French operatic culture: for instance, he washes his hands of Meyerbeer most fastidiously; and he puts Gluck, the hero of French musical classicism, most accurately in his true place.

And here let me give a piece of advice to readers of books about Wagner. Whenever you come to a statement that Wagner was an operatic reformer, and that in this capacity he was merely following in the footsteps of Gluck, who had anticipated some of his most important proposals, you may put your book in the waste-paper basket, as far as Wagner is concerned, with absolute confidence. Gluck was an opera composer who said to his contemporaries:

"Gentlemen, let us compose our operas more rationally. An opera is not a stage concert, as most of you seem to think. Let us give up our habit of sacrificing our common sense to the vanity of our singers, and let us compose and orchestrate our airs, our duets, our recitatives, and our sinfonias in such a way that they shall always be appropriate to the dramatic situation given to us by the librettist." And having given this excellent advice, he proceeded to shew how it could be followed. How well he did this we can judge, in spite of our scandalous ignorance of Gluck, from Orfeo, with which Giulia Ravogli has made us familiar lately.

When Wagner came on the scene, exactly a hundred years later, he found that the reform movement begun by Gluck had been carried to the utmost limits of possibility by Spontini, who told him flatly that after La Vestale, etc., there was nothing operatic left to be done. Wagner quite agreed with him, and never had the smallest intention of beginning the reform of opera over again at the very moment when it had just been finished. On the contrary, he took the fully reformed opera, with all its improvements, and asked the nineteenth century to look calmly at it and say whether all this patchwork of stage effects on a purely musical form had really done anything for it but expose the absurd unreality of its pretence to be a form of drama, and whether, in fact, Rossini had not shewn sound common sense in virtually throwing over that pretence and, like Gluck's Italian contemporaries, treating an opera as a stage concert. The nineteenth century took a long time to make up its mind on the question, which it was at first perfectly incapable of understanding. Verdi and Gounod kept on trying to get beyond Spontini on operatic lines, without the least success, except on the purely musical side; and Gounod never gave up the attempt, though Verdi did.

Meanwhile, however, Wagner, to shew what he meant, abandoned operatic composition altogether, and took to writing dramatic poems, and using all the resources of orchestral harmony and vocal tone to give them the utmost reality and intensity of expression, thereby producing the new art form which he called "music-drama," which is no more "reformed opera" than a cathedral is a reformed stone quarry. The whole secret of the amazing futility of the first attempts at Wagner criticism is the mistaking of this new form for an improved pattern of the old one. Once you conceive Wagner as the patentee of certain novel features in operas and librettos, you can demolish him point by point with impeccable logic, and without the least misgiving that you are publicly making a ludicrous exhibition of yourself.

The process is fatally easy, and consists mainly in shewing that the pretended novelties of reformed opera are no novelties at all. The "leading motives," regarded as operatic melodies recurring in connection with the entry of a certain character, are as old as opera itself; the instrumentation, regarded merely as instrumentation, is no better than Mozart's and much more expensive; whereas of those features that really tax the invention of the operatic composer, the airs, the duos, the quartets, the cabalettas to display the virtuosity of the trained Italian singer, the dances, the marches, the choruses, and so on, there is a deadly dearth, their place being taken by—of all things—an interminable dull recitative.

The plain conclusion follows that Wagner was a barren rascal whose whole reputation rested on a shop-ballad, O star of eve, and a march which he accidentally squeezed out when composing his interminable Tannhäuser. And so you go on, wading with fatuous self-satisfaction deeper and deeper into a morass of elaborately reasoned and highly conscientious error. You need fear nothing of this sort from Noufflard. He knows perfectly well the difference between music-drama and opera; and the result is that he not only does not tumble into blind hero-worship of Wagner, but is able to criticize him—a thing the blunderers never could do. Some of his criticisms: for example, his observation that in Wagner's earlier work the melody is by no means so original as Weber's, are indisputable—indeed he might have said Meyerbeer or anybody else; for Wagner's melody was never original at all in that sense, any more than Giotto's figures are picturesque or Shakespear's lines elegant.

But I entirely—though quite respectfully—dissent from Noufflard's suggestion that in composing Tristan Wagner turned his back on the theoretic basis of Siegfried, and returned to "absolute music." It is true, as Noufflard points out, that in Tristan, and even in Der Ring itself, Wagner sometimes got so rapt from the objective drama that he got away from the words too, and in Tristan came to writing music without coherent words at all. But wordless music is not absolute music. Absolute music is the purely decorative sound pattern: tone poetry is the musical expression of poetic feeling. When Tristan gives musical expression to an excess of feeling for which he can find no coherent words, he is no more uttering absolute music than the shepherd who carries on the drama at one of its most deeply felt passages by playing on his pipe.

Wagner regarded all Beethoven's important instrumental works as tone poems; and he himself, though he wrote so much for the orchestra alone in the course of his music-dramas, never wrote, or could write, a note of absolute music. The fact is, there is a great deal of feeling, highly poetic and highly dramatic, which cannot be expressed by mere words—because words are the counters of thinking, not of feeling—but which can be supremely expressed by music. The poet tries to make words serve his purpose by arranging them musically, but is hampered by the certainty of become absurd if he does not make his musically arranged words mean something to the intellect as well as to the feeling.

For example, the unfortunate Shakespear could not make Juliet say:

O Romeo, Romeo, Romeo, Romeo, Romeo;

and so on for twenty lines. He had to make her, in an extremity of unnaturalness, begin to argue the case in a sort of amatory legal fashion, thus:

O Romeo, Romeo, wherefore art thou Romeo?
Deny thy father and refuse they name,
Or, if thou wilt not, etc., etc., etc.

It is verbally decorative; but it is not love. And again:

Parting is such sweet sorrow
That I shall say goodnight till it be morrow;

which is a most ingenious conceit, but one which a woman would no more utter at such a moment than she would prove the rope ladder to be the shortest way out because any two sides of a triangle are together greater than the third.

Now these difficulties do not exist for the tone poet. He can make Isolde say nothing but "Tristan, Tristan, Tristan, Tristan, Tristan," and Tristan nothing but "Isolde, Isolde, Isolde, Isolde, Isolde," to their hearts' content without creating the smallest demand for more definite explanations; and as for the number of times a tenor and soprano can repeat "Addio, addio, addio," there is no limit to it. There is a great deal of this reduction of speech to mere ejaculation in Wagner; and it is a reduction directly pointed to in those very pages of Opera and Drama which seem to make the words all-important by putting the poem in the first place as the seed of the whole music-drama, and yet make a clean sweep of nine-tenths of the dictionary by insisting that it is only the language of feeling that craves for musical expression, or even is susceptible of it.

Nay, you may not only reduce the words to pure ejaculation, you may substitute mere roulade vocalization, or even balderdash, for them, provided the music sustains the feeling which is the real subject of the drama, as has been proved by many pages of genuinely dramatic music, both in opera and elsewhere, which either have no words at all, or else belie them. It is only when a thought interpenetrated with intense feeling has to be expressed, as in the Ode to Joy in the Ninth Symphony, that coherent words must come with the music. You have such words in Tristan; you have also ejaculations void of thought, though full of feeling; and you have plenty of instrumental music with no words at all. But you have no "absolute" music, and no "opera."

Nothing in the world convinces you more of the fact that a dramatic poem cannot possibly take the form of an opera libretto than listening to Tristan and comparing it with, say, Gounod's Romeo and Juliet. I submit, then, to Noufflard (whose two volumes I none the less cordially recommend to all amateurs who can appreciate a thinker) that the contradictions into which Wagner has fallen in this matter are merely such verbal ones as are inevitable from the imperfection of language as an instrument for conveying ideas; and that the progress from Der fliegende Holländer to Parsifal takes a perfectly straight line ahead in theory as well as in artistic execution.

· THE NINETEENTH CENTURY† ·

When Wagner was born in 1813, music had newly become the most astonishing, the most fascinating, the most miraculous art in the world. Mozart's Don Giovanni had made all musical Europe conscious of the enchantments of the modern orchestra and of the perfect adaptability of music to the subtlest needs of the dramatist. Beethoven had shown how those inarticulate mood-poems which surge through men who have, like himself, no exceptional command of words, can be written down in music as symphonies. Not that Mozart and Beethoven invented these applications of their art; but they were the first whose works made it clear that the dramatic and

†From *The Perfect Wagnerite*, 1898.

subjective powers of sound were enthralling enough to stand by themselves quite apart from the decorative musical structures of which they had hitherto been a mere feature. After the finales in Figaro and Don Giovanni, the possibility of the modern music drama lay bare. After the symphonies of Beethoven it was certain that the poetry that lies too deep for words does not lie too deep for music, and that the vicissitudes of the soul, from the roughest fun to the loftiest aspiration, can make symphonies without the aid of dance tunes. As much, perhaps, will be claimed for the preludes and fugues of Bach; but Bach's method was unattainable: his compositions were wonderful webs of exquisitely beautiful Gothic traceries in sound, quite beyond all ordinary human talent. Beethoven's far blunter craft was thoroughly popular and practicable: not to save his soul could he have drawn one long Gothic line in sound as Bach could, much less have woven several of them together with so apt a harmony that even when the composer is unmoved its progressions saturate themselves with the emotion which (as modern critics are a little apt to forget) springs as warmly from our delicately touched admiration as from our sympathies, and sometimes makes us give a composer credit for pathetic intentions which he does not entertain, just as a boy imagines a treasure of tenderness and noble wisdom in the beauty of a woman. Besides, Bach set comic dialogue to music exactly as he set the recitatives of the Passion, there being for him, apparently, only one recitative possible, and that the musically best. He reserved the expression of his merry mood for the regular set numbers in which he could make one of his wonderful contrapuntal traceries of pure ornament with the requisite gaiety of line and movement. Beethoven bowed to no ideal of beauty: he only sought the expression for his feeling. To him a joke was a joke; and if it sounded funny in music he was satisfied. Until the old habit of judging all music by its decorative symmetry had worn out, musicians were shocked by his symphonies, and, misunderstanding his integrity, openly questioned his sanity. But to those who were not looking for pretty new sound patterns, but were longing for the expression of their moods in music, he achieved a revelation, because, being single in his aim to express his own moods, he anticipated with revolutionary courage and frankness all the moods of the rising generations of the nineteenth century.

The result was inevitable. In the nineteenth century it was no longer necessary to be a born pattern designer in sound to be a composer. One had but to be a dramatist or a poet completely susceptible to the dramatic and descriptive powers of sound. A race of literary and theatrical musicians appeared; and Meyerbeer, the first of them, made an extraordinary impression. The frankly delirious description of his Robert the Devil in Balzac's short story entitled Gambara, and Goethe's astonishingly mistaken notion that he could have composed music for Faust, shew how completely the enchantments of the new dramatic music upset the judgment of artists of eminent discernment. Meyerbeer was, people said (old gentlemen still say so in Paris), the successor of Beethoven: he was, if a less perfect musician than Mozart, a profounder genius. Above all, he was original and daring. Wagner himself raved about the duet in the fourth act of Les Huguenots as wildly as anyone.

Yet all this effect of originality and profundity was produced by a quite limited talent for turning striking phrases, exploiting certain curious and rather catching rhythms and modulations, and devising suggestive or eccentric instrumentation. On its decorative side, it was the same phenomenon in music as the Baroque school in architecture: an energetic struggle to enliven organic decay by mechanical oddities and novelties. Meyerbeer was no symphonist. He could not apply the thematic system to his striking phrases, and so had to cobble them into metric patterns in the old style; and as he was no "absolute musician" either, he hardly got his metric patterns beyond mere quadrille tunes, which were either wholly undistinguished, or else made remarkable by certain brusqueries which, in the true rococo manner, owed their singularity to their senselessness. He could produce neither a thorough music drama nor a charming opera. But with all this, and worse, Meyerbeer had some genuine dramatic energy, and even passion; and sometimes rose to the occasion in a manner which, whilst the imagination of his contemporaries remained on fire with the novelties of dramatic music, led them to overrate him with an extravagance which provoked Wagner to conduct a long critical campaign against his supremacy. In the eighteen-sixties this was inevitably ascribed to the professional jealousy of a disappointed rival. Nowadays young people cannot understand how anyone could ever have taken Meyerbeer's influence seriously. The few who remember the reputation he built on The Huguenots and The Prophet, and who now realize what a no-thoroughfare the path he opened proved to be, even to himself, know how inevitable and how impersonal Wagner's attack was.

Wagner was the literary musician par excellence. He could not, like Mozart and Beethoven, produce decorative tone structures independently of any dramatic or poetic subject matter, because, that craft being no longer necessary for his purpose, he did not cultivate it. As Shakespear, compared with Tennyson, appears to have an exclusively dramatic talent, so exactly does Wagner compared with Mendelssohn. On the other hand, he had not to go to third rate literary hacks for "librettos" to set to music: he produced his own dramatic poems, thus giving dramatic integrity to opera, and making symphony articulate. A Beethoven symphony (except the articulate part of the ninth) expresses noble feeling, but not thought: it has moods, but no ideas. Wagner added thought and produced the music drama. Mozart's loftiest opera, his Ring, so to speak, The Magic Flute, has a libretto which, though none the worse for seeming, like The Rhine Gold, the merest Christmas tomfoolery to shallow spectators, is the product of a talent immeasurably inferior to Mozart's own. The libretto of Don Giovanni is coarse and trivial: its transfiguration by Mozart's music may be a marvel; but nobody will venture to contend that such transfigurations, however seductive, can be as satisfactory as tone poetry or drama in which the musician and the poet are at the same level. Here, then, we have the simple secret of Wagner's pre-eminence as a dramatic musician. He wrote the poems as well as composed the music of his "stage festival plays," as he called them.

Up to a certain point in his career Wagner paid the penalty of undertaking two arts instead of one. Mozart had his trade as a musician at his fingers' ends when he was twenty, because he had served an arduous apprenticeship to that trade and no other. Wagner was very far from having attained equal mastery at thirty-five: indeed he himself has told us that not until he had passed the age at which Mozart died did he compose with that complete spontaneity of musical expression which can only be attained by winning entire freedom from all preoccupation with the difficulties of technical processes. But when that time came, he was not only a consummate musician, like Mozart, but a dramatic poet and a critical and philosophical essayist, exercising a considerable influence on his century. The sign of this consummation was his ability at last to play with his art, and thus to add to his already famous achievements in sentimental drama that lighthearted art of comedy of which the greatest masters, like Molière and Mozart, are so much rarer than the tragedians and sentimentalists. It was then that he composed the first two acts of Siegfried, and later on The Mastersingers, a professedly comedic work, and a quite Mozartian garden of melody, hardly credible as the work of the straining artificer of Tannhäuser. Only, as no man ever learns to do one thing by doing something else, however closely allied the two things may be, Wagner still produced no music independently of his poems. The overture to The Mastersingers is delightful when you know what it is all about; but only those to whom it came as a concert piece without any such clue, and who judged its reckless counterpoint by the standard of Bach and of Mozart's Magic Flute overture, can realize how atrocious it used to sound to musicians of the old school. When I first heard it, with the clear march of the polyphony in Bach's B minor Mass fresh in my memory, I confess I thought that the parts had got dislocated, and that some of the band were half a bar behind the others. Perhaps they were; but now that I am familiar with the work, and with Wagner's harmony, I can still quite understand certain passages producing that effect on an admirer of Bach even when performed with perfect accuracy.

· THE OLD AND THE NEW MUSIC† ·

In the old-fashioned opera every separate number involved the composition of a fresh melody; but it is quite a mistake to suppose that this creative effort extended continuously throughout the number from the first to the last bar. When a musician composes according to a set metrical pattern, the selection of the pattern and the composition of the first stave (a stave in music corresponds to a line in verse) generally completes the creative effort. All the rest follows more or less mechanically to fill up the pattern, an air being very like a wall-paper design in this respect. Thus the second stave is usually a perfectly obvious consequence of the first; and the third and fourth an exact or very slightly varied repetition of the first and second. For example, given the first line of Pop Goes the Weasel or Yankee Doodle, any musical cobbler could supply the remaining three. There is very little tune-turning of this kind in The Ring; and it is noteworthy that where it does occur, as in Siegmund's spring song and Mimmy's croon, "Ein zullendes Kind," the effect of the symmetrical staves, recurring as a mere matter of form, is percepti-

†From *The Perfect Wagnerite*, 1898.

bly poor and platitudinous compared with the free flow of melody which prevails elsewhere.

The other and harder way of composing is to take a strain of free melody, and ring every variety of change of mood upon it as if it were a thought that sometimes brought hope, sometimes melancholy, sometimes exultation, sometimes raging despair and so on. To take several themes of this kind, and weave them together into a rich musical fabric passing panoramically before the ear with a continually varying flow of sentiment, is the highest feat of the musician: it is in this way that we get the fugue of Bach and the symphony of Beethoven. The admittedly inferior musician is the one who, like Auber and Offenbach, not to mention our purveyors of drawing room ballads, can produce an unlimited quantity of symmetrical tunes, but cannot weave themes symphonically.

When this is taken into account, it will be seen that the fact that there is a great deal of repetition in The Ring does not distinguish it from the old-fashioned operas. The real difference is that in them the repetition was used for the mechanical completion of conventional metric patterns, whereas in The Ring the recurrence of the theme is an intelligent and interesting consequence of the recurrence of the dramatic phenomenon which it denotes. It should be remembered also that the substitution of symphonically treated themes for tunes with symmetrical eight-bar staves and the like, has always been the rule in the highest forms of music. To describe it, or be affected by it, as an abandonment of melody, is to confess oneself an ignoramus conversant only with dance tunes and ballads.

The sort of stuff a purely dramatic musician produces when he hampers himself with metric patterns in composition is not unlike what might have resulted in literature if Carlyle (for example) had been compelled by convention to write his historical stories in rhymed stanzas. That is to say, it limits his fertility to an occasional phrase, and three quarters of the time exercises only his barren ingenuity in fitting rhymes and measures to it. In literature the great masters of the art have long emancipated themselves from metric patterns. Nobody claims that the hierarchy of modern impassioned prose writers, from Bunyan to Ruskin, should be placed below the writers of pretty lyrics, from Herrick to Mr Austin Dobson. Only in dramatic literature do we find the devastating tradition of blank verse still lingering, giving factitious prestige to the platitudes of dullards, and robbing the dramatic style of the genuine poet of its full natural endowment of variety, force, and simplicity.

This state of things, as we have seen, finds its parallel in musical art, since music can be written in prose themes or in versified tunes; only here nobody dreams of disputing the greater difficulty of the prose forms and the comparative triviality of versification. Yet in dramatic music, as in dramatic literature, the tradition of versification clings with the same pernicious results; and the opera, like the tragedy, is conventionally made like a wall paper. The theatre seems doomed to be in all things the last refuge of the hankering after cheap prettiness in art.

Unfortunately this confusion of the decorative with the dramatic element in both literature and music is maintained by the example of great masters in both arts. Very touching dramatic expression can be combined with decorative symmetry of versification when the artist happens to possess both the decorative and dramatic gifts, and to have cultivated both hand in hand. Shakespear and Shelley, for instance, far from being hampered by the conventional obligation to write their dramas in verse, found it much the easiest and cheapest way of producing them. But if Shakespear had been compelled by custom to write entirely in prose, all his ordinary dialogue might have been as good as the first scene of As You Like It; and all his lofty passages as fine as "What a piece of work is Man!"; thus sparing us a great deal of blank verse in which the thought is commonplace, and the expression, though catchingly turned, absurdly pompous. The Cenci might either have been a serious drama or might never have been written at all if Shelley had not been allowed to carry off its unreality by Elizabethan versification. Still, both poets have achieved many passages in which the decorative and dramatic qualities are not only reconciled, but seem to enhance one another to a pitch otherwise unattainable.

Just so in music. When we find, as in the case of Mozart, a prodigiously gifted and arduously trained musician who is also, by a happy accident, a dramatist comparable to Molière, the obligation to compose operas in versified numbers not only does not embarrass him, but actually saves him trouble and thought. No matter what his dramatic mood may be, he expresses it in exquisite musical verses more easily than a dramatist of ordinary singleness of talent can express it in prose. Accordingly, he too, like Shakespear and Shelley, leaves versified airs, like *Dalla sua pace,* or Gluck's *Che faro senza Euridice,* or Weber's *Leise, leise,* which are as dramatic from the first note to the last as the untrammelled themes of The Ring. In consequence, it used to be professorially demanded that all dramatic music should present the same double aspect. The demand was unreasonable, since symmetrical versification is no merit in dramatic music: one might as well stipulate that a dinner fork should be constructed so as to serve also as a tablecloth. It was an ignorant demand too, because it is not true that the composers of these exceptional examples were always, or even often, able to combine dramatic expression with symmetrical versification. Side by side with *Dalla sua pace* we have *Il mio tesoro* and *Non mi dir,* in which exquisitely expressive opening phrases lead to decorative passages which are as grotesque from the dramatic point of view as the music which Alberic sings when he is slipping and sneezing in the Rhine mud is from the decorative point of view. Further, there is to be considered the mass of shapeless "dry recitative" which separates these symmetrical numbers, and which might have been raised to considerable dramatic and musical importance had it been incorporated into a continuous musical fabric by thematic treatment. Finally, Mozart's most dramatic finales and concerted numbers are more or less in sonata form, like symphonic movements, and must therefore be classed as musical prose. And sonata form dictates repetitions and recapitulations from which the perfectly unconventional form adopted by Wagner is free. On the whole, there is more scope for both repetition and convention in the old form than in the new; and the poorer a composer's musical gift is, the surer he is to resort to the eighteenth century patterns to eke out his invention.

· WAGNER IN BAYREUTH ·

The English Illustrated Magazine, October 1889 (*)

There are many reasons for going to Bayreuth to see the Wagner Festival plays. Curiosity, for instance, or love of music, or hero-worship of Wagner, or adept Wagnerism—a much more complicated business—or a desire to see and be seen in a vortex of culture. But a few of us go to Bayreuth because it is a capital stick to beat a dog with. He who has once been there can crush all admirers of Die Meistersinger at Covent Garden with—"Ah, you should see it at Bayreuth," or, if the occasion be the Parsifal prelude at a Richter concert, "Have you heard Levi conduct it at Bayreuth?" And when the answer comes sorrowfully in the negative, the delinquent is made to feel that in that case he does not know what Parsifal is, and that the Bayreuth tourist does. These little triumphs are indulged in without the slightest remorse on the score of Richter's great superiority to Herr Levi as a Wagnerian conductor, and of the fact that a performance of the Parsifal prelude by a London orchestra under his direction is often much better worth a trip from Bayreuth to London than a performance by a German orchestra under Levi is ever worth a trip from London to Bayreuth. It is not in human nature to be honest in these matters—at least not yet.

Those who have never been in Germany, and cannot afford to go thither, will not be sorry when the inevitable revolt of English Wagnerism against Bayreuth breaks out; and the sooner they are gratified, the better. Ever since the death of Beethoven, the champions of Music have been desperately fighting to obtain a full hearing for her in spite of professorship, pedantry, superstition, literary men's acquiescent reports of concerts, and butcherly stage management—all trading on public ignorance and diffidence. Wagner, the greatest of these champions, did not fight for his own hand alone, but for Mozart, Beethoven, and Weber as well. All authority was opposed to him until he made his own paramount. Mendelssohn was against him at a time when to assert that Mendelssohn's opinion was of less weight than his seemed as monstrous as it would seem today to deny it. People do not discriminate in music as much as they do in other arts. They can see that Lord Tennyson is hardly the man to say the deepest word about Goethe, or Sir Frederick Leighton about Michael Angelo; but Mendelssohn's opinion about Beethoven was accepted as final, since the composer of Elijah must evidently know all about music. In England, since not only Mendelssohn, but Costa, the Philharmonic Society, The Times, and The Athenæum were satisfied when they had dried Mozart into a trivial musical box, when the overture to Le Nozze di Figaro was finished within three and a half minutes, when the beautiful trio of Beethoven's Eighth Symphony was made a mere practical joke on the violoncellists, when the famous theme in the Freischütz was played exactly in the style of the popular second subject in the Masaniello overture, the public could only conclude that these must be the classical ways of conducting, and that dulness was a necessary part of the classicism. Wagner did not succeed in putting dulness out of countenance until he became a classic himself. And now that he is a classic, who is to do for him what he did for his predecessors? For he is not going to escape their fate. The "poor and pretentious pietism" which he complained of as "shutting out every breath of fresh air from the musical atmosphere," is closing round his own music. At Bayreuth, where the Master's widow, it is said, sits in the wing as the jealous guardian of the traditions of his own personal direction, there is already a perceptible numbness—the symptom of paralysis.

The London branch of the Wagner Society, unobservant of this danger signal, seems to have come to the conclusion that the best thing it can do for its cause is to support Bayreuth. It has not yet dawned on it that the traditional way of playing Tristan und Isolde will, in the common course of mortality, inevitably come to what the traditional way of playing Mozart's G minor symphony had come to when Wagner heard Lachner conduct it; or, to take instances which appeal to our own experience, what Don Giovanni came to be under Costa in his later days, or what the C minor symphony is today at a Philharmonic concert. The law of traditional performances is, "Do what was done last time": the law of all living and fruitful performance is, "Obey the innermost impulse which the music gives, and obey it to the most exhaustive satisfaction." And as that impulse is never, in a fertile artistic nature, the impulse to do what was done last time, the two laws are incompatible, being virtually laws respectively of death and life in art. Bayreuth has chosen the law of death. Its boast is that it alone knows what was done last time, and that therefore it alone has the pure and complete tradition—or, as I prefer to put it, that it alone is in a position to strangle Wagner's lyric dramas note by note, bar by bar, *nuance* by *nuance*. It is in vain for Bayreuth to contend that by faithfully doing what was done last time it arrives at an exact phonograph of what was done the first time, when Wagner was alive, present, and approving. The difference consists just in this, that Wagner is now dead, absent, and indifferent. The powerful, magnetic personality, with all the tension it maintained, is gone; and no manipulation of the dead hand on the keys can ever reproduce the living touch. Even if such reproduction were possible, who, outside Bayreuth, would be imposed on by the shallow assumption that the Bayreuth performances fulfilled Wagner's whole desire? We can well believe that in justice to those who so loyally helped him, he professed himself satisfied when the most that could be had been done—nay, that after the desperate makeshifts with which he had had to put up in his long theatrical experience, he was genuinely delighted to find that so much was possible. But the unwieldy toy dragon, emitting its puff of steam when its mouth opened, about as impressively as a mechanical doll says "Mamma":

did that realize the poet's vision of Fafner? And the trees which walk off the stage in Parsifal: can the poorest imagination see nothing better by the light of Wagner's stage direction in the score than that? Is the gaudy ballet and unspeakable flower garden in the second act to be the final interpretation of the visionary bowers of Klingsor? The Philistine cockney laughs at these provincial conceits, and recommends Bayreuth to send for Mr Irving, Mr Hare, Mr Wilson Barrett, or Mr Augustus Harris to set the stage to rights. It is extremely likely that when A Midsummer Night's Dream was first produced, Shakespear complimented the stage manager, tipped the carpenters, patted Puck on the head, shook hands with Oberon, and wondered that the make-believe was no worse; but even if this were an established historical fact, no sane manager would therefore attempt to reproduce the Elizabethan *mise en scène* on the ground that it had fulfilled Shakespear's design. Yet if we had had a Shakespear theatre on foot since the seventeenth century, conducted on the Bayreuth plan, that is the very absurdity in which tradition would by this time have landed us.[1]

Tradition in scenery and stage management is, however, plausible in comparison with tradition in acting, singing, and playing. If Wagner had been able to say of any scene, "I am satisfied," meaning, not "I am satisfied that nothing better can be done for me; and I am heartily grateful to you—the painter—for having done more than I had hoped for," but "This is what I saw in my mind's eye when I wrote my poem," then successive scene manufacturers might mechanically copy the painting from cloth to cloth with sufficient accuracy to fix at least a good copy of the original scene for posterity to look at with new eyes and altered minds. At any rate the new cloth would not rebel, since it could be woven and cut at will to the pattern of the old picture. But when it is further sought to reproduce the old figures with new persons, then comes to light the absurdity of playing Procrustes with a dramatic representation. I remember once laughing at a provincial Iago who pointed the words "Trifles light as air," by twitching his handkerchief into space much as street hawkers now twitch the toy parachute made fashionable by Mr Baldwin. An

---

[1] The *Comédie Française*, in performing the plays of Molière, still keeps as closely as possible to the stage arrangements of the author's own time. Even in this instance, where the tradition has the excuse of being the most trustworthy record of the manners of the period represented, the effect on the plays themselves is sufficiently depressing; and its reaction on the French stage at large is a main factor of the immense superiority of English acting, undrilled and inartistic as our novices are, to French. [Shaw's note.]

experienced theatrical acquaintance rebuked me, assuring me that the actor was right, because he had been accustomed to rehearse the part of Charles Kean, and therefore had learnt every step, gesture, and inflection of that eminent tragedian's play. Unfortunately, he was not Charles Kean: consequently Charles Kean's play no more fitted him than Charles Kean's clothes. His Iago was a ridiculous misfit, even from his own shallow view of acting as a mere external affectation. In the old provincial stock companies, most of which have by this time died the death they richly deserved, there was often to be found an old lady who played Lady Macbeth when the star Shakespearean actor came his usual round. She played it exactly as Mrs Siddons played it, with the important difference that, as she was not Mrs Siddons, the way which was the right way for Mrs Siddons was the wrong way for her. Thoroughly sophisticated theatre fanciers carried the fool's logic of tradition to the extremity of admiring these performances. But of those with natural appetites, the young laughed and the old yawned. Consideration of these cases suggests the question whether we are to be made [to] laugh and yawn at Bayreuth by a line of mock Maternas and sham Maltens? If not, what can Bayreuth do that cannot be done as well elsewhere—that cannot be done much more conveniently for Englishmen in England? If Bayreuth repudiates tradition, there is no mortal reason why we should go so far to hear Wagner's lyric dramas. If it clings to it, then that is the strongest possible reason for avoiding it. Every fresh representation of Parsifal (for example) should be an original artistic creation, and not an imitation of the last one. The proper document to place in the hands of the artists is the complete work. Let the scene-painter paint the scenes he sees in the poem. Let the conductor express with his orchestra what the score expresses to him. Let the tenor do after the nature of that part of himself which he recognizes in Parsifal; and let the *prima donna* similarly realize herself as Kundry. The true Wagner Theatre is that in which this shall be done, though it stands on Primrose Hill or in California. And wherever the traditional method is substituted, there Wagner is not. The conclusion that the Bayreuth theatre cannot remain the true Wagner Theatre is obvious. The whole place reeks of tradition—boasts of it—bases its claims to fitness upon it. Frau Cosima Wagner, who has no function to perform except the illegitimate one of chief remembrancer, sits on guard there. When the veterans of 1876 retire, Wagner will be in the condition of Titurel in the third act of Parsifal.

After Wagner

7 February 1894 (III)

In order to save myself from having to cry Music, Music, when there is no music—for there is nothing beyond the barest routine going on—I diligently attend the Popular Concerts and saturate myself with Brahms. I have been accused of indifference to, and even of aversion from, that composer; but there never was a greater mistake: I can sit with infinite satisfaction for three-quarters of an hour listening to his quintets or sestets—four instruments cannot produce effects rich enough for him—in which he wanders with his eyes shut from barcarolle to pastoral, and from pastoral to elegy, these definite forms appearing for a moment on the surface of the rich harmony like figures in the fire or in the passing clouds. But such works are not the successors of the quintets of Mozart or the quartets of Beethoven. They are the direct and greatly enriched descendants of what the eighteenth-century masters used to call serenades—things to delight the senses, not to be thought about.

When a German Brahmsite critic proclaims them the latest products of the great school in chamber music, I feel exactly as if a gorgeous Oriental carpet were being nailed up on the wall at South Kensington as a continuation of the Raphael cartoons for the Sistine tapestry. It seems to me that anyone who can see the difference between Monticelli and Mantegna, or between Mr Swinburne and Shakespear, should also be able to perceive the absurdity of classing one of these big serenades of Brahms' with Mozart's quartets. Brahms, feeling his way from one sensuous moment to another, turning from every obstacle and embracing every amenity, produces a whole that has no more form than a mountain brook has, though every successive nook and corner as you wander along its brink may be as charming as possible.

Mozart never follows his inspiration in this manner: he leads it, makes its course for it, removes obstacles, holds it in from gadding erratically after this or that passing fancy, thinks for it, and finally produces with it an admirable whole, the full appreciation of which keeps every faculty on the alert from beginning to end. And though Haydn was a much commoner man than Mozart, and Beethoven a much less clearheaded one, both of them were, on the whole, also masters of their genius, and were able to think and sing at the same time, and so to produce chamber music which no one would dream of describing as merely sensuous. Brahms is built quite otherwise.

Nature inexorably offers him the alternative of Music without Mind, or Mind without Music; and even this hard alternative is not fairly presented, since the mind is of very ordinary quality, whereas the music is as good as mindless music can be. Sometimes Brahms submits to Nature, and, declaring for Music without Mind, produces the charming serenades which Lady Hallé and Piatti, with Messrs Ries, Gibson, Hobday, and Whitehead, have been playing at recent Monday Popular Concerts, to the unbounded delight of the audiences, including myself. Sometimes he rebels, and proceeds to shew his mental mastery, in which case we have Requiems and general yawning.

· FRENCH MUSIC ·

28 February 1894 (III)

An interesting book has just come into my hands—Mr Arthur Hervey's Masters of French Music (published by Messrs Osgood, McIlvaine and Co.). Mr Hervey is just the man for the work: he loves France and French music; he is an enthusiast and a composer; and I know nothing against him except that he is a musical critic, which, as Mr Riderhood remarked of his three months imprisonment, might happen to any man. I will not say that Mr Hervey expresses my own feelings about French music; for no book could be abusive enough for that and at the same time be entirely fit for publication. But then I should write a very bad book on the subject. To my mind, the French would be a very tolerable nation if only they would let art alone. It is the one thing for which they have no sort of capacity; and their perpetual affectation of it is in them what hypocrisy is in the English, an all-pervading falsehood which puts one out of patience with them in spite of their realities and efficiencies.

Mr Hervey has certain engaging qualities of kindliness and

modesty which prevent him from forming these violent opinions. He takes a warm interest in the French school, and, if the score of a grand opera has only as much as a pretty waltz in it, will relent over that instead of throwing the score at the composer's head. In sketching the men themselves he is wonderfully lively and sympathetic considering their superficiality and barrenness from that deeper artistic point of view which he takes when expressing his own feelings, whether as writer or composer. For instance, his sixty-five pages about Saint-Saëns give the pleasantest impression of that composer's cleverness, his technical ingenuity, his elegant and fanciful handling of the orchestra, his facility, his wit, his wide knowledge of modern music, his charming execution as pianist and organist, and his triumphs at the Opera and elsewhere as a "master of French music"—observe, not a French master of music: Mr Hervey, instinctively or intentionally, has guarded himself well in turning that phase. Mr Hervey even declares that Samson et Dalila, with its one heartless, fashionably sensuous love duet, and its whistling Abimelech in the vilest Meyerbeerian manner, ought to be imported to these shores.

Altogether, you would never guess from him that if you take away from Saint-Saëns' music what he has borrowed from Meyerbeer, Gounod, and Bach, or rather from that poetically ornamental vein of Bach which is best sampled in the prelude to the organ fugue in A minor, you will find nothing left but graceful nicknacks—barcarolles, serenades, ballets, and the like, with, of course, the regulation crescendos, aspiring modulations, and instrumental climaxes ending with a crash of the cymbals, which do duty for "symphonic poetry" when Phaeton has to be hurled from his car or some other sublimity taken in hand.

But Mr Hervey, all the same, allows him to sum himself up in these significant words: "I admire the works of Richard Wagner profoundly, in spite of their *bizarrerie*. They are superior and powerful, *which suffices for me*. But I have never belonged, I do not belong, and I never shall belong, to the Wagnerian religion." Here you have the French composer all over. To be "superior and powerful": that is enough for him. Accordingly, he imitates Meyerbeer, who deliberately cultivated *bizarrerie* in order to impress the French with the idea that he was "superior and powerful" (and succeeded); he complains of the *bizarrerie* of Wagner, the most sincere and straightforward of composers, whose hatred of *bizarrerie* amounted to loathing; and he then solemnly disclaims "the Wagnerian religion," as if, in any other country in the world except France, he could be suspected for a moment of even knowing what it means.

Bruneau himself, a far abler composer, who is really a tone-poet in his way, is quoted as saying, "Owing to Wagner's prodigious genius, the musical drama has entered into a new era—an era of true reason, of vigorous good sense, and of perfect logic." Imagine a man admiring Die Walküre for its good sense and its logic! What Bruneau catches is not the peotry and philosophy of Die Walküre, but the *system* of its composition—the system of representative themes, which he finds perfectly intelligible and reasonable, therefore admirable. Not that he stops here: on the contrary, he goes on to discourse very feelingly on the difference between music-drama and opera; but I cannot help suspecting that he thinks the superiority of the Wagnerian drama is the result instead of the cause of the superior logic of the Wagnerian system.

The most notable saying of Massenet's in the book is his avowal that it was at Rome that he felt his first stirrings of admiration of Nature and for Art. The point of this lies in the fact that he ran away from home at fourteen to be a musician, and played the drums at the Théâtre Lyrique for six years at two pounds fifteen a month before he won the *prix de Rome*. Therefore he recognizes in the above avowal the fact that musical propensity and faculty is one thing and artistic feeling another. Should Massenet require any instances to prove this proposition, England can supply him with several eminent professors who have been musicians by irresistable vocation all their lives, without ever having been artists for five minutes.

One of Mr Hervey's stories about Massenet is too characteristically French to be passed over. When he had to give a "reading" of his Werther to the artists and officials of the Imperial Opera House in Vienna, they all looked so imposing as they sat in a magnificent room round the piano, that when he came in, an unfortunate stranger with a reputation to live up to, and was received with appalling solemnity by the director, he naturally wanted to sit down and cry, just like an Englishman. But an Englishman would have died rather than have expressed his feelings: he would have chilled the assembly by an air of stiff unconcern, and played badly until he had recovered his nerve. Massenet, with frankness entirely honorable to him, promptly sat down and cried away to his heart's content, whereby throwing his audience into the most sympathetic condition.

Another anecdote tells us that "the impression made upon Vincent d'Indy by Brahms' Requiem in 1873 was such that he forthwith started for Germany in order to become acquainted with the master." I had a precisely similar impulse when I first heard that unspeakable work; but I restrained myself, whereas Vincent appears to have actually accomplished his fell purpose. "The result," says Mr Hervey naïvely, "does not seem to have been so satisfactory as it might have been, the German composer receiving the young enthusiast with a certain amount of reserve."

Finally, I cannot take leave of Mr Hervey without asking him to reconsider his remarks about "rules" of composition on pages 231–233. After shewing conclusively, in defence of Bruneau's Le Rêve, that there are no valid "rules" whatsoever, he adds, "Undoubtedly there must be rules of some kind," and proceeds to quote some delusively open-minded remarks from the preface to Mr Ebenezer Prout's work on harmony. Now, in so far as Mr Prout's preface means that his own rules are all nonsense, I agree with him. But I submit to Mr Hervey that he must either give up Mr Prout's treatise and its rules unreservedly, or else give up, not only Bruneau, but Mozart, whose conduct in making "a passing note" jump down a whole fifth in his E flat symphony is treated by Mr Prout as a regrettable impropriety which the student must on no account permit himself to imitate.

The fact is, there are no rules, and there never were any rules, and there never will be any rules of musical composition except rules of thumb; and thumbs vary in length, like ears. Doubtless it is bold of me to differ from such great musicians as Albrechtsberger, Marpurg, Kiel, Richter, Ouseley, and Macfarren as against such notoriously licentious musical anarchists as Bach, Handel, Haydn, Mozart, Beethoven, and Wagner; but the fact is, I prefer the music of these insubordinate persons; and I strongly suspect that Mr Prout does too, in spite of his scruples about "passing notes."

· PARRY'S *THE ART OF MUSIC* ·

4 April 1894 (III)

On my way down to the country for the Easter holidays I disbursed the respectable sum of twelve shillings to Messrs Kegan Paul & Co. for a copy of The Art of Music, by C. Hubert H. Parry, Master of Arts at Oxford; Doctor of Music at Oxford, Cambridge, and Dublin; and composer of—among other works—those two famous oratories, Judith and Job. Dr Parry occupies a position in the history of English art not unlike that occupied by Charles I in English politics. Any objection to his public compositions is immediately met by a reference to the extraordinary amiability of his private character. It is my firm belief that Hampden himself would have paid any assessment of ship money rather than sit out Judith a second time; and the attempt to arrest the five members seems to me a trifle in comparison with Job. But the defence is always the same—that Dr Parry sums up in his person every excellence that the best type of private gentleman can pretend to.

Now it should be remembered that long before people began to get tired of Judith they got tired of hearing Aristides called the Just; and if Dr Parry is not to end his days in St Helena, somebody must act as devil's advocate in his case. Out of pure friendliness, therefore, let me try to find fault a little with his book. If I do not do this, nobody else will; for, if I may blurt out the truth for once, without regard to the feelings of my colleagues, those musical critics who have sufficient culture and scholarship to grapple with Dr Parry's learning have been driven by mere isolation to associate themselves with the more scholarly of our musicians and artists on terms of personal intimacy which practically involve mutual admiration and logrolling.

These are not the objects of the intimacy, which is perfectly natural and honest, and in some ways beneficial to the public as well as to the principal parties; but they are among its inevitable consequences; and, frankly, I would not give a rap more for any public utterance of our best critics concerning Professor Stanford, Dr Parry, and the rest of their musical friends, than I would advise them to give for any public utterance that I could be persuaded to make concerning those friends of mine with whom I have been closely and specially allied for years past in political matters.

In reading Dr Parry's book I began at the end (my invariable custom with histories of music); and I have not yet quite reached the beginning. However, that does not matter, since it is not with the remoter history of the art that I am now concerned. In the later chapters I find, along with a great deal of criticism with which I agree, and a mass of information which my position as a critic obliges me to pretend that I knew all along, certain observations which smack, to me, of the commoner sort of analytic concert program. Most of these are due to the disturbance of Dr Parry's judgment by his love for Beethoven, which sets him pointing out as choice merits of that composer such features as "insisting on his key," and "often casting his leading idea in terms of the common chord."

If this be a mark of genius, let us not ignore it in Donizetti's choruses, in our comic songs and army trumpet-calls, and in such pretentious platitudes as the first movement of Rubinstein's Ocean symphony. But as it most certainly is not a mark of genius at all, I suggest that Dr Parry should cut all such special pleading out of his second edition, and replace it by a few words as to the manner in which melody follows the development of harmony. When I was a boy, an overture beginning emphatically with an unprepared discord made me expect something tremendous, provided the discord was not more extreme than a third inversion of the dominant seventh (play the common chord C, E, G, C with your right hand, dear lady, and hit B flat as hard as you can in octaves with your left: that's the effect I mean), which I was familiar with from the overture to Prometheus and Trema, trema in Don Giovanni. Later on, the crashing major ninths in the prelude to the second act of Tannhäuser sounded extraordinary to me; and Schumann imposed on me as an enigmatical genius of unfathomable depth, simply because his chords, being strange, were mysterious.

At present nothing surprises me: you may begin the next act of your opera with the sixth inversion of a full chord of the major thirteenth without making me turn a hair. Now the moment I get sufficiently used to a discord to tolerate it unprepared, and to recognize its key and destination, I am ready to accept a figuration of that discord and its resolution as a "popular" melody. When other lips, which everybody recognizes as popular, begins, practically, with a figuration of the resolution of the dominant seventh. Now that the finale of the first act of Lohengrin has educated the common ear to the extension of that familiar discord by another major third, any modern Balfe can manufacture an equally acceptable melody by substituting a figuration of the ninth for the seventh, though I doubt whether Dr Parry will compliment him on his "insistence on the key."

The fact is, it is the enormous part which figuration and rum-tum play in modern music—harmonic music, as Dr Parry calls it—that makes it wear so badly in comparison with the old contrapuntal

music, I had rather hear the most conventional, fashionable overture that Handel ever wrote than the once brilliant and novel overture to Zampa, with its "insistence on the key"; and I here prophesy
that the extent to which Wagner, like all the composers of the harmonic school, resorted to figuration of chords that are daily becoming more familiar and even platitudinous, will one day make many
pages of his mere *melodrame* sound stale and obvious when Bach's
polyphony will be as fresh as when it first came from his hand. Why,
then, should we hold up this "insistence on the key," which is really
nothing but reliance on the chord, as a merit, and, for example,
praise the finale to Beethoven's symphony in C minor for the features in which it so strongly resembles Cheer, boys, cheer?

It seems to me that all this part of the book wants restating. The
very interesting contrast made in it between Beethoven's first
pianoforte sonata and the finale to Mozart's G minor symphony is
spoiled by an attempt to represent the difference as a superiority on
Beethoven's part? Similarly, some very suggestive passages on Bach's
refusal to join the harmonic movement are weakened by an assumption that the harmonic school was a higher development than the
contrapuntal one. Surely the truth is that the so-called "development" was really the birth of the modern "tone poetry" or "music-
drama" with which the old music had long been pregnant. The
separation was concealed by the extraordinary genius of Mozart,
who could produce a piece of music which at once presented to the
theatre-goer the most perfect musical reflection of the vagaries of a
scene from a farce, and to the professor a "movement" in strict form;
but Mozart, none the less, made a European revolution in music with
the statue scene in Don Giovanni, unmentioned by Dr Parry, which
represents the most sensational manifestation of the only side of his
work which was followed up.

Beethoven could not touch Mozart as an "absolute musician": a
comparison of his attempts at contrapuntal writing with such examples as the minuets in Mozart's quintets or the Recordare in the
Requiem seems to me to shew a striking falling off in this respect.
Finally we come to Wagner, who, like Weber, could not write absolute music at all—not even an overture; for the Tannhäuser overture is no more an overture than our old friend William Tell; and the
Faust is simply a horrible reduction to absurdity of the attempt to
combine the new art with the old, the beginnings of the said reduction being already plain in the first allegro of no less respectable a

classic than Mozart's Hafner symphony. But before Wagner died, "absolute music" was reviving in the hands of men who were musicians alone, and not wits, dramatists, poets, or romancers, seizing on music as the most intense expression of their genius.

Mozart, Beethoven, and Wagner, with all the "program-music" men, practised a delightful and highly compound art which can be understood without any musicianship at all, and which so fascinated the world that it swept genuine absolute music out of existence for nearly a century. But now absolute music has been revived with enormous power by Brahms, and is being followed up in this country by Dr Parry himself, and by Professor Stanford. Unfortunately, neither of them sees this as clearly as I, the critic, see it. Dr Parry knocks the end of an admirable book to pieces by following up the technical development of music, which is, of course, continuous from generation to generation, instead of the development and differentiation of the purposes of the men who composed music. Thus, he treats Mozart as the successor of Bach, and Brahms as the successor of Wagner.

The truth is that Brahms is the son of Bach and only Wagner's second-cousin. Not understanding this, Brahms feels bound to try to be great in the way of Beethoven and Wagner. But for an absolute musician without dramatic genius to write for the theatre is to court instant detection and failure, besides facing a horribly irksome job. Therefore he falls back on a form of art which enables absolute music of the driest mechanical kind to be tacked on to a literary composition and performed under circumstances where boredom is expected, tolerated, and even piously relished. That is to say, he writes requiems or oratorios. Hence Brahms' requiem, Job, and Eden! Eden is evidently the work alluded to in this volume as "one of the finest of recent oratorios, in which the choruses of angels and of devils sing passages which express the characteristic impulses of angelic and diabolic natures to a nicety." O those mixo-Ionian, hypo-Phrygian angels, and those honest major and minor devils! shall I ever forget them?

The future is bright, however: Dr Parry's latest composition is an "overture to an *unwritten* drama"—precisely the right sort of drama for an absolute musician to write an overture to. In process of time he will see that his particular "art of music," though a very noble art, has nothing to do with tragedies, written or unwritten, or with Jobs, or Judiths, or Hypatias, or anything of the kind. In the meantime I must acknowledge my deep obligation to him for having written a book from which I have learned much. No critic can afford to leave it unread.

· THE MUSIC OF THE FUTURE† ·

The ultimate success of Wagner was so prodigious that to his dazzled disciples it seemed that the age of what he called "absolute" music must be at an end, and the musical future destined to be an exclusively Wagnerian one inaugurated at Bayreuth. All great geniuses produce this illusion. Wagner did not begin a movement: he consummated it. He was the summit of the nineteenth century school of dramatic music in the same sense as Mozart was the summit (the word is Gounod's) of the eighteenth century school. All those who attempted to carry on his Bayreuth tradition have shared the fate of the forgotten purveyors of second-hand Mozart a hundred years ago. As to the expected supersession of absolute music, Wagner's successors in European rank were Brahms, Elgar, and Richard Strauss. The reputation of Brahms rests on his absolute music alone: such works as his German Requiem endear themselves to us as being musically great fun; but to take them quite seriously is to make them oppressively dull. Elgar followed Beethoven and Schumann: he owes nothing essential to Wagner, and secured his niche in the temple by his symphonies and his Enigma Variations, which are as absolutely musical as any modern music can be. Although Strauss produced works for the musical theatre which maintained it at the level to which Wagner had raised it, his new departure was a form of musical drama, comic epic, and soul autobiography in which stage, singers, and all the rest of the theatrical material of Bayreuth save only the orchestra are thrown overboard, and the work effected by instrumental music alone, even Beethoven's final innovation of a chorus being discarded. Just the same thing happened when Elgar took as his theme Shakespear's Henry IV, with Falstaff as its chief figure. He made the band do it all, and with such masterful success that one cannot bear to think of what would have been the result of a mere attempt to turn the play into an opera.

The Russian composers whose vogue succeeded that of Wagner were not in the least Wagnerian: they developed from the romantic

---

†Added to the fourth edition of *The Perfect Wagnerite,* 1922.

school, from Weber and Meyerbeer, from Berlioz and Liszt, much as they might have done had Wagner never existed except as a propagandist of the importance of their art. A disparaging attitude towards Wagner resembling that of Chopin to Beethoven, and a very similar escape from his influence even in technique, was quite common among the composers whose early lives overlapped the last part of his. In England the composers who are the juniors of Elgar, but the seniors of (for example) Bax and Ireland, the most notable of whom are Mr Granville Bantock and Mr Rutland Boughton, were heavily Wagnerized in their youth, and began by Tristanizing and Götterdämmerunging heroically; but when they found themselves their Wagnerism vanished. The younger men do not begin with Wagner nor even with Strauss: they are mostly bent on producing curiosities of absolute music until they settle down into a serious style of their own. All that can be said for the Wagner tradition is that it finally killed the confusion between decorative pattern music and dramatic music which muddled Meyerbeer and imposed absurd repetitions on the heroes and heroines of Handel and Mozart. Even in absolute music, the post-Wagnerite sonata form has become so much less mechanical and thoughtless that the fact that it still persists in essentials is hardly worth asserting.

Writing before any of these developments had happened, I said in the first edition of this book that there was no more hope in attempts to out-Wagner Wagner in music drama than there had been in the old attempts to make Handel the starting point of a great school of oratorio. How true this was is now so obvious that my younger readers may wonder why I thought it worth while to say it. But if veterans did not indulge in these day-before-yesterdayisms Music would lose the thread of its history.

· WAGNERISM IN RETROSPECT 1935† ·

I reprint Bassetto's stuff shamefacedly after long hesitation with a reluctance which has been overcome only by my wife, who has found some amusement in reading it through, a drudgery which I could not bring myself to undertake. . . .

You may be puzzled . . . to find that the very music I was brought up on: the pre-Wagner school of formal melody in separate

†From Shaw's preface to *London Music in 1888–89 as Heard by Corno di Bassetto.*

numbers which seemed laid out to catch the encores that were then fashionable, was treated by me with contemptuous levity as something to be swept into the dustbin as soon as possible. The explanation is that these works were standing in the way of Wagner, who was then the furiously abused coming man in London. Only his early works were known or tolerated. Half a dozen bars of Tristan or The Mastersingers were made professional musicians put their fingers in their ears. The Ride of the Valkyries was played at the Promenade Concerts, and always encored, but only as an insanely rampagious curiosity. The Daily Telegraph steadily preached Wagner down as a discordant notoriety-hunting charlatan in six silk dressing-gowns, who could not write a bar of melody, and made an abominable noise with the orchestra. In pantomime harlequinades the clown produced a trombone, played a bit of the pilgrims' march from Tannhäuser fortissimo as well as he could, and said "The music of the future!" The wars of religion were not more bloodthirsty than the discussions of the Wagnerites and the Anti-Wagnerites. I was, of course, a violent Wagnerite; and I had the advantage of knowing the music to which Wagner grew up, whereas many of the most fanatical Wagnerites (Ashton Ellis, who translated the Master's prose works, was a conspicuous example) knew no other music than Wagner's, and believed that the music of Donizetti and Meyerbeer had no dramatic quality whatever. "A few arpeggios" was the description Ellis gave me of his notion of Les Huguenots.

Nowadays the reaction is all the other way. Our young lions have no use for Wagner the Liberator. His harmonies, which once seemed monstrous cacophonies, are the commonplaces of the variety theatres. Audacious young critics disparage his grandeurs as tawdry. When the wireless strikes up the Tannhäuser overture I hasten to switch it off, though I can always listen with pleasure to Rossini's overture to William Tell, hackneyed to death in Bassetto's time. The funeral march from Die Götterdämmerung hardly keeps my attention, though Handel's march from Saul is greater than ever. Though I used to scarify the fools who said that Wagner's music was formless, I should not now think the worse of Wagner if, like Bach and Mozart, he had combined the most poignant dramatic expression with the most elaborate decorative design. It was necessary for him to smash the superstition that this was obligatory; to free dramatic melody from the tyranny of arabesques; and to give the orchestra symphonic work instead of rosalias and rum-tum; but now that this and all the other musical superstitions are in the dustbin, and the post-Wagnerian harmonic and contrapuntal anarchy is so complete that it is easier technically to compose another Parsifal than another Bach's Mass in B Minor or Don Giovanni I am no longer a combatant anarchist in music, not to mention that I have learnt that a successful revolution's first task is to shoot all revolutionists. This means that I am no longer Corno di Bassetto. He was pre- and pro-Wagner; unfamiliar with Brahms; and unaware that a young musician named Elgar was chuckling over his irreverent boutades. As to Cyril Scott, Bax, Ireland, Goossens, Bliss, Walton, Schönberg, Hindemith, or even Richard Strauss and Sibelius, their idioms would have been quite outside Bassetto's conception of music, though today they seem natural enough.

PART TWO

The Concert Hall

Handel

· HANDEL IN ENGLAND† ·

Ainslee's Magazine, May 1913 (*)

Handel is not a mere composer in England: he is an institution. What is more, he is a sacred institution. When his Messiah is performed, the audience stands up, as if in church, while the Hallelujah chorus is being sung. It is the nearest sensation to the elevation of the Host known to English Protestants. Every three years there is a Handel Festival, at which his oratorios are performed by four thousand executants, collected from all the choirs in England. The effect is horrible; and everybody declares it sublime. Many of the songs in these oratorios were taken by Handel from his operas and set to pious words: for example, *Rende sereno il ciglio, madre: non piange più* has become Lord, remember David: teach him to know Thy ways. If anyone in England were to take the song from the oratorio and set it back again to secular words, he would probably be prosecuted for blasphemy. Occasionally a writer attempts to spell Handel's name properly as Händel or Haendel. This produces just the same shock as the attempts to spell Jehovah as Jahve. The effect is one of brazen impiety.

I do not know of any parallel case in France. Gluck, almost unknown in England until Giulia Ravogli made a success here some twenty years ago in Orfeo, was, and perhaps still is, an institution in France; but he was an operatic, not a religious, institution. Still, there is some resemblance between the two cases. Gluck and Handel were contemporaries. Both were Germans. Both were very great composers. Both achieved a special vogue in a country not their own, and each of them remained almost unknown in the country which the other had conquered. I can think of no other instance of this.

Handel's music is the least French music in the world, and the most English. If Doctor Johnson had been a composer he would have composed like Handel. So would Cobbett. It was from Handel

†Written to be read to a society of musicians in France.

that I learned that style consists in force of assertion. If you can say a thing with one stroke unanswerably you have style; if not, you are at best a *marchand de plaisir;* a decorative *littérateur,* or a musical confectioner, or a painter of fans with cupids and *cocottes.* Handel has this power. When he sets the words Fixed in His everlasting seat, the atheist is struck dumb: God is there, fixed in his everlasting seat by Handel, even if you live in an Avenue Paul Bert, and despise such superstitions. You may despise what you like; but you cannot contradict Handel. All the sermons of Bossuet could not convince Grimm that God existed. The four bars in which Handel finally affirms "the Everlasting Father, the Prince of Peace," would have struck Grimm into the gutter, as by a thunderbolt. When he tells you that when the Israelites went out of Egypt, "there was not one feeble person in all their tribes," it is utterly useless for you to plead that there must have been at least one case of influenza. Handel will not have it: "There was not one, not one feeble person in all their tribes," and the orchestra repeats it in curt, smashing chords that leave you speechless. This is why every Englishman believes that Handel now occupies an important position in heaven. If so, *le bon Dieu* must feel toward him very much as Louis Treize felt toward Richelieu.

Yet in England his music is murdered by the tradition of the big chorus! People think that four thousand singers must be four thousand times as impressive as one. This is a mistake: they are not even louder. You can hear the footsteps of four thousand people any day in the Rue de Rivoli—I mention it because it is the only street in Paris known to English tourists—but they are not so impressive as the march of a single well-trained actor down the stage of the Théâtre Français. It might as well be said that four thousand starving men are four thousand times as hungry as one, or four thousand slim *ingénues* four thousand times as slim as one. You can get a tremendously powerful *fortissimo* from twenty good singers—I have heard it done by the Dutch conductor, De Lange—because you can get twenty people into what is for practical purposes the same spot; but all the efforts of the conductors to get a *fortissimo* from the four thousand Handel Festival choristers are in vain: they occupy too large a space; and even when the conductor succeeds in making them sing a note simultaneously, no person can hear them simultaneously, because the sound takes an appreciable time to travel along a battle front four thousand strong; and in rapid passages the semiquaver of the singer farthest from you does not reach you until that of the singer nearest you has passed you by. If I were a member of the House of Commons I would propose a law making it a capital offence to perform an oratorio by Handel with more than eighty performers in the chorus and orchestra, allowing fortyeight singers and thirtytwo instrumentalists. Nothing short of that will revive Handel's music in England. It lies dead under the weight of his huge reputation and the silly notion that big music requires big bands and choruses. Little as Handel's music is played in France, the French must be better Handelians than the English—they could not possibly be worse—as they have no festival choirs. Perhaps they even know his operas, in which much of his best music lies buried.

The strangest recent fact in connection with Handel in England is the craze he inspired in Samuel Butler. You do not yet know in France that Samuel Butler was one of the greatest English and, indeed, European writers of the second half of the nineteenth century. You will find out all about him in a couple of hundred years or so. Paris is never in a hurry to discover great men; she is still too much occupied with Victor Hugo and Meyerbeer and Ingres to pay any attention to more recent upstarts. Or stay! I am unjust; there are advanced Parisians who know about Delacroix and the Barbizon school, and even about Wagner; and I once met a Parisian who had heard of Debussy, and even had a theory that he must have been employed in an organ factory, because of his love of the scale of whole tones.

However, I am forgetting Handel and Butler. Butler was so infatuated with Handel that he actually composed two oratorios, Narcissus and Ulysses, in the closest imitation of his style, with *fugato* choruses on the cries of the Bourse, the oddest combination imaginable. Butler's books are full of references to Handel, and quotations from his music. But, as I have said, what do the French care for Butler? Only Henri Bergson can understand the importance of his work. I should explain that Mr Bergson is a French philosopher, well known in England. When he has been as long dead as Descartes or Leibnitz, his reputation will reach Paris. Dear old Paris!

· ISRAEL IN EGYPT ·

29 November 1893 (III)

At the Albert Hall on Thursday last the Royal Choral Society was much more at home with Handel than it had been at the previous concert with Berlioz. The crisp and vigorous stroke of Handel, and the strength and audacity of his style, were of course lacking, partly because these huge lumbering choirs of which we are so proud always seem to oppress conductors with a sense of their unwieldiness, partly because Sir Joseph Barnby's style is so measured and complacent. He evidently enjoys Handel's high spirits; but as he invariably stops to dwell on them, and, what is more, stops longer as the movement gathers momentum on the paper before him, its qualities remain hidden in his own imagination, and the actual performance gets slower and heavier.

But if the choir is not impetuously led it is certainly well trained. There is a certain vulgarity of speech about it, especially on the part of the men; but the tone is remarkably good and free from incidental noises; the soft passages are pretty and effective; and the execution is careful and precise. If only some spontaneity and forward spring could be substituted for the perpetual leaning back of both the conductor and the choir, the oratorio performances at the Albert Hall would become about as good as it is in the nature of such things to be. Israel in Egypt is an extraordinary example of the way in which a musical giant can carry off an enterprise which is in its own nature a monumental bore, consisting as it does, to a great extent, of passages of cold narrative which not only do not yearn for the intensity of musical expression, but positively make it impossible.

How can any composer set to music the statement that Egypt was glad when they departed? If the fact were exhibited dramatically, and the actual exclamations of gladness uttered by the Egyptians given, something might be done with them; but the mere bald narrative statement is musically out of the question. Handel therefore falls back here on a purely formal display of his professional skill in fugue writing, and in that sort of experimenting with the old modes which consists in writing in the key of E minor and leaving the sharp out of the signature and occasionally out of the music. The result is extremely interesting to deaf persons whose hobby is counterpoint and the ecclesiastical modes; but to the unsophisticated ear it is deadly dull; and it is hard to refrain from laughing outright at the thousands of people sitting decorously at the Albert Hall listening to the choir trudging through And believe-ed the Lord and his ser-vant Mo-oh-zez, and then through And! I! will exaw-aw-aw-aw-alt Him, as if the gross absurdity of these highly scholastic choruses, considered as an expression of the text, were any the less ridiculous because they were perpetrated by a great musician who could not do even an unmusical thing quite unmusically.

The situation was heightened on Thursday by the recollection that at the last concert the joke of the evening was a parody of just such choral writing. Indeed, Berlioz' burlesque Amen is far less laughable than He led them through the deep as through a wilderness, the insane contrapuntal vagaries of the last four words surpassing in irreverent grotesqueness anything that the boldest buffoon dare offer as professedly comic composition.

While the world lasts these choruses will make a complete performance of Israel a very mixed joy indeed, to be endured only for the sake of the moments in which Handel made a chance for his genius by forcing a vividly descriptive character on the narrative. He could do little with the frogs and flies, and nothing with the blotches and blains, the rinderpest, and the lice; but the thick darkness that might be felt, the hailstones and the fire mingled with the hail running along the ground, the waters overwhelming the enemy, the floods standing upright as a heap, and the depths congealed in the heart of the sea—these he worked up into tone-picutres that make it impossible to leave Israel unperformed, and that bribe us to sit out in patience the obsolete pedantries in which he took refuge when the narrative beat him. One likes, too, to be heartened with the indomitable affirmation that "there was not one—*not one* feeble person among their tribes," and to exult over the "chosen captains" drowned in the Red Sea.

I wish, by the bye, it were possible for Sir Joseph Barnby to find two singers capable of dealing with those chosen captains, instead of falling back on his four hundred tenors and basses, whom at such moments I am guilty of wishing in the Red Sea themselves, so prosaically do they let the great war-song down. On Thursday they broke my spirit so that I went home forthwith, and so heard hardly anything of the soloists except Miss Butt, who sang Their land brought forth frogs, with some little awkwardness and nervousness and misplaced breaths which she will some day learn to avoid. All the same, she sang it magnificently. The last fourteen bars came with the true musical and dramatic passion which reduces all purely technical criticism to a mere matter of detail—such detail, however, as Miss Butt would do well not to neglect. All those long phrases on single words *can* be sung in one breath if only you know how to do it.

· MESSIAH ·

1 July 1891 (I)

Fundamentally my view of the Handel Festival is that of a convinced and ardent admirer of Handel. My favorite oratorio is The Messiah, with which I have spent many of the hours which others give to Shakespear, or Scott, or Dickens. But for all this primary bias in favor of Handel, my business is still to be that of the critic, who, invited to pronounce an opinion on the merits of a performance by four thousand executants, must judge these abnormal conditions by their effect on the work as open-mindedly as if there were only four hundred, or forty, or four. And I am bound to add that he who, so judging, delivers a single and unqualified verdict on the Festival, stultifies himself. The very same conditions which make one choral number majestic, imposing, even sublime, make another heavy, mechanical, meaningless. For instance, no host could be too mighty for the Hallelujah Chorus, or See the Conquering Hero. In them every individual chorister knows without study or instruction what he has to do and how he has to feel. The impulse to sing spreads even to the audience; and those who are old hands at choral singing do not always restrain it.

I saw more than one of my neighbors joining in the Hallelujah on the first day; and if my feelings at that moment had permitted me to make a properly controlled artistic effort, I think I should have been no more able to remain silent than Santley was. Under the circumstances, however, I followed the example of Albani, who, knowing that she had to save her voice for I know that my Redeemer liveth, kept a vocal score tightly on her mouth the whole time, and looked over it with the expression of a child confronted with some intolerably tempting sweetmeat which it knows it must not touch.

But The Messiah is not all Hallelujah. Compare such a moment as I have just described with the experience of listening to the fiercely tumultuous He trusted in God, with its alternations of sullen mockery with high-pitched derision, and its savage shouts of Let him deliver him if he delight in him, jogging along at about half the proper speed, with an expression of the deepest respect and propriety, as if a large body of the leading citizens, headed by the mayor, were presenting a surpassingly dull address to somebody. There may be, in the way of the proper presentation of such a chorus as this, something of the difficulty which confronted Wagner at the rehearsals of Tannhäuser in Paris in 1861, when he asked the ballet master to make his forces attack the Bacchanal in a bacchanalian way. "I understand perfectly what you mean," said the functionary; "but only to a whole ballet of *premiers sujets* dare I breathe such suggestions."

No doubt Mr Manns's three thousand five hundred choristers might better his instructions so heartily as to go considerably beyond the utmost licence of art if he told them that unless they sang that chorus like a howling bloodthirsty mob, the utter loneliness of Thy rebuke hath broken his heart, and Behold and see, must be lost, and with it the whole force of the tragic climax of the oratorio. Besides which, there is the physical difficulty, which only a skilled and powerful orator could fully surmount, of giving instruction of that kind to such a host. But I see no reason why matters should not be vastly improved if Mr Manns would adopt throughout the bolder policy as to speed which was forced on him after four on Selection day by the silent urgency of the clock, and persisted in to some extent—always with convincing effect—in Israel. Increased speed, however, is not all that is wanted. To get rid completely of the insufferable lumbering which is the curse of English Handelian choral singing, a spirited reform in style is needed.

For instance, Handel, in his vigorous moods, is fond of launching the whole mass of voices into florid passages of great brillancy and impetuosity. In one of the most splended choruses in The Messiah, For He shall purify the sons of Levi, the syllable "fy" comes out in a single trait consisting of no less than thirty-two semiquavers. That trait should be sung with one impulse from end to end without an instant's hesitation. How is it actually done in England? Just as if the thirty-two semiquavers were eight bars of crotchets taken *alla breve* in a not very lively tempo. The effect, of course, is to make the chorus so dull that all the reputation of Handel is needed to persuade Englishmen that they ought to enjoy it, whilst Frenchmen go away from our festivals confirmed in their scepticism as to our pet musical classic. When I had been listening for some minutes on Wednesday to the festival choristers trudging with ludicrous gravity through what they called Tellit Outa Mongthe Hea-ea Then, I could not help wishing that Santley, who roused them to boundless enthusiasm by his singing of Why do the nations, had given them a taste of their own quality by delivering those chains of triplets on the words "rage" and "counsel," as quavers in twelve-eight time in the tempo of the pastoral symphony. The celestial Lift up your heads, O ye gates, lost half its triumphant exultation from this heaviness of gait.

Again, in the beginning of For unto us, the tenors and basses told each other the news in a prosaic, methodical way which made the chorus quite comic until the thundering Wonderful, Counsellor, one of Handel's mightiest strokes, was reached; and even here the effect was disappointing, because the chorus, having held nothing in reserve, could make no climax. The orchestra needed at that point about twenty more of the biggest of big drums. Another lost opportunity was the pathetically grand conclusion of All we like sheep. Nothing in the whole work needs to be sung with more intense expression than But the Lord hath laid on Him the iniquity of us all. Unless it sounds as if the singers were touched to their very hearts, they had better not sing it at all. On that Monday it came as mechanically as if the four entries of the voices had been produced by drawing four stops in an organ. This was the greater pity, because it must be conceded to our young Handel-sceptics that the preceding musical portraiture of the sheep going astray has no great claims on their reverence.

I am aware that many people who feel the shortcomings of our choral style bear with it under the impression, first, that the English people are naturally too slow and shy in their musical ways, and, second, that *bravura* vocalization and impetuous speed are not possible or safe with large choruses. To this I reply, first, that the natural fault of the English when they are singing with genuine feeling is not slowness, but rowdiness, as the neighbors of the Salvation Army know; second, that it would undoubtedly be as risky to venture far in the *bravura* direction with a very small chorus as to attempt the Walküre fire-music or Liszt's Mezeppa in an ordinary theatre orchestra with its little handful of strings. But both these compositions are safe with sixteen first and sixteen second violins, because, though notes are dropped and mistakes made, they are not all made simultaneously, and the result is that at any given instant an overwhelming majority of the violins are right. For the same reason, I do not see why nine hundred basses, even if they were the stiffest and slowest in the world, could not be safely sent at full speed in the *bravura* style through Handel's easy diatonic semiquaver traits, as safely as our violinists are now sent through Wagner's demisemiquavers.

Bach

The Dramatic Review, 28 March 1885 (*)

The Bach choir is a body of ladies and gentlemen associated under the direction of Mr Otto Goldschmidt "for the practice and performance of choral works of excellence of various schools." It made itself famous on the 26th April 1876, by achieving the first complete performance in England of John Sebastian Bach's setting of the High Mass in B minor. The work disappointed some people, precisely as the Atlantic Ocean disappointed Mr Wilde. Others, fond of a good tune, missed in it those compact little airs that can be learnt by ear and accompanied by tonic, sub-dominant, tonic, dominant, and tonic harmonies in the order stated; or, pedantry apart, by the three useful chords with which professors of the banjo teach their pupils, in one lesson, to accompany songs (usually in the key of G), without any previous knowledge of thoroughbass. As there was nothing for those unfortunate persons who did not like the Mass but to listen to it again and again until their state became more gracious, the Bach choir repeated it in 1877, in 1879, and again on Saturday last. As that day is supposed to be the 200th anniversary of Bach's birthday, a special effort was made; the performance was given in the Albert Hall; the society was reinforced by picked choristers from Henry Leslie's and other noted choirs, to the total number of over five hundred singers; and orchestral instruments that have fallen into disuse since Bach's time were specially manufactured and studied by eminent players for the occasion.

Those faults in the performance for which the conductor and the choir can fairly be held responsible were not due to any want of care of earnestness in preparation. One chorus, *Credo in Unum Deum*, fell into confusion, the singers being apparently bewildered by the burst of applause with which the audience had just received the *Cum Sancto Spiritu*. This, however, was an accident: the number was sung accurately at the last rehearsal; and had the conductor been in a position to stop and start afresh, or to repeat the chorus, the mistake would have been remedied. Here, for once, was an opportunity for the British public to set matters right by an *encore*. It is needless to add that the British public did not rise to the very simple occasion. Among the inevitable shortcomings may be classed the loss of effect in some of the brighter numbers—notably the *Pleni sunt cœli*—by the jog trot which seems to be Mr Goldschmidt's *prestissimo*. It is ungracious to complain of a conductor who has achieved a result so admirable and difficult as a good performance of the great Mass; and it is quite possible that Mr Goldschmidt may have experimentally determined that a single extra beat per second would endanger the precision upon which so much depends in Bach's polyphony; but there were moments on Saturday when the audience must have longed that Mr Goldschmidt would go ahead a little—when some may have profanely felt that one glass of champagne administered to the conductor would have made an acceptable difference in the effect. Mr Goldschmidt has, however, well earned his right to have his own opinion on the question; and he shewed when, in the *Gloria* and the *Cum Sancto Spiritu*, he got from B minor into D major, that he is capable, on occasion, of a flash of that spirit which earned for Bach himself the compliment that "in conducting he was very accurate; and in time, *which he generally took at a very lively pace*, he was always sure."

24 December 1890 (I)

The Bach Choir gave a concert on the 16th. I was not present. There are some sacrifices which should not be demanded twice from any man; and one of them is listening to Brahms' Requiem. On some future evening, perhaps, when the weather is balmy, and I can be accommodated with a comfortable armchair, an interesting book, and all the evening papers, I may venture; but last week I should have required a requiem for myself if I had attempted such a feat of endurance. I am sorry to have to play the "disgruntled" critic over a composition so learnedly contrapuntal, not to say so fugacious; but I really cannot stand Brahms as a serious composer. It is nothing short of a European misfortune that such prodigious musical powers should have nothing better in the way of ideas to express than incoherent commonplace. However, that is what is always happening in music: the world is full of great musicians who are no composers, and great composers who are no musicians.

In his youth, Brahms when writing songs or serenades, or trifles of one kind or another, seemed a giant at play; and he still does small things well. I listened to his cleverly harmonized gipsy songs at the last Monday Popular Concert of the year with respectful satisfaction, though I shall not attempt to deny that fifteen minutes of them would have been better than twenty-five. This last remark, by the bye, shews that I am full of malice against "holy John," as Wagner called Brahms, even when he does what I have admitted his fitness for. Consequently my criticism, though it relieves my mind, is not likely to be of much value. Let me therefore drop the subject, and recall the attention of the Bach Choir to a composer of whom I entertain a very different opinion, to wit, John Sebastian Bach himself. It is the special business of this society to hammer away at Bach's works until it at last masters them to the point of being able to sing them as Bach meant them to be sung. For instance, there is the great Mass in B minor. The choir has given several public performances of that; but all have been timid, mechanical, and intolerably slow. And when the elderly German conductor who got up the first performances was succeeded by a young and talented Irishman, the Mass became duller and slower than ever. The public did not take to the work as performed in this manner. It satisfied its curiosity, received an impression of vast magnitude, yawned, and felt no great impatience for a repetition of the experience. If the society thinks that this was the fault of Bach, it is most unspeakably mistaken.

Nothing can be more ruinous to the spirited action of the individual parts in Bach's music, or to the sublime march of his polyphony, than the dragging, tentative, unintelligent, half-bewildered operations of a choir still in the stage of feeling its way from interval to interval and counting one, two, three, four, for dear life. Yet the Bach Choir never got far beyond this stage with the B minor Mass. Even at the great bi-centenary performance at the Albert Hall no attempt was made to attain the proper speed; and the work, as far as it came to light at all, loomed dimly and hugely through a gloomy, comfortless atmosphere of stolid awkwardness and anxiety. The effect the slow movements would make if executed with delicacy of touch and depth of expression, and of the quick ones if taken in the true Bach major mood, energetic, spontaneous, vivid, jubilant, was left to the imagination of the audience; and I fear that for the most part they rather declined to take it on trust. All this can be remedied by the Bach choristers if they stick at it, and are led with sufficient faith and courage. There is more reason than ever for persevering with their task at present; for Bach belongs, not to the past, but to the future—perhaps the near future. When he wrote such works as Wachet auf, for example, we were no more ready for them than the children for whom we are now buying Christmas gift-books of fairy tales are to receive volumes of Goethe and Ibsen. Acis and Galatea and Alexander's Feast, the ever-charming child literature of music, were what we were fit for then.

But now we are growing up we require passion, romance, picturesqueness, and a few easy bits of psychology. We are actually able to relish Faust and Carmen. And beyond Faust there is Tristan und Isolde, which is at last music for grown men. Mr Augustus Harris has never heard of it, as it is only thirty years old; but as he goes about a good deal, I cannot doubt that in the course of the next ten years or so he will not only have it mentioned to him by some ambitious prima donna who aspires to eclipse Frau Sucher, but may even be moved to try whether a performance of it would not be better business than a revival of Favorita. Now the reaction of Tristan on Wachet auf will be a notable one. The Bach cantata, which seemed as dry and archaic after Acis and Galatea as Emperor and Galilean would after Cinderella, will, after Tristan, suddenly send forth leaves, blossoms, and perfume from every one of its seemingly dry sticks, which have yet more sap in them than all the groves of the temple of Gounod. Provided, that is—and here I ask the ladies and gentlemen of the Bach Choir to favor me with their best attention for a moment—provided always that there shall be at that time a choir capable of singing Wachet auf as it ought to be sung.

·ST. MATTHEW PASSION·

14 October 1891 (I)

I cannot say that I am unmixedly grateful to the Birmingham Festival people. They brought me all the way from Venice by a polite assurance that a packet of tickets awaited my arrival. But when, after a headlong rush over the Alps and far away into the Midlands, I reached the Town Hall, insufferable indignities were put upon me. The stewards on the floor declared that my seat was in the gallery; the stewards in the gallery insisted that it was on the floor; and finally, when it became plain that no seat at all had been reserved, I was thrust ignominiously into a corner in company with a couple of

draughts and an echo, and left to brood vengefully over the performance. On the Passion Music day I escaped the corner, and shared a
knifeboard at the back of the gallery with a steward who kept Bach
off by reading the Birmingham Daily Post, and breathed so hard
when he came to the bankruptcy list that it was plain that every firm
mentioned in it was heavily in his debt.

Under these circumstances, no right-minded person will grudge
me a certain vindictive satisfaction in recording that the performance of the St Matthew Passion, which was what I came from
Venice to hear, was not, on the whole, a success. No doubt it was
something to have brought the chorus to the point of singing such
difficult music accurately and steadily. But a note-perfect performance is only the raw material of an artistic performance; and what
the Birmingham Festival achieved was very little more than such raw
material. In the opening chorus, the plaintive, poignant melody in
triple time got trampled to pieces by the stolid trudging of the choir
from beat to beat. The violins in the orchestra shewed the singers
how it ought to be done; but the lesson was thrown away; the trudging continued; and Richter, whom we have so often seen beating
twelve-eight time for his orchestra with a dozen sensitive beats in
every bar, made no attempt to cope with the British chorister, and
simply marked one, two, three, four, like a drill-sergeant. The rest
of the performance did nothing to shew any special sympathy with
Bach's religious music on Richter's part.

It is, of course, to be considered that the necessity for having the
Passion sung from Sterndale Bennett's edition, no other being available with the English words, may have compelled him to be content
with the best performance, according to that edition, attainable in
the time at his disposal; so that he, whilst wishing to give the work "à
la Wagner," as the Dresdeners used to say, may have had to put up
with it "à la Mendelssohn" in despair of getting anything better. But,
then why did he let those piteous questions from the second chorus
to the first come out with a shout like the *sforzandos* in the roughest
and most vigorous pages of Beethoven? And why did he allow the
remonstrances of the disciples about the pot of ointment to be sung
by the same mass of voices, and with the same savage turbulence, as
the outbursts of wrath and mockery from the crowd at Pilate's house
and Golgotha? Such matters as these might have been quite easily set
right. Perhaps the safest conclusion is that half the shortcoming was
due to Richter not having taken Bach's Passion Music to heart, and
the other half to Sterndale Bennett, to lack of time for rehearsal, and

to the impregnable density of that most terrific of human institutions, the British chorus.

For no one who knows Bach intimately will need to be told that our plan of compensating for the absence of some ten or eleven skilful and sympathetic singers by substituting ten or eleven hundred stolid and maladroit ones will not answer with his music, however strong-lunged the ten or eleven hundred may be. One comparatively easy thing the Birmingham chorus could do well, and that was to sing the chorales. These, accordingly, were excellently given. The rest was leather and prunella. Even the thunder and lightning chorus had no electricity in it.

Mozart

The Illustrated London News, 12 December 1891 (*)

Wolfgang Mozart, the centenary of whose death on December 5, 1791, we are now celebrating, was born on January 27, 1756. He was the grandson of an Augsburg bookbinder, and the son of Leopold Mozart, a composer, author, and violinist of good standing in the service of the Archbishop of Salzburg. When he was three years old he shewed such an interest in the music lessons of his sister, four and a half years his senior, that his father allowed him to play at learning music as he might have allowed him to play at horses. But the child was quite in earnest, and was soon composing minuets as eagerly as Mr Ruskin, at the same age, used to compose little poems. Leopold Mozart was a clever man up to a certain point, "self-made," untroubled by diffidence or shyness, conscious of being master of his profession, a practical, pushing man, ready to lay down an ambitious program for his son and bustle him through it. Seeing that Wolfgang had talent enough to qualify him for the highest attainable worldly success as a composer and *virtuoso,* he at once set about founding a European reputation for the future great man by making a grand tour through Vienna, Paris, London, Amsterdam, and many other towns, exhibiting his two children at Court and in public as "prodigies of nature." When the boy made a couple of tours in Italy in 1769–71, he knew everything that the most learned musicians in Europe could teach him; he became an unsurpassed harpsichord and pianoforte player; and as an organist he made old musicians declare that Sebastian Bach had come again. As a violinist he did not succeed in pleasing himself. Leopold insisted that nothing but self-confidence was needed to place him at the head of European violinists; and he may have been right; but Mozart never followed up his successes as a concerto player, and finally only used his skill to play the viola in quartets. On the whole, it must be admitted that the father, though incapable of conceiving the full range of his son's genius, did his utmost, according to his lights, to make the best of him; and although Mozart must, in his latter years, have once or twice speculated as to whether he might not have managed better as an orphan, he never bore any grudge against his father on that account.

Mozart's worldly propserity ended with his boyhood. From the time when he began the world as a young man of twenty-one by making a trip to Paris with his mother (who died there) to the day of his early death, fourteen years later, he lived the life of a very great man in a very small world. When he returned to settle in Vienna and get married there, he burst out crying with emotion after the ceremony. His wife cried too; and so did all the spectators. They cried more wisely than they knew, considering what the future of the couple was to be. Mozart had three means of getting money— teaching, giving concerts, and using such aristocratic influence as he could enlist to obtain either a Court appointment or commissions to compose for the church or the theatre. None of these ways were fruitful for him, though between them all, and a good deal of borrowing, he just managed to die leaving his wife in possession of £5, exactly £15 short of what they owed to the doctor. As a teacher, he got on very well while he was giving lessons for nothing to people who interested him: as a fashionable music-master he was comparatively a failure. The concerts paid a little better: he wrote one pianoforte concerto after another for them, and always improvised a *fantasia,* and was overwhelmed with applause. But there was then no great public, as we understand the term, to steadily support subscription concerts of classical music. His subscribers were people of fashion, inconstant except in their determination only to patronize music in "the season." His failure to obtain anything except a wretched pittance at Court for writing dance music was due to the extreme dread in which he was held by the cabal of musicians who had the ear of the Emperor. Salieri frankly said afterwards, "His death was a good job for us. If he had lived longer not a soul would have given us a crumb for our compositions." Mozart was badly worn out by hard work and incessant anxiety when his last fever attacked him. He even believed that someone had poisoned him. A great deal of false sentiment has been wasted on the fact that the weather was so bad on the day of his funeral that none of the friends who attended the funeral service at St Stephen's Church went with the hearse as far as the distant graveyard of St Mark's. The driver of the hearse, the assistant gravedigger, and a woman who was attached to the place as "authorized beggar," were the only persons who saw the coffin put on top of two others into a pauper grave of the third class. Except to shew how poor Mozart was, the incident is of no importance whatever. Its alleged pathos is really pure snobbery. Mozart would certainly not have disdained to lie down for his last sleep in the grave of the poor. He would probably have been of the same mind as old Buchanan, who on his deathbed told his servant to give all the money left in the house away in charity instead of spending it on a funeral, adding, in his characteristic way, that the parish would have a pressing reason to bury him if they left him lying there too long.

It must not be supposed, however, that Mozart's life was one of actual want in the ordinary sense. He had immense powers, both of work and enjoyment; joked, laughed, told stories, talked, traveled, played, sang, rhymed, danced, masqueraded, acted, and played billiards well enough to delight in them all; and he had the charm of a child at thirty just as he had had the seriousness of a man at five. One gathers that many of his friends did not relish his superiority much more than Salieri did, and that, in spite of society and domesticity, he, on his highest plane, lived and died lonely and unhelpable. Still, on his more attainable planes, he had many enthusiastic friends and worshipers. What he lacked was opportunity to do the best he felt capable of in his art—a tragic privation.

It is not possible to give here any adequate account of Mozart's claims to greatness as a composer. At present his music is hardly known in England except to those who study it in private. Public performances of it are few and far between, and, until Richter conducted the E flat symphony here, nobody could have gathered from the vapid, hasty, trivial readings which were customary in our concert rooms that Mozart, judged by nineteenth-century standards, had any serious claim to his old-fashioned reputation. One reason among many for this mistake may be given. Leopold Mozart undoubtedly did his son the great harm of imposing his own narrow musical ideal on him, instead of allowing him to find out the full capacities of the art for himself. He taught the boy that when a piece of music sounded beautifully, and was symmetrically, ingeniously, and interestingly worked out in sonata form, nothing more was to be expected or even permitted. Mozart, if left untutored, would probably have arrived at the conclusion that a composition without a poetic or dramatic basis was a mere luxury, and not a serious work of art at all. As it was, he was trained to consider the production of "absolute music" as the normal end of composition, and when his genius drove him to make his instrumental music mean something, he wasted the most extraordinary ingenuity in giving it expression through the forms and without violating the usages of absolute music, bending these forms and usages to his poetic purpose with such success that the same piece of music serves as a pet passage of tone poetry to the amateur who knows nothing of musical formalism, while the pedant who is insensible to poetry or drama holds them up as models of classic composition to his pupils.

This combination of formalism with poetic significance has been much applauded, not only for its ingenuity, as is natural, but as a merit in the music, which is perverse and absurd. Mozart apologizing to his father for some unusual modulation which he could not justify except on poetic grounds cut but a foolish figure. If he had written his G minor quintet, for instance, in the free form contrived by Liszt for his symphonic poems, the death of his father, which immediately followed the composition of that work, would, no doubt, have been attributed to his horror on reading the score; but there is not the slightest ground for pretending, with Wagner's works to instruct us, that the quintet would have been one whit less admirable. Later on, when Mozart had quite freed himself, and come to recognize that the forbidden thing was exactly what he was born to do, he still, from mere habit and mastery, kept to the old forms closely enough to pass with us for a formalist, although he scared his contemporaries into abusing him exactly as Wagner has been abused within our own time. The result is that since Mozart, under his father's influence, produced a vast quantity of instrumental music which is absolute music and nothing else, and since even the great dramatic and poetic works of his later years were cast mainly in the moulds of that music, we have hastily concluded that all his work is of one piece, and that an intelligent dramatic handling of his great symphonies would be an anachronism. In his very operas it is hard, nowadays, to get the most obvious dramatic points in his orchestration attended to, even the churchyard scene in Don Juan being invariably rattled through at Covent Garden as if it were a surprisingly vapid quadrille.

Fortunately, the persistence with which Wagner fought all his life for a reform of orchestral execution as to Mozart's works, the example set by the conductors inspired by him, and such authoritative utterances as those of Gounod on the subject of Don Giovanni, not to mention social influences which cannot be so simply stated, are at last letting the public into the important secret that the incompetence and superficiality of Mozart's interpreters are the true and only causes of the apparent triviality of his greatest music. Properly executed, Mozart's work never disappointed anybody yet. Its popularity is increasing at present, after a long interval. The appetite for riotous, passionate, wilful, heroic music has been appeased; and we are now beginning to feel that we cannot go on listening to Beethoven's Seventh Symphony and the Tannhäuser overture for ever. When we have quite worn them out, and have become conscious that there are grades of quality in emotion as well as variations of intensity, then we shall be on the way to become true Mozart connoisseurs and to value Wagner's best work apart from its mere novelty. The obstacle to that at present is the dulness of our daily lives, which makes us intemperate in our demands for sensation in art, and the bluntness of mind which prevents us from perceiving or relishing the essentially intellectual quality of the very finest music. Both these disqualifications are the result of deficient culture; and while that lasts Mozart will have to lie on the shelf. But that is so much the worse for the uncultured generation—not for the composer of Don Juan.

9 December 1891 (I)

The Mozart Centenary has made a good deal of literary and musical business this week. Part of this is easy enough, especially for the illustrated papers. Likenesses of Mozart at all ages; view of Salzburg; portrait of Marie Antoinette (described in the text as "the ill-fated"), to whom he proposed marriage at an early age; picture of the young composer, two and a half feet high, crushing the Pompadour with his "Who is this woman that refuses to kiss me? The Queen kissed me! (Sensation)"; facsimile of the original MS. of the first four bars of Là ci darem, and the like. These, with copious paraphrases of the English translation of Otto Jahn's great biography, will pull the journalists proper through the Centenary with credit. The critic's task is not quite so easy.

The word is, of course, Admire, admire, admire; but unless you frankly trade on the ignorance of the public, and cite as illustrations of his unique genius feats that come easily to dozens of organists and choir-boys who never wrote, and never will write, a bar of original music in their lives; or pay his symphonies and operas empty compliments that might be transferred word for word, without the least incongruity, to the symphonies of Spohr and the operas of Offenbach; or represent him as composing as spontaneously as a bird sings, on the strength of his habit of perfecting his greater compositions in his mind before he wrote them down—unless you try these well-worn dodges, you will find nothing to admire that is peculiar to Mozart: the fact being that he, like Praxiteles, Raphael, Molière, or Shakespear, was no leader of a new departure or founder of a school.

He came at the end of a development, not at the beginning of one; and although there are operas and symphonies, and even pianoforte sonatas and pages of instrumental scoring of his, on which you can put your finger and say, "Here is final perfection in this manner; and nobody, whatever his genius may be, will ever get a step further on these lines," you cannot say, "Here is an entirely new vein of musical art, of which nobody ever dreamt before Mozart." Haydn, who made the mould for Mozart's symphonies, was proud of Mozart's genius because he felt his own part in it: he would have written the E flat symphony if he could, and, though he could not, was at least able to feel that the man who had reached that preeminence was standing on his old shoulders. Now, Haydn would have recoiled from the idea of composing—or perpetrating, as he would have put it—the first movement of Beethoven's Eroica, and would have repudiated all part in leading music to such a pass.

The more far-sighted Gluck not only carried Mozart in his arms to within sight of the goal of his career as an opera composer, but even cleared a little of the new path into which Mozart's finality drove all those successors of his who were too gifted to waste their lives in making weak dilutions of Mozart's scores, and serving them up as "classics." Many Mozart worshippers cannot bear to be told that their hero was not the founder of a dynasty. But in art the highest success is to be the last of your race, not the first. Anybody, almost, can make a beginning: the difficulty is to make an end—to do what cannot be bettered.

For instance, if the beginner were to be ranked above the consummator, we should, in literary fiction, have to place Captain Mayne Reid, who certainly struck a new vein, above Dickens, who simply took the novel as he found it, and achieved the feat of compelling his successor (whoever he may be), either to create quite another sort of novel, or else to fall behind his predecessor as at best a superfluous imitator. Surely, if so great a composer as Haydn could say, out of his greatness as a man, "I am not the best of my school, though I was the first," Mozart's worshippers can afford to acknowledge, with equal gladness of spirit, that their hero was not the first, though he was the best. It is always like that. Praxiteles, Raphael and Co., have great men for their pioneers, and only fools for their followers.

So far everybody will agree with me. This proves either that I am hopelessly wrong or that the world has had at least half a century to think the matter over in. And, sure enough, a hundred years ago Mozart was considered a desperate innovator: it was his reputation in this respect that set so many composers—Meyerbeer, for example—cultivating innovation for its own sake. Let us, therefore, jump a hundred years forward, right up to date, and see whether there is any phenomenon of the same nature in view today. We have not to look far. Here, under our very noses, is Wagner held up on all hands as the founder of a school and the arch-musical innovator of our age. He himself knew better; but since his death I appear to be the only person who shares his view of the matter. I assert with the utmost confidence that in 1991 it will be seen quite clearly that Wagner was the end of the nineteenth-century, or Beethoven school, instead of the beginning of the twentieth-century school; just as Mozart's most perfect music is the last word of the eighteenth century, and not the first of the nineteenth. It is none the less plain because everyone knows that Il Seraglio was the beginning of the school of nineteenth-century German operas of Mozart, Beethoven, Weber, and Wagner; that Das Veilchen is the beginning of the nineteenth century German song of Schubert, Mendelssohn, and Schumann; and that Die Zauberflöte is the ancestor, not only of the Ninth Symphony, but of the Wagnerian allegorical music-drama, with personified abstractions instead of individualized characters as *dramatis personæ*. But Il Seraglio and Die Zauberflöte do not belong to the group of works which constitute Mozart's consummate achievement—Don Juan, Le Nozze di Figaro, and his three or four perfect symphonies. They are nineteenth-century music heard advancing in the distance, as his Masses are seventeenth-century music retreating in the distance. And, similarly, though the future fossiliferous critics of 1991, after having done their utmost, without success, to crush twentieth-century music, will be able to shew that Wagner (their chief classic) made one or two experiments in that direction, yet the world will rightly persist in thinking of him as a characteristically nineteenth-century composer of the school of Beethoven, greater than Beethoven by as much as Mozart was greater than Haydn. And now I hope I have saved my reputation by saying something at which everybody will exclaim, "Bless me! what nonsense!" Nevertheless, it is true; and our would-be Wagners had better look to it; for all their efforts to exploit the apparently inexhaustible wealth of musical material opened up at Bayreuth only prove that Wagner used it up to the last ounce, and that secondhand Wagner is more insufferable, because usually more pretentious, than even secondhand Mozart used to be.

For my own part, if I do not care to rhapsodize much about Mozart, it is because I am so violently prepossessed in his favor that I am capable of supplying any possible deficiency in his work by my imagination. Gounod has devoutly declared that Don Giovanni has been to him all his life a revelation of perfection, a miracle, a work without fault. I smile indulgently at Gounod, since I cannot afford to give myself away so generously (there being, no doubt, less of me); but I am afraid my fundamental attitude towards Mozart is the same as his. In my small-boyhood I by good luck had an opportunity of learning the Don thoroughly, and if it were only for the sense of the value of fine workmanship which I gained from it, I should still esteem that lesson the most important part of my education. Indeed, it educated me artistically in all sorts of ways, and disqualified me only in one—that of criticizing Mozart fairly. Everyone appears a sentimental, hysterical bungler in comparison when anything brings his finest work vividly back to me. Let me take warning by the follies of Oublicheff, and hold my tongue.

The people most to be pitied at this moment are the unfortunate singers, players, and conductors who are suddenly called upon to make the public *hear* the wonders which the newspapers are describing so lavishly. At ordinary times they simply refuse to do this. It is quite a mistake to suppose that Mozart's music is not in demand. I know of more than one concert-giver who asks every singer he engages for some song by Mozart, and is invariably met with the plea of excessive difficulty. You cannot "make an effect" with Mozart, or work your audience up by playing on their hysterical susceptibilities.

Nothing but the finest execution—beautiful, expressive, and intelligent—will serve; and the worst of it is, that the phrases are so perfectly clear and straightforward, that you are found out the moment you swerve by a hair's breadth from perfection, whilst, at the same time, your work is so obvious, that everyone thinks it must be easy, and puts you down remorselessly as a duffer for botching it. Naturally, then, we do not hear much of Mozart; and what we do hear goes far to destroy his reputation. But there was no getting out of the centenary: something had to be done. Accordingly, the Crystal Palace committed itself to the Jupiter Symphony and the Requiem; and the Albert Hall, by way of varying the entertainment, announced the Requiem and the Jupiter Symphony.

The Requiem satisfied that spirit of pious melancholy in which we celebrate great occasions; but I think the public ought to be made rather more sharply aware of the fact that Mozart died before the Requiem was half finished, and that his widow, in order to secure the stipulated price, got one of her husband's pupils, whose handwriting resembled his, to forge enough music to complete it. Undoubtedly Mozart gave a good start to most of the movements; but, suggestive as these are, very few of them are artistically so satisfactory as the pretty Benedictus, in which the forger escaped from the taskwork of cobbling up his master's hints to the free work of original composition. There are only about four numbers in the score which have any right to be included in a centenary program. As to the two performances, I cannot compare them, as I was late for the one at the Albert Hall. . . . The highest proof of Richter's ability as a conductor was his success with Mozart's symphony in E flat. Many of our conductors, who gain considerable credit by their achievements in our grandiose and sensational nineteenth-century music, are so completely beaten by Mozart that their performances have undermined the composer's immense reputation instead of confirming it. Herr Richter, however, held his own masterfully; and the only reputations damaged were those of the composers whose works were close enough to the E flat symphony in the program to suffer from the inevitable comparison. It was curious to observe in the two last movements of this work that the power of music to produce hysterical excitement when used—or abused—solely as a nerve stimulant, which is the only power that the nineteenth century seems to value it for, is used by Mozart with exquisite taste and irresistible good humor to relieve the audience from the earnest attention compelled by the more serious part of his work. Could he have foreseen that this half jocular side of his art would be that most seriously elaborated by his successors, and that his great compositions would appear as tame to some musicians of a later generation as a recitation from Shakespear presumably is to a howling dervish, his too early death might not have lacked consolation.

·SYMPHONY NO. 39·

11 June 1890 (I)

I see that the Bishop of Ripon's description of Mozart as "first in music" has been too much for Mr Labouchere,† who intimates that it is quite enough to have to admit the pre-eminence of Shakespear in drama, and to leave uncontradicted the compliment paid by the Bishop in the department of morals. I do not blame Mr Labouchere for rushing to the conclusion that the Bishop was wrong; for Bishops generally are wrong, just as Judges are always wrong. Such is the violence of anti-prelatic prejudice in me (for the Bishop never harmed me, and may be, for what I know, a most earnest and accomplished musician), that though I happen to agree with him in the present instance, yet I take his declaration rather as a belated conventional remark surviving from the Mozart mania of the first quarter of the century, than as expressing an original conviction. The mania was followed, like other manias, by a reaction, through which we have been living, and which will be succeeded next century by a reaction against Wagner. This sort of thing happens to all great men.

I once possessed an edition of Shakespear with a preface by that portentous dullard Rowe, wherein Nicholas apologized for William as for a naïve ignoramus who, "by a mere light of nature," had hit out a few accidental samples of what he might have done had he enjoyed the educational advantages of the author of Jane Shore. I kept Rowe for a long time as a curiosity; but when I found a fashion setting in of talking about Mozart as a vapidly tuneful infant phenomenon, I felt that Rowe was outdone, and so let him drop into the dust-bin. Of course all the men of Rowe's time who knew chalk from cheese in dramatic poetry understood Shakespear's true position well enough, just as Wagner understood Mozart's, and laughed at the small fry who quite believed that Schumann and Brahms—not to mention Beethoven—had left Mozart far behind. For my part, I should not like to call Schumann a sentimental trifler and Brahms a

---

†The Bishop had declared in a sermon, "As Mozart was first in Music; as Shakespeare was first in the Drama; so Christ was first in Morals." Henry Labouchère, the radical journalist and member of parliament, had demurred in *Truth* (May 29, 1890).

pretentious blockhead; but if the average man was a Mozart, that is how they would be generally described.

Unfortunately, Mozart's music is not everybody's affair when it comes to conducting it. His scores do not play themselves by their own physical weight, as many heavy modern scores do. When a sense of duty occasionally urges Mr Manns or the Philharmonic to put the G minor or the E flat or the Jupiter Symphony in the bill, the band, seeing nothing before them but easy diatonic scale passages and cadences smoothly turned on dominant discords, races through with the general effect of a couple of Brixton schoolgirls playing one of Diabelli's pianoforte duets. The audience fidgets during the allegro; yawns desperately through the andante; wakes up for a moment at the minuet, finding the trio rather pretty; sustains itself during the finale by looking forward to the end; and finishes by taking Mr Labouchere's side against the Bishop of Ripon, and voting me stark mad when I speak of Mozart as the peer of Bach and Wagner, and, in his highest achievements, the manifest superior of Beethoven.

I remember going one night to a Richter concert, at which an overture or prelude to nothing in particular, composed in a moment of jejune Wagner-worship by Mr Eugene d'Albert, was supposed to be the special event. But it was preceded, to its utter ruin, by the E flat Symphony; and that was the first time, as far as I know, that any living Londoner of reasonable age was reached by the true Mozart enchantment. It was an exploit that shewed Richter to be a master of his art as no Valkyrie ride or fire-charm could have done. And yet he has been kept mainly at the exciting obviousnesses of the Valkyrie ride and the fire-charm ever since, with Beethoven's seventh symphony for the hundredth time by special request for a wind-up to them.

Last week, however, came the announcement that the Richter concert would end with Mozart's Symphony in C—not the Jupiter, but that known as No. 6. I left the Opera to hear it, and was fortunate enough to arrive just in time to catch the symphony, and to miss an attempt to give the thundering Gibichung chorus from the Götter-dämmerung with a handful of feeble gentlemen, whose native woodnotes wild must have been cut to ribbons by the orchestra. The performance of the symphony was a repetition of Richter's old triumph. The slow movement and the finale were magnificent: the middle section of the latter, which I confess had quite taken me in by its innocent look on paper, astonished me by its majesty, and by a combination of vivacity with grandeur.

Beethoven

In thus certifying that Mr Henschel was fully equal to an important occasion, I feel impelled to confess that I cannot say as much for
myself. The fact is, I am not always fortunate enough to arrive at
these specially solemn concerts in the frame of mind proper to the
occasion. The funeral march in the Eroica symphony, for instance, is
extremely impressive to a man susceptible to the funereal emotions.
Unluckily, my early training in this respect was not what it should
have been. To begin with, I was born with an unreasonably large
stock of relations, who have increased and multiplied ever since. My
aunts and uncles were legion, and my cousins as the sands of the sea
without number. Consequently, even a low death-rate meant, in the
course of mere natural decay, a tolerably steady supply of funerals
for a by no means affectionate but exceedingly clannish family to go
to. Add to this that the town we lived in, being divided in religious
opinion, buried its dead in two great cemeteries, each of which was
held by the opposite faction to be the antechamber of perdition, and
by its own patrons to be the gate of paradise. These two cemeteries
lay a mile or two outside the town; and this circumstance, insig-
nificant as it appears, had a marked effect on the funerals, because a
considerable portion of the journey to the tomb, especially when the
deceased had lived in the suburbs, was made along country roads.
Now the sorest bereavement does not cause men to forget wholly
that time is money. Hence, though we used to proceed slowly and
sadly enough through the streets or terraces at the early stages of our
progress, when we got into the open a change came over the spirit in
which the coachmen drove. Encouraging words were addressed to
the horses; whips were flicked; a jerk all along the line warned us to
slip our arms through the broad elbow-straps of the mourning-
coaches, which were balanced on longitudinal poles by enormous

and totally inelastic springs; and then the funeral began in earnest. Many a clinking run have I had through that bit of country at the heels of some deceased uncle who had himself many a time enjoyed the same sport. But in the immediate neighborhood of the cemetery the houses recommenced; and at that point our grief returned upon us with overwhelming force: we were able barely to crawl along to the great iron gates where a demoniacal black pony was waiting with a sort of primitive gun-carriage and a pall to convey our burden up the avenue to the mortuary chapel, looking as if he might be expected at every step to snort fire, spread a pair of gigantic bat's wings, and vanish, coffin and all, in thunder and brimstone. Such were the scenes which have disqualified me for life from feeling the march in the Eroica symphony as others do. It is that fatal episode where the oboe carries the march into the major key and the whole composition brightens and steps out, so to speak, that ruins me. The moment it begins, I instinctively look beside me for an elbow-strap; and the voices of the orchestra are lost in those of three men, all holding on tight as we jolt and swing madly to and fro, the youngest, a cousin, telling me a romantic tale of an encounter with the Lord Lieutenant's beautiful consort in the hunting-field (an entirely imaginary incident); the eldest, an uncle, giving my father an interminable account of an old verge watch which cost five shillings and kept perfect time for forty years subsequently; and my father speculating as to how far the deceased was cut short by his wife's temper, how far by alcohol, and how far by what might be called natural causes. When the sudden and somewhat unprepared relapse of the movement into the minor key takes place, then I imagine that we have come to the houses again. Finally I wake up completely, and realize that for the last page or two of the score I have not been listening critically to a note of the performance. I do not defend my conduct, present or past: I merely describe it so that my infirmities may be duly taken into account in weighing my critical verdicts. Boyhood takes its fun where it finds it, without looking beneath the surface; and, since society chose to dispose of its dead with a grotesque pageant out of which farcical incidents sprang naturally and inevitably at every turn, it is not to be wondered at that funerals made me laugh when I was a boy nearly as much as they disgust me now that I am older, and have had glimpses from behind the scenes of the horrors of what a sentimental public likes to hear described as "God's acre." I will even go further and confess that this was not the only ritual as to which my faculty of reverence was permanently disabled at an early age by the scandalous ugliness and insincerity with which I always saw it performed. And for this reason I do not in my inmost soul care for that large part of Parsifal which consists spectacularly of pure ritual, and musically of the feeling which ritual inspires in the genuine ritualist. With Siegfried lying under his tree listening to the sounds of the forest I can utterly sympathize; but Parsifal gazing motionless on the ceremony of the Grail with nothing but an open door between him and the free air makes me feel that he is served right when Gurnemanz calls him a goose and pitches him out. And here let me urge upon pious parents, in the interests of thousands of unfortunate children of whom I once was one, that if you take a child and imprison it in a church under strict injunctions not to talk or fidget, at an age when the sole consciousness that the place can produce is the consciousness of imprisonment and consequently of longing for freedom, you are laying the foundation, not of a lifetime of exemplary church-going, but of an ineradicable antipathy to all temples built with hands, and to all rituals whatsoever. That certainly was the effect on me; and one of the secondary consequences was that at this London Symphony Concert, being in a very active and objective state of mind, I became so preoccupied with the ritualistic aspect of the Parsifal music and of the slow movement of the Eroica that I could get into no sort of true communion with the composers, and so cannot say whether Mr Henschel did them justice at these points or not.

· PASTORAL SYMPHONY ·

8 February 1893 (II)

Mr Henschel is to be congratulated on his last Symphony Concert, not only for having brought a really practicable choir into the field, but for having shewn by an exceptionally good performance of the Pastoral Symphony that he had fully completed his first labor of forming a first-rate orchestra before attempting to add a choir to it. In the long intervals between the visits of Richter it is an unspeakable relief to hear a London band in St James's Hall that has spirit and purpose in its execution, and in its tone a firmness, and at need a depth and richness, which it can sustain for as many bars as you please in the broadest movements without flinching or trailing off.

When we last heard the Pastoral Symphony from the Philharmonic (potentially and by common consent of the profession—on strictly reciprocal terms—the finest band in the world, and actually the most futile), the conductor had to apologize for the performance beforehand. On Thursday last Mr Henschel had to return to the platform twice *after* the performance to be tremendously applauded. This is the second time that he has deliberately picked a specially remarkable orchestral work out of the Philharmonic program in order to shew us the difference between the Philharmonic accomplishment of reading band parts at sight and the true art of orchestral execution. In Raff's Lenore he achieved a comparatively easy and certain success. In Beethoven he has gone deeper and been more conclusively successful. The first two movements were presented in a masterly way: I have not yet heard Mr Henschel accomplish so convincing a reading of a classic. In the third movement he was a little hampered by individual shortcomings in the band, the oboe being painfully out of tune; and the climax to the storm was a trifle discounted by letting the band explode too freely before it was reached; but these blemishes were outweighed by the bringing out of many touches which usually go for nothing.

The only thing that was old-fashioned about the concert was the inevitable remark in the analytic program that Beethoven had "*descended* to positive imitation" (of the quail, cuckoo, and nightingale) in the andante. Now I appeal to Mr Bennett as a man and a brother whether we need keep waving this snippet of impertinent small-talk over the Pastoral Symphony for ever. There is no more beautiful bar in the work than that which consists of the "imitations" in question. It is exquisitely constructed and infinitely poetic; and we all like it and wait for it expectantly, and shiver with agony whenever some confounded flautist who never appreciated the nightingale—perhaps never even heard one—dots half the quavers and turns the other half into semiquavers. And then we go and gravely reproach Beethoven for having "descended" to the low and inartistic device of imitating a vulgar bird that never had a proper singing lesson in its life.

I can only say that after many years of attentive observation, devoted to determining which of the two parties—Beethoven or the critic—cut the more foolish figure after each repetition of the rebuke, I have reluctantly come to the conclusion that we had better drop it. Our profession affords us so many suitable and unobtrusive opportunities for making donkeys of ourselves when we are so disposed, that there is no excuse for our clinging to the most conspicuous and unpopular of them all.

· EIGHTH SYMPHONY ·

The Daily Chronicle, 6 November 1895 (*)

In the last instalment of Mr Ashton Ellis's translation of the prose works of Richard Wagner occurs a well-known story about the third movement of Beethoven's Eighth Symphony. Says Wagner:—

> I once was in Mendelssohn's company at a performance of this symphony in Dresden, conducted by the now deceased Kapellmeister Reissiger, and told him how I had—as I believed —arranged for its right performance by Reissiger, since he had promised open-eyed to take the trio of the minuet slower than of wont. Mendelssohn quite agreed with me. We listened. The third movement began, and I was horrified to hear the old familiar Laendler tempo once again. Before I could express my wrath, Mendelssohn was rocking his head in pleased approval, and smiling to me: "That's capital! Bravo!" So I fell from horror into stupefaction. Mendelssohn's callousness towards this curious artistic *contretemps* inspired me with very natural doubts as to whether the thing presented any difference at all to him. I fancied I was peering into a veritable abyss of superficiality— an utter void.

A quarter of a century ago, when this was written, and for long enough after it, every conductor in England used to murder the Eighth Symphony exactly as Reissiger murdered it; and every violoncellist in the Philharmonic orchestra used to dread the trio of the third movement. It was not likely that we were going to alter our ways at the suggestion of a man blasphemous enough to consider the composer of Elijah superficial, [and] who produced abominably cacophonous music like that of Tannhäuser. For we little thought then that before the century was over the man who thought Mendelssohn superior to Wagner would enjoy about as much authority in musical criticism as a literary critic who should assume that Longfellow was obviously greater than Shakespear, still less that on the wettest day in winter, with the stalls at 15s., St Jame's Hall could be sold out on the announcement of an orchestral program three-fifths Wagner and the rest Beethoven and Berlioz, without even an allusion to Mendelssohn's Italian Symphony or Spohr's Consecration of Sound, which we used to call The Power of Sound because consecration was too metaphysical to seem good sense to us. That happened last Monday, and was by no means a remarkable or unprecedented event. It is mentioned here solely because the concert began with that very Eighth Symphony whereby the Mendelssohn tale hangs.

Last year, it will be remembered, Siegfried Wagner visited us for the first time, and was handsomely received. But on his second visit he conducted the Eighth Symphony and the overture to Der Freischütz—also much mentioned in the Essay on Conducting quoted above—and conducted them, of course, "*à la* Wagner" as best he could. Unhappily this time the band was in a bad temper; and the youthful conductor, staggering under the weight of a great name, yet had the hardihood to introduce himself as a composer by a symphonic poem which, though certainly a good deal better than his father used to turn out at his age, might have been replaced with great advantage by the Italian Symphony. The result was that, though Richter sat in the front row and applauded demonstratively, especially after the *allegretto* of the Eighth Symphony, the press turned and rent poor Siegfried; so that for a moment it seemed as though he would share the fate of the son of Mozart, and be crushed by a name to which no mere mortal could live up. The fact is, however, that Siegfried scored many charming points both in the symphony and the overture, and seems to need nothing but the tact and authority which a very young man necessarily lacks to hold his own in London, where, to confess the truth, we have not only put up with, *faute de mieux,* but wantonly glorified and bragged of much worse conductors than the one who stands in Siegfried's shoes.

We are still, with all our crowding to hear Richter and Mottl, a horribly unmusical city. You can tell this by our Gargantuan musical digestion. When a Theatre Royal performs nightly a favorite *comédietta*, a celebrated sensational drama, a Shakespearean tragedy, a grand Christmas pantomime, and a screaming farce to wind up with, you do not conclude that the taste for dramatic literature is in a flourishing condition in that town: quite the contrary. But what then

must we say of the program of the last Richter concert? Let us premise that a single Beethoven Symphony is quite as full a meal as any
real musician can digest at one sitting. Now for the horrible particulars. The Eighth Symphony, Berlioz's King Lear overture, the Tannhäuser overture with the Venusberg bacchanal, the first act of Die
Walküre from the exit of Hunding to the end, and, by way of a
liqueur at the end, the Ride of the Valkyries. Will future ages be able
to credit such monstrous, undiscriminating gorging and gormandiz-
ing? Even the Ninth Symphony is not enough for one concert—an
overture and a concerto, or perhaps Schubert's Unfinished Symphony, with Adelaida sandwiched between, must be thrown in to
give the audience value for its money. This means, of course, that the
British amateur does not follow the development of a symphony at
all: he only listens for a pretty bit here and there, like a child picking
raisins out of a stodgy cake. How schoolboyish he is can be seen by his
love of the Ride of the Valkyries and the Venusberg orgy, which have
no business in a concert room at all. Indeed, the popularity of the
Seventh Symphony, which Richter repeats *ad nauseam,* is evidently
due to the galloping rhythm of the first movement, and the stamping, racing vigor of the last, not to mention the simple hymn-tune
form of the pretty *allegretto.* In all subtler respects the Eighth is
better, with its immense cheerfulness and exquisite playfulness, its
perfect candor and naturalness, its filaments of heavenly melody
suddenly streaming up from the mass of sound, and flying away
cloudlike, and the cunning harmonic coquetry with which the irresistibly high-spirited themes, after innumerable feints and tan-
talizing invitations and promises, suddenly come at you round the
most unexpected corners, and sweep you away with a delightful
burst of joyous energy. The man who, being accessible to all this, asks
for more—and such a lot more—or even supposes himself capable
of entertaining it, is an inconceivable person.

Richter, by his handling of the Eighth Symphony, again shewed
himself a consummate Beethoven conductor. There was no
Reissiger-Mendelssohn mistake about the trio, no confusion of the
movement "in the time of a minuet" (as danced) with the old brisk
Haydn Symphony minuet, which is such a very different thing. It
goes without saying that the unforgetable second theme of the last
movement—perhaps the most ravishing of those aforesaid filaments of melody—was divine; but what unhappily does not go with-

out saying in this unhappy country was the masterly phrasing of the chain of passages which follows it. It is at such points that the connoisseur in finely intelligent execution recognizes the master.

· NINTH SYMPHONY ·

23 July 1890 (I)

It is a pity that a statistical department cannot be started at St James's Hall to ascertain how many of the crowd which the Ninth Symphony always draws really like the work. If a question to this effect were supplemented by another as to whether the catechumen had studied the symphony for himself or had derived his knowledge of it wholly from public performances, I am afraid that the answers (in the unlikely event of their being unaffectedly true) would shew that the line of cleavage between those whom it puzzles or bores, and those who cherish it among their greatest treasures, coincides exactly with that between the concert students and the home students. That terrible first movement is the rub. At the Richter concerts we are convinced but unsatisfied; at the Crystal Palace grateful but hardly convinced; at the Philharmonic wearied and embittered. The whole cause of the shortcoming in Richter's case is insufficient rehearsal.

Wagner assures us that the perfect performances which he heard in Paris by the Conservatoire orchestra under Habeneck in 1838 were achieved, not in the least by Habeneck's genius, for he had none, but because he had the perseverance to rehearse the first movement until he understood it. This took two years; but, in the end, the band had not only got hold of the obviously melodic themes, but had discovered that much of what had at the first blush seemed mere figurated accompaniment, to be played with the usual tum-tum accents, was true and poignantly expressive melody.

My own conviction is that if any band gets hold of this melody, the melody will get hold of the band so effectually that the symphony will play itself if the conductor will only let it, to ensure which it is necessary that he, too, should be equally saturated. But since the process does not pay as a commercial speculation, and the only national provision for orchestral music in this country is made by merely securing to every speculator full freedom to try his luck, a good performance of the first movement is never heard in London.

Richter himself is duly saturated and super-saturated; but in spite of all he can do in the time at his disposal, the perfect balance, the consentaneous inspiration, the felt omnipresence of melody in its highest sensitiveness, remain unachieved: you find the strings stumbling over the *forte* passages in a dry excited way, detaching themselves angrily from the turbid uncertain song of the wood and horns, and producing a worry which suggests that the movement, however heroic by nature, is teething, and cannot help going into convulsions occasionally. Richter strained every nerve to get it as nearly right as possible at his last concert, and he certainly got the uttermost that his material and opportunities admitted; but the uttermost was none too good. The rest was comparatively plain sailing. The Scherzo went perhaps a shade too slowly: he took it at from 110 to 112 bars per minute; and I stand out for 115 at least myself.

It was remarkable, by the bye, to hear the young people bursting prematurely into applause at the end of the Presto, before the repetition of the Scherzo. The reason was that the repeat is omitted in the familiar Peters edition arrangement of the symphonies as pianoforte duets; and these enthusiasts thought accordingly that the movement ended with the little rally at the end of the Presto. Nothing could be more welcome than a blunder which shewed that young England is not depending on the Philharmonic for its notions of Beethoven. The performance attained its highest pitch during the slow movement. Obvious as the relation between the Adagio and Andante sections seems, I have heard it misconceived in all manner of ways by conductors, from Mr Manns, who only misses it by a hair's breadth, to Signor Arditi, who, on being confronted with it for the first time one night at a "classical" Promenade Concert, went at it with the greatest intrepidity, taking the Andante at a supernaturally slow lento, and rattling the Adagio along at a lively allegretto, the whole producing the effect of a chastened selection from Il Barbiere for use on Sundays. Richter made no such mistakes. At the *reprise* of the Andante the movement was going so divinely that when the first violins went at a passage with an unmistakeable intention of overdoing it, Richter flung out an imploring hand with a gesture of the most appealing natural eloquence; and they forbore. There was one other magical instant—the announcement of the choral theme by the bass strings in an ethereal *piano*. Then the choir was unchained and led forth to havoc, in which I am bound to add that the four soloists, who began merrily enough, did not escape scathless. But badly as it was sung, this great hymn to happiness, with its noble and heartfelt glorification of joy and love, was at least better than an oratorio.

8 March 1893 (II)

A performance of the Ninth Symphony always brings a special audience to St James's Hall; for it is known to be the masterpiece of modern tone poetry, and the literary man comes to complete his culture by listening to it. I always pity him as he sits there, bothered and exhausted, wondering how soon the choir will begin to sing those verses which are the only part of the analytic program of which he can make head or tail, and hardly able to believe that the conductor can be serious in keeping the band moodling on for forty-five mortal minutes before the singers get to business. Time was when the conductor himself was often still more astray than the literary man as to the intention of Beethoven, and when those who knew the work by heart sat snorting in contemptuous rage, or enduring with the habitual resignation of tamed despair, whilst the dreary ceremony of reading through the band parts was proceeding.

When I say "time *was*," I do not for a moment question the ability of London to reproduce the same discouraging results still: no doubt anyone who may be curious to know exactly what I mean will find sufficient opportunity before we have lost all the traditions of the time when the Ninth Symphony was treated exactly as if it were a quintet for pianoforte, flute, etc., by Hummel, re-scored for full orchestra by Beethoven. But it has now become a matter of tolerably common knowledge that this sort of handling stamps a conductor, not as a leading authority on Beethoven, but as a nincompoop. How far the work has become really popular it would be hard to determine, because, as I have said, so many people come whenever it is in the bills, not to enjoy themselves, but to improve themselves. To them the culmination of its boredom in an Ode to Joy must seem a wanton mockery, since they always hear it for the first time; for a man does not sacrifice himself in that way twice, just as he does not read Daniel Deronda twice; and consequently, since it is preeminently true of the Ninth Symphony as of the hero of the musichall song, that it is all right when you know it but youve got to know it first, he never becomes sufficiently familiar with the work to delight in it.

On the other hand, there must be a growing number of persons who, like myself, would rather have the Ninth Symphony, even from the purely musical point of view, than all the other eight put together, and to whom, besides, it is religious music, and its performance a celebration rather than an entertainment. I am highly susceptible to the force of all truly religious music, no matter to what Church it belongs; but the music of my own Church—for which I may be allowed, like other people, to have a partiality—is to be found in the Die Zauberflöte and the Ninth Symphony. I was born into evil days, when Les Huguenots was considered a sublime creation, and Die Zauberflöte "a damned pantomime" (as they say nowadays of its legitimate successor, Das Rheingold), and when the Ninth Symphony was regarded as a too long and perversely ugly and difficult concert-piece, much inferior to such august neo-classics as Spohr's Consecration of Sound and Mendelssohn's Italian Symphony; and if I had won all my knowledge of the great Singspiel and the great Symphony from their interpreters, instead of from Mozart and Beethoven themselves, small and darkened would that knowledge have been. . . .

As to Mr Henschel and his performance of the Ninth Symphony last Thursday, when I say that he quite understood the nature of the work, and was not for a moment in danger of the old fundamental error of treating it as mere musical arabesque, I imply that the performance was a success; for, with a good band and a right understanding, the obscurities and difficulties of the Ninth Symphony vanish, and a child may lead it. The concert began with Schubert's unfinished symphony, which on this occasion ought to have been his uncommenced symphony. The Ninth Symphony is quite enough for one evening; and I purposely came late for the first movement of the Schubert part of the program, and did not listen to the second. When we got to Beethoven our minds were soon set at ease as to Mr Henschel's grasp of the situation by the vigor and decision with which we got the first subject, especially those two final bars with which Beethoven so powerfully clinches it. But though the main point was thus secured, the handling of the movement as it proceeded was not by any means above criticism.

Mr Henschel, like Ibsen's Master Builder, and like all good conductors, has a troll in him; and this troll occasionally takes to rampaging and filibustering, at which seasons Mr Henschel will not only tolerate, and even relish, rough and blatant attacks on imposing passages, but will overdrive his band in a manner recalling some of the most remarkable achievements of Bevignani. Now, Beethoven must have known well that this was one of the common faults of the qualities he required in a conductor; and it seems clear to me that it was his dread lest any vulgar urgency or excitement should mar the grandeur of his symphonic masterpiece that led him to give the *tempo* of the first movement not merely as *allegro*, but as "*allegro*, but not too much so—rather majestically." Mr Henschel certainly missed the full significance of this "un poco maestoso." He made more than one undignified spurt; and at each of these incontinences the execution became blurred and confused, even to the point, if I mistake not, of notes being dropped and hasty recoveries made in the next bar by the wood-wind.

In the Scherzo, which lends itself to impetuous treatment, the *tempo* was perfect, varying between a normal hundred and seventeen bars per minute and an exceptional hundred and twenty. There were many admirable points in the execution of the slow movement, notably the cantabile of the second violins in the first of the andante sections, and the only matter on which I found myself at odds with the conductor was the concluding twelve-eight section, where the fact, hardly noticeable at first in the common time, that the pace was a shade too fast for a true Beethoven adagio, became quite obvious. Later on, Mr Henschel rather astonished some of us by the apparently very slow *tempo* he adopted for the *allegro assai*, in which the basses give out the theme of the Ode to Joy. We are so accustomed to hear this played exactly twice too fast, as if the minims and crotchets were quavers and semiquavers, and treated as a Haydn allegro instead of as an expressive melody, that some of the older listeners felt a little indignant with Mr Henschel for not taking the usual wrong course.

I will even confess that I myself think that the thirty-three bars per minute, increasing to thirty-six at the *forte*, might have been changed to thirty-six and forty respectively without any worse effect than the correction of a slight failing that leaned to virtue's side. The choral portion was perhaps as well done as was possible under the circumstances at English concert pitch; but the strain was inhuman; and the florid variation beat both the choir and the principals, since it required smooth vocal execution as well as mere pluck, which quality the choir shewed abundantly as they held on desperately to high A after high A. On the whole, if we cannot get the pitch down, I am prepared to face the transposition of the choral section a semitone rather than have it marred by tearing and straining at impossibilities. The best points in the vocal work were the charming *piano* on the lines Who can not, oh let him, weeping, Steal away and live alone; the great chorus, Oh! embrace now all ye millions, and the martial tenor solo, which was sung with intelligence and spirit by Mr Henry McKinley.

· LAST QUARTETS ·

The Hornet, 28 March 1877 (*)

An extra Popular Concert was given on the afternoon of the 21st, for the performance of the first and fifth of Beethoven's post-humous quartets. The selection was an admirable one, for the two works in question illustrate some phases of feeling which belong peculiarly to the great master's individuality, and have been ex-pressed in music by no other composer. The quartet in F major, Op. 135, contains one of these majestic slow movements which occur in Beethoven's earliest and latest works, and in which he has conveyed intense melancholy without any sacrifice of dignity or suggestion of morbid sentimentality. In the *scherzo* and *finale* of the E flat quartet is expressed the riotous humor which seems to have increased in reck-lessness with the years and troubles of the writer. In both works are to be found other beauties, of which it would be impossible to treat with the pen; but the characteristics above-mentioned contrast so strongly that they produce a striking effect when heard in succes-sion, as was the case on Wednesday last. The executants were MM. Joachim, Ries, Straus, and Piatti.

21 February 1894 (III)

The great attraction for me at this concert was Beethoven's posthumous quartet in C sharp minor. Why should I be asked to listen to the intentional intellectualities, profundities, theatrical fits and starts, and wayward caprices of self-conscious genius which make up those features of the middle period Beethovenism of which we all have to speak so very seriously, when I much prefer these beautiful, simple, straightforward, unpretentious, perfectly intelli-gible posthumous quartets? Are they to be always avoided because the professors once pronounced them obscure and impossible?

Surely the disapproval of these infatuated persons must by this time prejudice all intelligent persons in favor of the works objected to.

The performance, though the opening *adagio* was taken at a tolerably active *andante,* was an enjoyable one—another proof, by the way, that the difficulties of these later works of Beethoven are superstitiously exaggerated. As a matter of fact, they fail much seldomer in performance nowadays than the works of his middle age.

Schubert

23 March 1892 (II)

At the Crystal Palace there is an understanding among the regular frequenters that a performance of Schubert's Symphony in C is one of the specialities of the place. The analytic program of it is one of Sir George Grove's masterpieces; and Mr Manns always receives a special ovation at the end. The band rises to the occasion with its greatest splendor; and I have to make a point of looking interested and pleased, lest Sir George should turn my way, and, reading my inmost thoughts, cut me dead for ever afterwards. For it seems to me all but wicked to give the public so irresistible a description of all the manifold charms and winningnesses of this astonishing symphony, and not tell them, on the other side of the question, the lamentable truth that a more exasperatingly brainless composition was never put on paper. Fresh as I was this time from the Rossini centenary, I could not help thinking, as I listened to those outrageously overdone and often abortive climaxes in the last movement, how much better than Schubert the wily composer of Tancredi could engineer this sort of sensationalism. It was not only his simple mechanism and the infallible certainty with which it wound you up to striking-point in exactly sixteen bars: it was his cool appreciation of the precise worth of the trick when he had done it.

Poor Schubert, who laughed at Rossini's overtures, and even burlesqued them, here lays out crescendo after crescendo, double after quickstep, gallopade after gallopade, with an absurdly sincere and excited conviction that if he only hurries fast enough he will presently overtake Mozart and Beethoven, who are not to be caught up in a thousand miles by any man with second-rate brains, however wonderful his musical endowment. Much as I appreciate the doughtiness with which Sir George Grove fought Schubert's battle in England, yet now that it is won I instinctively bear back a little, feeling that before any artist, whatever his branch may be, can take his place with the highest, there is a certain price to be paid in head-work, and that Schubert never paid that price. Let that be admitted, and we may play the Symphony in C until we are all black in the face: I shall not be the first to tire of it.

· OFFERTORIUM AND TANTUM ERGO ·

18 March 1891 (I)

The last two numbers at this Bach concert were curiously contrasted. One was an Offertorium and Tantum Ergo by Schubert, the other the Choral Fantasia. Beethoven's genuinely religious music, without a shadow of fear or mistrust on it from beginning to end, fit for happy and free people to sing with the most buoyant conviction, came with an extraordinarily refreshing effect after the hypochondriacal tromboning [which] Schubert, in a perverse fit, devised to set miserable sinners grovelling. It would be too much to suspect the Bach Choir of any satiric intention in the arrangement of its program: in fact, I suspect it of thinking the Tantum Ergo rather a fine piece of music. If that is so, I will take the liberty of urging them to remember that it is not the cowl that makes the monk, and that some of the most frivolous, the most inane, and even the most wicked music in the world is to be found in such forms as the oratorio, the Mass, and anthem, or the like. Any musician can turn out to order as much church music as you please, from a whole service to a Christmas carol, just as a domestic engineer can turn out a heating apparatus; but how is it likely to compare, as religious music, with Mozart's Die Zauberflöte, for instance, which professes to be no more than a mere profane Singspiel?

Berlioz

· THE DAMNATION OF FAUST ·

The Star, 9 July 1889 (C)

Call no conductor sensitive in the highest degree to musical impressions until you have heard him in Berlioz and Mozart. I never unreservedly took off my hat to Richter until I saw him conduct Mozart's great symphony in E flat. Now, having heard him conduct Berlioz's Faust, I repeat the salutation. I never go to hear that work without fearing that, instead of exquisite threads of melody, wonderful in their tenuity and delicacy, and the surpassingly strange and curious sounds and measures, ghostly in touch and quaint in trend, unearthly, unexpected, unaccountable, and full of pictures and stories, I shall hear a medley of thumps and bumps and whistles and commonplaces: one, two, three, four: one, two, three, four; and for Heaven's sake dont stop to think about what you are doing, gentlemen, or we shall never keep the thing together. Last night there was no such disappointment. The Hungarian March I pass over, though I felt towards the end that if it were to last another minute I must charge out and capture Trafalgar Square single-handed. But when the scene on the banks of the Elbe began—more slowly than any but a great conductor would have dared to take it—then I knew that I might dream the scene without fear of awakening a disenchanted man. As to the dance of will-o'-the-wisps in the third part, Richter's interpretation of that most supernatural minuet was a masterpiece of conducting. I need say no more. The man who succeeds with these numbers does not make the usual failure with the Easter Hymn or the Ride to Hell.

31 October 1889 (I)

A stroll round the gallery of the Albert Hall last night during the first part of Berlioz's Faust brought me past so many wage-working men of a type unknown at oratorio performances that I must at once say something which members of the Church Establishment had better skip lest they be shocked beyond recovery. It is nothing short of this—that a large section of the most alert-minded, forward, and culture-capable of the London artisan class are eager to gratify their curiosity about this wonderful art of music, if only they can get it dissociated from the detested names—dont be shocked, reader, it is quite true—of St Paul, Elijah, Saul, and the other terrors of the poor man's Sunday school. It is useless to blink the fact. Just as the workman, long after he wanted to give up bad beer and spirits for coffee and cocoa, yet refused to enter the coffee tavern until he could get what he wanted there without a tract and an inquiry as to whether he was saved, so he will keep out of the concert room until he feels certain that he will not be reminded there of the hated "religious instruction" to the hypocrisy of which his own poverty bears unanswerable testimony. He hates fugues because they remind him of anthems; an oratorio makes him feel as if he were in church, which is the most horrible sensation known to him short of actual bodily pain, because there is no place where he is forced to feel the shabbiness of his clothes and the unsocial contempt in which he is held by church-going respectability, as he is forced to feel it there. Therefore, I plead for more secular music for the workman—for picturesque dramatic music that will hold him as a novel holds him, whilst his ear is automatically acquiring the training that will eventually make him conscious of purely musical beauty. Faust he evidently likes, and he would perhaps relish it even more if Mr Barnby could be persuaded to conduct a trifle less canonically. Berlioz has told us how the audience rose in a wild tumult of patriotic enthusiasm when he first gave them his version of the Rákóczy March. At the Albert Hall last night the audience, with admirable self-control, kept their seats, and did not even encore the march. Mr Barnby is certain to be made a knight some day in the ordinary course; but before it is too late let me suggest that he should be made a bishop instead. At the same time I must again bear testimony to the enormous pains he has taken to drill that huge and stolid choir, and to the success with which he has taught them to produce genuine vocal tone and to do their duty with precision and some delicacy, if not with intelligence. I wonder he was not killed by the struggle with their thousandfold pigheadedness (this is not polite, I know; but, bless you, the Albert Hall choristers never read Radical newspapers). I had to leave at the end of the first part, and so did not hear Margaret. Mr Iver McKay, the Faust of the evening, was not in brilliant voice; he was more often flat than not. Mr Henschel sang the Mephistopheles music, which suits his peculiarities, cleverly—more cleverly, perhaps, than could any of his rivals in the part, except Mr Max Heinrich. Mr Ben Grove was an excellent Brander, again shewing himself to be what I declared him when he sang King Mark's music at Mr Armbruster's recital of Tristan, a capable, trustworthy, self-respecting, and Art-respecting singer.

8 November 1893 (III)

When the fierce strain put by my critical work on my powers of attention makes it necessary for me to allow my mind to ramble a little by way of relief, I like to go to the Albert Hall to hear one of the performances of the Royal Choral Society. I know nothing more interesting in its way than to wake up occasionally from a nap in the amphitheatre stalls, or to come out of a train of political or philosophic speculation, to listen for a few moments to an adaptation of some masterpiece of music to the tastes of what is called "the oratorio public." Berlioz' Faust is a particularly stiff subject for Albert Hall treatment. To comb that wild composer's hair, stuff him into a frock-coat and tall hat, stick a hymn-book in his hand, and obtain reverent applause for his ribald burlesque of an Amen chorus as if it were a genuine Handelian solemnity, is really a remarkable feat, and one which few conductors except Sir Joseph Barnby could achieve. Instead of the brimstonish orgy in Auerbach's cellar we have a *soirée* of the Young Men's Christian Association; the drunken blackguardism of Brander is replaced by the decorous conviviality of a respectable young bank clerk obliging with a display of his baritone voice (pronounced by the local pianoforte tuner equal to Hayden Coffin's); Faust reminds one of the gentleman in Sullivan's Sweethearts; the whiskered pandoors and the fierce hussars on the banks of the Danube become a Volunteer corps on the banks of the Serpentine; and all Brixton votes Berlioz a great composer, and finds a sulphurous sublimity in the whistles on the piccolo and clashes of the cymbals which bring Mr Henschel, as Mephistopheles, out of his chair. This does not mean that Berlioz has converted Brixton: it means that Brixton has converted Berlioz. Such conversions are always going on. The African heathen "embrace" the Christian religion by singing a Te Deum instead of dancing a wardance after "wetting their spears" in the blood of the tribe next door; the English heathen (a much more numerous body) take to reading the Bible when it is edited for them by Miss Marie Corelli; the masses,

sceptical as to Scott and Dumas, are converted to an appreciation
of romantic literature by Mr Rider Haggard; Shakespear and
Goethe become world-famous on the strength of "acting versions"
that must have set them fairly spinning in their graves; and there is a
general appearance of tempering the wind to the shorn lamb, which
turns out, on closer examination, to be really effected by building a
badly ventilated suburban villa round the silly animal, and telling
him that the frowsy warmth he begins to feel is that of the sunbeam
playing on Parnassus, or the peace of mind that passeth all understanding, according to circumstances. When I was young, I was like
all immature critics: I used to throw stones at the windows of the
villa, and thrust in my head and bawl at the lamb that he was a fool,
and that the villa builders—honest people enough, according to
their lights—were swindlers and hypocrites, and nincompoops and
sixth-raters. But the lamb got on better with them than with me; and
at last it struck me that he was happier and more civilized in his villa
than shivering in the keen Parnassian winds that delighted my har-
dier bones; so that now I have become quite fond of him, and love to
lead him out when the weather is exceptionally mild (the wind being
in the Festival cantata quarter perhaps), and talk to him a bit without
letting him see too plainly what a deplorable mutton-head he is.
Dropping the metaphor, which is becoming unmanageable, let me
point out that the title of Berlioz' work is The Damnation of Faust,
and that the most natural abbreviation would be, not Berlioz' Faust,
but Berlioz' Damnation. Now the Albert Hall audience would certainly not feel easy with such a phrase in their mouths. I have even
noticed a certain reluctance on the part of mixed assemblies of ladies
and gentlemen unfamiliar with the German language to tolerate
discussions of Wagner's Götterdämmerung, unless it were mentioned only as The Dusk of the Gods. Well, the sole criticism I have to
make of the Albert Hall performance is that the damnation has been
lifted from the work. It has been "saved," so to speak, and jogs along
in a most respectable manner. The march, which suggests household troops cheered by enthusiastic nursemaids, is encored; and so is
the dance of sylphs, which squeaks like a tune on the hurdy-gurdy.
The students' Jam nox stellata sounds as though middleaged commercial travellers were having a turn at it. On the whole the performance, though all the materials and forces for a good one are at the
conductor's disposal, is dull and suburban. The fact is, Berlioz is not
Sir Joseph Barnby's affair.

Mendelssohn

·QUARTET IN E FLAT MAJOR·

23 February 1889 (C)

What I really bring this concert in for is to ask why Mendelssohn's quartet in E flat major is to be thrust into our ears at the point of the analytical programme, as one of "the happiest productions of the composer's genius." Also why Mendelssohn is described as "a master yielding to none in the highest qualifications that warrant the name." The man who would say these things nowadays would say anything. Long ago, when the Mendelssohn power was at its height they were excusable; but programs dating from that period are out of date by this time. We now see plainly enough that Mendelssohn, though he expressed himself in music with touching tenderness and refinement, and sometimes with a nobility and pure fire that makes us forget all his kid glove gentility, his conventional sentimentality, and his despicable oratorio mongering, was not in the foremost rank of great composers. He was more intelligent than Schumann, as Tennyson is more intelligent than Browning: he is, indeed, the great composer of the century for all those to whom Tennyson is the great poet of the century. He was more vigorous, more inventive, more inspired than Spohr, and a much abler and better educated man than Schubert. But compare him with Bach, Handel, Haydn, Mozart, Beethoven, or Wagner; and then settle, if you can, what ought to be done to the fanatic who proclaims him "a master yeilding to," etc., etc., etc.

These remarks will doubtless have the effect of instantaneously inducing Messrs Chappell to discard their stereotyped program of the E flat quartet. To replace it they should select some person who is not only void of superstition as to Mendelssohn, but also as to the sacredness of sonata form. If the first movement of this quartet was not "a model of construction," it would perhaps be a genuine piece of music instead of the mere dummy that it is. Surely the musical critics ought to leave to their inferiors, the literary reviewers, the folly of supposing that "forms" are anything more than the shells of

works of art. Though Bach's natural shell was the fugue, and Beethoven's the sonata, can anybody but an academy professor be infatuated enough to suppose that musical composition consists in the
imitation of these shells: a sort of exercise that is as trivial as it is
tedious? The fugue form is as dead as the sonata form; and the
sonata form is as dead as Beethoven himself. Their deadliness kills
Mendelssohn's St Paul and the "regular" movements in his symphonies and chamber music. Fortunately, the people are sound on
this question. They are not indifferent to the merits of the first and
second subjects in a formal sonata; but to the twaddling "passages"
connecting them, to the superfluous repeat, the idiotic "working
out," and the tiresome recapitulation they are either deaf or wish
they were. I once asked an energetic and liberal-minded young conductor what he thought of Liszt's music. He replied with the inelegant but expressive monosyllable, "Rot." I was much less scandalized
than I should have been had he applied that term to Mendelssohn's
music; and yet I have no hesitation in saying that we have in Liszt's
Preludes a far better example of appropriate form than any of the
"regularly constructed" works of Mendelssohn.

· ST. PAUL ·

27 September 1889 (C)

The 16th November will be a dreadful afternoon at the Crystal
Palace Saturday concerts. It is to be devoted to Mendelssohn's St
Paul. I suppose this would not occur unless there were people capable of enjoying such musical atavisms as nineteenth-century scriptural oratorios. There is no accounting for taste. In the last century
people used to like sham Shakespear: tragedies in five acts and in
blank verse, in which the hero, usually a compound of Macbeth,
Richard III, and Iago, used to die declaiming "Whip me, ye grinning
fiends" at the ghosts of his murdered victims. In the same way le-
gions of organists and academy professors have turned out sham
Handel for the use of festival committees anxious to vindicate themselves from the charge of neglecting English art. Now I grant that
Mendelssohn is better than the organist, the professor, the
Mus.Bac., and the Mus.Doc.; just as Tennyson is better than Cum-
berland or Colman. But compared with Handel he is what Tennyson
is compared with Shakespear. If you are shocked at these sentiments,
I challenge you to go to the Crystal Palace on 16th November; to set all

that dreary fugue manufacture, with its Sunday-school sentimentalities and its Music-school ornamentalities, against your recollection of the expressive and vigorous choruses of Handel; and to ask yourself on your honor whether there is the slightest difference in kind between "Stone him to death" and "Under the pump, with a kick and a thump," in Dorothy. Then blame me, if you can, for objecting to the Palace people pestering mankind with Mendelssohnic St Pauls and Gounodic Redemptions and Parrysiac Judiths and the like, when one hardly ever hears Jephtha or a Bach cantata. But of what use is it to complain? If my cry were heeded, the Palace directors would simply say: "Oh, he likes Handel, does he? How nice! We rather think we can meet his views in that direction." And they would straightway kidnap five or six thousand choristers; put Israel in Egypt into rehearsal; and treat me to a dose of machine thunder in the Handel orchestra. It would be utterly in vain: I should complain worse than ever: the machine thunder is as unimpressive as the noise of the thousand footsteps in Oxford St.

· ELIJAH ·

11 May 1892 (II)

The performance of Elijah at the Albert Hall last Wednesday was one of remarkable excellence. The tone from the choir was clean and unadulterated: there was no screaming from the sopranos, nor brawling from the tenors, nor growling from the basses. In dispensing with these three staple ingredients of English choral singing Mr Barnby has achieved a triumph which can only be appreciated by those who remember as well as I do what the choir was like in its comparatively raw state some fifteen years ago. Nowadays he gets the high notes taken *piano* as easily as the middle ones; and the sharpness of attack and the willing vigor and consentaneousness of the singing when the music in hand is as familiar to the singers and as congenial to the conductor as Mendelssohn's, are all that could be desired.

I sat out the performance on Wednesday to the last note, an act of professional devotion which was by no means part of my plan for the evening; and I did not feel disposed to quarrel with Mr Barnby more than twice. The first time was over the chorus Hear us, Baal, which he quite spoiled by taking *allegro molto*. If he had taken it as Mendelssohn directed, *allegro non troppo*, with the quaver accompaniment excessively detached, and the theme struck out in pompous, stately strokes, the result would have convinced him that Mendelssohn knew quite well what he was about; and the chorus would not have discounted, by anticipation, the effect of the startled Hear our cry, O Baal, or of the frantic Baal, hear and answer. The second occasion was of the same kind. The chorus Then did Elijah the prophet break forth like a fire was taken almost twice too fast, in spite of Mendelssohn's instructions. For surely no difference of opinion as to the right *tempo* can extend to making a rattling *allegro* of a movement marked *moderato maestoso.* The consequence was that the unaccompanied phrase And when the Lord would take him away to heaven sounded ludicrously hasty; and there was no sensation at the end like that after Thanks be to God: He laveth the thirsty land, which, taken as Mendelssohn ordered it to be taken, roused the audience to enthusiasm. Madame Albani hardly needed the apology which was circulated for her on the ground of a "severe cold" which she simply had not got, though I have no doubt she was suffering, as we all were, from the abominable east wind. The selection of Mr Ben Davies and Madame Belle Cole for the tenor and contralto parts could not easily have been improved on; and though Mr Watkin Mills began badly, and did not at any time exactly break forth like a fire, he was not too far overparted.

The audience was a huge one, shewing, after all deductions for the numbers of the foolish people who only run after the reputations of the solo singers, that there is no falling off in the great popularity of Elijah. This need not be regretted so long as it is understood that our pet oratorio, as a work of religious art, stands together with the pictures of Scheffer and Paton, and the poems of Longfellow and Tennyson, sensuously beautiful in the most refined and fastidiously decorous way, but thoughtless. That is to say, it is not really religious music at all. The best of it is seraphic music, like the best of Gounod's; but you have only to think of Parsifal, of the Ninth Symphony, of Die Zauberflöte, of the inspired moments of Handel and Bach, to see the great gulf that lies between the true religious sentiment and our delight in Mendelssohn's exquisite prettiness. The British public is convinced in its middle age that Then shall the righteous shine forth as the sun is divine, on grounds no better and no worse than those on which, in its callow youth, it adores beautiful girls as angels. Far from desiring to belittle such innocent enthusiasm, I rather echo Mr Weller's plea that "Arter all, gen'lmen, it's an amiable weakness."

At the same time, a vigorous protest should be entered whenever an attempt is made to scrape a layer off the praise due to the seraphs in order to spread it over the prophet in evening dress, who, in feeble rivalry with the Handelian prophet's song of the power that is "like a refiner's fire," informs the audience, with a vicious exultation worthy of Mrs Clennam, that "God is angry with the wicked every day." That is the worst of your thoughtlessly seraphic composer: he is a wonder whilst he is flying; but when his wings fail him, he walks like a parrot.

· ATHALIE ·

2 July 1889 (C)

The Handel orchestra at the Crystal Palace is not the right place for work so delicately and finely concentrated as Mendelssohn's Athalie. Nor is it, as many people seem to think, a favorable arena for the display of choral excellence. The more fiddlers you have in your orchestra and the more singers you have in any section of your chorus, the less likelihood is there of any defects being noticed, since at any given moment there will be enough performers right to drown a considerable minority who may be wrong. The proportion of error can only be guessed at by the magnitude of the mere indeterminate noise—the buzz and rattle—that comes along with the definite vocal tone. From this the tonic sol-faists on Saturday were commendably free: the tone was clean and the intonation very good indeed: much better, I venture to assert, than is usual in staff-notation choirs, where practice mostly begins by taking the reading powers of the members for granted. In volume and penetration the vocal mass was fully up to the ordinary standard; but then the ordinary standard is absurdly low. Considering what a formidable sound can be produced by a single properly trained man or woman of ordinary physique, the mildness of the result of combining 2500 of them on an orchestra is almost ridiculous. It is not too much to say that nine-tenths of the potential efficiency of our choirs is wasted through the diffidence that comes from conscious want of individual skill. The way in which the tone from the sopranos dwindled at every G and A shewed that a large number of these healthy young Englishwomen were deliberately shirking every note above F. Now a soprano, or even a mezzosoprano, who is afraid of an occasional A simply does not know how to sing; and I would respectfully put it to these fair solfaists whether it is of much public use to know how to read if you cannot sing what you read. If a soprano breaks down over Mendelssohn, what sort of a figure would she cut if she were put at, say, the Choral Symphony?

As an exhibition of choral singing the concert was interesting enough: as a performance of Athalie it was neither here nor there. The work is one of Mendelssohn's finest; and it can only be mastered by a conductor who studies his part as seriously as he might study the part of Hamlet if he were an actor. Mr Venables confined himself to beating time for the choir with steadiness, spirit, and—except in one number—with judgment. That number, unfortunately, was the duet with chorus, "Ever blessed child," an inspired composition, standing with "I waited for the Lord" among the most beautiful and touching utterances of Mendelssohn. But, alas! it is in six-eight time; and whenever an English conductor sees six-eight, he exclaims: "Ha! Sir Roger de Coverley!" and scampers off up the middle and down again, reckless whether it is "Ever blessed child" or "O thou that tellest" that he is murdering. When Mr Venables had duly dragged the duet through by the hair, he changed his mood just in time to quench the fire of the fiercely impetuous "Behold, Zion, behold." Otherwise I have nothing to reproach him with. The orchestral effects, notably those striking *fortissimo* chords in "The sinner's joys decay", were feeble and scattered in the vast space. The unpublished fugue, which was performed for the first time at the end, is just like any other fugue by a master of Mendelssohn's calibre. The subject begins with the usual skip, and the parts solemnly trudge along to the pedal, after which climax of insanity the welcome end comes with due gravity of cadence.

· MIDSUMMER NIGHT'S DREAM ·

10 January 1890 (C)

About the music, however, I may venture on a word. Mendelssohn's score, even when eked out by Cooke's Over hill, over dale, and Horn's I Know a Bank, falls short of Mr Benson's requirements. Accordingly, not only are two "songs without words," the Spring Song and the so-called Bee's Wedding, pressed into the service, but the Fingal's Cave overture has been cheerfully annexed for the last *entr' acte*. I fully expected a selection from Elijah to crop up in the course of the fifth act. But how different this music is from the oratorio music! how original, how exquisitely happy, how radiant with pure light, absolutely without shadow! Nineteenth-century civilization had a job after its own pocket in knocking all that out of Mendelssohn, and setting him to work on Stone Him to Death and the like.

Schumann

2 March 1892 (II)

The Schumann symphony† might have been more delicately played; but the result, as far as I am concerned, would have been much the same in any case. I cannot understand why we take ourselves and Schumann seriously over a work the last half of which is so forced and bungled as to be almost intolerable. I wish someone would extract all the noble passages from Schumann's symphonies, and combine them into a single instrumental fantasia—Reminiscences of Schumann as the military bandmasters would call it—so that we might enjoy them without the drudgery of listening to their elaboration into heavy separate works in which, during three-quarters of the performance, there is nothing to admire except the composer's devoted perserverance, which you wish he had not exercised. We all have a deep regard for Schumann; but it is really not in human nature to refrain from occasionally making it clear that he was greater as a musical enthusiast than as a constructive musician. If he had only had Rossini's genius, or Rossini his conscience, what a composer we should have had!

· FAUST ·

The Hornet, 28 March 1877 (*)

At the third concert of the Philharmonic Society, on the 22nd inst., Schumann's music to the last scenes of Geothe's Faust was performed for the first time in London. It probably astonished many hearers, in whose minds music to Faust was associated in idea with limelight and earthly passion. It may safely be asserted that there are fifty English readers familiar with the story of Gretchen for one who is acquainted with that strange flight into purely ideal regions,

---

†Symphony no. 4, in D minor; see *ML*, I, 136; III, 165.

wherein the poet depicts the opening of the uneasy philosopher's immortal career. Speculations on the "eternal feminine" are more congenial to the German than to the English temperatment. It is, consequently, improbable that many of the audience on Thursday last knew very clearly what they were to look for. When the object and scope of Schumann's music become more familiar to us, we will be better able to appreciate its thoroughness; for sustainedly earnest and beautiful as it undoubtedly is, it never once rises to a sublimity independent of the poem.

1 March 1893 (II)

Why not let us hear Schumann's Faust, with Mr Santley in the title part, or, if he does not care for it, Mr Bispham? Years ago I remember the Philharmonic producing the third section, and gravely informing the public that the first and second were not worth doing. As a matter of fact, the scene in which Faust is dazzled by the rising sun, with the trio of Want, Care, and Guilt, Faust's blindness, his orders to build the great dyke, the digging of the grave by the Lemures under the direction of Mephistopheles, Faust's quiet exultation at what he believes to be the progress of his great work, his declaration that life and freedom are for those alone who can fight every day for them, and his death in the moment of his fulfilled aspiration: all these are in the second part, which is the summit of Schumann's achievement in dramatic music, and is far superior to the rest of the work. I have often wondered that no baritone singer has succeeded in inducing one of our societies to undertake a performance; and it seems to me that at the Crystal Palace, where Schumann is especially beloved, and where the conductor is far more successful with him and more in sympathy with him than with Berlioz, Schumann's Faust would be heard to special advantage.

Liszt

· DANTE SYMPHONY ·

The Dramatic Review, 15 February 1885 (*)

Mr Walter Bache has now given us a dozen opportunities of hearing the serious products of Franz Liszt. His twelfth orchestral concert of the works of that eminent pianist, biographer, essayist, patron of genius, Hungarian rhapsodist, and musical enthusiast took place on the 3rd instant. The chief composition in the program was "a symphony to Dante's Inferno, Purgatorio, and Paradiso," particularly the Inferno. When, in order that allowance may be made for my personal bias, I declare at once that I do not like this symphony, I consider that I am expressing myself very moderately indeed; and were I to act strictly upon critical precedents, I should proceed to prove to my own satisfaction that the form of the symphony is wrong, the progressions forbidden, the decay of modern music largely attributable to its influence, and the total result lamentably different to what might have been expected had it occurred to Mozart to set the Divine Comedy to music. But as all these remarks would be equally appropriate to much modern music of which I am very fond, I will forgo them, and content myself with thanking Mr Bache for the opportunity of making up my mind that the Dante symphony, though doubtless a treat to the composer's disciples, is not suited to my constitution. I shall justify as best I can my opinion that the work is shallowly conceived and detestably expressed; and the reader, if curious on the subject, can study the very different view advanced by Richard Pohl in his book about Franz Liszt, and judge between us. The shortest way would undoubtedly be to go and hear the symphony played; but this, with my experience of Mr Bache's concert fresh in my recollection, I distinctly decline to advise any sober person to attempt.

It is hard to say what the characteristics of Dante's Hell are. Turmoil, hurry, incessant movement, fire, roaring wind, and utter discomfort are there; but so they are also in a London house when the kitchen chimney is on fire. Convey these by music, and the music

131

will be just as appropriate to the one situation as to the other. To convey nothing else is to miss the characteristic which differentiates the Inferno from any other noisy and unpleasant place; and this is what, as I think, Liszt has done: therefore I call his conception a shallow one. I am seriously of opinion that if the symphony were dubbed anew The Conflagration, and a careful analytical program compiled, assigning the various episodes of the *allegro* to The Alarm, The Fire Gaining Ground, Awakening of the Inmates and their Flight, Gathering of the Crowd, Arrival of the Engines, Exertions of Firemen and Struggle of Police with the Mob, with the Falling in of the Roof as a climax, not one of the audience would perceive the slightest incongruity between the music and the subject. The plan could be carried out to the end of the symphony. The Francesca episode might be labeled Complaint of the Lady of the House to Captain Shaw. To that gallant officer might be attributed the soothing recitative-like passage for the bass clarionet, at present supposed to represent the poet's sympathetic address to the unfortunate lovers. The *andante* would be appropriate to the mingled feelings of relief and regret following the extinction of the flames; the incidental fugue might portray the firemen searching the blackened ruins by lantern light; whilst the vocal conclusion would be in its place as the Thanksgiving of the Householder. The music is far more adequate to this program than to that of the composer, whose logic is like that of Shakespear's Welshman. "I warrant you shall find," says Fluellen, "in the comparisons between Macedon and Monmouth, that the situations, look you, is both alike. There is a river in Macedon; and there is also moreover a river in Monmouth; and there is salmons in both." There is haste, confusion, and discord in Dante's Hell; and there is haste, confusion, and discord in Liszt's symphony. So far, "the situations, look you, is both alike." But not a whit more alike than dozens of situations even more remote from the Divine Comedy than the one I have suggested. Dante's poem is unique because of those features of it that are not to be found elsewhere. Liszt's symphony is commonplace because disturbance and noise are commonplace. But to do justice to it on its own level, I admit that the degree of noise is not altogether commonplace. The symphony is exceptionally loud.

The proceedings begin at the gate of Hell with a phrase founded on that useful old favorite formerly known as the chord of the diminished seventh. This is delivered *fortissimo* by the three trombones and the tuba in unison, and repeated twice with modifications of increasing harshness. The effect is purely a question of the power of the trombones. Such as it is, it is just half what six trombones and two tubas would produce. As additional instruments could easily be procured from the band of the Grenadier Guards, who are accustomed to enhance similar effects at Promenade Concerts, Mr Bache, if he really likes this description of music, might find the reinforcement worth its cost. As it is, the result of the opening is to deafen and irritate the listener, and to leave him more than ever convinced that the art of using the trombone to express the terrors of the supernatural was born and died with Mozart, who would certainly have regarded a *fortissimo* passage for three trombones in unison in a serious work as an outrage on public decency. It is impossible, from lack of space, to follow the symphony point by point. The trombones go from bad to worse. Their parts, at first marked *ff*, soon appear with the three f's, in his enthusiasm for which Liszt outdoes the Farmers' Alliance. Volleys of strident barks from the brass alternate with shuddering triplets from the strings, and mingle with clarionets buzzing in their lowest register on the hackneyed Der Freischütz model; drum rolls that soon cease to convey anything to the worried ear except a monotonous thumping and stamping, like applause at a public meeting in a hotel breaking out on the floor above your bedroom in the middle of your first sleep; and all the howling and hurrying commonplaces of orchestral *diablerie* piled upon one-another to exasperation point. When it was over on Friday evening, a majority of the audience, in spite of their disposition (which I shared) to make much of Mr Bache in return for his enterprise and devotion, shewed by their silence that the composer had gone too far in offering them this obscene instrumental orgy as a serious comment on a great poem.

The remainder of the work was so far Dantesque that it produced an impression which ordinary readers of the Divine Comedy often confess having experienced. They find the Purgatorio duller than the Inferno, and the Paradiso duller than either. For my own part I was in no humor to be consoled by elaborate prettinesses from harp and English horn, viola and flute, and so forth, for what I had just suffered. The choir of ladies, among whom were Mr Malcolm Lawson's votaresses of St Cecilia, furnished a pretty background to the orchestra; but they did not seem well accustomed to sing together; and the final Magnificat, monotonously exalting itself by modulations from one key to another a tone above, and accompanied by muted violins hissing like a badly-adjusted limelight, was not so soothing as it was intended to be. At last a senseless episode, like the duel in Don Giovanni gone mad, turned out to be the *coda;* and, with a final Hallelujah, the welcome end came.

Putting Dante and the pretensions of the composer to illustrate him out of the question, and regarding the work merely as an example of the resources of the orchestra, the symphony seems to me useless even from a student's point of view. Qualities of tone which have never been made effective except when used very sparingly are resorted to almost continuously. Combinations which have been used with delightful results elsewhere occur only to fall flat upon ears tortured beyond the desire of any orchestral combination except a few bars rest. Though in many places ethereal sweetness and smoothness have been so elaborately planned that a glance at the score raises pleasant expectations, the effect proves to be only a paper one; or perhaps the players are too far demoralized by the violence and strain of the context to do justice to the pretty platitudes which the composer has sought to worry, by mere stress of orchestration, into melody and beauty. If there be any of those charmingly piquant effects which decorate the Hungarian rhapsodies, they are so discounted as to be unnoticeable. Comparisons with Berlioz are suggested by the fact that his aims and method are imitated by Liszt, as they have been by Raff. But Liszt's range is very narrow as compared with that of Berlioz. He produces certain vigorous and strident effects which are acceptable until he gives you too much of them, which he invariably does: a notable example being his setting of the Rákóczy March, which was also in the program the other evening. But though he aims strenuously at Berlioz's formidable maximum of tone, he has not the secret of it, and degenerates into intolerable noise in the attempt to reach it. He never surprises you, as Berlioz does, by producing several different effects from combinations of the same instruments. He outdoes Berlioz in bidding for the diabolical by noise and fury; but he quite misses the strange nightmare sensation, the smell of brimstone, as Schumann called it, which characterized Berlioz's exploits in the infernal field. Preeminence in the infernal is, perhaps, hardly worth disputing; but one must compare Liszt with a composer against whom he is perceptibly measurable. To compare his works with those of Bach, Handel, and Mozart, or even with the occasional savage aberrations of Wagner and Beethoven, would dwarf him too absurdly.

· LISZT IN ENGLAND ·

The Dramatic Review, 10 April 1886 (I)

"The favorite of Fortune" has revisited us at last, and is installed as the Grand Old Man of music. Many persons of literary and artistic tastes are now reading with genuine enthusiasm the newspaper chronicles of his pilgrimage—in all human probability his last pilgrimage—to the land of Purcell. Sonnets will spring—are springing daily, perhaps—from irrepressible impulses to worship the white-haired hero; the contemporary of Schumann, Berlioz, Chopin, Mendelssohn, and Goetz; who was sped on his career by Beethoven; who was the cherished friend of Wagner; who has all his life conversed with the immortals, and been envied by most of them for his pianoforte playing and his pluck before the public. You cannot read about such a man without emotion. If music be to you only a glorious dream, an unknown language transcending all articulate poesy, a rapture of angelic song, a storm-cloud of sublimity discharging itself into your inmost soul with thrilling harmonious thunder; then for you especially the voice of man's innate godhead will speak in whatever Liszt plays, whether he extemporizes variations on Pop goes the Weasel or faithfully re-utters for you the chromatic *fantasia* of Bach. The great player is to you no mere pianist: he is a host of associations—George Sand, Lamartine, Victor Hugo, Paris in the days of the Romantic movement, and what not and who not? Happy hero-worshiper! No generous infidel will grudge you your ecstasy, or untimely urge that it is intense in inverse ratio to your knowledge of music. Indeed, if one felt disposed to throw cold water on such genial transports, it would be difficult to find any just now to throw: Liszt having the gift that was laid as a curse upon the Scotch laird who made icy water bubble and boil by touching it.

Yet Liszt's associations do not by themselves entitle him to take precedence of many worthy citizens whose very names are unknown to history. The servant who opened Balzac's door to his visitors, and who must have been no mean connoisseur in creditors, was perhaps more interesting from this point of view than Liszt. As to the gentlemen who turn over the leaves for the pianists at St James's Hall, is there a great *virtuoso* with whom they are not familiar? What exciting tales they could tell of their breathless efforts to follow incredibly swift *prestos;* and what pleasant reminiscences they must enjoy of delicious naps stolen in the midst of dreamy *adagios* with a nice long repeat included within one open folio. For they sleep, these men: I have seen one of them do it at the elbow of a great artist, and have forgotten the music in contemplating the unfathomable satiety of the slumberer, and in speculating on the chances of his waking up in time for the *volte subito*. The eyes did not fail to open punctually; and their expression, unmistakeably that of the sleeper awakened, relieved me of the last doubt as to whether he had not been ecstatically drinking in the music with his eyes shut. What are Liszt's experiences compared to those of a man so prodigiously *blasé* that not Madame Schumann herself can fix his attention for the brief space of two pages? Clearly it is by his merit as a player or composer that Liszt's reputation must stand or fade.

There are not many people of anything like a reasonable age in England who have heard Liszt play. This statement may become false by the time it is printed—I hope it will; but at present it is true. That he was once a great player, one who far more than any interpreter of his time could play a sonata as the composer thought it, reading into every quaver the intention with which it was written there, is proved to us, as firmly as any such thing can be proved, by the crowning testimony of Wagner. Having the gift of governing men too, he was a great conductor as well as a great pianist. Whether he is as great as he was is just what we are all at present very curious to ascertain. We cannot expect him to formally undertake a public performance of Beethoven's Opus 106, his playing of which was ranked by Wagner as a creative effort; but there is abundant hope that he may be tempted to touch the keyboard at some concert at which only his presence can be promised. Already he has yielded to the desire of the Academy students; and the public wishes itself, for the nonce, a corps of Academy students and not a mob of mere ticket purchasers, whose applause and lionizing an artist is bound to mistrust if not to despise. Perhaps, under the circumstances, the best policy would be one of exasperation. Treat the master to a few examples of average British pianism; and a desperate longing to take the sound of it out of his ears, tempered by a paternal willingness to shew us what real playing is, may urge him to fulfil our hearts' desire.

Of Liszt's merits as a composer, those who heard his St Elizabeth at St James's Hall last Tuesday have, no doubt, their own opinion. To some of us his devotion to serious composition seems as hopeless a struggle against natural incapacity as was Benjamin Haydon's determination to be a great painter. To others the Dante symphony and the symphonic poems are masterpieces slowly but surely making their way to full recognition. Mr Bache has pressed the latter opinion hard upon us, and has backed it heavily. The present is not the time to insist with any grace on the former view. Fortunately, much of Liszt's music is admired on all hands. Sceptics who think it no more than brilliant, inspiriting, amusing, applaud as loudly as believers who revere it as significant, profound, and destined to endure with the works of Bach and Mozart. So, since we all enjoy it from one point of view or the other, we can very well unite in making as pleasant as possible the sojourn among us of an artist who has come clean-handed out of the press of three generations of frenzied nineteenth-century scramblers for pelf, and of whom even hostile critics say no worse than that he has failed only by aiming too high.

· RETROSPECTIVE ·

Pall Mall Gazette, 2 August 1886 (*)

The foreboding that many of us must have felt last spring when Liszt left England with a promise to return has been verified by the news of his death at Bayreuth. Such news always comes too soon; but in this cast Time has exacted less than his traditional due: three score and fifteen years were allowed to Liszt to work out what was in him. He had twice as long to utter himself as had Mendelssohn, who was only two and a half years his senior; or Mozart, who might have done things quite unimaginable in their effect on modern music if he had been allowed another thirty years of life. Of Liszt, we at least know that he said his say fully, such as it was. He was a Hungarian, born at Raiding in 1811, with the pianoforte at his fingers' ends. His career as a public player began when he was nine years old; and his success led him to Vienna and then to Paris, where he was excluded by his nationality from the Conservatoire and Cherubini's instruction. Of his plunge into the Romantic movement; his Saint-Simonianism; his Roman Catholicism; his connection with the Countess d'Agoult (Daniel Stern); his career in his middle age at Weimar, where he did for the opera what Goethe had done before for the theatre; his championship of Wagner, who became his son-in-law, and whose widow is his sole surviving child; his unique position as the idol of all the pianoforte students in the world—of all these we have been lately put in mind by the great overhauling of his history, which took place when he revisited us this year after nearly half a century's absence. He first played here at the Philharmonic Concerts in 1827. Fifteen years later he gave us another trial out of which we did not come with perfect credit. That was, perhaps, why he stayed away fortyfour years before he came again, and as an old man, half priest, half musician, stirred up all the hero-worship in our little world of music and all the lionizing in our big world of fashion. That little world will grieve awhile to learn that his third absence must be the longest of all. The big world will probably feel none the worse for having had something to talk about at breakfast this morning. Between it and the dead artist there was little genuine love lost. He cared so little for even dazzling it that he adopted the profession of pianist with repugnance, and abandoned it for that of conductor and composer as soon as he could afford to.

It was as a composer that Liszt wished to stand high in the esteem of his contemporaries, or—failing their appreciation—of posterity. Many musicians of good credit think that he judged himself rightly. Mr Bache, for instance, has given us concert after concert of his favorite master's works with a devotion that has extorted applause from audiences for the most part quite convinced that Liszt and Mr Bache were mistaken. Wagner, who spoke very highly of Liszt as a conductor, declared that his playing of Beethoven's greater sonatas was essentially an act of composition as well as of interpretation; he did not, however, commit himself on the subject of the Dante symphony or Mazeppa. There is a consensus of opinion in favor of Liszt as a player. His songs, too, have affected many musicians deeply; and though they are not generally familiar, their merit has not been at all emphatically questioned. His studies and transcriptions, if not wholly irreproachable in point of taste, shew an exhaustive knowledge of the pianoforte; and, unplayable as they are to people who attack a pianoforte with stiff wrists and clenched teeth, they are not dreaded by good pianists. The brilliancy and impetuous fantasy of his Hungarian Rhapsodies are irresistible, as Herr Richter has proved again and again at St James's Hall. But his oratorios and symphonic poems—especially the latter—have not yet won the place which he claimed for them. A man can hardly be so impressionable as Liszt was and yet be sturdy enough to be original. He could conduct Lohengrin like Wagner's other self, and could play Beethoven as if the sonatas were of his own molding; but as an original composer he was like a child, delighting in noise, speed, and stirring modulation, and indulging in such irritating excesses and repetitions of them, that decorous concert-goers find his Infernos, his battles, and his Mazeppa rides first amusing, then rather scandalous, and finally quite unbearable. A pleasanter idea of the man can be derived from the many eulogies, some of them mere schoolgirl raptures, others balanced verdicts of great composers and critics, which, whether the symphonic poems live or die, will preserve a niche for him in the history of music as a man who loved his art, despised money, attracted everybody worth knowing in the nineteenth century, lived through the worst of it, and got away from it at last with his hands unstained.

Gounod

The Dramatic Review, 8 May 1886 (*)

Why should the Handel Festival occur only once in every three years? Would it pay to make it biennial, annual, half-yearly, quarterly, weekly? Cannot something be made out of our gold-laden visitors from the colonies this year by a festival or two? An experiment in the direction of answering these questions was made last Saturday at the Crystal Palace, when M. Gounod's Redemption was performed at the Crystal Palace by the Handel orchestra, with three thousand singers in the choir, and four hundred players in the orchestra. Additional solemnity was given to the occasion by the prohibition of the sale of intoxicating liquor at the refreshment bars during the performance (so I was assured by a neighbor on his return from a short and unsuccessful absence); and nothing was allowed to distract the attention of the audience from the oratorio except a large signboard with the inscription "OYSTERS," which was conspicuous on the left of the orchestra. The audience behaved much like a church congregation, stolid, unintelligent, and silent, except once, when Madame Albani took her place in the orchestra after the first part, and again when one of her highest notes excited the representatives of that large and influential section of the public which regards a vocalist as an interesting variety of locomotive with a powerful whistle.

M. Gounod is almost as hard to dispraise as the President of the Royal Academy. Both produce works so graceful, so harmonious, so smooth, so delicate, so refined, and so handsomely sentimental, that it is difficult to convey, without appearing ungracious or insensible, the exact measure of disparagement needed to prevent the reader from concluding that M. Gounod is another Handel, or Sir Frederick Leighton another Raphael. And indeed M. Gounod does not express his ideas worse than Handel; but then he has fewer ideas to express. No one has ever been bored by an adequate performance of The Messiah. Even a Good Friday tumble through it at the Albert

Hall—ordinarily the worst thing of its kind in the whole cosmos—inspires rage and longing for justice to Handel rather than weariness. But the best conceivable performance of the Redemption would not hold an audience to the last note if the half-past five train back to town from Sydenham were at stake, much less make them impatient for a repetition of the oratorio, which is, in truth, an extremely tedious work, not because any particular number is dull or repulsive, but because its beauties are repeated *ad nauseam*. We all remember how, at the awakening of Margaret in the prison scene of Faust, we were delighted by the harmonic transitions from phrase to phrase by minor ninths resolving on stirring inversions of the common chord of a new tonic (technically unskilled readers will kindly excuse this jargon), as her voice rose semitone by semitone to the final cadence. It was a charming device; and M. Gounod used it again and again in his other operas. But when he gives us a long oratorio, consisting for the most part of these phrases on successive degrees of the chromatic scale, not only do we get thoroughly tired of them, but the pious among us may well feel scandalized at hearing the central figure in the tragedy of the atonement delivering himself exactly in the love-sick manner of Romeo, Faust, and Cinq Mars. No one expected M. Gounod to succeed in making the Redeemer differ from Romeo as Sarastro, for example, differs from Don Giovanni; but he might at least have made him as impressive as Friar Lawrence. Instead, he has limited himself to making the Prince of Peace a gentleman; and one cannot help adding that he could have done no less for the Prince of Darkness.

And such a smooth-spoken gentleman! There is a plague of smoothness over the whole work. The fact that M. Gounod has put too much sugar in it for the palate of a British Protestant might be condoned if the music were not so very horizontal. There is nearly always a pedal flowing along, and the other parts are slipping chromatically down to merge in it. Mr Compton Reade used to be fond of calling Handel the great Dagon of music. But when, at the end of the second part of the trilogy, the celestial choir demands Who is the King of Glory? words cannot express the longing that arises to have done with M. Gounod's sweetly grandiose periods, and to hear great Dagon answer concerning The Lord strong and mighty; the Lord mighty in battle. And again, in the chorus of mockers at the crucifixion, Ah, thou that dost declare, though the composer's dramatic instinct does make a faint struggle against his love of suave harmony, the lamenting listener's memory reverts enviously to the sinister turbulence of great Dagon's sardonic He trusted in God that he would deliver him. If Mr Compton Reade, or anyone else, still doubts that M. Gounod is to Handel as a Parisian duel is to Armageddon, let him seek greater wisdom at the next Crystal Palace performance of the Redemption or Mors et Vita. Depend upon it, he will be forced either to change his opinion, or to accuse Handel of an extraordinary lack of variety in rhythm and harmonic treatment, and an essentially frivolous sentimental piety in dealing with a subject which, to a genuinely religious Christian composer, must be the most tremendous in universal history.

Brahms

16 May 1890 (C)

I desire to thank Mr William Stead publicly for getting out The Review of Reviews in time for the Bach Choir concert on Saturday afternoon, and so lightening for me the intolerable tedium of sitting unoccupied whilst the Bachists conscientiously maundered through Brahms' Requiem. Mind, I do not deny that the Requiem is a solid piece of music manufacture. You feel at once that it could only have come from the establishment of a first-class undertaker. But I object to requiems altogether. The Dead March in Saul is just as long as a soul in perfect health ought to meditate on the grave before turning lifewards again to a gay quickstep, as the soldiers do. A requiem overdoes it, even when there is an actual bereavement to be sympathized with; but in a concert-room when there is nobody dead, it is the very wantonness of make-believe. On such occasions the earnest musician reads The Review of Reviews; and the Culture Humbug sits with his longest face, pretending to drink in that "solemn joy at the commencement of a higher life" which Mr Bennett, in the analytical programme, assures him is the correct emotion for the occasion. By the bye, I must quote Mr Bennett's opening remark, as it put me into high spirits for the whole afternoon. "This Requiem," he writes, "was composed in 1867 as a tribute by the composer to the memory of his mother, a sentiment which lends especial interest to the soprano solo." For boldness of syntactical ellipsis, and farfetched subtlety of psychologic association, Mr Bennett must be admitted the master of us all.

Somebody is sure to write to me now demanding, "Do you mean Mozart's Requiem?" I reply, that in the few numbers—or parts of numbers—in that work which are pure Mozart, the corpse is left out. There is no shadow of death anywhere on Mozart's music. Even his own funeral was a failure. It was dispersed by a shower of rain; and to this day nobody knows where he was buried or whether he was buried at all or not. My own belief is that he was not. Depend on it, they had no sooner put up their umbrellas and bolted for the nearest shelter than he got up, shook off his bones into the common grave of the people, and soared off into universality. It is characteristic of the British middle class that whenever they write a book about Mozart, the crowning tragedy is always the dreadful thought that instead of having a respectable vault all to himself to moulder in for the edification of the British tourist, he should have been interred cheaply among the bodies of the lower classes. Was it not the Rev. H. R. Haweis who waxed quite pathetic over this lamentable miscarriage of propriety, and then called his book Music and Morals!?

24 June 1891 (I)

The admirers of Brahms had a succulent treat at the Richter concert last week. His German Requiem was done from end to end, and done quite well enough to bring out all its qualities. What those qualities are could have been guessed by a deaf man from the mountainous tedium of the unfortunate audience, who yet listened with a perverse belief that Brahms is a great composer, and the performance of this masterpiece of his an infinitely solemn and important function. I am afraid that this delusion was not confined to those who, having found by experience that good music bores them, have rashly concluded that all music that bores them must be good. It raged also among the learned musicians, who know what a *point d' orgue* is, and are delighted to be able to explain what is happening when Brahms sets a pedal pipe booming and a drum thumping the dominant of the key for ten minutes at a stretch, whilst the other instruments and the voices plough along through every practicable progression in or near the key, up hill from syncopation to syncopation, and down dale from suspension to suspension in an elaborately modernized manner that only makes the whole operation seem more desperately old-fashioned and empty.

Brahms seems to have been impressed by the fact that Beethoven produced remarkable effects by persisting with his pedal points long after Mozart would have resolved them, and to have convinced himself by an obvious logical process that it must be possible to produce still more remarkable results by outdoing Beethoven in persistency. And so indeed it is, as Bach proved before Mozart was born. Only somehow it has not come off in Brahms' hands, though he has prolonged and persisted to the verge of human endurance. Yet, as I say, the academic gentlemen like it, and seem pleased even by those endless repetitions, which are only the "rosalias" of the old Italian masses in a heavy and pretentious disguise. I can only say, with due respect, that I disagree with the academic gentlemen.

The fact is, there is nothing a genuine musician regards with more jealousy than an attempt to pass off the forms of music for music itself, especially those forms which have received a sort of consecration from their use by great composers in the past. Unfortunately, such impostures are sure of support from the sort of people—pretty numerous in this country as far as art is concerned—who think that it is the cowl that makes the monk. Any conspiracy between a musician and a literary man to set Wardour Street Jacobean English to Wardour Street Handelian counter-point will find ready victims in this class, which may be seen at any festival impartially applauding the music of Handel and the profane interpolations of any opera singer who has learned by experience how to turn its ignorant hero-worship to account.

Sometimes, of course, we have, for the sake of some respected professor, to put up with performances of honest pieces of pedantry like the oratorios of Kiel of Berlin, or Macfarren, not to mention names of the living. But I altogether demur to making concessions of this kind to Brahms. It will only end in his doing it again; for his extraordinary mechanical power of turning out the most ponderous description of music positively by tons, and the stupendous seriousness with which he takes this gift, are unrestrained by any consciousness on his part of the commonplaceness of his ideas, which makes his tone poetry all but worthless, or of the lack of constructive capacity which makes his "absolute music" incoherent. He is quite capable of writing half a dozen more Requiems, all as insufferable as this one, if we hail him as "the most prominent living representative of the classical school," as some enthusiastic simpleton did the other day on the strength of a couple of motets which were inferior in every essential characteristic of the classical school to the best bits of part-writing in Sir Arthur Sullivan's comic operas.

There are not gracious things to say of a composer who has written so many really pretty trifles; but self-defence is the first law of Nature; and though I am at this moment lying broiling on the sands at Broadstairs, at peace with all mankind, and indulgently disposed even towards Brahms, I can say no less when I think of that dreary Requiem, and of the imminent danger of its being repeated next season.

· VOCAL QUARTETS ·

The World, 23 December 1891 (*)

The admirers of Brahms are to be congratulated on the set of vocal quartets which have just been sung at the Popular Concerts for the first time by Mrs Henschel, Miss Fassett, Mr Shakespeare, and Mr Henschel. For once in a way, Johannes has really distinguished himself. In these quartets we have, it goes without saying, the extraordinary facility of harmonic workmanship which Brahms shews in everything he does, from the colossally stupid Requiem, which has made so many of us wish ourselves dead, to those unmitigated minor bores, the Liebeslieder Waltzes. But we have also in them a feeling which is thoroughly roused—a vivacious, positively romantic feeling—graceful, tender, spontaneous—something as different as possible from his usual unaroused state, his heavy, all-pervading unintelligent German sentimentality. Besides, they shew good handicraft in another sense than that of doing easily what other men find very difficult. Brahms has always had the mere brute force of his amazing musical faculty. No one can deny that he all but equals our most famous native orators in respect of having a power of utterance that would place him above the greatest masters if only he had anything particular to say. But this time he has shewn imaginative workmanship, especially in the play of color of the four voices, which are combined and contrasted and crossed and interwoven in a delightful way. Much of the effect was, no doubt, due to the four singers, each of them a soloist of distinguished merit; but that does not account for everything, since quite as much has been done for previous compositions of Brahms without for a moment producing the same charm. He evidently composed the quartets in one of those fortunately-inspired moments to which we owe all that is valuable in his work.

· FOURTH SYMPHONY ·

18 June 1890 (I)

My temper was not improved by Brahms' Symphony in E minor, though I have no fault to find with the execution of it. Euphuism, which is the beginning and end of Brahms' big works, is no more to my taste in music than in literature. Brahms takes an essentially commonplace theme; gives it a strange air by dressing it in the most elaborate and far-fetched harmonies; keeps his countenance severely (which at once convinces an English audience that he must have a great deal in him); and finds that a good many wiseacres are ready to guarantee him as deep as Wagner, and the true heir of Beethoven. The spectacle of the British public listening with its inchurchiest expression to one of the long and heavy fantasias which he calls his symphonies always reminds me of the yokel in As You Like It quailing before the big words of the fool. Strip off the euphuism from these symphonies, and you will find a string of incomplete dance and ballad tunes, following one another with no more organic coherence than the succession of passing images reflected in a shop window in Piccadilly during any twenty minutes in the day. That is why Brahms is so enjoyable when he merely tries to be pleasant or naïvely sentimental, and so insufferably tedious when he tries to be profound. His symphonies are endured at the Richter concerts as sermons are endured, and his Requiem is patiently borne only by the corpse; but Mr Orton Bradley, who gave a Brahms concert the other day at Steinway Hall, "his custom always of an afternoon" in the season, was able to entertain us happily enough by reverently letting alone the more ponderous nothings of his favorite composer.

· CLARINET QUINTET ·

11 May 1892 (II)

Only the other day I remarked that I was sure to come across Brahms' new clarionet quintet sooner or later. And, sure enough, my fate overtook me last week at Mr G. Clinton's Wind Concert at Steinway Hall. I shall not attempt to describe this latest exploit of the Leviathan Maunderer. It surpassed my utmost expectations: I never heard such a work in my life. Brahms' enormous gift of music is paralleled by nothing on earth but Mr Gladstone's gift of words: it is a verbosity which outfaces its own commonplaceness by dint of sheer magnitude. The first movement of the quintet is the best; and had the string players been on sufficiently easy terms with it, they might have softened it and given effect to its occasional sentimental excursions into dreamland. Unluckily they were all preoccupied with the difficulty of keeping together; and they were led by a violinist whose bold, free, slashing style, though useful in a general way, does more harm than good when the strings need to be touched with great tenderness and sensitiveness.

Mr Clinton played the clarionet part with scrupulous care, but without giving any clue to his private view of the work, which, though it shews off the compass and contrasts the registers of the instrument in the usual way, contains none of the haunting phrases which Weber, for instance, was able to find for the expression of its idiosyncrasy. The presto of the third movement is a ridiculously dismal version of a lately popular hornpipe. I first heard it at the pantomime which was produced at Her Majesty's Theatre a few years ago; and I have always supposed it to be a composition of Mr Solomon's. Anyhow, the street-pianos went through an epidemic of it; and it certainly deserved a merrier fate than burying alive in a Brahms quintet.

· PIANO CONCERTO ·

12 December 1888 (C)

The other day a small but select audience assembled in one of Messrs Broadwood's rooms to hear Miss Florence May play a pianoforte concerto by Brahms. An orchestra being out of the question, Mr Otto Goldschmidt and Mr Kemp played an arrangement of the band parts on two pianofortes. Brahms's music is at bottom only a prodigiously elaborated compound of incoherent reminiscences, and it is quite possible for a young lady with one of those wonderful "techniques," which are freely manufactured at Leipzig and other places, to struggle with his music for an hour at a stretch without giving such an insight to her higher powers as half a dozen bars of a sonata by Mozart. All that can be said confidently of Miss May is that her technique is undeniable. The ensemble of the three Broadwood grands was not so dreadful as might have been expected, and the pretty finale pleased everybody.

[*The above hasty (not to say silly) description of Brahms's music will, I hope, be a warning to critics who know too much. In every composer's work there are passages that are part of the common stock of music of the time; and when a new genius arises, and his idiom is still unfamilar and therefore even disagreeable, it is easy for a critic who knows that stock to recognize its contributions to the new work and fail to take in the original complexion put upon it. Beethoven denounced Weber's Euryanthe overture as a string of diminished sevenths. I had not yet got hold of the idiosyncratic Brahms. I apologize. (1936).*]

·CHAMBER MUSIC·

21 June 1893 (III)

A concert of chamber music selected exclusively from the works of Johannes Brahms is not supposed to be the sort of entertainment to put me into the highest good-humor. Herein, however, I am wronged. Such a reputation as that of Brahms is not to be won without great talent. Unfortunately, music is still so much of a mystery in this country that people get bewildered if they are told that the same man has produced an execrable requiem and an excellent sonata. There seems to them to be no sense in going on in this inconsistent way; for clearly a requiem is a musical composition, and if a man composes it badly he is a bad composer; and a bad composer cannot compose a good sonata, since that also is a musical composition. Yet these very people can often see plainly enough that in pictorial art the same man may be an admirable decorative designer, colorist, or landscape painter, and an atrocious figure draughtsman; or, in literature, that good stories and bad plays, charming poems and fatuous criticisms, may come from the same hand.

The departments of music are not less various than those of the other arts; and Brahms is no more to be disposed of by the condemnation as tedious, commonplace, and incoherent, of those works of his which profess an intellectual or poetic basis than—well, the comparisons which offer themselves are numerous and tempting; but perhaps I had better leave them alone. Suffice it to say that whilst Brahms is successful neither as an intellectual nor a poetic composer, but only as a purely sensuous musician, his musical sense is so much more developed than that of the average audience that many of the harmonies and rhythms which are too him simply voluptuous and impetuous, sound puzzling and imposing to the public, and are therefore surmised to be profoundly intellectual.

To me it seems quite obvious that the real Brahms is nothing more than a sentimental voluptuary with a wonderful ear. For respectability's sake he adopts the forms academically supposed to be proper to great composers, since it gives him no trouble to pile up *points d' orgue,* as in the Requiem, or to call a childishly sensuous reverie on a few simple chords, arranged into the simplest of strains for chaconne purposes by Handel, a set of variations on a theme by that master, or to adapt a ramble in search of fresh delights more or less to sonata form; but you have only to compare his symphonies and quintets with those of Beethoven or Mozart to become conscious that he is the most wanton of composers, that he is only ingenious in his wantonness, and that when his ambition leads him to turn his industry in any other direction his charm does not turn with it, and he becomes the most superficial and irrelevant of formalists.

Only, his wantonness is not vicious: it is that of a great baby, gifted enough to play with harmonies that would baffle most grown-up men, but still a baby, never more happy than when he has a crooning song to play with, always ready for the rockinghorse and the sugar-stick, and rather tiresomely addicted to dressing himself up as Handel or Beethoven and making a prolonged and intolerable noise. That this masquerade of his has taken in a considerable number of persons in Berlin and London is easily explicable on the hypothesis that they see no more in Handel or Beethoven that Brahms can imitate; but again you have only to compare the agonies of lassitude undergone by a Requiem audience with the general purring over his violin concerto, or the encores Miss Lehmann gets for his cradle songs, to see that Monsieur Tout-le-Monde is not in the least taken in, though he does not venture to say so in the teeth of eminent counsel's opinion to the effect that he ought to be.

Goetz

22 November 1893 (III)

The gem of the concert was Goetz' symphony, which has fallen into neglect because, I suppose, it is the only real symphony that has been composed since Beethoven died. Beside it Mendelssohn's Scotch symphony is no symphony at all, but only an enchanting *suite de pièces*; Schubert's symphonies seem mere debauches of exquisitely musical thoughtlessness; and Schumann's, though genuinely symphonic in ambition, fall short in actual composition. Goetz alone among the modern symphonists is easily and unaffectedly successful from beginning to end.

He has the charm of Schubert without his brainlessness, the refinement and inspiration of Mendelssohn without his limitation and timid gentility, Schumann's sense of harmonic expression without his laboriousness, shortcoming, and dependence on external poetic stimulus; while as to unembarrassed mastery of the material of music, shewing itself in the Mozartian grace and responsiveness of his polyphony, he leaves all three of them simply nowhere. Brahms, who alone touches him in mere brute musical faculty, is a dolt in comparison to him.

You have to go to Mozart's finest quartets and quintets on the one hand, and to Die Meistersinger on the other, for work of the quality we find, not here and there, but continuously, in the symphony in F and in The Taming of the Shrew, two masterpieces which place Goetz securely above all other German composers of the last hundred years, save only Mozart and Beethoven, Weber and Wagner. Of course, if Goetz were alive this would be an excellent reason for opposing him tooth and nail, for the same reasons that moved Salieri to oppose Mozart. A very little Goetz would certainly spoil the market for Festival symphonies; but now that the man is dead, why may we not have the symphony made a stock-piece at the London Symphony and Richter concerts, and performed oftener than once in four years at the Crystal Palace?

151

Tchaikowsky

·CONCERTO NO. 2·

2 May 1890 (C)

Although Mr Manns was inconsiderate enough to select the very wettest day he could find for his benefit, the audience was of the largest; and as they all had umbrellas to thump with, the applause was exceptionally effective. Not so the program. The Freischütz overture, played without the Wagnerian interpretation of the *decrescendo* mark over the chord preceding the entry of the "feminine theme" in the coda, was as fresh as ever; though, with all respect to Mr Manns, Wagner was assuredly right. The Tannhäuser overture was equally welcome. But then the Freischütz was played at three and the Tannhäuser at five; and between the two were two mortal hours of music which did nothing to restore that alacrity of spirit which the rain had washed out of me.

There was Dr Sapellnikoff's playing of Tschaikowsky's pianoforte concerto in G (No. 2) for the first time in England. The apology made by Sir George Grove in the program for the absence of an analysis was the less needed because the work contains nothing new. It is impulsive, copious, difficult, and pretentious; but it has no distinction, no originality, no feeling for the solo instrument, nothing to rouse the attention or to occupy the memory. It left me without any notion of Sapellnikoff's rank as a player: he is, of course, swift and powerful with his fingers; but six bars of a Mozart sonata would have told me more about his artistic gift than twenty whole concertos of the Tschaikowsky sort.

And here let me remark that whenever you hear of a great composer from Russia, or from Hungary, or from any other country which is far behind us in social development, the safest plan is not to believe in him. You cannot be too intensely insular on the art question in England. If England wants music to reach her own highest standard, she must make it for herself. The adolescent enthusiasms, the revolutionary ardors, the belated romanticism of Slav and Czech can produce nothing for England except toys for her young people.

· SIXTH SYMPHONY ·

7 March 1894 (III)

For all that, the opening concert of the season on Wednesday last was a great success, thanks to Tchaikowsky's last symphony, which was very interesting, and far too novel and difficult to leave the band any middle course between playing it well and not playing it at all. Tchaikowsky had a thoroughly Byronic power of being tragic, momentous, romantic about nothing at all. Like Childe Harold, who was more tragic when there was nothing whatever the matter with him than an ordinary Englishman is when he is going to be executed, Tchaikowsky could set the fateful drum rolling and make the trombones utter the sepulchral voice of destiny without any conceivable provocation.

This last symphony of his is a veritable Castle of Otranto, with no real depth of mood anywhere in it, but full of tragic and supernatural episodes which, though unmotived, and produced by a glaringly obvious machinery, are nevertheless impressive and entertaining. There are, besides, abundant passages of romance and revelry, with the usual Tchaikowskian allowance of orchestral effects which are so purely that and nothing else that they have absolutely no sense if played on a pianoforte. Take, for instance, the basso ostinato at the end of the first movement, and the rushing scale passages for strings and wind in the march. These are, from the symphonic point of view, simple humbug. There is no separate slow movement, its place being taken by the second subject of the opening allegro, which appears as an andante, fully developed as such. The innovation is so successful in its effect that I shall not be surprised if it be generally adopted.

By way of schetzo, there is a charming movement in five-four time, which brought the house down. Most musicians, if asked to note it by ear off-hand, would have written the first eight bars of five-four time as twenty bars of two-four, taking the second note as the beginning of the first bar, and dividing the theme into strains of five bars instead of the usual four. No doubt such a scoring would produce a number of accents which Tchaikowsky did not intend; but our sense of this five-in-a-bar rhythm is still so undeveloped that as I listened I found myself repeatedly breaking the movement into two-four and three-four bars; and, what is more, the band was doing exactly the same thing. After this five-four movement comes a very elaborate and brilliant march, with, it must be confessed, a good deal of nonsense about it. The finale brings us back to the Castle of Otranto, and ends in a sufficiently melancholy manner to enable us critics (Tchaikowsky having opportunely died) to give our "swan song" stereo an airing.

Grieg

16 March 1889 (C)

Hitherto I have not been a great admirer of Edvard Grieg. He is a "national" composer; and I am not to be imposed on by that sort of thing. I do not cry out "How Norwegian!" whenever I hear an augmented triad; not "How Bohemian!" when I hear a tune proceeding by intervals of augmented seconds; nor "How Irish!" when Mr Villiers Stanford plays certain tricks on subdominant harmonies; nor "How Scotch!" when somebody goes to the piano and drones away on E flat and B flat with his left hand, meanwhile jigging at random on the other black keys with his right. All good "folk music" is as international as the story of Jack the Giant Killer, or the Ninth Symphony. Grieg is very fond of the augmented triad; but his music does not remind me of Norway, perhaps because I have never been there. And his sweet but very cosmopolitan modulations, and his inability to get beyond a very pretty snatch of melody, do not go very far with me: for I despise pretty music. Give me a good, solid, long-winded, classical lump of composition, with time to go to sleep and wake up two or three times in each movement, say I.

However, let us be just. The pretty snatches are not only pretty, but both delicately and deeply felt by the composer. And they are, at least, long enough to make exquisite little songs, which Madame Grieg sings in such a way as to bring out everything that is in them. There is a certain quaintness about the pair. Grieg is a small, swift, busy earnest man, with the eyes of a rhapsode, and in his hair and complexion the indescribably ashen tint that marks a certain type of modern Norseman. For Madame's appearance I cannot answer so fully, as I have had no opportunity of observing her quite closely; but she holds herself oddly and sings with unrestrained expression. The voice, unluckily, does not help her much. I know half a dozen commonplace young ladies with better, fresher, more flexible voices; but they will not take Madame Grieg's place yet awhile. Most of them, too, would regard a habit of musical composition on their husband's

155

part as one of the conceited follies to which men are subject. It is really a stupendous feat, this of making your wife believe in you.

Grieg's Peer Gynt suite, which he conducted at the Philharmonic on Thursday, was written for use in the theatre at the performance of the play. Now Peer Gynt (Pare Yoont is about as near as you can get to it in English) is a great play: a masterpiece of Norwegian literature, as Faust is a masterpiece of German literature. Like Faust, it is a fantastic drama in rhymed verse. Like Faust, again, it is full of scenes that haunt a composer and compel him to give them musical expression. Grieg, however, has not attempted to wrestle with a giant like Ibsen. His Aase's death music, for instance, does not deal with that wonderful imaginary ride to the castle east of the sun and west of the moon with which Peer, having harnessed the cat to his mother's deathbed, beguiles the worn-out old woman painlessly from the world. Grieg deals rather with the earlier part of the scene, where Aase lies deserted, awaiting her last hour. The music, a quiet crooning harmonic motive, is deeply pathetic. On Thursday it moved an audience which knew nothing of Peer Gynt. For the rest, the dawn music is charming, and so is Anitra's dance, which begins like the waltz in Berlioz's Fantastic Symphony. The Dovregubben orgy is a riotous piece of weird fun. All four numbers are simply frank repetitions, in various keys and with different instrumentation, of some short phrase, trivial certainly, but graceful and fancifully expressive. But they pleased the Philharmonic audience more and more as they went on; and finally Grieg, after two recalls, had to repeat the Dovregubben piece.

PART THREE

The Opera House

Gluck

12 November 1890 (I)

Is Gluck, the conqueror of Paris, at last going to conquer London? I hope so; for the man was a great master, one for whom we are hardly ready even yet. Hitherto our plan of sweeping together a sackful of opera-singers from Milan, Vienna, Monte Video, Chicago, Clapham, China, and Peru, and emptying them on to the Covent Garden stage to tumble through Trovatore or Traviata as best they can, has not succeeded with Gluck. This Orfeo, for instance! Anyone can see before the curtain is half-a-minute up that it grew by the introduction of vocal music, not into chaos, but into an elaborate existing organization of ballet. The opening chorus, S' in questo bosco, sounds nobly to people who are looking at groups of figures in poetic motion or eloquent pose, at draperies falling in graceful lines and flowing in harmonious colors, and at scenery binding the whole into a complete and single picture.

Under such circumstances, our old friend Monseigneur of the Œil de Bœuf, when he had a taste that way, no doubt enjoyed himself. But when we, to wit, Smith and Jones, with our suburban traditions, going to the Opera full of that sense of unaccustomed adventure which the fine arts give us, are dumbfounded by the spectacle of our old original choristers appealing with every feature and limb against the unreasonableness of asking them to look like classical shepherds and shepherdesses—when their desperate Theocritean weeds have the promiscuity of Rag Fair without its picturesqueness—when even Katti Lanner's young ladies move awkwardly and uncertainly, put out of step by these long-drawn elegiac strains—when the scene suggests Wimbledon on a cold day, and Euridice's tomb is something between a Druidic cromlech and a milestone, bearing the name of the deceased in the tallest advertising stencil—then it must be confessed that S' in questo bosco affects its new acquaintances far from cheerfully.

These drawbacks were in full force at Covent Garden last Wednesday; but Orfeo triumphed in spite of them. Gluck and Giulia Ravogli were too many even for the shabby sofa, apparently borrowed from a decayed seaside lodging, which was shamelessly placed in the middle of the stage, just outside the mouth of Hades, for Euridice to die conveniently on. It was the stage-manager's last insult; and when it failed, he collected all his forces behind the scenes and set them talking at the top of their voices, so as to drown the singing and distract the attention of the audience. What a thing it is to live in the richest capital in the world, and yet have to take your grand opera, at its largest and most expensive theatre, with the makeshifts and absurdities of the barn and the booth! And to add to the exasperation of it, you are kept waiting longer between the acts for the dumping down of this miserable sofa on the bare boards than would be required for the setting of the most elaborate stage-picture at the Lyceum or Drury Lane.

I am not sure that Gluck is not in a better way to be understood now than he has been any time since the French Revolution. Listening to the strains in the Elysian Fields the other night, I could not help feeling that music had strayed far away from them, and only regained them the other day when Wagner wrote the Good Friday music in Parsifal. No musical experience in the journey between these two havens of rest seems better than either. The Zauberflöte and the Ninth Symphony have a discomforting consciousness of virture, an uphill effort of aspiration, about them; but in the Elysian Fields, in the Good Friday meadows, virtue and effort are transcended: there is no need to be good or to strive upward any more: one has arrived, and all those accursed hygienics of the soul are done with and forgotten. Not that they were without a priggish ecstasy of their own: I am far from denying that. Virtue, like vice, has its attractions. It was well worth while to slip through the Elysian hedge into the domain of Klingsor, and be shewn the enchantments of his magic gardens by Weber, plunged into his struggles and hopes by Beethoven, introduced to polite society in his castle drawing room by Mendelssohn, besides being led by Mozart through many unforgettable episodes of comedy and romance—episodes producing no bitter reaction like that which was apt to follow the scenes of tragic passion or rapturous sentimentality which Meyerbeer, Verdi, and Gounod managed so well for Klingsor. I do not forget these for a moment; and yet I am glad to be in the Elysian Fields again. And it is because I have also been in the Good Friday meadows that I can now see, more clearly than anyone could before Parsifal, how exactly Gluck was the Wagner of his day—a thing that would have been violently disputed by Berlioz, who was, nevertheless, almost as good a critic as I. Listen to Orfeo, and you hear that perfect union of the poem and the music—that growth of every musical form, melodic interval, harmonic progression, and orchestral tone out of some feeling or purpose belonging to the drama—which you have only heard before in the cantatas of Bach and the music dramas of Wagner. Instead of the mere opera-making musician, tied to his poem as to a stake, and breaking loose whenever it gives him an excuse for a soldiers' chorus, or a waltz, or a crashing finale, we have the poet-musician who has no lower use for music than the expression of poetry.

Though it is easy to see all this in Orfeo during such numbers as Che faro? it might not have been so apparent last Wednesday in the ballet-music, although that never loses its poetic character, but for Giulia Ravogli, about whom I now confess myself infatuated. It is no longer anything to me that her diction is not always so pure as Salvini's, that her roulade is inferior in certainty and spontaneity to Signor Foli's, that the dress in which I first saw her as Amneris ought to have had ever so many yards more stuff in the train, that she would not put on the grey eyebrows and wrinkles of Azucena, and even that she is capable of coming out of a stage faint to bow to the applause it evokes. Ah, that heart-searching pantomime, saturated with feeling beyond all possibility of shortcoming in grace, as Orfeo came into those Elysian Fields, and stole from shade to shade, trying to identify by his sense of touch the one whom he was forbidden to seek with his eyes! Flagrant ballet-girls all those shades were; but it did not matter: Giulia awakened in us the power by which a child sees a living being in its rag doll. Even the *première danseuse* was transfigured to a possible Euridice as Giulia's hand, trembling with a restrained caress, passed over her eyes! And then the entry into Hades, the passionate pleading with the Furies, and, later on, the eloquence of the famous aria in the last act! I was hardly surprised, though I was alarmed, to see a gentleman in a stagebox, with frenzy in his eye, seize a substantial-looking bouquet and hurl it straight at her head, which would probably have been removed from her shoulders had not the missile fallen some yards short of its mark. Her success was immense. Nobody noticed that there were only two other solo-singers in the whole opera, both less than nothing beside her. She—and Gluck—sufficed. In the singer, as in the composer, we saw a perfectly original artistic impulse naïvely finding its way to the heart of the most artificial and complex of art forms.

Mozart

· THE MARRIAGE OF FIGARO ·

The Dramatic Review, 6 June 1885 (*)

On this day last week Mr Carl Rosa concluded his triumphant season at Drury Lane by conducting a performance of Mozart's opera, Le Nozze di Figaro, now a hundred years old. A century after Shakespear's death it was the fashion for men, otherwise sane, to ridicule the pretensions of the author of Hamlet to intellectual seriousness, and to publish editions of his works prefaced by apologies for his childishness and barbarism, with entreaties to the reader to judge him indulgently as a man who "worked by a mere light of nature." At present, a century after Mozart's death, we have among us men, only partially idiotic, who hold similar language of the composer of Figaro, Don Giovanni, and Die Zauberflöte. Now the truth about Shakespear was never forgotten—never even questioned by the silent masses who read poetry, but skip notes, comments, and criticisms. And that the many heads of the mob are perfectly "level" on the subject of Mozart, is shown by the fact that Figaro or The Don will still draw a house when nothing else will, though not a single perfectly satisfactory representation of either opera is on record. It is true that the infallibility of the mob is as yet only a dogma of Mr Sydney Grundy's; but this matter does not rest on mob authority alone: Wagner, when not directly expressing his unmitigated contempt for his own disciples, delighted to taunt them by extoling Mozart; and Gounod, standing undazzled before Wagner and Beethoven, has confessed that before Mozart his ambition turns to despair. Berlioz formed his taste in ignorance of Handel and Mozart, much as a sculptor might form his taste in ignorance of Phidias and Praxiteles; and when he subsequently became acquainted with Mozart in his works, he could not quite forgive him for possessing all the great qualities of his idol Gluck, and many others of which Gluck was destitute, besides surpassing him in technical skill. Yet Berlioz admitted the greatness of Mozart; and if he did not fully appreciate him as the most subtle and profound of all musical dramatists, much less as his own superior in the handling of his favorite instrument, the orchestra, he never was guilty of the stupid fashion that has since sprung up of treating him as a sort of Papageno among composers.

This exordium is intended to help a few readers, who may have been perverted by the Papageno propagandists, to realize the magnitude of the task which Mr Carl Rosa successfully attempted last Saturday. For his own part, he came forward as a conductor to carry out his own reading of the work, and not as Mr Randegger does—and does very well—merely to keep the band together and accompany the singers. There is an old tradition that the Figaro overture should be played against time so as to finish within three and a half minutes. There are two hundred and ninety four bars in the overture; and there are only two hundred and ten seconds in three and a half minutes. Consequently seven bars have to be played every five seconds. This gives the most effective speed. But the conductor must keep it uniform throughout: he must not indulge in *rallentandos*. Unfortunately this is just what Mr Carl Rosa did. He lingered affectionately over the delightful little theme in A just before the repeat, and then spurted to make up for lost time. The orchestra responded gamely; and the final chord was passed well within the two hundred and tenth second; but the finish was a scramble, which was the greater pity as the *rallentando* which necessitated it was in bad taste. Mr Carl Rosa's conducting is marred by two bad habits of his: he hurries at every *crescendo;* and he prolongs his pet passages as much as possible. Physically, he gives himself much unnecessary trouble. Throughout the overture he actually made two down beats in each bar, as if the music were written in two-four instead of common time. In a less familiar work the effect might have been to confuse the players, and Mr Carl Rosa can hardly have steadied his own nerves by slashing the unoffending air nearly six hundred times in less than four minutes. However, if he did those things which he ought not to have done, he at least did not leave undone those things which he ought to have done. He conducted the performance instead of allowing the performance to conduct him; and the largest share of the effect produced would not have been produced had he not been there. His treatment of the *allegro maestoso* movement in the baritone *aria, Vedro, mentr' io sospiro,* revealed all its dignity, which must have surprised many Italian opera-goers present. In this case he reduced the speed to which we have become accustomed; and he did the same, but with questionable judiciousness, in the first section of the great *finale* to the second act, where the *allegro,* interrupted by the discovery of Susanna, is resumed in B flat at the words *Susanna, son morta.* On the other hand, he took Figaro's *aria, Aprite un po',* at the beginning of the last act, at a rattling *allegro molto,* a quite unjustifiable proceeding, as it bothered Mr Barrington Foote and violated Mozart's direction *"moderato."* Later in the same act the movement marked *andante* in six-eight time, *Pace, pace, mio dolce tesoro,* was also taken far too quickly. There were three important omissions, besides those which have become customary. These were the duet *Via resti servita, madama brillante* for Susanna and Marcellina in the first act; the sestet *Riconosci in questo amplesso* in the third act, which was perceptibly weakened by the hiatus; and that extraordinary pæan of a base soul, *In quegl' anni,* for Don Basilio in the fourth act.

The Nation, London, 28 July 1917 (*)

Everyone who has seen the new production of Figaro's Wedding at Drury Lane will agree that it is quite the most delightful entertainment in London. It may without exaggeration be described as ravishing. To all Londoners who are at their last shilling and are perplexed as to how to spend it most economically I say unhesitatingly, spend it at the Drury Lane pay-box when next Figaro is in the bill. Can a critic say more? Can a gentleman say less?

And yet see what has just occurred. An able musical critic, well known to the readers of these columns, and with every reason to make the utter best of Sir Thomas Beecham's enterprise (as indeed what lover of music has not?), volunteers the curious suggestion that Sir Thomas should revive the operas of Paisiello and Cimarosa, in order to teach the public that what they are admiring and enjoying in the Drury Lane performance is a sweetness and a neatness, a featness and discreetness (pardon the vile jingle) that belongs to all the best eighteenth-century composers no less than to Mozart. This is a shot that hits Sir Thomas between wind and water. It means that he has given us the charm of the eighteenth century, but not that strange spell by virtue of which Mozart, being dead, yet liveth, whilst Paisiello and Cimarosa are in comparison as dead as mutton. It means that the same success might have been achieved by a revival of Paisiello.

The wily critic aforesaid has no difficulty in illustrating his suggestion by citing several numbers in Mozart's opera which might have been written by any of his popular contemporaries without adding a leaf to their now withered laurels. If you doubt it, turn to Don Giovanni, and pretend, if you can, that the contemporary specimens preserved in the supper scene by the Don's restaurant band are any worse than, or even distinguishable in style from *Ricevete O padroncina* or any of the numbers mentioned in Mr Newman's article. The truth is that the eighteenth century produced a good deal of the loveliest art known to us; and any of its masterpieces adequately presented to us now could not fail to make us ashamed of our own violent and vulgar attempts to entertain ourselves. When you are enchanted at Drury Lane, you must not say "What a wonderful man Mozart was!" but "What a wonderful century Mozart lived in!"; and so it was, for persons of quality, comfortably mounted on the backs of the poor.

Turn now to the eighteenth-century opinion of Mozart. Far from finding his contemporaries listening with half-closed eyes to his delicious strains of melody, and to the melting supertonic cadence that Wagner made fun of in Die Meistersinger, you are stunned and amazed by complaints of the horrible noisiness of his instrumentation, of having to climb an arid mountain of discord to pluck a single flower of melody, of "the statue in the orchestra and the pedestal on the stage," of "too many notes," of assaults on the human ear and the human tendency to slumber in the stalls after dinner. They suggest the Tannhäuser fiasco in Paris in 1860 or the reception of Ibsen's Ghosts in London in 1890 rather than *Voi che sapete* and *Deh vieni a la finestra*. What has become of all this disturbing power? In the case of Tannhäuser we can explain it by the fact that we have only lately become quite accustomed to the unprepared major ninths which made the joyous music of Elizabeth sound so horrible to our grandfather's ears. But the harmonies which disgruntled Mozart's contemporaries were not new. Mozart could take the common chord and make you jump by just doubling the third in the base; or he could put the hackneyed discord of the dominant seventh in a form so cunningly distributed and instrumented that it would sound as if it came straight from hell or from the Elysian fields across the Ionian Sea, according to his purpose. It is hardly an exaggeration to say that as far as mere grammar and vocabulary go, there is nothing more in the statue scene from Don Juan, which threw open the whole magic realm of modern orchestration first explored by Mozart's forerunner Gluck, than in the exquisite little song of Cherubino, *Non so più*. All the effects are still there, as fresh, and, on occasion, as terrible as the day they were composed: handle them properly, and Lohengrin and Tristan will taste like soothing syrup after them. Unfortunately, nobody seems able to handle them properly. After a long experience of many conductors and many composers, I have come to the conclusion that Mozart and Berlioz are, among the moderns, by far the most elusive and difficult in performance.

As I am only half a critic now, I act up to that character by going to only half an opera at a time. As in the case of Il Trovatore, I did not see the first two acts of Figaro's Wedding. When I entered, Sir Thomas Beecham struck up, by way of instrumental prelude to the third act, the *fandango* (at least Mozart, who had never been in Spain and can certainly never have heard a note of Spanish music, called it a *fandango*) from the wedding scene. What Mozart would have said if he had heard himself thus held up as a miserable nineteenth-century composer, so barren of invention as to have to fall back on tunes out of his opera for preludes, I will not try to imagine, though I hope he would simply have expressed a mild wish that people would not do silly things. However, I was not sorry to hear the *fandango* twice; and I suppose nobody else was, in spite of the bad form involved. Only I began instantly to suspect that Sir Thomas is very fond of eighteenth-century music and does not care twopence about the specific Mozart. When the great duet came presently, he treated the few eloquent notes of exordium as if they were merely pianist's chords to fix the key; and of the wonderful opening-out of feeling which comes with the first words of Susanna I could not detect a trace. The first section was just dapper and nothing else: not until the concerted part came did the conductor warm to it. But the conclusive test was the sestet following Figaro's discovery of his parentage. How fine a piece of music that is, and how much it makes of a rather trivial though affectionate situation Sir Thomas will never know until he has fulfilled his destiny by conducting some of Mozart's greatest church music: say the grand Mass in C which lay so long undiscovered. Nothing came of the sestet, absolutely nothing at all: it might just as well have been omitted, as it was by the Carl Rosa company. But when it came to *Dove sono*, the conductor was really great: he squeezed every drop of nectar it contains out for us to the very last drop, and never relaxed his care, not even for the tiniest fraction of a bar. I will not blame the singer for putting in a little *liaison* of her own at the reprise, though I hope she will creep up to it diatonically instead of chromatically in future; for the chromatic progression is a mannerism of Meyerbeer's, and a patch of Meyerbeer on Mozart does not match nicely. All the rest was like that. The sentimental parts were treated as so much purely decorative music, kept going very tightly and strictly and rapidly, and played with perfect precision and prettiness: that is to say, for Mozart's purpose, not played at all. The singers, in these rhetorical and dramatic passages, could do nothing but hold on hard lest they should find themselves in the last bar but one. Mr Newman's complaint that he could find none of the bitterness Beaumarchais gave to Figaro in the air *Aprite un po' gli occhi* was therefore not Mozart's fault. It is true that Mozart made no attempt to write political music in the sense of expressing not only wounded human feeling but the specific rancor of the class-conscious proletarian; but the wounded feeling is provided for very plentifully if only the conductor will allow the singer to put it in instead of treating him as if he were one of the second violins. That unlucky power of juggling with music which enabled Mozart to force dramatic expression upon purely decorative musical forms makes it possible for a conductor to treat any of his numbers as merely a sonata or *rondo* or what not; and this is very much what Sir Thomas Beecham does except when he comes to the beauty bits which appeal to him by their feminine sweetness. In conducting Wagner or Strauss he could not do so, because if he ignored the dramatic element there would be nothing left but senseless-sounding brass and tinkling cymbals. In Mozart's case what is left is a very elegant and pretty sonata movement; and with this Sir Thomas is quite satisfied. But even whilst securing a spirited and polished execution of the music on this plane, he shews a curious want of appreciation of Mozart's personal quality, especially his severe taste. After strangling his singers dramatically, he allows them to debase the music by substituting for what Mozart wrote what he no doubt might have written if he had been, not a great composer, but a conceited singer. Sir Thomas thinks that his singers are better composers than Mozart; he allows Susanna not only to transpose passages an octave up, as if he could not stand her quite adequate low notes, but to alter wantonly the end of *Deh vieni non tardar,* a miracle of perfect simplicity [and] beauty, into what seems by contrast a miracle of artificial commonplace, not to say vulgarity. After conducting Basilio's *aria*—that quaint pæan of meanness which only a great actor could make intelligible—so completely in the spirit of abstract music that not even the roar of the tempest or the growl of the lion is suggested by the orchestra, he allows him to perpetrate the most third-class of all operatic tricks, the bawling of the last note an octave up in order to beg a foolish *encore* by a high B flat. As this is not weakness on Sir Thomas Beecham's part, for he is strict to tyranny in getting what his artistic conscience demands, he must really consider that his singers are improving Mozart. He actually lays himself open to the suspicion of having suggested the improvements. In that case there is nothing more to be said. What is clear so far is that he likes eighteenth-century music in its eighteenth-century form; and that this taste of his, highly creditable so far as it goes, has brought him accidentally into contact with Mozart; but of and for the specific Mozart who was not for the eighteenth century but for all time he knows and cares nothing.

Now this opinion of mine is only an opinion unless it can be brought to the test of experiment. Who am I that I should criticize a conductor of Sir Thomas Beecham's experience, and an artistic director of his proved enterprise and popularity? Simply nobody but a man of letters of no musical authority at all. Well, I propose an experiment, and a very interesting one. Let Sir Thomas Beecham induce Sir Edward Elgar to take over Figaro for just one night. Elgar has not only the technical tradition (which is being so rapidly lost that I wish the Government would at once commission him to edit all Mozart's operas for State publication) but he understands the heroic side of Mozart, which includes the dramatic side. It is sometimes rather a rough side; but Elgar would not be afraid of that. If Sir Thomas does not, after one hearing, blush to the roots of his hair and exclaim "Great Heavens! And I took this great composer for a mere confectioner!" I will pay a penny to any war charity he likes to name.

Mozart's opera scoring does in truth need some editing; for our conductors are spoiled by the copious and minute instructions which have been provided for them ever since they ceased to be a socially humble, professional caste fortified with an elaborate technical tradition instead of coming in from the general body of cultivated gentlemen amateurs. Mozart jotted down *f* or *sf* in his score where Meyerbeer would have written *con esplosione.* He wrote *p* where Verdi would have written *ppppp*! He did not resort to abbreviations to anything like the extent that the seventeenth-century and earlier composers did; but compared to nineteenth-century composers, who wrote down every note they meant to be sung, he used conventional musical shorthand to a considerable extent; and we want someone to fill in his scores as Arnold Dolmetsch has filled in the scores of Mozart's predecessors. Sir Thomas Beecham, relying on the existing scores, seems to have no conception of the dynamic range of Mozart's effects, of the fierceness of his *fortepianos,* the *élan* of his whipping-up triplets, the volume of his *fortes.* Even when Mozart writes *pp,* by which he means silence made barely audible (as in the first section of the Wedding March, for instance), we get at Drury Lane the same *mezzo forte* that prevails, except at a few blessed moments, during the whole performance. When the audience should be holding its breath to listen, or reeling from the thunder of the whole band and all the singers at their amplest, it still gets the same monotonous pretty fiddling that is neither high nor low, loud nor soft.

Yet on Thursday night, when I returned to hear the first two acts, I was carried away by the superb virtuosity of the orchestral execution, and the irresistible vigor and brilliancy of the great *finale* to the first act. Everything except this *finale* was far too fast even for all the instrumental effects, not to mention the dramatic ones; but I could not grudge the conductor his musical triumph; and I was positively grateful to him for audaciously forcing on us between the acts a slow movement for strings that had nothing to do with the opera, so finely was it played. It was pathetic and delightful to see the extraordinary pleasure of the audience, many of whom seemed to be discovering Mozart and going almost silly with the enchantment of it.

I repeat, the Drury Lane performance is charming; and very little additional care and understanding would make it great. It is, by the way, partly a performance of Beaumarchais' Mariage de Figaro; and I think it probable that if Mozart could be consulted as to the propriety of this attempt to make the best of both theatrical worlds, he would say that what he had taken from Beaumarchais he had taken and ennobled, and what he had left he had left for good reasons. To drag the Countess of *Porgi amor* and *Dove sono,* and the Cherubino of *Non so più* and *Voi che sapete* back into an atmosphere of scandalous intrigue was dangerous, but it is not unsuccessful: Mozart carries everything before him. The scenery and costumes are rich and amusing. The idea seems to have been to do something in the style of Mr Charles Ricketts; and the rose-pink crinoline petticoats are certainly as much in the style of Mr Ricketts as the sestet was in the style of Mozart: that is, Ricketts with Ricketts left out. Mr Nigel Playfair did what a man could in looking after Beaumarchais; but it was Mozart that needed looking after, and Mr Playfair could not supersede the conductor. However, I cannot bear to grumble; only I wish a little more thought had been added to all the money and time and trouble lavished. That last scene, for instance, which should be so cunningly fitted to the music, and is not fitted to anything at all but a vague idea that it would make a pretty picture cover for a summer number of something. When I think of—but there! I think too much to be a reasonable critic.

· DON GIOVANNI ·

Pall Mall Gazette, 31 October 1887 (*)

When I was requested by the Pall Mall Gazette to attend the centenary concert recital of Don Giovanni on Saturday last at the Crystal Palace, I felt strongly disposed to write curtly to the Editor expressing my unworthiness to do justice to the beauties of eighteenth-century opera. However, I was by no means sure that the Editor would have appreciated the sarcasm (editors, as a class, being shocking examples of neglected musical education); and, besides, I was somewhat curious to hear the performance. For though we are all agreed as to the prettiness of Mozart's melodies, his *naive* touches of mild fun, and the touch, ingenuity, and grace with which he rang his few stereotyped changes on the old-fashioned forms, yet I have observed that some modern musicians, in the face of a great technical development of harmony and instrumentation, and an enlargement even to world spaciousness of our views of the mission of art, yet persist in claiming for Mozart powers simply impossible to a man who had never read a line of Hegel or a stave of Wagner. I am not now thinking of the maudlin Mozart idolatry of M. Gounod, whom I of course do not consider a great musician; but rather of the unaccountable fact that even Richard Wagner seems to have regarded Mozart as in some respects the greatest of his predecessors. To me it is obvious that Mozart was a mere child in comparison with Schumann, Liszt, or Johannes Brahms; and yet I believe that I could not have expressed myself to that effect in the presence of the great master without considerable risk of contemptuous abuse, if not of bodily violence.

So I resolved finally to venture hearing poor old Rossini's pet *dramma giocosa*. Before starting, I took a glance at the score, and found exactly what I expected—commonplace melodies, diatonic harmonies and dominant discords, ridiculous old closes and half-closes at every eighth bar or so, "florid" accompaniments consisting of tum-tum in the bass and scales like pianoforte finger studies in the treble, and a ludicrously thin instrumentation, without trombones or clarionets except in two or three exceptionally pretentious numbers; the string quartet, with a couple of horns and oboes, seeming quite to satisfy the Mozartian notion of instrumentation. These are facts—facts which can be verified at any time by a reference to the score; and they must weigh more with any advanced musician than the hasty opinions which I formed at the concert when in a sort of delirium, induced, I have no doubt, by the heat of the room.

For I am bound to admit that the heat of the room produced a most extraordinary effect upon me. The commonplace melodies quite confounded me by acquiring subtlety, nobility, and dramatic truth of expression; the hackneyed diatonic harmonies reminded me of nothing I had ever heard before; the dominant discords had a poignant expression which I have failed in my own compositions to attain even by forcibly sounding all the twelve notes of the chromatic scale simultaneously; the ridiculous cadences and half-closes came sometimes like answers to unspoken questions of the heart, sometimes like ghostly echoes from another world; and the feeble instrumentation—but that was what warned me that my senses were astray. Otherwise I must have declared that here was a master compared to whom Berlioz was a musical pastrycook. From Beethoven and Wagner I have learned that the orchestra can paint every aspect of nature, and turn impersonal but specific emotion into exquisite sound. But an orchestra that creates men and women as Shakespear and Molière did—that makes emotion not only specific but personal and characteristic (and this, mind, without clarionets, without trombones, without a second pair of horns): such a thing is madness: I must have been dreaming. When the trombones did come in for a while in a supernatural scene at the end, I felt more in my accustomed element; but presently they took an accent so inexpressibly awful, that I, who have sat and smiled through Liszt's Inferno with the keenest relish, felt forgotten superstitions reviving within me. The roots of my hair stirred; and I recoiled as from the actual presence of Hell. But enough of these delusions, which I have effectually dispelled by a dispassionate private performance at my own pianoforte. Of the concert technically, I can only say that it was practically little more than a rehearsal of the orchestral parts.

13 May 1891 (I)

Ever since I was a boy I have been in search of a satisfactory performance of Don Giovanni; and I have at last come to see that Mozart's turn will hardly be in my time. I have had no lack of opportunities and disappointments; for the Don is never left long on the shelf, since it is so far unlike the masterpieces of Wagner, Berlioz, and Bach that cannot be done at all without arduous preparation. Any opera singer can pick up the notes and tumble through the concerted pieces with one eye on the conductor: any band can scrape through the orchestral parts at sight. Last year and the year before, it was tried in this fashion for a night at Covent Garden, with D'Andrade as Don Juan, and anybody who came handy in the other parts. This year it has been recognized that trifling with Mozart can be carried too far even for the credit of the Royal Italian Opera.

At the performance last Thursday, the first three acts of the four (twice too many) into which the work is divided at Covent Garden shewed signs of rehearsal. Even the last had not been altogether neglected. In the orchestra especially the improvement was marked. Not that anything very wonderful was accomplished in this department: the vigorous passages were handled in the usual timid, conventional way; and the statue music, still as impressive as it was before Wagner and Berlioz were born, was muddled through like a vote of thanks at the end of a very belated public meeting. But the overture was at least attentively played; and in some of the quieter and simpler numbers the exhalations of the magical atmosphere of the Mozartian orchestra were much less scanty and foggy than last year, when I could not, without risk of being laughed at, have assured a novice that in the subtleties of dramatic instrumentation Mozart was the greatest master of them all. The cast was neither a very bad nor a very good one. Its weakest point was the Leporello of Isnardon. Lacking the necessary weight in the middle of his voice, as well as the personal force demanded by the character, he was quite unable to lead the final section of the great sextet, Mille torbidi pensieri, which, thus deprived of its stage significance, became a rather senseless piece of "absolute music." Again, in O statua gentilissima, he hardly seized a point from beginning to end.

Now if an artist has neither voice enough nor musical perception enough to interpret forcibly and intelligently such an obvious and simple dramatic transition as that which follows the incident of the statue nodding acceptance of the invitation to supper, he is not fit to meddle with Mozart. Isnardon certainly makes a considerable show of acting throughout the opera; but as he is only trying to be facetious—abstractly facetious, if I may say so—without the slightest feeling for his part, the effect is irritating and irrelevant. Such pieces of business as his pointing the words, Voi sapete quel che fa, by nudging Elvira with his elbow at the end of Madamina, almost make one's blood boil. Poor old Sganarelle-Leporello, with all his failings, was no Yellow-plush: he would not have presumed upon a familiarity of that character with Donna Elvira, even if she had been a much meeker and less distinguished person than Molière made her. There is one man in Mr Harris's company whose clear artistic duty it is to play Leporello; and he, unfortunately, is an arrant *fainéant,* whose identity I charitably hide under the designation of Brother Edouard,† which, I need hardly add, is not that under which he appears in the bills. In Leporello he would have one of the greatest parts ever written, exactly suited to his range, and full of points which his musical intelligence would seize instinctively without unaccustomed mental exertion. And now that I have begun sketching a new cast, I may as well complete it. Dalla sua pace is not an easy song to sing; but if Jean de Reszke were to do it justice, the memory thereof would abide when all his Gounod successes were lapsed and lost.

With Giulia Ravogli as Zerlina, and the rest of the parts allotted much as at present, a tremendous house would be drawn. Nevertheless the tremendous house would be bored and kept late for its trains unless the representation were brought up to date by the following measures. Take a pot of paste, a scissors and some tissue paper, and start on the *recitativo secco* by entirely expunging the first two dialogues after the duel and before Ah, chi mi dice mai. Reduce all

---

†Edouard de Reszke, the famous operatic bass, was a brother of the equally famous tenor, Jean de Reszke.

the rest to such sentences as are barely necessary to preserve the continuity of the action. Play the opera in two acts only. And use the time thus gained to restore not only the Don's song, Metà di voi, which Faure used to sing, but, above all, the last three movements of the second finale, thereby putting an end for ever to the sensational vulgarity of bringing down the curtain on the red fire and the ghost and the trapdoor. There are other suppressed pages of the score to be reconsidered—a capital song which gets Leporello off the stage after the sextet, a curiously old-fashioned tragic air, almost Handelian, for Elvira between Là ci darem and the quartet, and a comic duet for Zerlina and Leporello, one of the later Vienna interpolations, which, however, is a very dispensable piece of buffoonery.

To return to the actual Don Giovanni of Thursday last, I need say no more of Miss de Lussan, who does not grow more interesting as her voice loses freshness and sustaining power and her manner becomes perter and trickier, than that she is one of those Zerlinas who end Batti, batti, on the upper octave of the note written, as a sort of apology for having been unable to do anything else with the song. The effect of this suburban grace can be realized by anyone who will take the trouble to whistle Pop goes the Weasel with the last note displaced an octave.

I am sorry to add that alterations of Mozart's text were the order of the evening, every one of the singers lacking Mozart's exquisite sense of form and artistic dignity. Maurel, though he stopped short of reviving the traditional atrocity of going up to F sharp in the serenade, did worse things by dragging an F natural into the end of Finch' han del vino, and two unpardonable G's into the finale of the first ballroom scene, just before the final *stretto*, thereby anticipating and destroying the climax Odi il tuon from the sopranos. Madame Tavary still clings to that desolating run up and down the scale with which she contrives to make the conclusion of Non mi dir ridiculous; and Montariol, unable to evade Il mio tesoro by omitting it like Dalla sua pace, did strange things with it in his desperation. His Ottavio was altogether a melancholy performance, as he was put out of countenance from the beginning by being clothed in a seedy misfit which made him look lamentably down on his luck. Mr Harris would not dream of allowing such a costume to be seen on his stage in a modern opera; and I must really urge upon him that there are limits to the application even of the principle that anything is good enough for Mozart.

Maurel's Don Giovanni, though immeasurably better than any we have seen of late years, is not to be compared to his Rigoletto, his Iago, or, in short, to any of his melodramatic parts. Don Juan may be as handsome as irresistible, as adroit, as unscrupulous, as brave as you please; but the one thing that is not to be tolerated is that he should consciously parade these qualities as if they were elaborate accomplishments instead of his natural parts. And this is exactly where Maurel failed. He gave us a description of Don Juan rather than an impersonation of him. The confident smile, the heroic gesture, the splendid dress, even the intentionally seductive vocal inflexion which made such a success of Là ci darem in spite of Miss de Lussan's coquettish inanity, were all more or less artificial. A Don Juan who is continually aiming at being Don Juan may excite our admiration by the skill with which he does it; but he cannot convince us that he is the real man. I remember seeing Jean de Reszke play the part when he had less than a tenth of Maurel's present skill and experience; and yet I think Mozart would have found the younger man the more sympathetic interpreter.

It seems ungrateful to find fault with an artist who rescues a great rôle from the hands of such ignoble exponents as the common or Covent Garden Dons who swagger feebly through it like emancipated billiard-markers; but it would hardly be a compliment to Maurel to praise him for so cheap a superiority. And, indeed, there is no fault-finding in the matter. It is a question of temperament. When all is said, the fundamental impossibility remains that Maurel's artistic vein is not Mozartian. One or two points of detail may be mentioned. He was best in the love-making scenes and worst in those with Leporello, whom he treated with a familiarity which was rather that of Robert Macaire with Jacques Strop than of a gentleman with his valet. The scene of the exposure in the ballroom he played rather callously. Nothing in the score is clearer than that Don Juan is discomfited, confused, and at a loss from the moment in which they denounce him until, seeing that there is nothing for it but to fight his way out, he ceases to utter hasty exclamations of dismay, and recovers himself at the words Ma non manca in me coraggio. Maurel dehumanized and melodramatized the scene by missing this entirely, and maintaining a defiant and self-possessed bearing throughout.

And again, on the entry of the statue, which Don Juan, however stable his nerve may be imagined to have been, can hardly have witnessed without at least a dash of surprise and curiosity, Maurel behaved very much as if his uncle had dropped in unexpectedly in the middle of a bachelor's supper-party. The result was that the scene went for nothing, though it is beyond all comparison the most wonderful of the wonders of dramatic music. But if the audience is ever to be cured of the habit of treating it as a sort of voluntary to play them out, it must be very carefully studied by the artist playing Don Juan, upon whose pantomime the whole action of the scene depends, since the statue can only stand with a stony air of weighing several tons, whilst the orchestra makes him as awful as the conductor will allow it. Since Maurel let this scene slip completely through his fingers, I do not see how he can be classed with the great Don Juans (if there ever were any great ones). The problem of how to receive a call from a public statue does not seem to have struck him as worth solving.

The Elvira (Madame Rolla), whose B flat at the end of her aria was perhaps the most excusable of all the inexcusable interpolations, was as good as gold, not indulging once in a scream, and relying altogether on pure vocal tone of remarkable softness. In Mi tradi she succeeded in being more pleasing than any Elvira I can remember except Di Murska, who understood the full value of the part and played it incomparably, like the great artist she was. Madame Rolla does not act with the force of Nilsson; and in the quartet she failed to bring off the effect at the end, where Elvira gets louder and angrier whilst the wretched Don gets more and more agitated by the dread of her making a scene; but I think Maurel was a little unequal to the occasion here too. On the whole, Madame Rolla, whose voice reminds one somewhat of Marimon's, is a useful addition to the company. Mr Harris had better now turn his attention to achieving a really serious performance of Le Nozzi di Figaro.

2 May 1894 (III)

I have been indulging in five shillings' worth of Ruskin on Music, in a volume just published by Mr George Allen. As it happened, the first sentence I lighted on when I opened the book was "the oratorio, withering the life of religion into dead bones on the Syren sands." Immediately I woke up; for the fact that modern oratorio is mostly a combination of frivolity and sensuality with hypocrisy and the most oppressive dullness is still sufficiently a trade secret to make its discovery by an outsider interesting. A few pages off I found Mr Ruskin describing the singing he heard south of the Alps. Usually the Englishman in Italy, carefully primed beforehand with literary raptures concerning a nation of born musicians speaking the most vocal language in the world, is sufficiently careful of his own credit as a man of taste to discover a Giuglini in every gondolier and St Cecilia's lute in every accordion.

Mr Ruskin innovated so far as to use his own judgment; and here is the result: "Of bestial howling, and entirely frantic vomiting up of damned souls through their still carnal throats, I have heard more than, please God, I will ever endure the hearing of again, in one of His summers." I take the liberty of squeezing Mr Ruskin's hand in mute sympathy with the spirit of this passage. In Italy, where the chance of being picked up off the streets and brought out as *primo tenore* at the Opera occupies the same space in the imagination of the men as the chance of selecting a Derby winner does in England, you cannot get away from the ignoble bawling which Mr Ruskin describes so forcibly—and yet not too forcibly, or forcibly enough; for language will not hold the full pretentiousness and cupidity of the thing, let alone the unpleasantness of the noise it makes.

It is at once the strength and weakness of Mr Ruskin in dealing with music that he is in love with it. There is always a certain comedy in the contrast between people as they appear transfigured in the eyes of those who love them, and as they appear to those who are under no such inspiration—or, for the matter of that, as they appear to themselves. And the tragi-comedy of the love of men and women for one another is reproduced in their love for art.

Mr Ruskin is head and ears in love with Music; and so am I; but I am married to her, so to speak, as a professional critic, whereas he is still a wooer, and has the illusions of imperfect knowledge as well as the illuminations of perfect love. Listen to this, for example:

"True music is the natural expression of a lofty passion for a right cause. In proportion to the kingliness and force of any personality, the expression either of its joy or suffering becomes measured, chastened, calm, and capable of interpretation only by the majesty of ordered, beautiful, and worded sound. Exactly in proportion to the degree in which we become narrow in the cause and conception of our passions, incontinent in the utterance of them, feeble of perseverance in them, sullied or shameful in the indulgence of them, their expression by musical means becomes broken, mean, fatuitous, and at last impossible: the measured waves of heaven will not lend themselves to the expression of ultimate vice: it must be for ever sunk in discordance or silence."

I entirely agree with Mr Ruskin in this; but it will not hold water, for all that. "The measured waves of heaven" are not so particular as he thinks. Music will express any emotion, base or lofty. She is absolutely unmoral: we find her in Verdi's last work heightening to the utmost the expression of Falstaff's carnal gloating over a cup of sack, just as willingly as she heightened the expression of "a lofty passion for a right cause" for Beethoven in the Ninth Symphony. She mocked and prostituted the Orpheus legend for Offenbach just as keenly and effectively as she ennobled it for Gluck. Mr Ruskin himself has given an instance of this—a signally wrong instance, by the way; but let that pass for a moment:

"And yonder musician, who used the greatest power which (in the art he knew) the Father of Spirits ever yet breathed into the clay of this world; who used it, I say, to follow and fit with perfect sound the words of the Zauberflöte and of Don Giovanni—foolishest and most monstrous of conceivable human words and subjects of thought —for the future amusement of his race! No such spectacle of unconscious (and in that unconsciousness all the more fearful) moral degradation of the highest faculty to the lowest purpose can be found in history."

This is a capital instance of Mr Ruskin's besetting sin—virtuous indignation. If these two operas are examples of "foolishest and most monstrous" words fitted and followed with perfect sound— that is, with true music—what becomes of the definition which limits true music to "the natural expression of a lofty passion for a right cause"? Clearly, that will not do.

And now may I beg Mr Ruskin to mend his illustration, if not his argument? The generation which could see nothing in Die Zauberflöte but a silly extravaganza was one which Mr Ruskin certainly belonged to in point of time; and he has for once sunk to the average level of its thought in this shallow criticism of the work which Mozart deliberately devoted to the expression of his moral sympathies. Everything that is true and vital in his worship of music would be shattered if it were a fact—happily it is not—that the music of Sarastro came from a silly and trivial mood. If I were to assure Mr Ruskin that Bellini's Madonna with St Ursula, in Venice, was originally knocked off as a sign for a tavern by the painter, Mr Ruskin would simply refuse to entertain the story, no matter what the evidence might be, knowing that the thing was eternally impossible. Since he sees no such impossibility in the case of Die Zauberflöte, I must conclude that he does not know the masterpieces of music as he knows those of painting.

As to Don Giovanni, otherwise The Dissolute One Punished, the only immoral feature of it is its supernatural retributive morality. Gentlemen who break through the ordinary categories of good and evil, and come out at the other side singing Fin ch' han dal vino and La ci darem, do not, as a matter of fact, get called on by statues, and taken straight down through the floor to eternal torments; and to pretend that they do is to shirk the social problem they present. Nor is it yet by any means an established fact that the world owes more to its Don Ottavios than to its Don Juans.

It is, of course, impossible to make a serious stand on a libretto which is such an odd mixture of the old Punch tradition with the highly emancipated modern philosophy of Molière; but whether you apply Mr Ruskin's hasty criticism to Punch and Judy or to Le Festin de Pierre, you will, I think, see that it is fundamentally nothing but an explosion of pious horror of the best Denmark Hill brand. The hard fact is that Don Giovanni is eminent in virtue of its uncommon share of wisdom, beauty, and humor; and if any theory of morals leads to the conclusion that it is foolish and monstrous, so much the worse for the theory.

The Nation, London, 22 June 1918 (*)

Last week my old professional habit of opera-going reasserted itself for a moment. I heard the last two acts of Don Giovanni at the Shaftesbury Theatre by the Carl Rosa company, and The Valkyrie (Hunnishly known as Die Walküre) at Drury Lane. There was an immense difference between the two performances. One of them might have been an attempt on the part of an opera company, a conductor, and a number of bandsmen, all perfect strangers to one-another and accidentally marooned in the Shaftesbury Theatre, to wile away the time by reading at sight a bundle of band parts and vocal scores of a rather difficult opera which they had never heard before by a young and very puzzling composer. The other had been rehearsed to the point of achieving, at its best moments, a superb fulfilment of the composer's intention; and the repeated storms of applause which broke out, until the conductor was forced to make several reluctant appearances before the curtain, were not, and could not have been, more generous than he deserved.

And yet they were both scratch performances.

When I was a child I heard certain operas rehearsed by a company of amateurs who, having everything to learn, could not have achieved a performance at all if they had not been coached and trained and rehearsed with a thoroughness impossible in professional music. It would cost too much. These amateurs rehearsed an opera for six months. There were all sorts of weaknesses about their performances; and yet I have never since, even in the course of several years' experience as a professional critic in London, with occasional excursions to Paris, Italy, and the German capitals, heard any performances as perfect, except some of the most thoroughly prepared productions at Bayreuth and Munich. I may be asked whether the brothers De Reszke, playing Gounod's Faust for the fifty millionth time at Covent Garden, did not display a tolerable familiarity with that work; and, of course, I cannot deny that they did; but the Valentines and Marguerites and Siebels came and went; and there was always the scratch habit which is so hard to throw off. In the ordinary theatre, where thorough rehearsal is the rule, and the conductor (called the producer) and the company have nothing else to do for six weeks or more than to work at the play, I have sometimes had to deal with an actor whose lot has been cast in theatres where a new play had to be presented every week or even every night. In such actors the scratch habit is an incurable disease. At the first rehearsal they astonish everyone, just as London orchestras always astonish foreign conductors and composers, by being almost letter-perfect, and giving such a capable and promising reading of their parts that one feels that after a fortnight's work they will be magnificent, and leave all the others nowhere. And they never get a step further. The fortnight's work is to them useless, unnecessary, and irritating. Even the letter-perfection vanishes: it deteriorates into appeals to the prompter or appalling improvisations. The same thing occurs with opera singers. You hear a performance of some hackneyed opera by singers who have sung in it hundreds of times. It is never accurate. The individual singers are not so accurate, or even nearly so accurate, as when they performed the part nervously and anxiously for the first time, and were much too young to have found out how little accuracy they could make shift with. They could no more give such a performances as Mr Du Maurier's company at Wyndham's Theatre gives of Dear Brutus than a hotel waiter can behave like an old family servant. All experienced travelers have noticed that, however generously they may tip, hotel servants get tired of them if they attempt to reside in the hotel instead of passing on like all the others. There is a hotel psychology, a stock company psychology, and an opera psychology; and all three are modes of the scratch psychology, which is incompatible with thorough excellence.

I sometimes ask myself whether a thorough representation of an opera is worth while. I do not mean commercially: commercially it is impossible under existing conditions. But suppose money were no object, would the final degrees of perfection be worth the trouble they would cost? I go further than merely saying baldly that I think they would. I am strongly of opinion that nothing but superlative excellence in art can excuse a man or woman for being an artist at all. It is not a light thing in a world of drudgery for any citizen to say, "I am not going to do what you others must: I am going to do what I like." I think we are entitled to reply, "Then we shall expect you to do it devilish well, my friend, if we are not to treat you as a rogue and a vagabond." I have a large charity for loose morals: they are often more virtuous than straitlaced ones. But for loose art I have no charity at all. When I hear a fiddler playing *mezzo forte* when his part is marked *pianissimo* or *fortissimo* (as the English orchestral fiddler is apt to do if he can trifle with the conductor), or a trombone player shirking the trouble of phrasing intelligently, I hate him. Yet I could forgive him quite easily for being a bigamist.

The difference between the Don Giovanni and the Valkyrie performances was that the Carl Rosa company had better not have played Don Giovanni at all than played it as they did, whereas it would have been a positive national loss to us if we had not had the Beecham performance. I grant that there are extenuating circumstances. Mozart's music is enormously more difficult than Wagner's; and his tragi-comedy is even more so. With Mozart you either hit the bull's-eye or miss; and a miss is as bad as a mile. With Wagner the target is so large and the charge so heavy that if you get the notes out anyhow, you are bound to do some execution. It takes a Coquelin, combined with a first-rate *basso cantante,* to play Leporello; but any heavyweight bass, with the voice of a wolf, and very little more power of vocal execution, can put up a quite impressive Hund-

ing. Roll Forbes-Robertson and Vladimir Rosing into one, and you
will have an adequate Don Juan; but which of all the famous Wotans
could have touched Don Juan with the tips of his fingers? It is the
same with the conducting: what conductor of any talent, with the
tradition of Wagner and Richter to prompt him, could fail with the
scene between Siegmund and Brynhild in the second act of Die
Walküre, or with the fire music at the close? Try him with the two
symphonic scenes in which Don Juan invites the statue to supper,
and in which the statue avails himself of the invitation, and he is as
likely as not to be hopelessly beaten. Felix Mottl was one of the very
best Wagner conductors produced by Bayreuth. I have heard him
conduct Mozart's Nozze di Figaro, Così fan Tutte, and Clemenza di
Tito to perfection in Munich. But he was utterly beaten by Don
Giovanni. Senor de la Fuente, the Carl Rosa conductor, when he
conducted Le Nozze di Figaro last year, handled it brilliantly. It is an
easily learnt work: the execution may require exquisite delicacy and
immaculate taste; but there is no touch of tragedy in it, nor any touch
of passion of the tragic quality. Now, Don Juan is a tragic hero or
nothing: his destiny is announced by Mozart from the very first
chord of the overture. That the opera is called a *dramma giocosa,* and
that there was an early Don Juan who was only a squalid drunkard
and libertine, does not weigh against the evidence of the score. Before Shakespear touched Hamlet there was a zany Hamlet who
mopped and mowed, and nailed down the courtiers under the arras
and set them on fire, going through all the pitiable antics with which
the village idiot amused heartless visitors when he was one of the
sights of the village instead of an inmate of the county asylum. Well,
Mozart abolished the drunken Don Juan as completely and finally as
Shakespear abolished the zany Hamlet. Unfortunately, the operatic
conductors and stars do not seem to have found this out. When the
singer who impersonates Don Juan happens to be a gentleman, he
takes the greatest pains to make himself a cad for the occasion.
Leporello's agonies of terror are replaced by silly and ineptly executed buffooneries which the Brothers Griffith could do, in their
proper place, artistically and funnily. Everyone, the conductor included, is nosing through the score for the vulgar fun which is not
there, and overlooking the tragic and supernatural atmosphere
which is there. And the result is that they all feel that the thing is not
going, that they are missing instead of hitting. They do not know
what is the matter, and yet know that something is the matter. They

find the music frightfully difficult; cling with their eyes to the conductor; become rattled and flurried and panic-stricken; until at last their passages sound like nothing at all. The conductor has to keep up an air of assurance, but is secretly almost equally puzzled: you know it by the infirmity of the rhythm. Even the ruthless march of the statue music, a rhythm which no conductor ever misses in the music of Wotan or of Rossini's Moses, dwindles into an irresolute buzzing. For example, the terrible address of the statue, which begins *Tu m'invitasti a cena,* is preceded by two ominous bars in which this rhythm is thundered through dead vocal silence as emphatically as the opening of Beethoven's symphony in C minor. The conductor must mark this with Handelian conviction and power; for it is quite as necessary to the effect as the more sensational orchestration of the hellish blasts which follow it, and which only a deaf conductor could underrate. But Senor de la Fuente noticed nothing in it but commonplace rum-tum, which he was too worried to attend to. That is only one instance of the sort of thing that went on all through the symphonic numbers, and that always will go on until some conductor will take the work in tragic seriousness, search the score for what Mozart put into it and not for what he made his reputation by leaving out of it, and finally rehearse it hard for a year or so before letting the public in.

He will find other things besides the tragic intensity of the overture and the statue music. He will find that the window *trio, Ah, taci, ingiusto core,* is not a comic accompaniment to the unauthorized tomfoolery of Don Juan making a marionet of Leporello, but perhaps the most lovely nocturne in the whole range of musical literature. And he may also be led to the discovery, greatly needed by all English conductors, and apparently by one Spanish one, that six-eight time does not always mean that the piece is a country dance. In German music it often means an *andantino* of intense and noble sentiment.

I must in fairness make it clear that the shortcomings in the Carl Rosa performance were not the fault of the singers. They were asked to perform under scratch conditions a work which has never yet been satisfactorily or even decently performed under such conditions, and never will. At Covent Garden the directors used to throw it over to some *ripieno* conductor to run through once a season as an easy routine job, and were perfectly successful in making it appear worthy of the ignorant contempt with which they were treating it.

The Carl Rosa company at least know it to be an important work; but as they know little else about it except the mere notes, and some of its silliest would-be comic traditions, the result is no better. Why not leave Don Giovanni in peace on the shelf? It is so easy not to perform it.

By the way, there was one original point made. Mr James Pursail is the first Don, as far as I know, to notice that, as Don Juan was not a professional singer, however masterfully he may sing all the dramatic music, he should sing the serenade like an amateur. And this was just what Mr Pursail did. I do not mean that he sang it badly: on the contrary, he sang it very nicely; and I do not quarrel with his unauthorized F sharp at the end, because, for a high baritone with an F sharp which is better than his low D, it is a pardonable flourish, and is not in any case a vulgarity like shouting the last note an octave up, with which Mr Edward Davies discredited an otherwise excellent performance of *Il mio tesoro*. I mean that Mr Pursail sang it, not in the traditionally ardent and accomplished manner, but in the manner of a modest amateur. This is a real new reading which deserves to be noted.

Weber

18 July 1894 (III)

The production of Der Freischütz and Fidelio at the German Opera momentarily transferred the centre of operatic interest, for me at least, from Covent Garden to Drury Lane. It was amusing to find these two masterpieces arousing quite a patronizing interest as old-fashioned curiosities, somewhat dowdy perhaps, but still deserving of indulgence for the sake of tradition. As to the Freischütz, hardly anyone could remember its last performance in London; and I was astonished when the questions addressed to me on this point made me conscious that although the work is familiar to me as the most familiar of Shakespear's plays, and counts, indeed, as a permanent factor in my consciousness, I could only clearly recollect two actual representations of it, one in Munich, and the other in my native town, which is not in England. I will not swear that I have not seen it oftener; for I have long since given free play to my inestimable gift of forgetting, and have lost count of the performances I have witnessed almost as completely as I have lost count of my headaches; but still, even in my case, it is somewhat significant that I should be unable to recall a representation of Der Freischütz in London. Such a doubt as to the abysmally inferior Carmen would be a ridiculous affectation.

Perhaps, therefore, the first question to answer is. "How has Der Freischütz worn?" To which I am happy to be able to reply that its freshness and charm delighted everyone as much as its unaffected sincerity of sentiment impressed them. I will not, of course, pretend that the hermit strikes the popular imagination as he did in the days when hermits habitually trod the stage, and were deferred to, at sight of their brown gowns, rope girdles, and white beards, by all the civil and military authorities, exactly as if they were modern French deputies exhibiting their scarves to the police in *émeutes*.

And it would be vain to conceal the fact that the terrors of the Wolf's Gulch and the casting of the magic bullets were received with audible chuckling, although Sir Augustus Harris had made a supreme effort to ensure the unearthliness of the incantation by making the stage a sort of museum of all the effects of magic and devilry known in the modern theatre. He had illuminated steam clouds from Bayreuth, and fiery rain from the Lyceum Faust; he had red fire, glowing hell-mouth caverns, apparitions, skeletons, vampire bats, explosions, conflagrations, besides the traditional wheels, the skulls, the owl, and the charmed circle.

And yet nobody could help laughing, least of all, I should imagine, Sir Augustus himself. The owl alone would have sufficed to set me off, because, though its eyes were not red like those of previous stage owls, and it was therefore not so irresistibly suggestive of a railway signal as I had expected, one of its eyes was much larger than the other, so that it seemed to contemplate the house derisively through a single eyeglass. This quaint monocle notwithstanding, the scene produced some effect until the other phenomena supervened. If they had been omitted—if the apparitions had been left to our imaginations and to Weber's music, the effect would have been enormously heightened. Owls, bats, ravens, and skeletons have no supernatural associations for our rising generations: the only function an owl or a bat can now fulfil in such a scene is to heighten that sense of night in a forest which is one of Nature's most wonderful effects.

But this change in public susceptibility makes it necessary to take much greater pains with stage illusions than formerly. When the bat was a mere bogy to terrify an audience of grown-up children, it was, no doubt, sufficient to dangle something like a stuffed bustard with huge moth's wings at the end of a string from the flies to make the pit's flesh creep. Nowadays, unless a manager can devise some sort of aerial top that will imitate the peculiar flitting of the real flittermouse he must forgo bats altogether.

To appeal to our extinct sense of the supernatural by means that outrage our heightened sense of the natural is to court ridicule. Pasteboard pies and paper flowers are being banished from the stage by the growth of that power of accurate observation which is commonly called cynicism by those who have not got it; and impossible bats and owls must be banished with them. Der Freischütz may be depended on to suggest plenty of phantasmagoria without help from out-of-date stage-machinists and property-masters.

Except during the absurdities of the Wolf's Gulch, the performance appeared to me to be an exceptionally successful one. The orchestra has improved greatly since the first week; and though Lohse has one trick which I greatly dislike—that of hurrying at every crescendo—he is equal to his weighty duties as Wagner and Beethoven conductor. His handling of Fidelio was at many points admirable. Beethoven had not any bats or skeletons to contend with; but he had what was quite as bad in its way: to wit, an execrable chorus of prisoners who, on catching sight of the sentinels, would break in on the German text with mistuned howls of "Silenzio, silenzio." In both operas there were moments when the singing was beyond all apology.

Rossini

The Illustrated London News, 5 March 1892 (*)

Fifty years ago Rossini would have been described as one of the greatest of modern composers, the equal, if not the superior, of Beethoven. At present, such an estimate of him seems as ridiculous to us all as it seemed then to Berlioz and Wagner; and the danger now is that all the centenary notices of him which are not mere compilations from the musical dictionaries will revenge upon his memory the excesses of the Rossinian age, when even scholarly musicians regarded him as an Italian Handel. Mendelssohn himself was captivated by his genius, although it is not too much to say that Rossini never produced a single secular composition of any length without padding or spicing it with some gross claptrap which Mendelssohn would have hanged himself rather than put before the public as his own work. Indeed, Rossini was one of the greatest masters of claptrap that ever lived. His moral deficiencies as an artist were quite extraordinary. When he found the natural superiority of his genius in conflict with the ignorance and frivolity of the public—and the musical ignorance and frivolity of the Venetians and Neapolitans can hardly be overstated—he surrendered without a struggle. Although he was so able a man that it was easier and pleasanter to him to do his work intelligently than to conventionalize it and write down to the popular taste, he never persevered in any innovation that was not well received; and it is hardly possible to doubt that the superiority of William Tell to his other operas is due solely to the fact that it was written for the Grand Opéra in Paris, where the public had been educated by Gluck to expect at least a show of seriousness in an *opera seria.* He rose to the occasion then as a matter of business, just as he would have sunk to it had the commission come from Venice; and it was characteristic of him that he did not rise an inch beyond it: in fact, he adapted all the old claptrap to the new conditions instead of discarding it. This may be seen plainly enough in the overture which every reader of these lines probably knows by heart. Rossini's previous overtures had all been composed

189

according to a formula of his own. First came a majestic and often beautiful exordium, sometimes extending, as in Semiramide, to the dimensions of a slow movement. Then he fell to business with an irresistibly piquant "first subject," usually a *galop* more or less thinly disguised, working up into the conventional *tutti*, with the strings rushing up and down the scales and the brass blaring vigorously. Then a striking half-close, announcing a fresh treat in the shape of a "second subject," not a *galop* this time, but a spirited little march tune, leading to the celebrated Rossini *crescendo*, in which one of the *arabesques* of the march pattern would be repeated and repeated, with the pace of the accompaniment doubling and redoubling, and the orchestration thickening and warming, until finally the big drum and the trombones were in full play, and every true Italian was ready to shout *Viva il gran' maestro!* in wild enthusiasm. And then, since everybody wanted to hear it all again, the whole affair, except, of course, the introduction, was repeated note for note, and finished off with a Pelion of a *coda* piled on the Ossa of the *crescendo*, the last flourish being always a rush up the scale by the fiddles, and a final thump and crash for the whole band. As Rossini's invention never flagged in the matter of *galops* and marches, he was able to turn out overtures of this sort without a second thought. They soon overran Europe; and those to Tancredi, L' Italiana in Algeri, La Gazza Ladra, and especially Semiramide, are still as familiar to military bandsmen as God Save the Queen. When William Tell was ordered, Rossini understood that Paris would expect something more than a mere reshaking of his old box of tricks; but he knew better than to risk his popularity by giving them any really novel or profound work. All he abandoned was the wholesale repetition and the *crescendo*. By way of repudiating all noisy pomp in the exordium, he made it a charming concerted piece for the violoncellos alone. The *galop* and the *tutti* he presented in the most ingenious metamorphosis as the approach and final bursting of a tremendous storm. The second subject was a charming pastorale, with variations on the flute which no schoolgirl could misunderstand. Suddenly came a trumpet-call, and then such a quickstep as the world had never heard before. Not one of his old *galopades* or *crescendos* could keep pace with it for a moment: it was the very quintessence of all his claptrap. Hackneyed as it has become, it is hard to this day to keep an audience from encoring it when it is well played. The whole opera bears the same relation to his other operas as the overture to his other overtures. It was meant for an audience which included a certain percentage of serious and cultivated musicians. He just surpasses himself far enough to compel the admiration, if not the respect, of these few, without losing his hold of the rest. Had the percentage been higher, he would have taken a little more trouble: if it had been lower, he would have taken less. The success of William Tell, added to the results of a prudent marriage, and the friendship of the Rothschilds, who looked after his savings for him, secured his future pecuniarily. From that time, although he had not turned thirtynine, he wrote no more operas. For the forty years of life which remained to him he could afford to be idle, and he was idle, except that he composed a mass and a Stabat Mater, in which again he rose with consummate ease just to the requirements of his church, still without sacrificing a jot of his popularity. The Stabat, with its *Cujus animam* set to a stirring march tune, its theatrically sublime *Inflammatus,* and the ingenious sham fugue at the end, shews that he was the same man in the church as in the theatre. In so far as he was ever great, he was great in spite of himself. When he was a lad learning counterpoint, his master one day disparaged him as only knowing enough to compose mere operas. He immediately replied that all he wanted was to compose operas, and refused to carry his studies a step further. Among musicians, therefore, his name is famous, but not sacred. He was captivating and exhilarating; he was imposing to the last degree in his splendid moments; he was clever, and full of fun; his practicality was largely due to good sense; he did not settle down to offering the public frivolous work until it had snubbed him for taking himself more seriously; he may be credited with some sincerity in his admissions that he was not a great composer as Mozart was a great composer; and it cannot be denied that he was exceptionally unfortunate in respect of the illiteracy, the Bohemianism, the ignorance, narrowness, and squalor of his environment during childhood. On all these grounds, and some others, there is a case to be made out on Rossini's side which cannot be adequately stated here; but when the utmost has been made of it, it will not entitle him to pre-eminence even among modern Italian composers, whilst as to a place in the hierarchy of the greatest modern masters, from Bach to Wagner, that is quite out of the question.

9 March 1892 (II)

The Rossini Centenary passed without any celebration in London (as far as I know) except an afternoon concert at the Crystal

Palace, whither I went, partly for the sake of old times, and partly because the concert afforded me an opportunity, now very rare, of hearing Rossini's overtures, not from a military band, or from a careless promenade-concert orchestra with an enormous preponderance of string quartet, but from a first-rate wind-band, balanced by about as many strings as the composer reckoned upon. The program was made up of no fewer than four overtures—Siege of Corinth, La Gazza Ladra, Semiramide, and William Tell—with an admirable arrangement of the prayer from Moses for orchestra and organ by Mr Manns, and two vocal pieces, Di piacer and Una voce, curiously chosen, since one is almost an inversion of the intervals of the other. There was, besides, a selection from William Tell, arranged for the band alone.

This was rather too much for the endurance of the orchestra, which became a little demoralized towards the end. Rossini's band parts consist mostly of uninteresting stretches of rum-tum, relieved here and there by some abominably inconvenient melodic trait; for he was the most "absolute" of musicians: his tunes came into his head unconnected with any particular quality of tone, and were handed over to the instrument they would sound prettiest on, without the least regard to the technical convenience of the player—further, of course, than to recognize the physical limits of possibility, and not write piccolo parts down to sixteen-foot C, or trombone parts up to C in altissimo. Consequently, though the scores of Berlioz and Wagner are in a sense far more difficult than those of Rossini, you do not hear during performances of their works any of those little hitches or hair-breadth escapes which are apt to occur when a player has to achieve a feat, however trifling, which is foreign to the genius of his instrument.

It is true that what I call the genius of the instrument varies with the nationality of the player; so that a French horn, though most refractory to a compatriot of its own, or to an Englishman, will be quite docile in the hands of a German; or twelve violins played by Italians will have less weight in an orchestra than five played by Englishmen, not to mention other and subtler differences. Yet the fact remains that we have at present a sort of international school of orchestration, through which an English player, whatever his instrument may be, finds much the same class of work set for him, whether the composer be the Italian Verdi, the French Gounod or Massenet, the Jew Max Bruch, the Bohemian Dvořák, the Norwegian Grieg, the Dutchman Benoit, and so on to the Irish Villiers Stanford, the Scotch Hamish MacCunn, and the English—well, perhaps I had better not mention names in the case of England. Rossini's scores, especially those which he wrote from Venice and Naples, run off these lines; and the result is, that at a Rossini concert there is more likelihood of actual slips in execution than at a Wagner or Beethoven concert; whilst the eventual worrying, fatiguing, and boring of the executants is a certainty when the program is a long one.

The Crystal Palace band held out brilliantly until the final number, which was the overture and selection from William Tell, in the course of which it occurred to most of them that they had had about enough of the Swan of Pesaro. Yet the Swan came off more triumphantly than one could have imagined possible at this time of day. Dal tuo stellato soglio was as sublime as ever. Mr Manns conducted it as he had arranged it, with perfect judgment and sympathy with its inspiration; and in spite of myself I so wanted to hear it again that after a careful look round to see that none of my brother-critics were watching me I wore away about an eighth of an inch from the ferrule of my umbrella in abetting an encore. Another encore, of which I am guiltless, was elicited by the cabaletta of Una voce, which, however, Miss Thudichum did not sing so well as Di piacer. The repeats in the overtures were, strange to say, not in the least tedious: we were perfectly well content to hear the whole bag of tricks turned out a second time. Nobody was disgusted, *à la* Berlioz, by "the brutal crescendo and big drum." On the contrary, we were exhilarated and amused; and I, for one, was astonished to find it all still so fresh, so imposing, so clever, and even, in the few serious passages, so really fine.

I felt, not without dread, that the nails were coming out of Rossini's coffin as the performance proceeded; and if I had been seated a little nearer the platform, there is no saying that I might not have seized Mr Manns's arm and exclaimed, "You know not what you do. Ten minutes more and you will have this evil genius of music alive again, and undoing the last thirty years of your work." But after the third overture and the second aria, when we had had six doses of crescendo, and three, including one encore, of cabaletta, I breathed again. We have not heard the last of the overture to Semiramide; but we shall not in future hear grave critics speaking of it as if it were first-cousin to Beethoven's No. 3 Leonora. The general opinion, especially among literary men who affected music, used to be that there was an Egyptian grandeur about Semiramide, a massiveness as of the Great Pyramid, a Ninevesque power and terror far beyond anything that Beethoven had ever achieved. And when Madame Trebelli, as a handsome chieftain in a panther-skin, used to come down to the footlights, exclaiming, "Here I am at last in Babylon," and give us Ah quel giorno, with a cabaletta not to be distinguished without close scrutiny from that to Rosina's aria in Il Barbiere, we took it as part of the course of Nature on the operatic stage. We are apt to wonder nowadays why the public should have been so impressed at first by the apparent originality, dramatic genius, depth and daring of Meyerbeer as to be mystified and scandalized when Mendelssohn, Schumann, and Wagner treated him with no more respect than if he had been an old clo' man from Houndsditch.

But the explanation is very simple. We compare Meyerbeer with Wagner: amateurs of 1840 compared him with Rossini; and that made all the difference. If we are to have any Rossini celebrations during the opera season, the best opera for the purpose will be Otello, partly because the comparison between it and Verdi's latest work would be interesting, and partly because it is one of the least obsolete of his operas. When it was last played here at Her Majesty's, with Nilsson, Faure, and Tamberlik, it proved highly bearable, although Faure was then almost at the end of his capacity for singing on his reputation, and Tamberlik was a mere creaking wreck, whose boasted *ut de poitrine* was an eldritch screech which might just as well have been aimed an octave higher, for all the claim it had to be received as a vocal note in the artistic sense. The only difficulty at present would be to replace Nilsson, who sang Desdemona's music beautifully.

William Tell, of course, we may have: Sir Augustus Harris's attempts with it have always ranked among his triumphs from the artistic point of view, probably because (like Rienzi) it is an opera not of heroes and heroines, but of crowds and armies. He is therefore able to deal with it as he deals with his pantomimes and melodramas, which he takes so much more seriously and artistically than he is able to take those unfortunate operas in which his spoiled children of the Paris Opera, lazier than Rossini himself, have to be petted at every turn. However, enough of Rossini for the present. I cannot say "Rest his soul," for he had none; but I may at least be allowed the fervent aspiration that we may never look upon his like again.

Meyerbeer

10 May 1893 (II)

If you try to form a critical scheme of the development of English poetry from Pope to Walt Whitman, you cannot by any stretch of ingenuity make a place in it for Thomas Moore, who is accordingly either ignored in such schemes or else contemptuously dismissed as a flowery trifler. In the same way you cannot get Meyerbeer into the Wagnerian scheme except as the Autolycus of the piece. But this proves nothing except that criticism cannot give an absolutely true and just account of any artist: it can at best explain its point of view and then describe the artist from that point of view. You have only to shift yourself an inch to the right or left of my own point of view to find this column full of grotesque exaggerations and distortions; and if you read the musical papers you will sometimes find some *naif* doing this, and verdantly assuming that *his* point of view commands the absolute truth and that I am the father of lies.

Let me therefore make it clear that I am not [looking at] Meyerbeer from the Wagnerian point of view. I am thinking of Meyerbeer's individual characteristics as a composer: for instance, the singularity which is not always originality, the inventiveness which is not always fecundity, the love of the curious and piquant, the fastidious industry and cleverness, the intense and jealous individualism with its resultant treatment of the executants as mere instruments and not as artistic comrades and co-operators, the retreating from any effect that cannot be exactly and mechanically planned by himself as from an impossibility, the love of the fantastic, legendary, non-human element in folk-music . . . and the almost selfishly concentrated feeling, the fire, the distinction, the passion that flash out occasionally through much artifice and much trifling.

· LES HUGUENOTS ·

The Hornet, 1 August 1877 (*)

Few operas have suffered more from the pruning-knife of the stage manager than Meyerbeer's historical romance [Les Huguenots]. The fifth act, performed as it usually is with the opening scene excised and the *finale* recklessly mutilated, rarely induces an audience to sit after midnight for its sake. This season it vanished entirely from the boards, its omission being justifiable on the principle that what cannot be done properly is best left undone. The remaining acts are so extensively and tastelessly curtailed that many critics, unacquainted with the score, have denounced the opera as a fragmentary arrangement of musical odds and ends. In its original form the work is undoubtedly too long for the most patient audience. But the method which has been adopted of extracting central portions from the concerted pieces, as in the *finale* to the second and third acts, is so barbarous that a reconstruction of the version for performance would be extremely desirable, until the public are prepared to devote two nights to one opera. The score contains nothing unworthy of a hearing. We are acquainted with no work of similar length which is more highly finished in all its parts; which contains such a profusion of original and varied melody without being eked out by conventional manufacture; which displays greater fertility in orchestral device; and which at the same time bears so exclusive a stamp of one individuality. The merits of Meyerbeer are now rarely disputed. The conservative critics, having glorified Mayer and Paisiello in order to disparage Rossini, at length praised Rossini at the expense of Meyerbeer; and now, nothing discouraged, invent rhapsodies about Meyerbeer for the purpose of depreciating Wagner.

· LE PROPHÈTE ·

2 July 1890 (I)

At the revival of Meyerbeer's Prophète many critics, including myself, were reduced to the humiliating necessity of buying books of the play, containing a French and an English version, both different in arrangement from the one used on the stage. I had never seen the opera except on paper. The three Anabaptists rather interested me

when they started an open-air revolutionary agitation, as I am a bit
of an amateur in that line myself; but when they turned out badly in
the end I felt much as the mottle-faced man in Pickwick did when
Sam Weller sang of the Bishop's coachman running away from Dick
Turpin. "I say," said the mottle-faced man on that occasion, "that
that coachman did not run away, but that he died game—game as
pheasants; and I wont hear nothing said to the contrary." In a similar
spirit I affirm that the Anabaptists died "game as pheasants," and
that Scribe's history is trash.

But, indeed, Scribe never shewed his radical incapacity for anything deeper than his deadly "well-made plays" more conclusively
than when he mistook for a great musical delineator of the passions
of the multitude the composer who, in Les Huguenots, set forth the
Reformation as a strife between a Rataplan chorus and an Ave Maria, the two factions subsequently having it out in alternate strains
of a waltz. The Prophet, meant to be luridly historical, is in fact the
oddest medley of drinking songs, tinder-box trios, sleigh rides, and
skating quadrilles imaginable; and even John of Leyden, whose part
detaches itself from the dead mass of machinery as something alive
and romantic, if not exactly human, is at the disadvantage of being a
hero without having anything heroic to do, and of having finally to
degrade himself by shouting a vile drinking song amid a pack of
absurd nautch-girls. The orchestra seemed to feel this on Monday;
for they brought the scene to an end in ruin and confusion by differing on the subject of the last cut in the score. Jean de Reszke, though
a little hoarse, made as much as was possible of the part under the
circumstances; and Mlle Richard's Fidès was at least more credible
than her Favorita. Madame Nuovina, on the other hand, seems to
have gone completely to pieces. The shrillness of her highest notes is
worse than ever; and she has developed a tremolo which sounds like
a burlesque of Madame Tetrazzini's. It is a pity; for her first appearance as Margaret in Faust promised better things.

Schumann

13 December 1893 (III)

The chief musical event of last week was the performance of
Schumann's Genoveva for the first time on the English stage by the
students of the Royal College of Music. The pit and galleries of
Drury Lane (handsomely lent for the occasion) were crammed with
students. Parents and uncles and aunts of students were everywhere,
interrupting the performance in the wrongest possible places by
untimely applause, and feeling that such incomprehensible and solemn music as Schumann's must be excellent training for young
people. The stalls and boxes were full of critics and other distinguished persons. Speaking as one of them, may I suggest that when
we are so numerous, and consequently so tightly packed, the management should have a steam crane on the site of the prompter's box
between the acts, so that any critic desiring to leave his place during
the intervals could hook himself by the waistband to the end of the
chain and be hoisted out of his seat, swung round, and dropped at
the door nearest the refreshment bar?

The orchestra, being nearly eighty strong, was responsible for
some of the packing. It was quite the most brilliant part of the house,
as thirty-four out of fifty of the strings were young women, most of
them so attractive that for once the average of personal beauty was
higher in the band than on the stage. The swarming and chattering
when they assembled, and the irreverent waving of bows to friends
in the house, put everybody into good humor—even those critics
who were furious at having to begin their afternoon's work as early
as half-past one.

Genoveva was an excellent selection for the College to make.
Since it is commercially valueless as an opera, we should never have
heard it at all if it had not been taken in hand by a purely academic
institution; and yet, being by Schumann, it was certain that some

198

interesting music lay buried in it. For Schumann had at least one gift which we have now come to rank very highly among the qualifications of a composer for the stage: to wit, a strong feeling for harmony as a means of emotional expression. There are passages in Genoveva which are in this respect genuinely Wagnerian—and I am not one of those incorrigible people who cry out Wagner whenever they hear an unprepared major "tonic discord."

Unfortunately, in the other qualifications of the music-dramatist, Schumann is as far behind Beethoven as Beethoven was behind Mozart and Wagner. To begin with, he gives away all pretension to seriousness in his enterprise by providing as its subject a book which is nakedly silly. He may have persuaded himself—such a folly would have been just like him—that he could make his heroine do for his opera what Beethoven made Leonora do for Fidelio. But Fidelio, though commonplace and homely, is not silly. Its few harmless stage conventions do not prevent it from being credible and human from beginning to end; whereas Genoveva, from the moment when the witch enters in the first act, degenerates into pure bosh, and remains mostly at that level to the end. The witch's music is frivolous and serio-comic, the orchestration sprouting at the top into an outrageous piccolo part which would hardly be let off with mere indulgent laughter if it came from any less well-beloved composer.

In one place, the villain being left with the heroine, who has fainted, he exclaims: "We are alone." Immediately—the witch being round the corner—the piccolo utters a prolonged and derisive squawk, as if a cockatoo were reminding him that it had its eye on him. Instrumentation, as we all know, was not Schumann's strong point; and there is plenty of his characteristic orchestral muddling in Genoveva; but I can remember no other instance of his scoring being foolish in its intention. The witch is perhaps not much worse in the early scenes than Sir Arthur Sullivan's Ulrica in Ivanhoe, or in the incantation scene than Verdi's Ulrica in Un Ballo; but one has only to think of Ortrud in Lohengrin to realize the distance that separates Schumann's second-hand ideas from those of a really creative genius.

Another of the failures of Genoveva is Golo, the villain. As he is, unfortunately, a sentimental villain, it would require a Mozartian subtlety of characterization to differentiate him from the other sentimental people in the opera—the hero and the heroine, for instance. This subtlety Schumann did not possess: accordingly, Siegfried or Genoveva might sing every bar of Golo's music without the smallest incongruity. Imagine the effect of Don Giovanni singing Leporello's music, Elvira Zerlina's, Wotan Loki's, or Alberich Mime's!

Even Beethoven, whose powers in this respect were so blunt that, like a veritable Procrustes, he levelled four different characters in his Fidelio by writing a quartet in canon for them (conceive Non ti fidar or Un di si ben in canon!), not to mention that his prison porter and gaoler's daughter are absolutely indistinguishable in kind from his Florestan and Leonora—even Beethoven made Pizarro an unmistakeable scoundrel. He could not, like Wagner or Mozart, have given us half a dozen scoundrels, each as distinct from the other as Tartuffe from Harpagon or Rogue Riderhood from Silas Wegg; but he could at least distinguish an amiable person from an unamiable one. But this moderate feat has baffled Schumann in Genoveva.

It is obvious, then, that we must fall back on the symphonic, descriptive, and lyrical pages of the score for such merits as it possesses. In none of these can anything be found that need be heard by anyone who knows Schumann's songs, pianoforte pieces, and symphonies. In the nonsensical magic mirror and ghost scenes of the third act, and the demented business in the ravine in the fourth, Schumann, for the most part, leaves the stage to get on as best it can, and retires into pure symphony, with an effect which is only tolerable on condition of dismissing as so much superfluous rubbish all of the actual drama shewn on the boards, except, perhaps, what may be barely necessary to motivate in the vaguest manner the emotions of Genoveva and her husband.

The opera is at its best when Genoveva is on the stage; and it is never absolutely vulgar and trivial except in the witch music. The departure of the troops in the first act is an effective piece of composition for the stage; and there are one or two episodes in the second act, when Genoveva is alone in her chamber, which are by no means unsuccessful. But the work, as a whole, is a failure; and glad as I am that I have heard it, I cannot blame the world for dropping its acquaintance, though it has left a good many less worthy names on its operatic visiting list.

Verdi

---

2 November 1892 (II)

After Caedmar, Signor Lago put up the third act of Ernani. Strange to say, a good many people did not wait for it.

Just imagine the situation. Here is a baritone singer, Signor Mario Ancona, who has attracted general notice by his performance of Telramund in Lohengrin and Alfonso in La Favorita. Signor Lago accordingly mounts a famous scene, the classic opportunity for lyric actors of the Italian school (baritone variety), a scene which is not only highly prized by all students of Italian opera, but which had its dramatic import well taught to Londoners by the Comédie Française when they crowded to see Sarah Bernhardt as Doña Sol, and incidentally saw Worms as Charles V. In the play Charles is sublime in feeling, but somewhat tedious in expression. In the opera he is equally sublime in feeling, but concise, grand, and touching in expression, thereby proving that the chief glory of Victor Hugo as a stage poet was to have provided libretti for Verdi.

Every opera-goer who knows chalk from cheese knows that to hear that scene finely done is worth hearing all the Mephistopheleses and Toreadors that ever grimaced or swaggered, and that when a new artist offers to play it, the occasion is a first-class one. Yet, when Caedmar was over there was a considerable exodus from the stalls, as if nothing remained but a harlequinade for the children and the novices. "Now this," thought I, "is pretty odd. If these people knew their Ernani, surely they would stay." Then I realized that they did not know their Ernani—that years of Faust, and Carmen, and Les Huguenots, and Mefistofele, and soi-disant Lohengrin had left them ignorant of that ultra-classical product of Romanticism, the grandiose Italian opera in which the executive art consists in a splendid display of personal heroics, and the drama arises out of the simplest and most universal stimulants to them.

Il Trovatore, Un Ballo, Ernani, etc., are no longer read at the piano at home as the works of the Carmen *genre* are, and as Wagner's are. The popular notion of them is therefore founded on performances in which the superb distinction and heroic force of the male characters, and the tragic beauty of the women, have been burlesqued by performers with every sort of disqualification for such parts, from age and obesity to the most excruciating phases of physical insignificance and modern cockney vulgarity. I used often to wonder why it was that whilst every asphalt contractor could get a man to tar the streets, and every tourist could find a gondolier rather above the average of the House of Lords in point of nobility of aspect, no operatic manager, after Mario vanished, seemed to be able to find a Manrico with whom any exclusively disposed Thames mudlark would care to be seen grubbing for pennies. When I get on this subject I really cannot contain myself. The thought of that dynasty of execrable imposters in tights and tunics, interpolating their loathsome B flats into the beautiful melodies they could not sing, and swelling with conceit when they were able to finish Di quella pira with a high C capable of making a stranded man-of-war recoil off a reef into mid-ocean, I demand the suspension of all rules as to decorum of language until I have heaped upon them some little instalment of the infinite abuse they deserve. Others, alas! have blamed Verdi, much as if Dickens had blamed Shakespear for the absurdities of Mr Wopsle.

The general improvement in operatic performances of late years has taken us still further away from the heroic school. But in due time its turn will come. Von Bülow, who once contemptuously refused the name of music to Verdi's works, has recanted in terms which would hardly have been out of place if addressed to Wagner; and many who now talk of the master as of a tuneful trifler who only half-redeemed a misspent life by the clever artificialities which are added in Aida and Otello to the power and freedom of his earlier works, will change their tone when his operas are once more seriously studied by great artists.

·RIGOLETTO·

2 July 1890 (I)

I cannot congratulate Lassale on his Rigoletto last Thursday at Covent Garden. A massive gentleman with all the empty pomposity of the Paris Opéra hampering him like an invisible chain and bullet tied to his ankle, and whose stock-in-trade as an actor consists of one mock-heroic attitude, cannot throw himself into a part which requires the activity of a leopard; nor, by merely screwing up his eyes in an ecstasy of self-approbation, convey the raging self-contempt, the superstitious terror, the impotent fury, the savage vindictiveness, the heartbroken grovelling of the crippled jester wounded in his one vulnerable point—his fierce love of his child, the only creature who does not either hate or despise him. In such a character, burnt into music as it has been by Verdi, Lassalle's bag of hackneyed Parisian tricks makes him egotistical and ridiculous.

Further, he spoils the effect of the great scene with the courtiers, and makes a most unreasonable demand on the orchestra, by transposing his music a whole tone down, a monstrous liberty to take. No one can blame a singer for requiring a transposition of half-a-tone from our Philharmonic pitch; but where, as at Covent Garden, the French pitch is adopted, a demand for "a tone down" could only be justified in the case of a singer of very limited range, but with sufficiently remarkable acting power to compensate for the injury to the musical effect. As Lassale has neither excuse, it seems to me that we are entitled to expect that he shall in future either sing the part as Verdi wrote it, or else let it alone. At the same time, it is but fair to add that when an unfortunate baritone has to sing fifty bars in what is practically twelve-eight time, *andante*, on the four or five highest notes in his compass, without a rest except for two bars, during which he is getting out of breath in a violent stage struggle, the composer has only himself to thank when the same artist, who sings the much longer part of Wagner's Hans Sachs without turning a hair, flatly declines to submit to the strain of Rigoletto.

As it was, the honors of the occasion were carried off by Madame Melba, who ended the famous quartet on a high D flat of the most beautiful quality, the licence in this instance justifying itself by its effect. Valero, if he did not realize the masterful egotist, full of *la joie de vivre*, as conceived by Victor Hugo and Verdi, yet played with such spirit and humor that he may put down the Duke as one of his London successes. His singing, to be sure, was only a tasty sort of yelling, without spontaneity or purity of tone; but it was pretty enough to bring down the house in La donna è mobile.

· IL TROVATORE ·

The Nation, London, 7 July 1917 (C)

Our orchestras become so stale with their endless repetitions of work which contains no durably interesting orchestral detail nor presents any technical difficulty, that nothing but a high standard of artistic self-respect and honesty in their public obligations will make them do their work seriously if the conductor either sympathizes with their attitude or lacks the authority which is not to be trifled with. When these saving conditions are lacking, you get spoof opera. The accompaniments are a derisive rum-tum. The fortissimo chords are music-hall crashes, pure charivari, in which the players play any note that comes uppermost, and then laugh to one another. The joke is kept from the audience, partly by its own ignorance, and partly by the fact that as the *farceurs* are in a minority, most of the players are playing the notes set down in their parts because that is the easiest thing to do, and because they are not all in the humor for horseplay, not to mention that some of them are artists to whose taste and conscience such tomfoolery is detestable.

V erdi was the victim of a riot of this sort which lately came under my ghostly notice. I haunted a famous London theatre one evening in time to hear the last two acts of what was the most popular opera of the nineteenth century until Gounod's Faust supplanted it: an opera so popular that people who never dreamt of going to the opera as a general habit, and never in all their lives went to any other opera, went again and again to hear Il Trovatore whenever they had a chance.

Il Trovatore is, in fact, unique, even among the works of its own composer and its own country. It has tragic power, poignant melancholy, impetuous vigor, and a sweet and intense pathos that never loses its dignity. It is swift in action, and perfectly homogeneous in atmosphere and feeling. It is absolutely void of intellectual interest: the appeal is to the instincts and to the senses all through. If it allowed you to think for a moment it would crumble into absurdity like the garden of Klingsor. The very orchestra is silenced as to every sound that has the irritant quality that awakens thought: for example, you never hear the oboe: all the scoring for the wind that is not mere noise is for the lower registers of the clarionets and flutes, and for the least reedy notes of the bassoon.

Let us admit that no man is bound to take Il Trovatore seriously. We are entirely within our rights in passing it by and turning to Bach and Handel, Mozart and Beethoven, Wagner and Strauss, for our music. But we must take it or leave it: we must not trifle with it. He who thinks that Il Trovatore can be performed without taking it with the most tragic solemnity is, for all the purposes of a romantic art, a fool. The production of a revival of Il Trovatore should be supervised by Bergson; for he alone could be trusted to value this perfect work of instinct, and defend its integrity from the restless encroachments of intelligence.

The costumes and scenery need to be studied and guarded with the most discriminating care. For example, there is only one costume possible for the Count di Luna. He must wear a stiff violet velvet tunic, white satin tights, velvet shoes, and a white turban hat, with a white puggaree falling on a white cloak. No other known costume can remove its wearer so completely from common humanity. No man could sit down in such a tunic and such tights; for the vulgar realism of sitting down is ten times more impossible for the Count di Luna than for the Venus of Milo. The gipsy must be decorated with sequins and Zodiacal signs: as well put a caravan on the stage at once as relate her by the smallest realistic detail to any gipsy that ever sold uncouth horses at St. Margaret's Fair or kept a shooting-gallery. The harp of Manrico must be, not "the harp that once," but the harp that never. It should be such an instrument as Adams decorated ceilings with, or modern piano-makers use as supports for the pedals of their instruments. Give Manrico an Erard harp—a thing that he could possibly play—and he is no longer Manrico, but simply Man; and the unplumbed depths of the opera dry up into an ascertained and disilluding shallow. And the scenes in which these unbounded and heart-satisfying figures move must be the scenery of Gustave Doré at his most romantic. The mountains must make us homesick, even if we are Cockneys who have never seen a mountain bigger or remoter than Primrose Hill. The garden must be an enchanted garden: the convent must be a sepulchre for the living: the towers of Castellor must proclaim the dungeons within.

I should say that a production of Il Trovatore is perhaps the most severe test a modern impresario has to face; and I suggest that if he cannot face it he had better run away from it; for if he pretends to make light of it no one will laugh with him.

· LA TRAVIATA ·

29 April 1891 (I)

After a fortnight of Gluck, Gounod, Bizet, and Wagner, Covent Garden relapsed exhausted into the arms of La Traviata; and the audience promptly dwindled. Albani played Violetta on the occasion; and it is proper, if somewhat personal, to say that on her part too there has been a certain dwindling which does much to reconcile the imagination to her impersonations of operatic heroines. Not, of course, that she can by any conceivable stretch of fancy be accepted as a typical case of pulmonary consumption. But one has only to recall the eminent prima donnas who began their careers needing only a touch of blue under the eyes to make them look plausibly phthisical, and progressed with appalling rapidity to a condition in which no art of the maker-up could prevent them from looking insistently dropsical, to feel abundantly grateful to Albani for having so trained herself that nobody can say anything worse of her than that she is pleasingly plump. Indeed, in one way her figure is just the thing for La Traviata, as it does away with the painful impression which the last act produces whenever there is the faintest realism about. Even in the agonies of death Albani robs the sick bed and the medicine bottles of half their terrors by her reassuring air of doing as well as can be expected. Still, I submit that though the representation is not painful, it is in the last degree ridiculous. In saying this I by no means endorse the verdict of those colleagues of mine who are declaring in all directions that the opera is antiquated, impossible, absurd, a relic of the old régime, and so on. Verdi's opera is one thing: the wilful folly of the Covent Garden parody of it is quite another. Take any drama ever written, and put it on a stage six times too large for its scenes, introducing the maddest incongruities of furniture, costume, and manners at every turn of it; and it will seem as nonsensical as La Traviata, even without the crowning burlesque of a robust, joyous, round-cheeked lady figuring as a moribund patient in decline. I have no doubt that when Mr Joseph Bennett is commissioned by Mr Harris to found a *libretto* for an opera by Signor Randegger on Hedda Gabler, and it is produced at Covent Garden with Hedda in modern costume, Tesman as a Dutch burgomaster after Rembrandt, Lövborg as a Louis XIII mousquetaire, Brack as the traditional notary, and Thea in black with a mantilla and a convulsive walk, Ibsen himself will be voted antiquated. The truth is that La Traviata, in spite of its conventionalities, is before its time at Covent Garden instead of behind it. It is a much more real and powerful work than Carmen, for instance, which everybody accepts as typically modern.

· UN BALLO IN MASCHERA ·

4 July 1888 (C)

To old opera-goers a performance of Verdi's Ballo in Maschera brings reminiscences of bygone days and forgotten singers: of Titiens in the trio in the cave scene and Giuglini in the quintet. Fortunately for you, dear reader, it produces no such effect on me; for I never heard the opera on the stage before, and never heard Giuglini, though I knew most of the music in my cradle or thereabouts. As to the young opera-goers, one can really only wonder what they think about it. Its interminable string of cavatinas, its absurdly Offenbachian finale to the first act, its inexhaustible vein of melodramatic anguish, its entire impossibility from any rational point of view from beginning to end, must all help to puzzle those who were never broken in to that strange survival of Richardson's show, the so-called acting of genuinely Italian opera. These are untimely reflections, perhaps; but they rise unbidden at a performance of Un Ballo. The work, nevertheless, contains one capital scene: that in which Samuel and Tom (who are called Armando and Angri in the bills in these squeamish days) meet Renato innocently escorting his own wife, veiled, from an assignation with his dearest friend, and force her to unveil. Verdi has done nothing better than the combination of the raillery of the two rascals, the humiliation of the woman, and the distress of the husband. But at Covent Garden they do not seem to think that there is much in this. Samuel and Tom were solemn as sextons; and M. Lassalle merely stretched forth his sword to the stalls, as if he were about to perform the familiar feat of cutting an apple in two on Signor Mancinelli's head. He sang the part very well from a French point of view, which the audience, it was most encouraging to observe, flatly declined to accept. Mdlle. Rolla does not understand the English people. She may sing consistently sharp here with impunity. Though the assembled Britons will not like it, they will pretend to, thinking that she knows best. But to begin a note in tune, and then force it up quarter of a tone is neither popular nor humane. It is better, on the whole, to sing in tune all through, as Mdlle. Rolla decided to do towards the end of the performance. Her acting consisted of the singular plunge, gasp, and stagger peculiar to the Verdi heroine, whose reason is permanently unsettled by grief.

Miss Arnoldson added Oscar to the list of her successes. Jean de Reszke was Riccardo. Some of the tediousness of the opera was due to the senseless conventionality of the representation and to the slow *tempi* adopted by Signor Mancinelli; but Mr Harris will do well to face the fact that, until fortune sends him an extraordinarily sensational dramatic soprano, he will do well to leave such old-fashioned affairs as Un Ballo on the shelf.

· AÏDA ·

16 July 1888 (C)

AÏDA filled the house at Covent Garden on Saturday quite as effectually as Il Trovatore emptied it earlier in the week. Not that Aïda, comparatively fresh and varied in interest as it is, is at bottom at all a more rational entertainment than Il Trovatore, but simply because Aïda is now put on to give the best artists in the company a chance, whereas Il Trovatore is put on only to give them a rest. The performance of the first two acts was unsatisfactory. Madame Nordica, brown enough as to face and arms, was colorless as to voice. Signor Mancinelli conducted the court and temple scenes barbarically, evidently believing that the ancient Egyptians were a tribe of savages, instead of, as far as one can ascertain, considerably more advanced than the society now nightly contemplating in "indispensable evening dress" the back of Signor Mancinelli's head. Not until the scene of the triumphal return of Radames from the war did the gallery begin to pluck up and applaud. Fortunately, an incident which occurred at the beginning of the fourth act confirmed the good humor thus set in. Ramphis, Amneris, and their escort were seen approaching the temple in a state barge. On its tall prow, which rose some five feet out of the water, stood an Egyptian oarsman, urging the craft along the moonlit bosom of the Nile. Now this was all very well whilst the royal party were on board to balance him: but when they stepped ashore on to the stage, the barge went head over heels; the native went heels over head; and Signor Navarrini's impressive exhortation to *Vieni d'Iside al tempio* was received with shrieks of laughter. Whether the operatic gods were appeased by the sacrifice of the luckless boatman (who never reappeared from beneath the wave), or whether his fate made his surviving colleagues more serious, is a matter for speculation; but the fact is beyond question that the representation greatly improved from that moment. Madame Nordica's voice, no longer colorless, began to ring with awakened feeling. Her admirable method, to which she is, unfortunately, not invariably faithful, was exemplified in the ease, skill, and perfect intonation with which the higher notes were produced. It is an inexpressible relief to the jaded opera-goer to hear notes above the treble stave taken otherwise than with the neck-or-nothing scream of the ordinary *prima donna ma ultima cantatrice.* M. Jean de Reszke also rose to the occasion, and so astonished the house by a magnificent delivery of *Io son disonorato! Per te tradii la patria! . . . Sacerdote, io resto a te,* that the curtain descended to an explosion of applause. It is true that M. de Reszke utterly missed the simple dignity of his part of the duet with Amneris in the first scene of the last act; but that did not obscure his great success: the audience, delighted with him, accepting his version with enthusiasm. Signor d'Andrade, in coffee color and tiger skins, ranted as Amonasro in a manner against which common sense ought to have guarded him. Why the Ethiopian captive king should be conceived on the Italian stage, not even as an antique Cetewayo, but as a frenzied Hottentot, is hard to understand. Verdi certainly had no such intention, as the character of the music proves. Madame Scalchi played Amneris with passion and a certain tragic grace that might make her an actress, if it were possible for anyone to become an actress in such an atmosphere of incongruity and nonsense as that which an operatic artist is condemned to breathe.

· OTELLO ·

22 July 1891 (I)

I CONFESS to having witnessed with a certain satisfaction the curious demonstrations which enlivened the first performance of Otello at Covent Garden. The first sign of tumult was a disposition to insist on applauding Maurel in season and out of season, even to the extent of causing ridiculous interruptions to the performance. The second was an almost equally strong disposition to disparage—I had almost said to hoot—Jean de Reszke, who was defended by vehement counter-demonstrations, in leading which Lassalle, standing in a box next to the stage on the grand tier, was the most conspicuous figure. Fortunately, the majority in an English audience generally declines to concern itself in greenroom politics; and at Covent Garden the majority is so huge that it is not possible to make much of a scene there. By the end of the second act matters relapsed into the usual routine, greatly, I should imagine, to the relief of Maurel. However, partial as the demonstration was, it was far too general to be the work of a claque; and I recommend it to the most serious consideration of Brother Jean. It is to his petulant laziness, and to nothing else, that we owe the frightful waste of artistic resources at Covent Garden on stale repetitions of worn-out operas night after night, when we might have been listening to Siegfried and Otello, not to mention half a dozen other works which are familiar in every second-rate German town, and of which we know nothing in London. The height of his ambition would be attained, as far as one can judge, if he were permitted to maintain his status as leading tenor at the Royal Italian Opera by a single performance of Romeo every year, leaving the rest of the work to be done by Perotti, Montariol, and Ravelli. And yet, at the beginning of this season, he had the—shall I say the ingenuousness?—to favor an interviewer with some observations about his devotion to Art. Can he wonder at the frequenters of the Opera shewing a little temper in the matter at last?

His acting as Otello was about equally remarkable for its amateurish ineptitudes and for its manifestations of the natural histrionic powers which he has so studiously neglected for the last fifteen years. Though he overcame his genius for being late so far as to get on the stage punctually for his first utterance in the storm, it reconquered him when he entered to interrupt the fight between Cassio and Montano; and in his sudden appearance at the masked door in Desdemona's bedroom, which depended for its effect on being timed exactly to a certain chord, he was a good half bar behindhand. His reluctance to determined physical action came out chiefly in his onslaught on Iago, which he managed in such a way as to make the audience feel how extremely obliging it was of Maurel to fall. And at the end of the third act, in simulating the epileptic fit in which Otello's fury culminates, he moved the gods to laughter by lying down with a much too obvious solicitude for his own comfort.

On the whole it may be said that throughout the first two acts his diffidence and irresolution again and again got the better of his more vigorous and passionate impulses. This was intensified no doubt by nervousness; but it was partly due also to his halting between a half-hearted attempt at the savage style of Tamagno and the quieter, more refined manner natural to himself. In the third act, when the atmosphere of the house had become friendly, he began to treat the part more in his own fashion, and at last got really into it, playing for the first time with sustained conviction instead of merely with fitful bursts of self-assertion. Indeed, but for that gingerly fall at the end, this third act would have been an unqualified success for him. As it was, it shewed, like his Don Jose and other post-Van Dyck performances, that when the rivalry of younger men and the decay of his old superficial charm with advancing years force him to make the most of all his powers, he may yet gain more as an actor than he will lose as a singer.

His Otello will never be like Tamagno's; but he need not regret that, as the same thing might have been said of Salvini. The Italian tenor's shrill screaming voice and fierce temper were tremendously effective here and there; but the nobler side of the Moor, which Salvini brought out with such admirable artistic quietude and self-containment, and which De Reszke shews a considerable, though only half cultivated, power of indicating in the same way, was left untouched by Tamagno, who on this and other accounts is the very last man a wise tenor would attempt to imitate.

There is less to be said as to the other principals. It is no compliment to Albani to declare that she was better than Madame Cattaneo, as she could hardly have been worse. Like De Reszke, she redeemed herself in the latter half of the opera. Her intonation improved; and her acting had the sincerity which so honorably distinguishes her from most of her rivals, and which so often leads her straight to the right vocal treatment of purely dramatic music. If she will only forgo that absurd little stage run with which she embraces Otello in the first act, she will have nothing to reproach herself with as far as her playing of the part is concerned. Maurel, tired out as to voice, dropping all the G's, and unable to make the pianissimo nuances tell at anything softer than a tolerably vigorous *mezzo forte,* was yet able to repeat his old success as Iago. His playing is as striking and picturesque as ever; but I have come to think that it requires a touch of realism here and there to relieve its somewhat mechanical grace and effectiveness. The excessive descriptiveness which is the fault in his method, and even in his conception of the actor's function, resulting in a tendency to be illustrative rather than impersonative, occasionally leads him to forget the natural consequences of the actions he represents on the stage.

For instance, when Otello half throttles Iago, it is a little disillusioning to see the victim rise from a faultless attitude, and declaim Divina grazia, difendimi, with his throat in perfect order. Nothing is easier to produce than the *voce soffocata;* and there are not many operatic passages in which it is more appropriate than here. Apart from these matters of detail, the chief objection to Maurel's Iago is that it is not Iago at all, but rather the Cæsar Borgia of romance. As far as it is human, it is a portrait of a distinguished officer, one who would not be passed over for Cassio when he was expecting his step. I am aware that this view of him falls in with the current impression in artistic circles that Iago was a very fine fellow. But in circles wherein men have to take one another seriously, there will not be much difference of opinion as to the fact that Iago must have been an ingrained blackguard and consequently an (if I may use a slightly Germanic adjective) obviously-to-everyone-but-himself-unpromotable person.

A certain bluffness and frankness, with that habit of looking you straight in the face which is the surest sign of a born liar, male or female, appear to me to be indispensable to "honest Iago"; and it is the absence of these, with the statuesque attitudes, the lofty carriage of the head, and the delicate play of the hands and wrists, that makes the figure created by Maurel irreconcilable with my notion of the essentially vulgar ancient who sang comic songs to Cassio and drank him, so to speak, under the table. There is too much of Lucifer, the fallen angel, about it—and this, be it remarked, by no means through the fault of Verdi, who has in several places given a quite Shakespearean tone to the part by *nuances* which Maurel refuses to execute, a striking instance being the famous Ecco il leon at the end of the fourth act, when Iago spurns the insensible body of the prostrate Otello.

Nobody, it seems to me, can escape the meaning of the descent to the rattling shake on the middle F which Verdi has written. It expresses to perfection the base envious exultation of the ass's kick at the helpless lion, and suggests nothing of the Satanic scorn with which Maurel, omitting the ugly shake, leaves the stage. His performance is to be admired rather as a powerfully executed fantasy of his own than as the Iago either of Verdi or Shakespear. If his successors in the part try to imitate him, their wisdom will be even less than their originality.

· FALSTAFF ·

12 April 1893 (II)

EASTER has afforded me an opportunity for a look through the vocal score of Verdi's Falstaff, now to be had at Ricordi's for sixteen shillings, a price which must obviously be reduced before the opera can get into the hands of the amateur at large. I did not go to Milan to hear the first performance for several reasons, the chief being that I am not enough of a first-nighter to face the huge tedium and probable sickness of the journey from Holborn to Basle (the rest I do not mind) in order merely to knock at the tradesman's door of Italy, so to speak, and turn back after hearing an opera half murdered by La Scala prima donnas with shattering tremolos, and witnessing a Grand Old Man demonstration conducted for the most part by people who know about as much of music as the average worshipper of Mr Gladstone does of statesmanship. In short, being lazy and heavily preoccupied, I cried sour grapes and stayed at home, knowing that the mountain would come to Mahomet soon enough.

Let it be understood, then, that since I have not been present at a complete performance of Falstaff I do not know the work: I only know some things about it. And of these I need not repeat what has already been sufficiently told: as, for instance, that Falstaff is a music drama, not an opera, and that consequently it is by Shakespear, Boito, and Verdi, and not by Verdi alone. The fact that it is a music drama explains the whole mystery of its composition by a man eighty years old. If there were another Il balen or La donna è mobile in it, I should have been greatly astonished; but there is nothing of the sort: the fire and heroism of his earlier works blazes up now only on strong provocation.

Falstaff is lighted and warmed only by the afterglow of the fierce noonday sun of Ernani; but the gain in beauty conceals the loss in heat—if, indeed, it be a loss to replace intensity of passion and spontaneity of song by fullness of insight and perfect mastery of workmanship. Verdi has exchanged the excess of his qualities for the wisdom to supply his deficiencies; his weaknesses have disappeared with his superfluous force; and he is now, in his dignified competence, the greatest of living dramatic composers. It is not often that a man's strength is so immense that he can remain an athlete after bartering half of it to old age for experience; but the thing happens occasionally, and need not so greatly surprise us in Verdi's case, especially those of us who, long ago, when Von Bülow and others were contemptuously repudiating him, were able to discern in him a man possessing more power than he knew how to use, or indeed was permitted to use by the old operatic forms imposed on him by circumstances.

I have noticed one or two exclamations of surprise at the supposed revelation in Falstaff of a "hitherto unsuspected" humorous force in the veteran tragic composer. This must be the result of the enormous popularity which Il Trovatore first and Aida afterwards attained in this country. I grant that these operas are quite guiltless of comic relief; but what about Un Ballo, with its exquisitely lighthearted E scherz' od è follia, and the finale to the third act, where Renato is sarcastically complimented on his domestic virtue by the conspirators who have just shewn him that the Duke's veiled mistress, whom he is defending from them after devotedly saving the Duke's life, is his own wife. Stupidly as that tragi-comic quartet and chorus has always been mishandled on our wretched operatic stage, I cannot understand anyone who knows it denying Verdi's gift of dramatic humor.

In the first act of Otello, the stretto made in the drinking song by Cassio when he gets drunk is very funny without being in the least unmusical. The grim humor of Sparafucile, the terrible ironic humor of Iago, the agonized humor of Rigoletto: these surely settled the question as to Verdi's capacity for Falstaff none the less because the works in which they occur are tragedies and not comedies. All that could be said on the other side was that Verdi was no Mozart, which was as idle as saying that Victor Hugo was no Molière. Verdi's vein of humor is all the more Shakespearean on that account.

Verdi's worst sins as a composer have been sins against the human voice. His habit of taking the upper fifth of the compass of an exceptionally high voice, and treating that fifth as the normal range, has a great deal to do with the fact that the Italian singer is now the worst singer in the world, just as Wagner's return to Handel's way of using the voice all over its compass and obtaining physical relief for the singer and artistic relief for the audience by the contrast of the upper and lower registers has made the Wagnerian singer now the best singer in the world. Verdi applied his system with special severity to baritones.

If you look at the score of Don Giovanni, you will find three different male voices written for on the bass clef, and so treated as to leave no doubt that Mozart, as he wrote the music, had a particular sort of voice for each part constantly in his head, and the one (Masetto's) was a rough peasant's bass, another (Leporello's) a ready, fluent, copious *basso contante;* and the third a light fine baritone, the voice of a gentleman. I have heard public meetings addressed successively by an agricultural laborer's delegate, a representative of the skilled artisans, and a university man; and they have taught me what all the treatises on singing in the world could not about the Mozartian differentiation between Masetto, Leporello, and Don Giovanni.

But now please remark that there is no difference of range between the three parts. Any man who can sing the notes of one of them can sing the notes of the others. Let Masetto and the Don exchange characters, and though the Don will be utterly ineffective in the concerted music on Masetto's lower G's and B flats, whilst Masetto will rob the serenade of all its delicacy, yet neither singer will encounter any more impossibility, or even inconvenience, in singing the notes than Mr Toole would have in reading the part of Hamlet. The same thing is true of the parts of Bartolo, Figaro, and Almaviva in Le Nozze; of San Bris and Nevers in Les Huguenots; of Wotan and Alberich in The Niblung's Ring; and of Amfortas and Klingsor in Parsifal. The dramatic distinction between these parts is so strong that only an artist of remarkable versatility could play one as well as the other; but there is practically no distinction of vocal range any more than there is a distinction of physical stature or strength.

But if we turn to Il Trovatore, we find two vocal parts written in the bass clef, of which the lower, Ferrando, is not a *basso profondo* like Osmin or Marcel, but a *basso cantante* like San Bris or Leporello; yet the baritone part (Di Luna) is beyond the reach of any normal *basso cantante,* and treats a baritone voice as consisting of about one effective octave, from G on the fourth space of the bass stave to the G above. In Il balen there are from two hundred and ten to two hundred and twenty notes, including the cadenza, etc. Barring five notes in the cadenza, which is never sung as written, only three are below F on the fourth line, whilst nearly one hundred and forty lie above the stave between B flat and the high G. The singing is practically continuous from end to end; and the strain on a normal baritone voice is frightful, even when the song is transposed half a tone as it usually is to bring it within the bare limits of possibility. Di Luna is in this respect a typical Verdi baritone; and the result has been that only singers with abnormally high voices have been able to sing it without effort.

As to the normal baritones who have made a specialty of bawling fiercely up to G sharp, they have so lost the power of producing an endurable tone in their lower octave, or of pitching its notes with even approximate accuracy, that they have all but destroyed the popularity of Mozart's operas by their occasional appearances as Don Giovanni, Figaro, etc. I have often wished that the law would permit me to destroy these unhappy wretches, whose lives must be a burden to them. It is easy to go into raptures over the superiority of the Italian master in vocal writing because his phrases are melodious, easily learned, symmetrical, and often grandiose; but when you have to sing the melodious well-turned phrases, and find that they lie a tone higher than you can comfortably manage them, and a third higher than you can keep on managing them for five minutes at a stretch (for music that *lies* rather high is much more trying than music that *ventures* very high occasionally), you begin to appreciate the sort of knowledge of and consideration for the voice shewn by Purcell, Handel, and Wagner, and to very decidedly resent Verdi's mere partiality for the top end of it.

Now comes the question, what sort of voice is needed for the part of Falstaff? Well, Ferrando and the Count di Luna rolled into one—Amonasro, in short. A rich *basso cantante,* who can knock out a vigorous high G and play with F sharp as Melba plays with B flat. Polyphemus in Handel's Acis and Valentine in Gounod's Faust might do it justice between them. Barely reasonable this, even at French pitch, and monstrous at Philharmonic pitch. And yet it is the fashion to say that Verdi is a master of the art of writing singable music.

The score is necessarily occupied to a great extent by the discourses of Falstaff, which are set with the most expert ingenuity and subtlety, the advance in this respect from the declamation of Charles V in Ernani to that of Falstaff being as great as from Tannhäuser's to Parsifal's, or from Vanderdecken's to Hans Sachs's. One capital effect—the negative answers in the manner of Mr Chadband to the repeated questions as to what honor is—is, musically, a happy adaptation from Boito's Mefistofele, and is, as far as I have discovered, the only direct Boitoism in the work, though I imagine that Verdi has profited generally by having so fine an artist and critic as Boito at his elbow when composing Otello and Falstaff. There are some amusing passages of instrumental music: for instance, a highly expressive accompaniment to a colossal drink taken by Falstaff.

During the abundant action and stage bustle of the piece we get a symphonic treatment, which belongs exclusively to Verdi's latest manner. Some tripping figuration, which creates perpetual motion by its ceaseless repetition in all sorts of ingenious sequences, as in Mendelssohn's scherzos or the finales to his concertos, is taken as the musical groundwork upon which the vocal parts are put in, the whole fabric being wrought with the most skilful elegance. This is a matter for some of our musical pundits to consider rather anxiously. For, if I had said ten years ago that Ernani was a much greater musical composition than Mendelssohn's Scotch symphony or any of his concertos, words could not have conveyed the scorn with which so gross an opinion would have been received. But here, today, is the scorned one, whom even Browning thought it safe to represent as an empty blusterer shrinking amid a torrent of vulgar applause from the grave eye of—of—of—well, of ROSSINI! (poor Browning!) falling back in his old age on the Mendelssohnian method, and employing it with ease and brilliancy.

Perhaps, when Verdi turns a hundred and feels too old for opera composition, he will take to concerto writing, and cut out Mendelssohn and Schumann in the pretty pattern work which the pundits love them for. Which will shew how very easy it is for a good musician, when he happens to be a bad critic, to admire a great composer for the wrong thing.

· A WORD MORE ·

Anglo-Saxon Review, March 1901†

I HAVE read most of the articles on Verdi elicited by his death, and I have blushed for my species. By this I mean the music-critic species; for though I have of late years disused this learned branch I am still entitled to say to my former colleagues "*Anch' io son critico.*" And when I find men whom I know otherwise honorable glibly pretending to an intimate acquaintance with Oberto, Conte di San Bonifacio, with Un Giorno di Regno, with La Battaglia de Legnano; actually comparing them with Falstaff and Aïda, and weighing, with a nicely judicial air, the differences made by the influence of Wagner, well knowing all the time that they know no more of Oberto than they do of the tunes Miriam timbrelled on the shores of the

---

†Reprinted in *London Music in 1888–89.*

divided Red Sea, I say again that I blush for our profession, and ask them, as an old friend who wishes them well, where they expect to go to after such shamelessly mendacious implications when they die.

For myself, I value a virtuous appearance above vain erudition; and I confess that the only operas of Verdi's I know honestly right through, as I know Dickens's novels, are Ernani, Rigoletto, Il Trovatore, Un Ballo, La Traviata, Aïda, Otello, and Falstaff. And quite enough too, provided one also knows enough of the works of Verdi's forerunners and contemporaries to see exactly when he came in and where he stood. It is inevitable that as younger and younger critics come into the field, more and more mistakes should be made about men who lived as long as Verdi and Wagner, not because the critics do not know their music, but because they do not know the operas that Wagner and Verdi heard when they were boys, and are consequently apt to credit them with the invention of many things which were familiar to their grandfathers.

For example, in all the articles I have read it is assumed that the difference between Ernani and Aïda is due to the influence of Wagner. Now I declare without reserve that there is no evidence in any bar of Aïda or the two later operas that Verdi ever heard a note of Wagner's music. There is evidence that he had heard Boito's music, Mendelssohn's music, and Beethoven's music; but the utmost that can be said to connect him with Wagner is that if Wagner had not got all Europe into the habit of using the whole series of dominant and tonic discords as freely as Rossini used the dominant seventh, it is possible that Falstaff might have been differently harmonized. But as much might be said of any modern pantomime score. Verdi uses the harmonic freedom of his time so thoroughly in his own way, and so consistently in terms of his old style, that if he had been as ignorant of Wagner as Berlioz was of Brahms there is no reason to suppose that the score of Falstaff would have been an unprepared thirteenth the worse.

I am, of course, aware that when Aïda first reached us, it produced a strong impression of Wagnerism. But at that time nothing of Wagner's later than Lohengrin was known to us. We thought the Evening Star song in Tannhäuser a precious Wagnerian gem. In short, we knew nothing of Wagner's own exclusive style, only his operatic style, which was much more mixed than we imagined. Everybody then thought that a recurring theme in an opera was a Wagnerian Leitmotif, especially if it stole in to a *tremolando* of the strings and was harmonized with major ninths instead of sub-dominants; so when this occurred in Aïda's scena, *Ritorna vincitor,* we all said "Aha! Wagner!" And, as very often happens, when we came to know better, we quite forgot to revise our premature conclusion. Accordingly, we find critics taking it for granted to-day that Aïda is Wagnerized Verdi, although, if they had not heard Aïda until after Siegfried and Die Meistersinger, they would never dream of con-necting the two composers or their styles.

The real secret of the change from the roughness of Il Trova-tore to the elaboration of the three last operas, is the inevitable natural drying up of Verdi's spontaneity and fertility. So long as an opera composer can pour forth melodies like *La donna è mobile* and *Il balen,* he does not stop to excogitate harmonic elegancies and or-chestral sonorities which are neither helpful to him dramatically nor demanded by the taste of his audience. But when in process of time the well begins to dry up; when instead of getting splashed with the bubbling over of *Ah si, ben mio,* he has to let down a bucket to drag up *Celeste Aida,* then it is time to be clever, to be nice, to be distinguished, to be impressive, to study instrumental confectionery, to bring thought and knowledge and seriousness to the rescue of failing vital-ity. In Aïda this is not very happily done: it is not until Otello that we get dignified accomplishment and fine critical taste; but here, too, we have unmistakably a new hand in the business, the hand of Boito. It is quite certain that Boito could not have written Otello; but certain touches in Iago's Credo were perhaps either suggested by Boito, or composed in his manner in fatherly compliment to him; and the whole work, even in its most authentic passages, shews that Verdi was responding to the claims of a more fastidious artistic conscience and even a finer sensitiveness to musical sound than his own was when he tried to turn Macbeth into another Trovatore, and made Lady Macbeth enliven the banquet scene with a florid drinking song. The advance from romantic intensity to dramatic seriousness is rev-olutionary. Nothing is more genial in Verdi's character than this docility, this respect for the demands of a younger man, this recogni-tion that the implied rebuke to his taste and his coarseness showed a greater tenderness for his own genius than he had shown to it himself.

But there is something else than Boito in Otello. In the third act there is a movement in six-eight time, Essa t'avvince, which is utterly unlike anything in the Trovatore period, and surprisingly like a rondo in the style of Beethoven. That is to say, it is pre-Wagnerian; which at such a date is almost equivalent to anti-Wagnerian. In *Falstaff*, again, in the buck-basket scene there is a light-fingered and humorous *moto perpetuo* which might have come straight out of a Mendelssohn concerto. Unfortunately it is ineffectively scored; for Verdi, brought up in the Italian practice of using the orchestra as pure accompaniment, was an unskilled beginner in German symphonic orchestration. These are the only passages in the later works which are not obviously the old Verdi developed into a careful and thoughtful composer under the influence of Boito and the effect of advancing age on his artistic resources. I think they would both be impossible to a composer who had not formed an affectionate acquaintance with German music. But the music of Beethoven and Mendelssohn is the music of a Germany still under that Franco-Italian influence which made the music of Mozart so amazingly unlike the music of Bach. Of the later music that was consciously and resolutely German and German only; that would not even write *allegro* at the head of its quick, or *adagio* at the head of its slow movements, because these words are not German; of the music of Schumann, Brahms, and Wagner, there is not anywhere in Verdi the faintest trace. In German music the Italian loved what Italy gave. What Germany offered of her own music he entirely ignored.

Having now, I hope, purged myself of the heresy that Verdi was Wagnerized, a heresy which would never have arisen if our foolish London Opera had been as punctual with Lohengrin as with Aïda, instead of being nearly a quarter of a century late with it, I may take Verdi on his own ground. Verdi's genius, like Victor Hugo's, was hyperbolical and grandiose: he expressed all the common passions with an impetuosity and intensity which produced an effect of sublimity. If you ask What is it all about? the answer must be that it is mostly about the police intelligence melodramatized. In the same way, if you check your excitement at the conclusion of the wedding scene in Il Trovatore to ask what, after all, *Di quella pira* is, the answer must be that it is only a common bolero tune, just as *Strida la vampa* is only a common waltz tune. Indeed, if you know these tunes only through the barrel organs, you will need no telling. But in the theatre, if the singers have the requisite power and spirit, one does not ask these questions: the bolero form passes as unnoticed as the saraband form in Handel's *Lascia ch'io pianga*, whereas in the more academic form of the aria with caballetto, which Rossini, Bellini, and

Donizetti accepted, the form reduces the matter to absurdity. Verdi, stronger and more singly dramatic, broke away from the Rossinian convention; developed the simpler cavatina form with an integral codetta instead of a separated cabaletto; combined it fearlessly with popular dance and ballad forms; and finally produced the once enormously popular, because concise, powerful, and comparatively natural and dramatic type of operatic solo which prevails in Il Trovatore and Un Ballo. A comparison of this Italian emancipation of dramatic music from decorative form with the Wagnerian emancipation shews in a moment the utter unthinkableness of any sort of connection between the two composers. No doubt the stimulus given to Verdi's self-respect and courage by his share in the political activity of his time, is to some extent paralleled by the effect of the 1848 revolution on Wagner; but this only accentuates the difference between the successful composer of a period of triumphant nationalism and the exiled communist-artist-philosopher of The Niblung's Ring. As Wagner contracted his views to a practicable nationalism at moments later on, I can conceive a critic epigrammatically dismissing the Kaiser March as a bit of Verdified Wagner. But the critic who can find Wagner in Otello must surely be related to the gentleman who accused Bach of putting forth the accompaniment to Gounod's Ave Maria as a prelude of his own composition.

By this Mascagni-facilitating emancipation of Italian opera, Verdi concentrated its qualities and got rid of its alloys. Il Trovatore is Italian opera in earnest and nothing else: Rossini's operas are musical entertainments which are only occasionally and secondarily dramatic. Moses in Egypt and Semiramis, for example, are ridiculous as dramas, though both of them contain one impressively splendid number to shew how nobly Rossini could have done if the silly conditions of the Italian opera houses had given their composers any chance of being sensible. "I could have achieved something had I been a German" said Rossini humbly to Wagner; *"car j'avais du talent."* Bellini, Donizetti, and the Italianized Jew Meyerbeer pushed the dramatic element in opera still further, making it possible for Verdi to end by being almost wholly dramatic. But until Verdi was induced by Boito to take Shakespear seriously they all exploited the same romantic stock-in-trade. They composed with perfect romantic sincerity, undesirous and intolerant of reality, untroubled by the philosophic faculty which, in the mind of Wagner, revolted against the demoralizing falseness of their dramatic material. They revelled in the luxury of stage woe, with its rhetorical loves and deaths and poisons and jealousies and murders, all of the most luscious, the most enjoyable, the most unreal kind. They did not, like Rossini, break suddenly off in the midst of their grandiosities to write *excusez du peu* at the top of the score, and finish with a galop. On the contrary, it was just where the stage business demanded something elegantly trivial that they became embarrassed and vulgar. This was especially the case with Verdi, who was nothing if not strenuous, whereas Bellini could be trivially simple and Donizetti thoughtlessly gay on occasion. Verdi, when he is simple or gay, is powerfully so. It has been said, on the strength of the alleged failure of a forgotten comic opera called Un Giorno di Regno, that Verdi was incapable of humor; and I can understand that an acquaintance limited to Ernani, Il Trovatore, La Traviata, and Aïda (and acquaintances of just this extent are very common) might support that opinion. But the parts of the Duke and Sparafucile in Rigoletto could not have been composed by a humorless man. In Un Ballo again we have in Riccardo the Duke's gaiety and gallantry without his callousness; and at the great moment of the melodrama Verdi achieves a master-stroke by his dramatic humor. The hero has made an assignation with the heroine in one of those romantically lonely spots which are always to be found in operas. A band of conspirators resolves to seize the opportunity to murder him. His friend Renato, getting wind of their design, arrives before them, and persuades him to fly, taking upon himself the charge of the lady. Renato defends her; but she, to save him from being killed, unveils herself and turns out to be Renato's own wife. This is no doubt a very thrilling stage climax: it is easy for a dramatist to work up to it. But it is not quite so easy to get away from it; for when the veil is off the bolt is shot; and the difficulty is what is to be said next. The librettist solves the problem by falling back on the chaffing of Renato by the conspirators. Verdi seizes on this with genuine humorous power in his most boldly popular style, giving just the right vein of blackguardly irony and mischievous mirth to the passage, and getting the necessary respite before the final storm, in which the woman's shame, the man's agony of jealousy and wounded friendship, and the malicious chuckling of the conspirators provide material for one of those concerted pieces in which Italian opera is at its best.

And here may I mildly protest that the quartet in Rigoletto, with its four people expressing different emotions simultaneously, was not, as the obituary notices almost all imply, an innovation of Verdi's. Such concerted pieces were *de rigueur* in Italian opera before he was born. The earliest example that holds the stage is the quartet in Don Giovanni, *Non ti fidar;* and between Don Giovanni and Rigoletto it would be difficult to find an Italian opera without a specimen. Several of them were quite as famous as the Rigoletto quartet became. They were burlesqued by Arthur Sullivan in Trial by Jury; but Verdi never, to the end of his life, saw anything ridiculous in them; nor do I. There are some charming examples in Un Ballo, of which but little seems to be remembered nowadays.

In Otello and Falstaff there is some deliberate and not unsuccessful fun. When Cassio gets too drunk to find his place in Iago's drinking song it is impossible not to burst out laughing, though the mistake is as pretty as it is comic. The fugue at the end of Falstaff so tickled Professor Villiers Stanford that he compromised himself to the extent of implying that it is a good fugue. It is neither a good fugue nor a good joke, except as a family joke among professional musicians; but since Mozart finished Don Giovanni with a whizzing fughetta, and Beethoven expressed his most wayward fits by scraps of fugato, and Berlioz made his solitary joke fugally, the Falstaff fugue may be allowed to pass.

However, to shew that Verdi was occasionally jocular does not prove that he had the gift of dramatic humor. For such a gift the main popular evidence must be taken from the serious part of Falstaff; for there is nothing so serious as great humor. Unfortunately, very few people know The Merry Wives of Windsor as it was when Falstaff was capably played according to the old tradition, and the playgoer went to hear the actor pile up a mighty climax, culminating in "Think of that, Master Brook." In those palmy days it was the vision of the man-mountain baked in the buck-basket and suddenly plunged hissing hot into the cool stream of the Thames at Datchet that focused the excitement of the pit; and if the two conversations between Ford and Falstaff were played for all they were worth, Shakespear was justified of his creation, and the rest was taken cheerfully as mere filling up. Now, it cannot be supposed that either Boito or Verdi had ever seen such a performance; and the criticisms of modern quite futile productions of The Merry Wives have shown that a mere literary acquaintance with the text will not yield up the secret to the ordinary unShakespearean man; yet it is just here, on Ford and Falstaff, that Verdi has concentrated his attack and trained his heaviest artillery. His Ford carries Shakespear's a step higher: it exhausts what Shakespear's resources could only suggest. And this seems to me to dispose of the matter in Verdi's favor.

The composition of Otello was a much less Shakespearean feat; for the truth is that instead of Otello being an Italian opera written in the style of Shakespear, Othello is a play written by Shakespear in the style of Italian opera. It is quite peculiar among his works in this aspect. Its characters are monsters: Desdemona is a prima donna, with handkerchief, confidante, and vocal solo all complete; and Iago, though certainly more anthropomorphic than the Count di Luna, is only so when he slips out of his stage villain's part. Othello's transports are conveyed by a magnificent but senseless music which rages from the Propontick to the Hellespont in an orgy of thundering sound and bounding rhythm; and the plot is a pure farce plot: that is to say, it is supported on an artificially manufactured and desperately precarious trick with a handkerchief which a chance word might upset at any moment. With such a libretto, Verdi was quite at home: his success with it proves, not that he could occupy Shakespear's plane, but that Shakespear could on occasion occupy his, which is a very different matter. Nevertheless, such as Othello is, Verdi does not belittle it as Donizetti would have done, nor conventionalize it as Rossini actually did. He often rises fully to it; he transcends it in his setting of the very stagey oath of Othello and Iago; and he enhances it by a charming return to the simplicity of real popular life in the episodes of the peasants singing over the fire after the storm in the first act, and their serenade to Desdemona in the second. When one compares these choruses with the choruses of gypsies and soldiers in Il Trovatore one realizes how much Verdi gained by the loss of his power to pour forth *Il balens* and *Ah, che la mortes*.

The decay and discredit which the Verdi operas of the Trovatore type undoubtedly brought on Italian opera in spite of their prodigious initial popularity was caused not at all by the advent of Wagner (for the decay was just as obvious before Lohengrin became familiar to us as it is now that Tristan has driven Manrico from the Covent Garden stage), but by Verdi's recklessness as to the effect of his works on their performers. Until Boito became his artistic conscience he wrote inhumanly for the voice and ferociously for the orchestra. The art of writing well for the voice is neither recondite nor difficult. It has nothing to do with the use or disuse of extreme high notes or low notes. Handel and Wagner, who are beyond all comparison the most skilled and considerate writers of dramatic vocal music, do not hesitate to employ extreme notes when they can get singers who possess them. But they never smash voices. On the contrary, the Handelian and Wagnerian singer thrives on his vocal exercises and lasts so long that one sometimes wishes that he would sing Il Trovatore once and die.

The whole secret of healthy vocal writing lies in keeping the normal plane of the music, and therefore the bulk of the singer's work, in the middle of the voice. Unfortunately, the middle or the voice is not the prettiest part of it; and in immature or badly and insufficiently trained voices it is often the weakest part. There is, therefore, a constant temptation to composers to use the upper fifth of the voice almost exclusively; and this is exactly what Verdi did without remorse. He practically treated that upper fifth as the whole voice, and pitched his melodies in the middle of it instead of in the middle of the entire compass, the result being a frightful strain on the singer. And this strain was not relieved, as Handel relieved his singers, by frequent rests of a bar or two and by long ritornellos: the voice has to keep going from one end of the song to the other. The upshot of that, except in the case of abnormally pitched voices, was displacement, fatigue, intolerable strain, shattering tremolo, and finally, not, as could have been wished, total annihilation, but the development of an unnatural trick of making an atrociously disagreeable noise and inflicting it on the public as Italian singing, with the result that the Italian opera singer is now execrated and banished from the boards of which he was once the undisputed master. He still imposes himself in obscure places; for, curiously enough, nothing dumbs him except well-written music. Handel he never attempts; but Wagner utterly destroys him; and this is why he spread the rumour through Europe that Wagner's music ruined voices.

To the unseductive bass voice, Verdi always behaved well; for since he could not make it sensuously attractive, it forced him to make the bass parts dramatically interesting. It is in Ferrando and Sparafucile, not in Charles V. and the Count di Luna, that one sees the future composer of Falstaff. As to the orchestra, until Boito came, it was for the most part nothing but the big guitar, with the whole wind playing the tune in unison or in thirds and sixths with the singer.[1] I am quite sure that as far as the brass was concerned this was a more sensible system, and less harshly crushing to the singer, than the dot and dash system of using trumpets and drums, to which the German school and its pupils in England clung pedantically long after the employment of valves had made it as unnecessary as it was ugly and absurd. But beyond this, I do not feel called upon to find excuses for Verdi's pre-Boitian handling of the orchestra. He used it unscrupulously to emphasize his immoderate demands for over-charged and superhuman passion, tempting the executants to un-natural and dangerous assumptions and exertions. It may have been exciting to see Edmund Kean revealing Shakspear "by flashes of lightning," and Robson rivalling him in burlesque; but when the flashes turned out to be tumblers of brandy, and the two thunder-wielders perished miserably of their excesses, the last excuse for the insufferable follies and vulgarities of the would-be Keans and Rob-sons vanished. I speak of Kean and Robson so as not to hurt the survivors of the interregnum between Mario and De Reszke, when bawling troopers, roaring Italian porters, and strangulating Italian newspaper criers made our summer nights horrible with Verdi's fortissimos. Those who remember them will understand.

But in his defects, as in his efficiencies, his directness, and his practical common sense, Verdi is a thorough unadulterated Italian. Nothing in his work needs tracing to any German source. His latter-day development of declamatory recitative can be traced back through the recitatives in Rossini's Moses right back to the beginning of Italian opera. You cannot trace a note of Wotan in Amonasro or Iago, though you can trace something of Moses in the rhythms of Wotan. The anxious northern genius is magnificently assimilative: the self-sufficient Italian genius is magnificently impervious. I doubt whether even Puccini really studies Schumann, in spite of his har-monic Schumannisms. Certainly, where you come to a strong Italian like Verdi you may be quite sure that if you cannot explain him with-out dragging in the great Germans, you cannot explain him at all.

---

[1]Elgar, the greatest of all orchestral technicians, maintained that the big guitar business has a genuine skilled technique, and that, for instance, such scores as Ros-sini's Stabar Mater, in the apparently crude and crushing accompaniment to *Cujus animam,* in performance sound exactly right, and help the singer instead of annihila-ting him. [Shaw's note.]

At all events, Verdi will stand among the greatest of the Italian composers. It may be that, as with Handel, his operas will pass out of fashion and be forgotten whilst the Manzoni Requiem remains his imperishable monument. Even so, that alone, like Messiah, will make his place safe among the immortals.

Wagner

The Hornet, 1 April 1877 (*)

The forthcoming Wagner Festival at the Albert Hall, announced by Messrs Hodge and Essex, ought to prove the genuineness of our appreciation of the greatest of modern composers, by presenting to us his music divested of the attractions of the stage. Our Wagnerian education has, by the force of circumstances, hitherto been retrogressive. Lohengrin was the first work of the advanced school with which we became familiar; and this was not in itself inappropriate, for Lohengrin in the first opera in which Wagner is all himself. Its form is complete and symmetrical, and its construction exhibits no trace of the disturbing influence of the old style of Weber and Meyerbeer, which may be regarded as Wagner's starting point. This disturbing influence is so palpable in the incongruous mixture of old forms and new effects throughout the Tannhäuser that those who represented Wagner's music as inconsistent and chaotic were, for once, enabled to gratify their prejudice against the master with some degree of truth.

Yet this opera formed the next step in our experience of what has been absurdly called "the music of the future." It was inefficiently presented to us; and its vague outline, the natural product of the period of transition during which it was composed, was unsatisfactory to an audience whose hopes had been inspired by the perfect form of Lohengrin. But the retrograde from Lohengrin to Tannhäuser found a sort of homeopathic remedy in a further step back to Der Fliegende Holländer, in which the conflicting elements are as yet accommodated to oneanother, and which possesses what the other operas of Wagner grievously lack—human interest.

Such is the curious course which constitutes our preparation for the most advanced works of the composer who will shortly revisit us. How far it will be successful remains to be seen.

228

The Hornet, 6 June 1877 (*)

On the 29th of last month the last concert of the Wagner Festival took place at the Albert Hall. It is not, however, our intention to criticize any of the concerts in particular, but simply to make a few remarks about the festival generally. Herr Wagner, as a conductor, must be very unsatisfactory to an orchestra unused to his peculiarities. He does not, as has been stated, lack vigor, but his beat is nervous and abrupt; the player's intuition is of no avail to warn him when it will come; and the *tempo* is capriciously hurried or retarded without any apparent reason. Herr Richter, whose assumption of the *bâton* was hailed by the band on each occasion with a relief rather unbecomingly expressed, is an excellent conductor, his beat being most intelligible in its method, and withal sufficiently spirited. The orchestra acquitted themselves imperfectly as a rule, the inner parts dragging sometimes so much as to destroy the effect, more especially in such brisk contrapuntal movements as occur in Die Meistersinger.

The vocalists were of exceptional excellence. Frau Materna justified her great reputation, not only as to the brilliancy of her tone and her great powers of endurance, but in the equally important matter of expressive delivery and distinct articulation. Frau von Sadler Grün's voice is of that rare quality which has some indefinable sympathy with melancholy. Her rendering of Brangäne's ominous warning in the Tristan and Isolde conveyed the spirit of the verse to perfection, and her performance of Senta's music in Der Fliegende Holländer has fixed for us a high standard for future reference. No less remarkable was her singing as the woodbird in Siegfried. Owing to a severe cold, the mellow and powerful voice of Herr Unger was heard at a disadvantage. Herr Karl Hill made good his claim as a singer of the first rank by his expressive and refined singing of the parts of Vanderdecken and King Mark.

At each concert Herr Wagner was received with tempestuous applause. On the 19th May he was presented with an address, and a laurel wreath was placed on his brow, which latter distinction was probably more gratifying to his feelings than favorable to the dignity of his appearance. After the last concert he made a brief speech to the orchestra, expressing a satisfaction at their performance which we hope was sincere. Addresses were also presented to Herren Richter and Wilhelmj.

The Dramatic Review, 8 February 1885 (*)

Herr Richter's popularity as an orchestral conductor began, not in the auditorium, but in the orchestra. It dates from his first visit here in 1877 to conduct the Wagner festivals at the Albert Hall. At these concerts there was a large and somewhat clumsy band of about 170 players, not well accustomed to the music, and not at all accustomed to the composer, who had contracted to heighten the sensation by conducting a portion of each concert. It is not easy to make an English orchestra nervous, but Wagner's tense neuralgic glare at the players as they waited for the beat with their bows poised above the strings was hard upon the sympathetic men, whilst the intolerable length of the pause exasperated the tougher spirits. When all were effectually disconcerted, the composer's *bâton* was suddenly jerked upwards, as if by a sharp twinge of gout in his elbow; and, after a moment of confusion, a scrambling start was made. During the performance Wagner's glare never relaxed: he never looked pleased. When he wanted more emphasis he stamped; when the division into bars was merely conventional he disdained counting, and looked daggers—spoke them too, sometimes—at innocent instrumentalists who were enjoying the last few bars of their rest without any suspicion that the impatient composer had just discounted half a stave or so and was angrily waiting for them. When he laid down the *bâton* it was with the air of a man who hoped he might never be condemned to listen to such a performance again. Then Herr Richter stepped into the conductor's desk; and the orchestra, tapping their desks noisily with their bows, revenged themselves by an ebullition of delight and deep relief, which scandalized Wagner's personal admirers, but which set the fashion of applauding the new conductor, whose broad, calm style was doubly reassuring after that of Wagner. He, meanwhile, sat humbly among the harps until he could no longer bear to listen quietly to his own music, when he would rise, get into the way of the players, seek flight by no throughfares and return discomfited, to escape at last into the stalls and prowl from chair to chair like a man lost and friendless. As it is difficult to remain in the room with the greatest living composer without watching his movements, even at the risk of missing some of his music—which, after all, you will have other chances of hearing—you perhaps paid less attention to Herr Richter than he deserved.

Pall Mall Budget, 15 November 1894 (C)

I DO not wish to hurt your feelings, O respectable reader; but do you really think a man of genius would feel much more at home in your company than you would in the galleys? Your objection to a galley-slave, after all, is only that he is a coarser fellow than yourself, insensible to the extremes of your points of honor in decency and morality; tolerant of sights, sounds, and deeds that are horrible to you; and callously reckless, even to bodily violence, of the delicacies and amenities which are to you the indispensable conditions of bearable human intercourse. Among such creatures, shrinking and constant apprehension would be your lot; and yet it would not be safe to shew your fear any more than if you were in a den of hyenas and jackals. I submit to you, then, as politely as such a thing may be submitted, that since Plato, Dante, Shakespear, Goethe, and men of that kind are esteemed great only because they exceed us average persons exactly as we exceed the galley-slave, it follows that they must walk through our world much as through a strange country full of dangerous beasts. It must, therefore, take something like a lion-tamer's nerve to be a man of genius; and when the man of genius is timid—and fear is the beginning of wisdom—he must suffer much more than the ordinary coward, who can, at any rate, choose a safer pursuit than lion-taming, whereas your hapless man of genius is born into the den and must stay there until he is carried out in his coffin.

Obviously, I have never seen Goethe or Shakespear or Plato: they were before my time. But I have seen Richard Wagner, who was so vehemently specialized by Nature as a man of genius that he was totally incapable of anything ordinary. He fought with the wild beasts all his life; and when you saw him coming through a crowded cage, even when they all felt about him as the lions felt about Daniel, he had an air of having his life in his hand, as it were, and of wandering in search of his right place and his own people, if any such there might be. When he had nothing else to do he would wander away to the walls and corners, apparently in search of some door or stairway or other exit from the world, not finding which he would return disconcerted, and either sit down in desperation for a moment before starting off on a fresh exploration, or else—being a most humane man—pet on one of the animals with a little conversation.

In 1883 Wagner wandered to Venice, and there at last stumbled upon that long-sought exit, since when he has not been seen by mortal man. You may well believe, then, how ghostly a sensation I had when, at Queen's Hall in London ten years later, I saw, making its guarded way through the crowd on the platform, a phantom Wagner, again, in Bunyan's phrase, "walking through the wilderness of this world." Of course I knew perfectly well that it was really Siegfried Wagner, son of Richard, and grandson of Liszt; for had I not come there expressly to see him? But, for all that, what appeared to me was the father in his habit as he lived, the old face with immortal youth in it, the set expression of endurance, the apprehensive step, and the unmistakable feeling of supernaturalness among the wild beasts.

· DIE FEEN ·

23 February 1889 (C)

ONE of the reflections suggested by the musical events of the last seven days is a comparison of Mr Hamish MacCunn's luck with Wagner's. It is exactly six years since Wagner died at Venice, aged 70. Mr Hamish MacCunn was born yesterday—or thereabouts. Yet whereas Mr MacCunn's Last Minstrel was performed at the Crystal Palace last Saturday, even the overture to Wagner's Die Feen was not heard in London until Tuesday last, when Mr Henschel kindly gave it at the London Symphony Concert. This Die Feen (The Fairies) was written in 1833 for the Wurzburg Theatre, where Wagner was chorus master at ten florins a month, which was probably considered a handsome thing for a young man of twenty. It must by no means be supposed that at that age he was a crude amateur. He was certainly a crude Wagner; but if his object had been to turn out a business-like opera overture, he could evidently have managed as well as Sir Arthur Sullivan or Mr Ebenezer Prout; for the shortcomings of Die Feen are not those of mere illiteracy in music. And there is something of the enchantment of twenty about it. At that age fairyland is not forgotten. The impulse to hear "the horns of elfland" is genuine and spontaneous. At twenty-six fairyland is gone: one is stronger, more dexterous, much more bumptious, but not yet much deeper: sometimes not so deep. Accordingly, it was not surprising to find a charm in this "Vorspiel" that is wanting in the empty and violently splendid overture to Rienzi. It is more Wagnerian, for one thing. For another, it has youthful grace and fancy as well as earnestness. At the end, after a little juvenile tearing and raging, it weakens off into an echo of Weber's jubilant mood, and the coda is spoilt by the boyish repetition of a piece of energetic commonplace. But the earlier part is well worth the trouble Mr Henschel took with it. The only later work foreshadowed in it is the Faust overture of 1840.

·LOHENGRIN·

8 August 1894 (III)

SITTING, as I am today, in a Surrey farmhouse with the sky overcast, and a big fire burning to keep me from shivering, it seems to me that it must be at least four or five months since I was breathing balmy airs in the scented pine-woods on the hills round Bayreuth. If I could only see the sun for five minutes I could better recall what I have to write about. As it is, I seem to have left it all far behind with the other vanities of the season. I no longer feel any impulse to describe Lohengrin and Tannhäuser as I promised, or to draw morals for Frau Wagner on the one hand, or Sir Augustus Harris on the other. For months I have held the whole subject of musical art in an intense grip, which never slackened even when I was asleep; but now the natural periodicity of my function asserts itself, and compels me to drop the subject in August and September, just as hens moult in November (so they tell me here in the farmhouse).

What I feel bound to record concerning the Bayreuth Lohengrin—remember that this is the first time the work has been done there, and probably the first time it has ever been thoroughly done at all, if we except the earliest attempt under Liszt at Weimar—is that its stage framework is immensely more entertaining, convincing, and natural than it has ever seemed before. This is mainly because the stage management is so good, especially with regard to the chorus. In Lohengrin there are only two comparatively short scenes in which the chorus is not present and in constant action.

The opera therefore suffers fearfully on ordinary occasions from the surprising power of the average Italian chorister to destroy all stage illusion the moment he shambles on the scene with his blue jaws, his reach-me-down costume, his foolish single gesture, his embarrassed eye on the prompter, and his general air of being in an opera chorus because he is fit for nothing better. At Covent Garden he is, in addition, generally an old acquaintance: it is not only that he is destroying the illusion of the opera you are looking at, but that he has destroyed the illusion of nearly all the operas you have ever seen; so that the conflict of his claim upon you as one of "the old familiar faces" with the claims of the art which he outrages finally weakens your mind and disturbs your conscience until you lose the power of making any serious effort to get rid of him. As to the ladies of our opera chorus, they have to be led by competent, sensible women; and as women at present can only acquire these qualities by a long experience as mothers of large families, our front row hardly helps the romance of the thing more than the men do.

Now I am not going to pretend that at Bayreuth the choristers produce an overwhelming impression of beauty and chivalry, or even to conceal the fact that the economic, social, and personal conditions which make the Covent Garden chorus what it is in spite of the earnest desire of everybody concerned that it should be something quite different, dominate Frau Wagner just as they dominate Sir Augustus Harris, and compel her to allot to Elsa a bevy of maidens, and to Henry the Fowler a band of warriors, about whose charms and prowess a good deal of make-believe is necessary. The stouter build of the men, the prevalence of a Teutonic cast among them, and their reinforcement by a physically and artistically superior class of singers who regard it as an honor to sing at Bayreuth, even in the chorus, certainly help the illusion as far as the Saxon and Brabantine warriors in Lohengrin are concerned; but this difference in raw material is as nothing compared with the difference made by the intelligent activity of the stage-manager.

One example of this will suffice. Those who know the score of Lohengrin are aware that in the finale to the first act there is a section, usually omitted in performance, in which the whole movement is somewhat unexpectedly repeated in a strongly contrasted key, the modulation being unaccountable from the point of view of the absolute musician, as it is not at all needed as a relief to the principal key. At Bayreuth its purpose is made clear. After the combat with Telramund and the solo for Elsa which serves musically as the exposition of the theme of the finale, the men, greatly excited and enthusiastic over the victory of the strange knight, range themselves in a sort of wheel formation, of which Lohengrin is the centre, and march round him as they take up the finale from Elsa in the principal key. When the modulation comes, the women, in their white robes, break into this triumphal circle, displace the men, and march round Elsa in the same way, the striking change of key being thus accompanied by a correspondingly striking change on the stage, one of the incidents of which is a particularly remarkable kaleidoscoping of the scheme of color produced by the dresses.

Here you have a piece of stage management of the true Wagnerian kind, combining into one stroke a dramatic effect, a scenic effect, and a musical effect, the total result being a popular effect the value of which was proved by the roar of excitement which burst forth as the curtains closed in. A more complex example of the same combination was afforded by the last act of Tannhäuser, which produced the same outburst from the audience, and which was all the more conclusive because none of the enthusiasm could be credited to the principal artists, who had, in the first two acts, effectually cleared themselves of all suspicion of being able to produce any effect except one of portentous boredom.

· THE RING OF THE NIBELUNGEN ·

Preface to *The Perfect Wagnerite* 1898

THIS book is a commentary on The Niblung's Ring, Richard Wagner's chief work. I offer it to those enthusiastic admirers of Wagner who are unable to follow his ideas, and do not in the least understand the dilemma of Wotan, though they are filled with indignation at the irreverence of the Philistines who frankly avow that they find the remarks of the god too often tedious and nonsensical. Now to be devoted to Wagner merely as a dog is devoted to his master, sharing a few elementary ideas, appetites and emotions with him, and, for the rest, reverencing his superiority without understanding it, is no true Wagnerism. Yet nothing better is possible without a stock of ideas common to master and disciple. Unfortunately, the ideas of the revolutionary Wagner of 1848 are taught neither by the education nor the experience of English and American gentleman-amateurs, who are almost always political mugwumps, and hardly ever associate with revolutionists. The earlier attempts to translate his numerous pamphlets and essays into English resulted in ludicrous mixtures of pure nonsense with the absurdest distortions of his ideas into the ideas of the translators. We now have a translation which is a masterpiece of interpretation and an eminent addition to our literature; but that is not because its author, Mr Ashton Ellis, knows the German dictionary better than his predecessors. He is simply in possession of Wagner's ideas, which were to them inconceivable.

All I pretend to do in this book is to impart the ideas which are most likely to be lacking in the conventional Englishman's equipment. I came by them myself much as Wagner did, having learnt more about music than about anything else in my youth, and sown my political wild oats subsequently in the revolutionary school. This combination is not common in England; and as I seem, so far, to be the only publicly articulate result of it, I venture to add my commentary to what has already been written by musicians who are no revolutionists, and revolutionists who are no musicians.

Preliminary Encouragements†

A few of these will be welcome to the ordinary citizen visiting the theatre to satisfy his curiosity, or his desire to be in the fashion, by witnessing a representation of Richard Wagner's famous tetralogy: The Niblung's Ring.

First, The Ring, with all its gods and giants and dwarfs, its water-maidens and Valkyries, its wishing-cap, magic ring, enchanted sword, and miraculous treasure, is a drama of today, and not of a remote and fabulous antiquity. It could not have been written before the second half of the nineteenth century, because it deals with events which were only then consummating themselves. Unless the spectator recognizes in it an image of the life he is himself fighting his way through, it must needs appear to him a monstrous development of the Christmas pantomimes, spun out here and there into intolerable lengths of dull conversation by the principal baritone. Fortunately, even from this point of view, The Ring is full of extraordinarily attractive episodes, both orchestral and dramatic. The nature music alone—music of river and rainbow, fire and forest—is enough to bribe people with any love of the country in them to endure the passages of political philosophy in the sure hope of a prettier page to come. Everybody, too, can enjoy the love music, the hammer and anvil music, the clumping of the giants, the tune of the young woodsman's horn, the trilling of the bird, the dragon music and nightmare music and thunder and lightning music, the profusion of simple melody, the sensuous charm of the orchestra-

†From *The Perfect Wagnerite*, 1898.

tion: in short, the vast extent of common ground between The Ring and the ordinary music we use for play and pleasure. Hence it is that the four separate music-plays of which it is built have become popular throughout Europe as operas. We shall presently see that one of them, Night Falls on The Gods, actually is an opera.

It is generally understood, however, that there is an inner ring of superior persons to whom the whole work has a most urgent and searching philosophic and social significance. I profess to be such a superior person; and I write this pamphlet for the assistance of those who wish to be introduced to the work on equal terms with that inner circle of adepts.

My second encouragement is addressed to modest citizens who may suppose themselves to be disqualified from enjoying The Ring by their technical ignorance of music. They may dismiss all such misgivings speedily and confidently. If the sound of music has any power to move them, they will find that Wagner exacts nothing further. There is not a single bar of "classical music" in The Ring— not a note in it that has any other point than the single direct point of giving musical expression to the drama. In classical music there are, as the analytical programs tell us, first subjects and second subjects, free fantasias, recapitulations, and codas; there are fugues, with counter-subjects, strettos, and pedal points; there are passacaglias on ground basses, canons and hypodiapente, and other ingenuities, which have, after all, stood or fallen by their prettiness as much as the simplest folktune. Wagner is never driving at anything of this sort any more than Shakespear in his plays is driving at such ingenuities of verse-making as sonnets, triolets, and the like. And this is why he is so easy for the natural musician who has had no academic teaching. The professors, when Wagner's music is played to them, exclaim at once "What is this? Is it aria, or recitative? Is there no cabaletta to it—not even a full close? Why was that discord not prepared: and why does he not resolve it correctly? How dare he indulge in those scandalous and illicit transitions into a key that has not one note in common with the key he has just left? Listen to those false relations! What does he want with six drums and eight horns when Mozart worked miracles with two of each? The man is no musician." The layman neither knows nor cares about any of these things. If Wagner were to turn aside from his straightforward dramatic purpose to propitiate the professor with correct exercises in sonata form, his music would at once become unintelligible to the unsophisticated spectator, upon whom the familiar and dreaded "classical" sensation would descend like the influenza. Nothing of the kind need be dreaded. The unskilled, untaught musician may approach Wagner boldly; for there is no possibility of a misunderstanding between them: the Ring music is perfectly single and simple. It is the adept musician of the old school who has everything to unlearn; and him I leave, unpitied, to his fate.

The Music of the Ring†

To be able to follow the music of The Ring, all that is necessary is to become familiar enough with the brief musical phrases out of which it is built to recognize them and attach a certain definite significance to them, exactly as any ordinary Englishman recognizes and attaches a definite significance to the opening bars of God Save the Queen. There is no difficulty here: every soldier is expected to learn and distinguish between different bugle calls and trumpet calls; and anyone who can do this can learn and distinguish between the representative themes or "leading motives" (Leitmotifs) of The Ring. They are the easier to learn because they are repeated again and again; and the main ones are so emphatically impressed on the ear whilst the spectator is looking for the first time at the objects, or witnessing the first strong dramatic expression of the ideas they denote, that the requisite association is formed unconsciously. The themes are neither long, nor complicated, nor difficult. Whoever can pick up the flourish of a coach-horn, the note of a bird, the rhythm of the postman's knock or of a horse's gallop, will be at no loss in picking up the themes of The Ring. No doubt, when it comes to forming the necessary mental association with the theme, it may happen that the spectator may find his ear conquering the tune more easily than his mind conquers the thought. But for the most part the themes do not denote thoughts at all, but either emotions of a quite simple universal kind, or the sights, sounds and fancies common enough to be familiar to children. Indeed some of them are as frankly childish as any of the funny little orchestral interludes which, in Haydn's Creation, introduce the horse, the deer, or the worm. We have both the horse and the worm in The Ring, treated exactly in Haydn's manner, and with an effect not a whit less ridiculous to superior people who decline to take it good-humoredly. Even the

---

†From *The Perfect Wagnerite*, 1898.

complaisance of good Wagnerites is occasionally rather overstrained by the way in which Brynhild's allusion to her charger Grani elicit from the band a little rum-ti-tum triplet which by itself is in no way suggestive of a horse, although a continuous rush of such triplets makes a very exciting musical gallop.

Other themes denote objects which cannot be imitatively suggested by music: for instance, music cannot suggest a ring, and cannot suggest gold; yet each of these has a representative theme which pervades the score in all directions. In the case of the gold the association is established by the very salient way in which the orchestra breaks into the pretty theme in the first act of The Rhine Gold at the moment when the sunrays strike down through the water and light up the glittering treasure, thitherto invisible. The reference of the strange little theme of the wishing cap is equally manifest from the first, since the spectator's attention is wholly taken up with the Tarnhelm and its magic when the theme is first pointedly uttered by the orchestra. The sword theme is introduced at the end of The Rhine Gold to express Wotan's hero inspiration; and I have already mentioned that Wagner, unable, when it came to practical stage management, to forego the appeal to the eye as well as to the thought, here made Wotan pick up a sword and brandish it, though no such instruction appears in the printed score. When this sacrifice to Wagner's scepticism as to the reality of any appeal to an audience that is not made through their bodily sense is omitted, the association of the theme with the sword is not formed until that point in the first act of The Valkyries at which Siegmund is left alone by Hunding's hearth, weaponless, with the assurance that he will have to fight for his life at dawn with his host. He recalls then how his father promised him a sword for his hour of need; and as he does so, a flicker from the dying fire is caught by the golden hilt of the sword in the tree, when the theme immediately begins to gleam through the quiver of sound from the orchestra, and only dies out as the fire sinks and the sword is once more hidden by the darkness. Later on, this theme, which is never silent whilst Sieglinda is dwelling on the story of the sword, leaps out into the most dazzling splendor the band can give it when Siegmund triumphantly draws the weapon from the tree. As it consists of seven notes only, with a very marked measure, and a melody like a simple flourish on a trumpet or post horn, nobody capable of catching a tune can easily miss it.

The Valhalla theme, sounded with solemn grandeur as the

home of the gods first appears to us and to Wotan at the beginning of the second scene of The Rhine Gold, also cannot be mistaken. It, too, has a memorable rhythm; and its majestic harmonies, far from presenting those novel or curious problems in polyphony of which Wagner still stands suspected by superstitious people, are just those three simple chords which festive students who vamp accompaniments to comic songs "by ear" soon find sufficient for nearly all the popular tunes in the world.

On the other hand, the ring theme, when it begins to hurtle through the third scene of The Rhine Gold, cannot possibly be referred to any special feature in the general gloom and turmoil of the den of the dwarfs. It is not a melody, but merely the displaced metric accent which musicians call syncopation, rung on the notes of the familiar chord formed by piling three minor thirds on top of one another (technically, the chord of the minor ninth, *ci-devant* diminished seventh). One soon picks it up and identifies it; but it does not get introduced in the unequivocally clear fashion of the themes described above, or of that malignant monstrosity, the theme which denotes the curse on the gold. Consequently it cannot be said that the musical design of the work is perfectly clear at the first hearing as regards all the themes; but it is so as regards most of them, the main lines being laid down as emphatically and intelligibly as the dramatic motives in a Shakespearean play. As to the coyer subtleties of the score, their discovery provides fresh interest for repeated hearings, giving The Ring a Beethovenian inexhaustibility and toughness of wear.

The themes associated with the individual characters get stamped on the memory easily by the simple association of the sound of the theme with the appearance of the person indicated. Its appropriateness is generally pretty obvious. Thus, the entry of the giants is made to a vigorous stumping, tramping measure. Mimmy, being a quaint, weird old creature, has a quaint, weird theme of two thin chords that creep down eerily one to the other. Gutruna's theme is pretty and caressing: Gunther's bold, rough, and commonplace. It is a favorite trick of Wagner's, when one of his characters is killed on the stage, to make the theme attached to that character weaken, fail, and fade away with a broken echo into silence.

All this, however, is the mere child's play of theme work. The more complex characters, instead of having a simple musical label attached to them, have their characteristic ideas and aspirations identified with special representative themes as they come into play in the drama; and the chief merit of the thematic structure of The Ring is the mastery with which the dramatic play of the ideas is reflected in the contrapuntal play of the themes. We do not find Wotan, like the dragon or the horse, or, for the matter of that, like the stage demon in Weber's Freischütz or Meyerbeer's Robert the Devil, with one fixed theme attached to him like a name plate to an umbrella, blaring unaltered from the orchestra whenever he steps on the stage. Sometimes we have the Valhalla theme used to express the greatness of the gods as an idea of Wotan's. Again, we have his spear, the symbol of his power, identified with another theme, on which Wagner finally exercises his favorite device by making it break and fail, cut through, as it were, by the tearing sound of the theme identified with the sword, when Siegfried shivers the spear with the stroke of Nothung. Yet another theme connected with Wotan is the Wanderer music which breaks with such a majestic reassurance on the nightmare terror of Mimmy when Wotan appears at the mouth of his cave in the scene of the three riddles. Thus not only are there several Wotan themes, but each varies in its inflexions and shades of tone color according to its dramatic circumstances. So, too, the merry horn tune of the young Siegfried changes its measure, loads itself with massive harmonies, and becomes an exordium of the most imposing splendor when it heralds his entry as full-fledged hero in the prologue to Night Falls on The Gods. Even Mimmy has his two or three themes; the weird one already described; the little one in triple measure imitating the tap of his hammer, and fiercely mocked in the savage laugh of Alberic at his death; and finally the crooning tune in which he details all his motherly kindnesses to the little foundling Siegfried. Besides this there are all manner of little musical blinkings and shamblings and whinings, the least hint of which from the orchestra at any moment instantly brings Mimmy to mind, whether he is on the stage at the time or not.

In truth, dramatic characterization in music cannot be carried very far by the use of representative themes. Mozart, the greatest of all masters of this art, never dreamt of employing them; and, extensively as they are used in The Ring, they do not enable Wagner to dispense with the Mozartian method. Apart from the themes, Siegfried and Mimmy are still as sharply distinguished from one another by the character of their music as Don Giovanni from Leporello, Wotan from Gutruna as Sarastro from Papagena. It is true that the themes attached to the characters have the same musical appropriateness as the rest of the music: for example, neither the Valhalla nor the spear themes could, without the most ludicrous incongruity, be used for the forest bird or the unstable, delusive Loki; but for all that the musical characterization must be regarded as independent of the specific themes, since the entire elimination of the thematic system from the score would have the characters as well distinguished musically as they are at present.

One more illustration of the way in which the thematic system is worked. There are two themes connected with Loki. One is a rapid, sinuous, twisting, shifty semiquaver figure suggested by the unsubstantial, elusive logic-spinning of the clever one's braincraft. The other is the fire theme. In the first act of Siegfried, Mimmy makes his unavailing attempt to explain fear to Siegfried. With the horror fresh upon him of the sort of nightmare into which he has fallen after the departure of the Wanderer, and which has taken the form, at once fanciful and symbolic, of a delirious dread of light, he asks Siegfried whether he has never, whilst wandering in the forest, had his heart set hammering in frantic dread by the mysterious lights of the gloaming. To this, Siegfried, greatly astonished, replies that on such occasions his heart is altogether healthy and his sensations perfectly normal. Here Mimmy's question is accompanied by the tremulous sounding of the fire theme with its harmonies most oppressively disturbed and troubled; whereas with Siegfried's reply they become quite clear and straightforward, making the theme sound bold, brilliant, and serene. This is a typical instance of the way in which the themes are used.

The thematic system gives symphonic interest, reasonableness and unity to the music, enabling the composer to exhaust every aspect and quality of his melodic material, and, in Beethoven's manner, to work miracles of beauty, expression and significance with the briefest phrases. As a set-off against this, it has led Wagner to indulge in repetitions that would be intolerable in a purely dramatic work. Almost the first thing that a dramatist has to learn in constructing a play is that the persons must not come on the stage in the second act and tell one another at great length what the audience has already seen pass before its eyes in the first act. The extent to which Wagner has been seduced into violating this rule by his affection for his themes is startling to a practised playwright. Siegfried inherits from Wotan a mania for autobiography which leads him to inflict on everyone he meets the story of Mimmy and the dragon, although the audience have spent a whole evening witnessing the events he is narrating. Hagen tells the story to Gunther; and that same night Alberic's ghost tells it over again to Hagen, who knows it already as well as the audience. Siegfried tells the Rhine maidens as much of it as they will listen to, and then keeps telling it to his hunting companions until they kill him. Wotan's autobiography on the second evening becomes his biography in the mouths of the Norns on the fourth. The little that the Norns add to it is repeated an hour later by Valtrauta. How far all this repetition is tolerable is a matter of individual taste. A good story will bear repetition; and if it has woven into it such pretty tunes as the Rhine maidens' yodel, Mimmy's tinkling anvil beat, the note of the forest bird, the call of Siegfried's horn, and so on, it will bear a good deal of rehearing. Those who have but newly learnt their way through The Ring will not readily admit that there is a bar too much repetition.

Wagner as Revolutionist

BEFORE leaving this explanation† of The Rhine Gold, I must have a word or two about it with the reader.

It is the least popular of the sections of The Ring. The reason is that its dramatic moments lie quite outside the consciousness of people whose joys and sorrows are all domestic and personal, and whose religions and political ideas are purely conventional and superstitious. To them it is a struggle between half a dozen fairytale personages for a ring, involving hours of scolding and cheating, and one long scene in a dark, gruesome mine, with gloomy, ugly music, and not a glimpse of a handsome young man or pretty woman. Only those of wider consciousness can follow it breathlessly, seeing in it the whole tragedy of human history and the whole horror of the dilemmas from which the world is shrinking today. At Bayreuth I have seen a party of English tourists, after enduring agonies of boredom from Alberic, rise in the middle of the third scene, and almost force their way out of the dark theatre into the sunlit pinewood without. And I have seen people who were deeply affected by the scene driven almost beside themselves by this disturbance. But it was a very natural thing for the unfortunate tourists to do, since in this Rhine Gold prologue there is no interval between the

†This analysis has been omitted. See "Note on the Selections."

acts for escape. Roughly speaking, people who have no general ideas, no touch of the concern of the philosopher and statesman for the race, cannot enjoy The Rhine Gold as a drama. They may find compensations in some exceedingly pretty music, at times even grand and glorious, which will enable them to escape occasionally from the struggle between Alberic and Wotan; but if their capacity for music should be as limited as their comprehension of the world, they had better stay away.

And now, attentive Reader, we have reached the point at which some foolish person is sure to interrupt us by declaring that The Rhine Gold is what they call "a work of art" pure and simple, and that Wagner never dreamt of shareholders, tall hats, whitelead factories, and industrial and political questions looked at from the socialistic and humanitarian points of view. We need not discuss these impertinences: it is easier to silence them with the facts of Wagner's life. In 1843 he obtained the position of conductor of the Opera at Dresden at a salary of £225 a year, with a pension. This was a first-rate permanent appointment in the service of the Saxon State, carrying an assured professional position and livelihood with it. In 1848, the year of revolutions, the discontented middle class, unable to rouse the Church-and-State governments of the day from their bondage to custom, caste, and law by appeals to morality or constitutional agitation for Liberal reforms, made common cause with the starving wage-working class, and resorted to armed rebellion, which reached Dresden in 1849. Had Wagner been the mere musical epicure and political mugwump that the term "artist" seems to suggest to so many critics and amateurs—that is, a creature in their own lazy likeness—he need have taken no more part in the political struggles of his day than Bishop took in the English Reform agitation of 1832, or Sterndale Bennett in the Chartist or Free Trade movements. What he did do was first to make a desperate appeal to the King to cast off his bonds and answer the need of the time by taking true kingship on himself and leading his people to the redress of their intolerable wrongs (fancy the poor monarch's feelings!), and then, when the crash came, to take his side with the right and the poor against the rich and the wrong. When the insurrection was defeated, three leaders of it were especially marked down for vengeance: August Roeckel, an old friend of Wagner's to whom he wrote a well-known series of letters; Michael Bakoonin, afterwards a famous apostle of revolutionary Anarchism; and Wagner himself. Wagner escaped to Switzerland: Roeckel and Bakoonin suffered long terms of imprisonment. Wagner was of course utterly ruined, pecuniarily and socially (to his own intense relief and satisfaction); and his exile lasted twelve years. His first idea was to get his Tannhäuser produced in Paris. With the notion of explaining himself to the Parisians he wrote a pamphlet entitled Art and Revolution, a glance through which will shew how thoroughly the socialistic side of the revolution had his sympathy, and how completely he had got free from the influence of the established Churches of his day. For three years he kept pouring forth pamphlets—some of them elaborate treatises in size and intellectual rank, but still essentially the pamphlets and manifestos of a born agitator—on social evolution, religion, life, art, and the influence of riches. In 1853 the poem of The Ring was privately printed; and in 1854, five years after the Dresden insurrection, The Rhine Gold score was completed to the last drum tap.

These facts are on official record in Germany, where the proclamation summing up Wagner as "a politically dangerous person" may be consulted to this day. The pamphlets are now accessible to English readers in the translation of Mr Ashton Ellis. This being so, any person who, having perhaps heard that I am a Socialist, attempts to persuade you that my interpretation of The Rhine Gold is only "my socialism" read into the works of a dilettantist who borrowed an idle tale from an old saga to make an opera book with, may safely be dismissed from your consideration as an ignoramus.

If you are now satisfied that The Rhine Gold is an allegory, do not forget that an allegory is never quite consistent except when it is written by someone without dramatic faculty, in which case it is unreadable. There is only one way of dramatizing an idea; and that is by putting on the stage a human being possessed by that idea, yet none the less a human being with all the human impulses which make him akin and therefore interesting to us. Bunyan, in his Pilgrim's Progress, does not, like his unread imitators, attempt to personify Christianity and Valour: he dramatizes for you the life of the Christian and the Valiant Man. Just so, though I have shewn that Wotan is Godhead and Kingship, and Loki Logic and Imagination without living Will (Brain without Heart, to put it vulgarly); yet in the drama Wotan is a religiously moral man, and Loki a witty, ingenious, imaginative and cynical one. As to Fricka, who stands for State Law, she does not assume her allegorical character in The Rhine Gold at all, but is simply Wotan's wife and Freia's sister: nay, she contradicts her allegorical self by conniving at all Wotan's rogueries. That, of course, is just what State Law would do; but we must not save the credit of the allegory by a quip. Not until she reappears in the next play (The Valkyries) does her function in the allegorical scheme become plain.

One preconception will bewilder the spectator hopelessly unless he has been warned against it or is naturally free from it. In the old-fashioned orders of creation, the supernatural personages are invariably conceived as greater than man, for good or evil. In the modern humanitarian order as adopted by Wagner, Man is the highest. In The Rhine Gold, it is pretended that there are as yet no men on the earth. There are dwarfs, giants, and gods. The danger is that you will jump to the conclusion that the gods, at least, are a higher order than the human order. On the contrary, the world is waiting for Man to redeem it from the lame and cramped government of the gods. Once grasp that; and the allegory becomes simple enough. Really, of course, the dwarfs, giants, and gods are dramatizations of the three main orders of men: to wit, the instinctive, predatory, lustful, greedy people; the patient, toiling, stupid, respectful, money-worshipping people; and the intellectual, moral, talented people who devise and administer States and Churches. History shews us only one order higher than the highest of these: namely, the order of Heroes.

Now it is quite clear—though you have perhaps never thought of it—that if the next generation of Englishmen consisted wholly of Julius Cæsars, all our political, ecclesiastical, and moral institutions would vanish, and the less perishable of their appurtenances be classed with Stonehenge and the cromlechs and round towers as inexplicable relics of a bygone social order. Julius Cæsars would no more trouble themselves about such contrivances as our codes and churches than a Fellow of the Royal Society will touch his hat to the squire and listen to the village curate's sermons. This is precisely what must happen some day if life continues thrusting towards higher and higher organization as it has hitherto done. As most of our English professional men are to Australian bushmen, so, we must suppose, will the average man of some future day be to Julius Cæsar. Let any man of middle age, pondering this prospect, consider what has happened within a single generation to the articles of faith his father regarded as eternal, nay, to the very scepticisms and blasphemies of his youth (Bishop Colenso's criticism of the Pentateuch, for example!); and he will begin to realize how much of our barbarous Theology and Law the man of the future will do without.

Bakoonin, the Dresden revolutionary leader with whom Wagner went out in 1849, put forward later on a program, often quoted with foolish horror, for the abolition of all institutions, religious, political, juridicial, financial, legal, academic, and so on, so as to leave the will of man free to find its own way. All the loftiest spirits of that time were burning to raise Man up, to give him self-respect, to shake him out of his habit of grovelling before the ideals created by his own imagination, of attributing the good that sprang from the ceaseless energy of the life within himself to some superior power in the clouds, and of making a fetish of self-sacrifice to justify his own cowardice.

Farther on in The Ring we shall see the Hero arrive and make an end of dwarfs, giants, and gods. Meanwhile, let us not forget that godhood means to Wagner infirmity and compromise, and manhood strength and integrity. Above all, we must understand—for it is the key to much that we are to see—that the god, since his desire is toward a higher and fuller life, must long in his inmost soul for the advent of that greater power whose first work, though this he does not see as yet, must be his own undoing.

In the midst of all these far-reaching ideas, it is amusing to find Wagner still full of his ingrained theatrical professionalism, and introducing effects which now seem old-fashioned and stagey with as much energy and earnestness as if they were his loftiest inspirations. When Wotan wrests the ring from Alberic, the dwarf delivers a lurid and blood-curdling stage curse, calling down on its every future possessor care, fear, and death. The musical phrase accompanying this outburst was a veritable harmonic and melodic bogey to mid-century ears, though time has now robbed it of its terrors. It sounds again when Fafnir slays Fasolt, and on every subsequent occasion when the ring brings death to its holder. This episode must justify itself purely as a piece of stage sensationalism. On deeper ground it is superfluous and confusing, as the ruin to which the pursuit of riches leads needs no curse to explain it; nor is there any sense in investing Alberic with providential powers in the matter.

Siegfried
15 June 1892 (II)

LAST Wednesday I was told that Siegfried was to be produced that evening at Covent Garden. I was incredulous, and asked my informant whether he did not mean Carmen, with Miss Zélie de Lussan in the title part. He said he thought not. I suggested Faust, Les Huguenots, even Die Meistersinger; but he stuck to his story: Siegfried, he said, was really and truly in the bills, and the house was sold out. Still doubting, I went to the box-office, where they confirmed the intelligence, except that they had just one stall left. I took it, and went away wondering and only half convinced. But when I reached the theatre in the evening a little late, fully expecting to find notices on the seats to the effect that Siegfried was unavoidably postponed, in consequence of the sudden indisposition of the dragon, and Philémon and Cavalleria substituted, I found the lights out and the belated stall-holders wandering like ghosts through the gloom in search of their numbers, helped only by the glimmer from the huge orchestra and some faint daylight from the ventilators.

The darkness was audible as well as visible; for there was no mistaking that cavernous music, with the tubas lowing like Plutonian bullocks, Mime's hammer rapping weirdly, and the drums muttering the subterranean thunder of Nibelheim. And before I left the house—to be exact, it was at half-past twelve next morning—I actually saw Rosa Sucher and Sir Augustus Harris hand in hand before the curtain, looking as if Covent Garden had been the birthplace of her reputation, and as if he had never heard La Favorita in his life. Perhaps it was all a dream; but it seemed real to me, and does so still. Assuming that I was awake, I may claim that at least one of those curtain-calls was not for the manager at all, but for me and for those colleagues of mine who so strongly urged Sir Augustus Harris to try this experiment in the golden years when money was plenty and there was no Dissolution impending, even at the cost of depriving London of the opportunity of witnessing the début of Signor Rawner as Manrico.

The performance was vigorous, complete, earnest—in short, all that was needed to make Siegfried enormously interesting to operatic starvelings like the Covent Garden frequenters. The German orchestra is rough; but the men know the work, and are under perfect and willing discipline. In readiness and certainty of execution they are fully equal, if not superior, to the ordinary Covent Garden orchestra. But I cannot say as much for them in the matter of purity and individuality of tone. After making every allowance for the difference between the German orchestral tradition, which is partly popular, and the English, which is purely classic, as well as for the effect, peculiar to the Nibelungen tetralogy, of the rugged and massive ground bass which pervades so much of the score, I still cannot accept this imported orchestra as being up to the standard of tone quality we have been accustomed to expect in London.

In that vast mass of brass, it seemed to me that instead of three distinct and finely contrasted families of thoroughbred trombones, horns, and tubas, we had a huge tribe of mongrels, differing chiefly in size. I felt that some ancestor of the trombones had been guilty of a *mésalliance* with a bombardon; that each cornet, though itself already an admittedly half-bred trumpet, was further disgracing itself by a leaning towards the flügel horn; and that the mother of the horns must have run away with a whole military band. Something of the same doubt hangs over the lineage of the wood-wind, the bass clarionet alone being above suspicion. Even in the strings, the 'cellos and tenors lack distinction, though here the thicker and heavier tone is partly due to the lower pitch, which is in every other respect a prodigious relief. I think it will not be disputed that the Covent Garden orchestra, if it had half the opportunities of the German one, could handle the score of Siegfried not only with much greater distinction of tone and consequent variety of effect, but also with a more delicate and finished execution of the phrases which make up the mosaic of leading-motives, and with a wider range of gradation from *pianissimo* to *fortissimo* than Herr Mahler's band achieved, excellent in many respects as its performance certainly was. This is no mere conjecture: we have already heard the Siegfried blacksmith music and forest music played by our own orchestras in concert selections better than it was played on Wednesday last.

And that is why I still complain that Sir Augustus Harris is no more establishing the Wagnerian music-drama in London than Mr Kiralfy is establishing the gondola. When he organized the performance of Die Meistersinger by his own company and his own orchestra, he achieved his greatest feat as an impresario. This time he has only sent for a German impresario and a German company to help him out of the difficulty; and for that I grudge him the smallest exaltation, as I could have done as much myself if I had the requisite commercial credit.

The impression created by the performance was extraordinary, the gallery cheering wildly at the end of each act. Everybody was delighted with the change from the tailor-made operatic tenor in velvet and tights to the wild young hero who forges his own weapons and tans his own coat and buskins. We all breathed that vast orchestral atmosphere of fire, air, earth, and water, with unbounded relief and invigoration; and I doubt if half-a-dozen people in the house were troubled with the critical reflections which occurred to me whenever the orchestra took a particularly rough spin over exquisitely delicate ground, as in the scene between Wotan and Erda. It is not to be doubted that all the women found Brynhild an improvement on Carmen and Co.

I say nothing of the great drama of world-forces which the Nibelung story symbolizes, because I must not pretend that the Covent Garden performance was judged on that ground; but considering how very large a proportion of the audience was still seated when the curtain came down at half-past twelve, I think it is fair to assume that the people to whom Wotan is nothing but an unmitigated bore were in a minority. At the same time, Herr Grengg, with his imposing presence, powerful voice, and perpetual fortissimo, did very little to break that ponderous monotony which is the besetting sin of the German Wotan. Lorent, who was on the stage for a few minutes as Alberich, was also earnest, but pointless and characterless. Fortunately Mime (Herr Lieban) saved the situation by his unflagging vivacity. It would be unreasonable to ask for a cleverer representation than his of the crafty, timid, covetous, and, one must admit, unmercifully bullied old dwarf. His singing shewed remarkable artistic ingenuity—exactly the quality which Mime's music requires.

There are two great points in the part: first, that awful nightmare which comes upon Mime after the question-and-answer scene in the first act, when he curses the shimmering light and falls into a growing terror which is just reaching an intolerable climax when it vanishes as if by magic at the voice of Siegfried in the wood outside; and, second, his attempt to poison Siegfried after the fight with the worm, when he involuntarily talks murder instead of the flattery he intends. Both of these passages were driven home forcibly by Lieban, especially the poison scene, where the effect depends more on the actor and less on the orchestra than in the other. Alvary, though he has something of that air of rather fancying himself in his part which distinguishes some of the most popular impersonations of Mr Wilson Barrett (whom Alvary rather resembles personally), attained a very considerable level of excellence as Siegfried, especially in the forest scene, the remembrance of which will, I think, prove more lasting than that of the first and last acts when we have seen a few rival Siegfrieds and grown a little more critical. Fräulein Traubmann, as the bird, was energetic, purposeful, human, and, in short, everything that a bird ought not to be. For so nice a stage illusion we need wilder and far more spontaneous wood-notes than hers.

As I have already intimated, Fräulein Heink, as Erda, had her scene rather roughly handled both by the orchestra and by Wotan; but she nevertheless succeeded in rescuing something of its ineffable charm by her expressive delivery and her rich contralto tones. As to Rosa Sucher, she was as prompt, as powerful, as vigorous, as perfect in her drill, as solid and gleaming in her tone as ever. Her efficiency, brilliancy, and strength have a charm that is rather military than feminine; and consequently they will fail to rouse the voluptuous enthusiasm of our devotees of that splendid and invariably repentant female, the Womanly Woman; but as Brynhild was no Magdalen, Frau Sucher can hardly be blamed for not making her one. Finally, I have to chronicle several curtain-calls for the energetic conductor, Herr Mahler.† He knows the score thoroughly, and sets the *tempi* with excellent judgment. That being so, I hope he will yet succeed in getting a finer quality of execution from his band.

The scenery is of the usual German type, majestic, but intensely prosaic. The dragon, whose vocal utterances were managed jointly by Herr Wiegand and a speaking-trumpet, was a little like Carpaccio's dragon at San Giorgio Schiavone, a little like the Temple Bar griffin, and a little like a camel about the ears, although the general foundation appeared to be an old and mangy donkey. As usual, people are complaining of the dragon as a mistake on Wagner's part, as if he were the man to have omitted a vital scene in his drama merely because our stage machinists are such duffers as to be unable, with all their resources, to make as good a dragon as I could improvise with two old umbrellas, a mackintosh, a clothes-horse, and a couple of towels. Surely it is within the scope of modern engineering to make a thing that will give its tail one smart swing round, and then rear up.

The stage effects throughout were punctual and conscientious (always excepting the flagrant exhibition of Brynhild in the last act as

---

†In the spring of 1892 Gustav Mahler presented a season of German opera in London (including Wagner's *Ring*) with artists from the Hamburg Stadttheater, where he was chief conductor.

the Sleeping Beauty instead of as an armed figure whose sex remains a mystery until Siegfried removes the helmet and cuts away the coat of mail); but they were not very imaginative. The stithy was lighted like a Board School; and the fires of Loge and the apparition of Erda might have been ordered from the gas company, for all the pictorial art they displayed. Sir Augustus Harris need not look to Bayreuth for a lead in this direction. Where Bayreuth surpasses us is not in picturesque stage composition, but in the seriousness, punctuality, and thoroughness with which it looks after the stage business, which is mostly left to take care of itself at Covent Garden.

Siegfried as Protestant†

THE philosophically fertile element in the original project of Siegfried's Death was the conception of Siegfried himself as a type of the healthy man raised to perfect confidence in his own impulses by an intense and joyous vitality which is above fear, sickliness of conscience, malice, and the makeshifts and moral crutches of law and order which accompany them. Such a character appears extraordinarily fascinating and exhilarating to our guilty and conscience-ridden generations, however little they may understand him. The world has always delighted in the man who is delivered from conscience. From Punch and Don Juan down to Robert Macaire, Jeremy Diddler and the pantomime down, he has always drawn large audiences; but hitherto he has been decorously given to the devil at the end. Indeed eternal punishment is sometimes deemed too high a compliment to his nature. When the late Lord Lytton, in his Strange Story, introduced a character personifying the joyousness of intense vitality, he felt bound to deny him the immortal soul which was at the time conceded even to the humblest characters in fiction, and to accept mischievousness, cruelty, and utter incapacity for sympathy as the inevitable consequence of his magnificent bodily and mental health.

In short, though men felt all the charm of abounding life and abandonment to its impulses, they dared not, in their deep self-mistrust, conceive it otherwise than as a force making for evil—one which must lead to universal ruin unless checked and literally mortified by self-renunciation in obedience to superhuman guidance, or at least to some reasoned system of morals. When it became appar-

†From *The Perfect Wagnerite,* 1898.

ent to the cleverest of them that no such superhuman guidance existed, and that their secularist systems had all the fictitiousness of "revelation" without its poetry, there was no escaping the conclusion that all the good that man had done must be put down to his arbitrary will as well as all the evil he had done; and it was also obvious that if progress were a reality, his beneficent impulses must be gaining on his destructive ones. It was under the influence of these ideas that we began to hear about the joy of life where we had formerly heard about the grace of God or the Age of Reason, and that the boldest spirits began to raise the question whether churches and laws and the like were not doing a great deal more harm than good by their action in limiting the freedom of the human will. Four hundred years ago, when belief in God and in revelation was general throughout Europe, a similar wave of thought led the strongest-hearted peoples to affirm that every man's private judgment was a more trustworthy interpreter of God and revelation than the Church. This was called Protestantism; and though the Protestants were not strong enough for their creed, and soon set up a Church of their own, yet the movement, on the whole, has justified the direction it took. Nowadays the supernatural element in Protestantism has perished; and if every man's private judgment is still to be justified as the most trustworthy interpreter of the will of Humanity (which is not a more extreme proposition than the old one about the will of God) Protestantism must take a fresh step in advance, and become Anarchism. Which it has accordingly done, Anarchism being one of the notable new creeds of the eighteenth and nineteenth centuries.

The weak place which experience finds out in the Anarchist theory is its reliance on the progress already achieved by "Man." There is no such thing as Man in the world: what we have to deal with is a multitude of men, some of them great rascals, some of them great statesmen, others both, with a vast majority capable of managing their personal affairs, but not of comprehending social organization, or grappling with the problems created by their association in enormous numbers. If "Man" means this majority, then "Man" has made no progress: he has, on the contrary, resisted it. He will not even pay the cost of existing institutions: the requisite money has to be filched from him by "indirect taxation." Such people, like Wagner's giants, must be governed by laws; and their assent to such government must be secured by deliberately filling them with prejudices and practising on their imaginations by pageantry and artificial eminences and dignities. The government is of course established by the few who are capable of government, though, its mechanism once complete, it may be, and generally is, carried on unintelligently by people who are incapable of it, the capable people repairing it from time to time when it gets too far behind the continuous advance or decay of civilization. All these capable people are thus in the position of Wotan, forced to maintain as sacred, and themselves submit to, laws which they privately know to be obsolescent makeshifts, and to affect the deepest veneration for creeds and ideals which they ridicule among themselves with cynical scepticism. No individual Siegfried can rescue them from this bondage and hypocrisy; in fact, the individual Siegfried has come often enough, only to find himself confronted with the alternative of governing those who are not Siegfrieds or risking destruction at their hands. And this dilemma will persist until Wotan's inspiration comes to our governors, and they see that their business is not the devising of laws and institutions to prop up the weaknesses of mobs and secure the survival of the unfittest, but the breeding of men whose wills and intelligences may be depended on to produce spontaneously the social wellbeing our clumsy laws now aim at and miss. The majority of men at present in Europe have no business to be alive; and no serious progress will be made until we address ourselves earnestly and scientifically to the task of producing trustworthy human material for society. In short, it is necessary to breed a race of men in whom the life-giving impulses predominate, before the New Protestantism becomes politically practicable.[1]

The most inevitable dramatic conception, then, of the nineteenth century is that of a perfectly naïve hero upsetting religion, law and order in all directions, and establishing in their place the unfettered action of Humanity doing exactly what it likes, and producing order instead of confusion thereby because it likes to do what is necessary for the good of the race. This conception, already incipient in Adam Smith's Wealth of Nations, was certain at last to

---

[1]The necessity for breeding the governing class from a selected stock has always been recognized by Aristocrats, however erroneous their methods of selection. We have changed our system from Aristocracy to Democracy without considering that we were at the same time changing, as regards our governing class, from Selection to Promiscuity. Those who have taken a practical part in modern politics best know how farcical the result is. [Shaw's note.]

reach some great artist, and be embodied by him in a masterpiece. It was also certain that if that master happened to be a German, he should take delight in describing his hero as the Freewiller of Necessity, thereby beyond measure exasperating Englishmen with a congenital incapacity for metaphysics.

PANACEA QUACKERY, OTHERWISE IDEALISM

Unfortunately, human enlightenment does not progress by nicer and nicer adjustments, but by violent corrective reactions which invariably send us clean over our saddle and would bring us to the ground on the other side if the next reaction did not send us back again with equally excessive zeal. Ecclesiasticism and Constitutionalism sends us one way, Protestantism and Anarchism the other; Order rescues us from confusion and lands us in Tyranny; Liberty then saves the situation and is presently found to be as great a nuisance as Despotism. A scientifically balanced application of these forces, theoretically possible, is practically incompatible with human passion. Besides, we have the same weakness in morals as in medicine: we cannot be cured of running after panaceas, or, as they are called in the sphere of morals, ideals. One generation sets up duty, renunciation, self-sacrifice as a panacea. The next generation, especially the women, wake up at the age of forty or thereabouts to the fact that their lives have been wasted in the worship of this ideal, and, what is still more aggravating, that the elders who imposed it on them did so in a fit of satiety with their own experiments in the other direction. Then that defrauded generation foams at the mouth at the very mention of duty, and sets up the alternative panacea of love, their deprivation of which seems to them to have been the most cruel and mischievous feature of their slavery to duty. It is useless to warn them that this reaction, if prescribed as a panacea, will prove as great a failure as all the other reactions have done; for they do not recognize its identity with any reaction that ever occurred before. Take for instance the hackneyed historic example of the austerity of the Commonwealth being followed by the licence of the Restoration. You cannot persuade any moral enthusiast to accept this as a pure oscillation from action to reaction. If he is a Puritan he looks upon the Restoration as a national disaster: if he is an artist he regards it as the salvation of the country from gloom, devil worship, and starvation of the affections. The Puritan is ready to try the Commonwealth again with a few modern improvements: the Amateur is equally ready to try the Restoration with modern enlightenments. And so for the present we must be content to proceed by reactions, hoping that each will establish some permanently practical and beneficial reform or moral habit that will survive the correction of its excesses by the next reaction.

DRAMATIC ORIGIN OF WOTAN

We can now see how a single drama in which Wotan does not appear, and of which Siegfried is the hero, expanded itself into a great fourfold drama of which Wotan is the hero. You cannot dramatize a reaction by personifying the reacting force only, any more than Archimedes could lift the world without a fulcrum for his lever. You must also personify the established power against which the new force is reacting; and in the conflict between them you get your drama, conflict being the essential ingredient in all drama. Siegfried, as the hero of Die Götterdämmerung, is only the *primo tenore robusto* of an opera book, deferring his death, after he has been stabbed in the last act, to sing rapturous love strains to the heroine exactly like Edgardo in Donizetti's Lucia. In order to make him intelligible in the wider significance which his joyous, fearless, conscienceless heroism soon assumed in Wagner's imagination, it was necessary to provide him with a much vaster dramatic antagonist than the operatic villain Hagen. Hence Wagner had to create Wotan as the anvil for Siegfried's hammer; and since there was no room for Wotan in the original opera book, Wagner had to work back to a preliminary drama reaching primarily to the very beginnings of human society. And since, on this world-embracing scale, it was clear that Siegfried must come into conflict with many baser and stupider forces than those lofty ones of supernatural religion and political constitutionalism typified by Wotan and his wife Fricka, these minor antagonists had to be dramatized also in the persons of Alberic, Mime, Fafnir, Loki, and the rest. None of these appear in Night Falls on The Gods save Alberic, whose weird dream-colloquy with Hagen, effective as it is, is as purely theatrical as the scene of the Ghost in Hamlet, or the statue in Don Giovanni. Cut the conference of the Norns and the visit of Valtrauta to Brynhild out of Night Falls on The Gods, and the drama remains coherent and complete without them. Retain them, and the play becomes connected by conversational references with the three music dramas; but the connection establishes no philosophic coherence, no real identity between the operatic Brynhild of the Gibichung episode (presently to be related) and the daughter of Wotan and the First Mother.

THE LOVE PANACEA

We shall now find that at the point where The Ring changes from music drama into opera, it also ceases to be philosophic, and becomes didactic. The philosophic part is a dramatic symbol of the world as Wagner observed it. In the didactic part the philosophy degenerates into the prescription of a romantic nostrum for all human ills. Wagner, only mortal after all, succumbed to the panacea mania when his philosophy was exhausted, like any of the rest of us.

The panacea is by no means an original one. Wagner was anticipated in the year 1819 by a young country gentleman from Sussex named Shelley, in a work of extraordinary artistic power and splendor. Prometheus Unbound is an English attempt at a Ring; and when it is taken into account that the author was only 27, whereas Wagner was 40 when he completed the poem of The Ring, our vulgar patriotism may find an envious satisfaction in insisting upon the comparison. Both works set forth the same conflict between humanity and its gods and governments, issuing in the redemption of man from their tyranny by the growth of his will into perfect strength and self-confidence; and both finish by a lapse into panacea-mongering didacticism by the holding up of Love as the remedy for all evils and the solvent of all social difficulties.

The differences between Prometheus Unbound and The Ring are as interesting as the likenesses. Shelley, caught in the pugnacity of his youth and the first impetuosity of his prodigious artistic power by the first fierce attack of the New Reformation, gave no quarter to the antagonist of his hero. His Wotan, whom he calls Jupiter, is the almighty fiend into whom the Englishman's God had degenerated during two centuries of ignorant Bible worship and shameless commercialism. He is Alberic, Fafnir, Loki and the ambitious side of Wotan all rolled into one melodramatic demon who is finally torn from his throne and hurled shrieking into the abyss by a spirit representing that conception of Eternal Law which has been replaced since by the conception of Evolution. Wagner, an older, more experienced man than the Shelley of 1819, understood Wotan and pardoned him, separating him tenderly from all the compromising alliances to which Shelley fiercely held him; making the truth and heroism which overthrow him the children of his inmost heart; and representing him as finally acquiescing in and working for his own supersession and annihilation. Shelley, in his later works, is seen progressing towards the same tolerance, justice, and humility of spirit, as he advanced towards the middle age he never reached. But there is no progress from Shelley to Wagner as regards the panacea, except that in Wagner there is a certain shadow of night and death come on it: nay, even a clear opinion that the supreme good of love is that it so completely satisfies the desire for life that after it the Will to Live ceases to trouble us, and we are at last content to achieve the highest happiness of death.

This reduction of the panacea to absurdity was not forced upon Shelley, because the love which acts as a universal solvent in his Prometheus Unbound is a sentiment of affectionate benevolence which has nothing to do with sexual passion. It might, and in fact does, exist in the absence of any sexual interest whatever. The words mercy and kindness connote it less ambiguously than the word love. But Wagner sought always for some point of contact between his ideas and the physical senses, so that people might not only think or imagine them in the eighteenth century fashion, but see them on the stage, hear them from the orchestra, and feel them through the infection of passionate emotion. Dr Johnson kicking the stone to confute Berkeley is not more bent on common-sense concreteness than Wagner: on all occasions he insists on the need for sensuous apprehension to give reality to abstract comprehension, maintaining, in fact, that reality has no other meaning. Now he could apply this process to poetic love only by following it back to its alleged origin in sexual passion, the emotional phenomena of which he has expressed in music with a frankness and forcible naturalism which would possibly have scandalized Shelley. The love duet in the first act of The Valkyries is brought to a point at which the conventions of our society demand the precipitate fall of the curtain; whilst the prelude to Tristan and Isolde is such an astonishingly intense and faithful translation into music of the emotions which accompany the union of a pair of lovers that it is questionable whether the great popularity of this piece at our orchestral concerts really means that our audiences are entirely catholic in their respect for life in all its beneficiently creative functions, or whether they simply enjoy the music without understanding it.

But however offensive and inhuman may be the superstition which brands such exaltations of natural passion as shameful and indecorous, there is at least as much common sense in disparaging love as in setting it up as a panacea. Even the mercy and loving-kindness of Shelley do not hold good as a universal law of conduct: Shelley himself makes extremely short work of Jupiter, just as Siegfried does of Fafnir, Mime, and Wotan; and the fact that Prometheus is saved from doing the destructive part of his work by the intervention of that very nebulous personification of Eternity called Demogorgon does not in the least save the situation, because, flatly, there is no such person as Demogorgon, and if Prometheus does not pull down Jupiter himself, no one else will. It would be exasperating, if it were not so funny, to see these poets leading their heroes through blood and destruction to the conclusion that, as Browning's David puts it (David of all people!), "All's Love; yet all's Law."

Certainly it is clear enough that such love as that implied by Siegfried's first taste of fear as he cuts through the mailed coat of the sleeping figure on the mountain, and discovers that it is a woman; by her fierce revolt against being touched by him when his terror gives way to ardor; by his manly transports of victory; and by the womanly mixture of rapture and horror with which she abandons herself to the passion which has seized on them both, is an experience which it is much better, like the vast majority of us, never to have passed through, than to allow it to play more than a recreative holiday part in our lives. It did not play a very large part in Wagner's own laborious life, and does not occupy more than two scenes of The Ring. Tristan and Isolde, wholly devoted to it, is a poem of destruction and death. The Mastersingers, a work full of health, fun, and happiness, contains not a single bar of love music that can be described as passionate: the hero of it is a widower who cobbles shoes, writes verses, and contents himself with looking on at the sweetheartings of his customers. Parsifal makes an end of it altogether. The truth is that the love panacea in Night Falls on The Gods and in the last act of Siegfried is a survival of the first crude operatic conception of the story, modified by an anticipation of Wagner's later, though not latest, conception of love as the fulfiller of our Will to Live and consequently our reconciler to night and death.

NOT LOVE, BUT LIFE

The only faith which any reasonable disciple can gain from The Ring is not in love, but in life itself as a tireless power which is continually driving onward and upward—not, please observe, being beckoned or drawn by *Das ewig Weibliche* or any other external sentimentality, but growing from within, by its own inexplicable energy, into ever higher and higher forms of organization, the strengths and the needs of which are continually superseding the institutions which were made to fit our former requirements. When your Bakoonins call out for the demolition of all these venerable institutions, there is no need to fly into a panic and lock them up in prison whilst your parliament is bit by bit doing exactly what they advised you to do. When your Siegfrieds melt down the old weapons into new ones, and with disrespectful words chop in twain the antiquated constable's staves in the hands of their elders, the end of the world is no nearer than it was before. If human nature, which is the highest organization of life reached on this planet, is really degenerating, then human society will decay; and no panic-begotten penal measures can possibly save it: we must, like Prometheus, set to work to make new men instead of vainly torturing old ones. On the other hand, if the energy of life is still carrying human nature to higher and higher levels, then the more young people shock their elders and deride and discard their pet institutions the better for the hopes of the world, since the apparent growth of anarchy is only the measure of the rate of improvement. History, as far as we are capable of history (which is not saying much as yet), shews that all changes from crudity of social organization to complexity, and from mechanical agencies in government to living ones, seems anarchic at first sight. No doubt it is natural to a snail to think that any evolution which threatens to do away with shells will result in general death from exposure. Nevertheless, the most elaborately housed beings today are born not only without houses on their backs but without even fur or feathers to clothe them.

The Incongruity of Die Götterdämmerung†

Die Götterdämmerung begins with an elaborate prologue. The three Norns sit in the night on Brynhild's mountain top spinning their thread of destiny, and telling the story of Wotan's sacrifice of his eye, and of his breaking off a bough from the World Ash to make a haft for his spear, also how the tree withered after suffering that violence. They have also some fresher news to discuss. Wotan, on the breaking of his spear by Siegfried, has called all his heroes to cut down the withered World Ash and stack its faggots in a mighty pyre

†From *The Perfect Wagnerite*, 1898. My title.

about Valhalla. Then, with his broken spear in his hand, he has seated himself in state in the great hall, with the Gods and Heroes assembled about him as if in council, solemnly waiting for the end. All this belongs to the old legendary materials with which Wagner began The Ring.

The tale is broken by the thread snapping in the hands of the third Norn; for the hour has arrived when man has taken his destiny in his own hands to shape it for himself, and no longer bows to circumstance, environment, necessity (which he now freely wills), and all the rest of the inevitables. So the Norns recognize that the world has no further use for them, and sink into the earth to return to the First Mother. Then the day dawns; and Siegfried and Brynhild come, and have another duet. He gives her his ring; and she gives him her horse. Away then he goes in search of more adventures; and she watches him from her crag until he disappears. The curtain falls; but we can still hear the trolling of his horn, and the merry clatter of his horse's shoes trotting gaily down the valley. The sound is lost in the grander rhythm of the Rhine as he reaches its banks. We hear again an echo of the lament of the Rhine maidens for the ravished gold; and then, finally, a new strain, which does not surge like the mighty flood of the river, but has an unmistakable tramp of hardy men and a strong land flavor about it. And on this the opera curtain at last goes up—for please remember that all that has gone before is only the overture.

THE FIRST ACT

We now understand the new tramping strain. We are in the Rhineside hall of the Gibichungs, in the presence of King Gunther, his sister Gutruna, and Gunther's grim half brother Hagen, the villain of the piece. Gunther is a fool, and has for Hagen's intelligence the respect a fool always has for the brains of a scoundrel. Feebly fishing for compliments, he appeals to Hagen to pronounce him a fine fellow and a glory to the race of Gibich. Hagen declares that it is impossible to contemplate him without envy, but thinks it a pity that he has not yet found a wife glorious enough for him. Gunther doubts whether so extraordinary a person can possibly exist. Hagen then tells him of Brynhild and her rampart of fire; also of Siegfried. Gunther takes this rather in bad part, since not only is he afraid of the fire, but Siegfried, according to Hagen, is not, and will therefore achieve this desirable match himself. But Hagen points out that since Siegfried is riding about in quest of adventures, he will certainly pay an early visit to the renowned chief of the Gibichungs. They can then give him a philtre which will make him fall in love with Gutruna and forget every other woman he has yet seen.

Gunther is transported with admiration of Hagen's cunning when he takes in this plan; and he has hardly assented to it when Siegfried, with operatic opportuneness, drops in just as Hagen expected, and is duly drugged into the heartiest love for Gutruna and total oblivion of Brynhild and his own past. When Gunther declares his longing for the bride who lies inaccessible within a palisade of flame, Siegfried at once offers to undertake the adventure for him. Hagen then explains to both of them that Siegfried can, after braving the fire, appear to Brynhild in the semblance of Gunther through the magic of the wishing cap (or Tarnhelm, as it is called throughout The Ring), the use of which Siegfried now learns for the first time. It is of course part of the bargain that Gunther shall give his sister to Siegfried in marriage. On that they swear blood-brotherhood; and at this opportunity the old operatic leaven breaks out amusingly in Wagner. With tremendous exordium of brass, the tenor and baritone go at it with a will, showing off the power of their voices, following each other in canonic imitation, singing together in thirds and sixths, and finishing with a lurid unison, quite in the manner of Ruy Gomez and Ernani, or Othello and Iago. Then without further ado Siegfried departs on his expedition, taking Gunther with him to the foot of the mountain, and leaving Hagen to guard the hall and sing a very fine solo which has often figured in the programs of the Richter concerts, explaining that his interest in the affair is that Siegfried will bring back the Ring, and that he, Hagen, will presently contrive to possess himself of that Ring and become Plutonic master of the world.

And now it will be asked how does Hagen know all about the Plutonic empire; and why was he able to tell Gunther about Brynhild and Siegfried, and to explain to Siegfried the trick of the Tarnhelm. The explanation is that though Hagen's mother was the mother of Gunther, his father was not the illustrious Gibich, but no less a person than our old friend Alberic, who, like Wotan, has begotten a son to do for him what he cannot do for himself.

In the above incidents, those gentle moralizers who find the serious philosophy of the music dramas too terrifying for them, may allegorize pleasingly on the philtre as the maddening chalice of passion which, once tasted, causes the respectable man to forget his lawfully wedded wife and plunge into adventures which eventually lead him headlong to destruction.

We now come upon a last relic of the tragedy of Wotan. Returning to Brynhild's mountain, we find her visited by her sister Valkyrie Valtrauta, who has witnessed Wotan's solemn preparations with terror. She repeats to Brynhild the account already given by the Norns. Clinging in anguish to Wotan's knees, she has heard him mutter that were the ring returned to the daughters of the deep Rhine, both Gods and world would be redeemed from the stage curse of Alberic's in The Rhine Gold. On this she has rushed on her warhorse through the air to beg Brynhild to give the Rhine back its ring. But this is asking Woman to give up love for the sake of Church and State. She declares that she will see them both perish first; and Valtrauta returns to Valhalla in despair. Whilst Brynhild is watching the course of the black thundercloud that marks her sister's flight, the fires of Loki again flame high round the mountain; and the horn of Siegfried is heard as he makes his way through them. But the man who now appears wears the Tarnhelm: his voice is a strange voice: his figure is the unknown one of the king of the Gibichungs. He tears the ring from her finger, and, claiming her as his wife, drives her into the cave without pity for her agony of horror, and sets Nothung between them in token of his loyalty to the friend he is impersonating. No explanation of this highway robbery of the ring is offered. Clearly, this Siegfried is not the Siegfried of the previous drama.

THE SECOND ACT

In the second act we return to the hall of Gibich, where Hagen, in the last hours of that night, still sits, his spear in his hand, and his shield beside him. At his knees crouches a dwarfish spectre, his father Alberic, still full of his old grievances against Wotan, and urging his son in his dreams to win back the ring for him. This Hagen swears to do; and as the apparition of his father vanishes, the sun rises and Siegfried suddenly comes from the river bank tucking into his belt the Tarnhelm, which has transported him from the mountain like the enchanted carpet of the Arabian tales. He describes his adventures to Gutruna until Gunther's boat is seen approaching, when Hagen seizes a cowhorn and calls the tribesmen to welcome their chief and his bride. It is most exhilarating, this colloquy with the startled and hastily armed clan, ending with a thunderous chorus, the drums marking the time with mighty pulses from dominant to tonic, much as Rossini would have made them do if he had been a pupil of Beethoven's.

A terrible scene follows. Gunther leads his captive bride straight into the presence of Siegfried, whom she claims as her husband by the ring, which she is astonished to see on his finger: Gunther, as she supposes, having torn it from her the night before. Turning on Gunther, she says, "Since you took that ring from me, and married me with it, tell him of your right to it; and make him give it back to you." Gunther stammers, "The ring! I gave him no ring—er—do you know him?" The rejoinder is obvious. "Then where are you hiding the ring that you had from me?" Gunther's confusion enlightens her; and she calls Siegfried trickster and thief to his face. In vain he declares that he got the ring from no woman, but from a dragon whom he slew; for he is manifestly puzzled; and she, seizing her opportunity, accuses him before the clan of having played Gunther false with her.

Hereupon we have another grandoise operatic oath, Siegfried attesting his innocence on Hagen's spear, and Brynhild rushing to the footlights and thrusting him aside to attest his guilt, whilst the clansmen call upon their gods to send down lightnings and silence the perjured. The gods do not respond; and Siegfried, after whispering to Gunther that the Tarnhelm seems to have been only half effectual after all, laughs his way out of the general embarrassment and goes off merrily to prepare for his wedding, with his arm round Gutruna's waist, followed by the clan. Gunther, Hagen, and Brynhild are left together to plot operatic vengeance. Brynhild, it appears, has enchanted Siegfried in such a fashion that no weapon can hurt him. She has, however, omitted to protect his back, since it is impossible that he should ever turn that to a foe. They agree accordingly that on the morrow a great hunt shall take place, at which Hagen shall thrust his spear into the hero's vulnerable back. The blame is to be laid on the tusk of a wild boar. Gunther, being a fool, is remorseful about his oath of blood-brotherhood and about his sister's bereavement, without having the strength of mind to prevent the murder. The three burst into a herculean trio, similar in conception to that of the three conspirators in Un Ballo in Maschera; and the act concludes with a joyous strain heralding the appearance of Siegfried's wedding procession, with strewing of flowers, sacrificing to the gods, and carrying bride and bridegroom in triumph.

It will be seen that in this act we have lost all connection with the earlier drama. Brynhild is not only not the Brynhild of The Valkyries, she is the Hiordis of Ibsen, a majestically savage woman, in whom jealousy and revenge are intensified to heroic proportions. That is the inevitable theatrical treatment of the murderous heroine of the Saga. Ibsen's aim in The Vikings was purely theatrical, and not, as in his later dramas, also philosophically symbolic. Wagner's aim in Siegfried's Death was equally theatrical, and not, as it afterwards became in the dramas of which Siegfried's antagonist Wotan is the hero, likewise philosophically symbolic. The two masterdramatists therefore produce practically the same version of Brynhild. Thus on the second evening of The Ring we see Brynhild in the character of the truth-divining instinct in religion, cast into an enchanted slumber and surrounded by the fires of hell lest she should overthrow a Church corrupted by its alliance with government. On the fourth evening, we find her swearing a malicious lie to gratify her personal jealousy, and then plotting a treacherous murder with a fool and a scoundrel. In the original draft of Siegfried's Death, the incongruity is carried still further by the conclusion, at which the dead Brynhild, restored to her godhead by Wotan, and again a Valkyrie, carries the slain Siegfried to Valhalla to live there happily ever after with its pious heroes.

As to Siegfried himself, he talks of women, both in this second act and the next, with the air of a man of the world. "Their tantrums," he says, "are soon over." Such speeches do not belong to the novice of the preceding drama, but to the original Siegfried's Tod, with its leading characters sketched on the ordinary romantic lines from the old Sagas, and not yet reminted as the original creations of Wagner's genius whose acquaintance we have made on the two previous evenings. The very title "Siegfried's Death" survives as a strong theatrical point in the following passage. Gunther, in his rage and despair, cries, "Save me, Hagen: save my honor and thy mother's who bore us both." "Nothing can save thee," replies Hagen: "neither brain nor hand, but *Siegfried's Death.*" And Gunther echoes with a shudder, "*Siegfried's Death!*"

A WAGNERIAN NEWSPAPER CONTROVERSY

The devotion which Wagner's work inspires has been illustrated lately in a public correspondence on this very point. A writer in The Daily Telegraph having commented on the falsehood uttered by Brynhild in accusing Siegfried of having betrayed Gunther with her, a correspondence in defence of the beloved heroine was opened in The Daily Chronicle. The imputation of falsehood to Brynhild was strongly resented and combated, in spite of the unanswerable evidence of the text. It was contended that Brynhild's statement must be taken as establishing the fact that she actually was ravished by somebody whom she believed to be Siegfried, he being as incapable of treachery to Gunther as she of falsehood, it must have been Gunther himself after a second exchange of personalities not mentioned in the text. The reply to this—if so obviously desperate a hypothesis needs a reply—is that the text is perfectly explicit as to Siegfried, disguised as Gunther, passing the night with Brynhild with Nothung dividing them, and in the morning bringing her down the mountain *through the fire* (an impassable obstacle to Gunther) and there transporting himself in a single breath, by the Tarnhelm's magic, back to the hall of the Gibichungs, leaving the real Gunther to bring Brynhild down the river after him. One controversialist actually pleaded for the expedition occupying two nights, on the second of which the alleged outrage might have taken place. But the time is accounted for to the last minute: it all takes place during the single night watch of Hagen. There is no possible way out of the plain fact that Brynhild's accusation is to her own knowledge false; and the impossible ways just cited are only interesting as examples of the fanatical worship which Wagner and his creations have been able to inspire in minds of exceptional power and culture.

More plausible was the line taken by those who admitted the falsehood. Their contention was that when Wotan deprived Brynhild of her Godhead, he also deprived her of her former high moral attributes; so that Siegfried's kiss awakened an ordinary mortal jealous woman. But a goddess can become mortal and jealous without plunging at once into perjury and murder. Besides, this explanation involves the sacrifice of the whole significance of the allegory, and the reduction of The Ring to the place of a child's conception of The Sleeping Beauty. Whoever does not understand that, in terms of The Ring philosophy, a change from godhead to humanity is a step higher and not a degradation, misses the whole point of The Ring. It is precisely because the truthfulness of Brynhild is proof against Wotan's spells that he has to contrive the fire palisade with Loki, to protect the fictions and conventions of Valhalla against her.

The only tolerable view is the one supported by the known history of The Ring, and also, for musicians of sufficiently fine judgment, by the evidence of the scores; of which more anon. As a matter of fact Wagner began, as I have said, with Siegfried's Death. Then, wanting to develop the idea of Siegfried as neo-Protestant, he went on to The Young Siegfried. As a Protestant cannot be dramatically projected without a pontifical antagonist, The Young Siegfried led to The Valkyries, and that again to its preface The Rhine Gold (the preface is always written after the book is finished). Finally, of course, the whole was revised. The revision, if carried out strictly, would have involved the cutting out of Siegfried's Death, now become inconsistent and superfluous; and that would have involved, in turn, the facing of the fact that The Ring was no longer a Niblung epic, and really demanded modern costumes, tall hats for Tarnhelms, factories for Nibelheims, villas for Valhallas, and so on—in short, a complete confession of the extent to which the old Niblung epic had become the merest pretext and name directory in the course of Wagner's travail. But, as Wagner's most eminent English interpreter once put it to me at Bayreuth between the acts of Night Falls on The Gods, the master wanted to "Lohengrinize" again after his long abstention from opera: and Siegfried's Death (first sketched in 1848, the year before the rising in Dresden and the subsequent events which so deepened Wagner's sense of life and the seriousness of art) gave him exactly the libretto he required for that outbreak of the old operatic Adam in him. So he changed it into Die Götterdämmerung, retaining the traditional plot of murder and jealousy, and with it, necessarily, his original second act, in spite of the incongruity of its Siegfried and Brynhild with the Siegfried and Brynhild of the allegory. As to the legendary matter about the world-ash and the destruction of Valhalla by Loki, it fitted in well enough; for though, allegorically, the blow by which Siegfried breaks the god's spear is the end of Wotan and of Valhalla, those who do not see the allegory, and take the story literally, like children, are sure to ask what becomes of Wotan after Seigfried gets past him up the mountain; and to this question the old tale told in Night Falls on The Gods is as good an answer as another. The very senselessness of the scenes of the Norns and of Valtrauta in relation to the three foregoing dramas, gives them a highly effective air of mystery; and no one ventures to challenge their consequentiality, because we are all more apt to pretend to understand great works of art than to confess that the meaning (if any) has escaped us. Valtrauta, however, betrays her irrelevance by explaining that the gods can be saved by the restoration of the ring to the Rhine daughters. This, considered as part of the previous allegory, is nonsense; so that even this scene, which has a more plausible air of organic connection with The Valkyries than any other in Night Falls on The Gods, is as clearly part of a different and earlier conception as the episode which concludes it, in which Siegfried actually robs Brynhild of her ring, though he has no recollection of having given it to her. Night Falls on The Gods, in fact, was not even revised into any real coherence with the world-poem which sprang from it; and that is the authentic solution of all the controversies which have arisen over it.

THE THIRD ACT

The hunting party comes off duly. Siegfried strays from it and meets the Rhine maidens, who almost succeed in coaxing the ring from him. He pretends to be afraid of his wife; and they chaff him as to her beating him and so forth; but when they add that the ring is accursed and will bring death upon him, he discloses to them, as unconsciously as Julius Cæsar disclosed it long ago, that secret of heroism, never to let your life be shaped by fear of its end.[1] So he keeps the ring; and they leave him to his fate. The hunting party now finds him; and they all sit down together to make a meal by the river side, Siegfried telling them meanwhile the story of his adventures. When he approaches the subject of Brynhild, as to whom his memory is a blank, Hagen pours an antidote to the love philtre into his drinking horn, whereupon, his memory returning, he proceeds to narrate the incident of the fiery mountain, to Gunther's intense mortification. Hagen then plunges his spear into the back of Siegfried, who falls dead on his shield, but gets up again, after the old operatic custom, to sing about thirty bars to his love before allowing himself to be finally carried off to the strains of the famous Trauermarsch.

The scene then changes to the hall of the Gibichungs by the Rhine. It is night; and Gutruna, unable to sleep, and haunted by all

---

[1] "We must learn to die, and to die in the fullest sense of the word. The fear of the end is the source of all lovelessness; and this fear is generated only when love begins to wane. How came it that this love, the highest blessedness to all things living, was so far lost sight of by the human race that at last it came to this: all that mankind did, ordered, and established, was conceived only in fear of the end? My poem sets this forth."—Wagner to Roeckel, 25th Jan. 1854.[Shaw's note.]

sorts of vague terrors, is waiting for the return of her husband, and wondering whether a ghostly figure she has seen gliding down to the river bank is Brynhild, whose room is empty. Then comes the cry of Hagen, returning with the hunting party to announce the death of Siegfried by the tusk of a wild boar. But Gutruna divines the truth; and Hagen does not deny it. Siegfried's body is brought in; Gunter claims the ring; Hagen will not suffer him to take it: they fight; and Gunther is slain. Hagen then attempts to take it; but the dead man's hand closes on it and raises itself threateningly. Then Brynhild comes; and a funeral pyre is raised whilst she declaims a prolonged scena, extremely moving and imposing, but yielding nothing to resolute intellectual criticism except a very powerful and elevated exploitation of theatrical pathos, psychologically identical with the scene of Cleopatra and the dead Antony in Shakespear's tragedy. Finally she flings a torch into the pyre, and rides her warhorse into the flames. The hall of the Gibichungs catches fire, as most halls would were a cremation attempted in the middle of the floor (I permit myself this gibe purposely to emphasize the excessive artificiality of the scene); but the Rhine overflows its banks to allow the three Rhine maidens to take the ring from Siegfried's finger, incidentally extinguishing the conflagration as it does so. Hagen attempts to snatch the ring from the maidens, who promptly drown him; and in the distant heavens the Gods and their castle are seen perishing in the fires of Loki as the curtain falls.

COLLAPSE OF THE ALLEGORY

In all this, it will be observed, there is nothing new. The musical fabric is enormously elaborate and gorgeous; but you cannot say, as you must in witnessing the Rhine Gold, The Valkyries, and the first two acts of Siegfried, that you have never seen anything like it before, and that the inspiration is entirely original. Not only the action; but most of the poetry, might conceivably belong to an Elizabethan drama. The situation of Cleopatra and Anthony is unconsciously reproduced without being bettered, or even equalled in point of majesty and musical expression. The loss of all simplicity and dignity, the impossibility of any credible scenic presentation of the incidents, and the extreme staginess of the conventions by which these impossibilities are got over, are no doubt covered from the popular eye by the overwhelming prestige of Die Götterdämmerung as part of so great a work as The Ring, and by the extraordinary storm of emotion and excitement which the music keeps up. But the very qualities that intoxicate the novice in music enlighten the adept. In spite of the fulness of the composer's technical accomplishment, the finished style and effortless mastery of harmony and instrumentation displayed, there is not a bar in the work which moves us as the same themes moved us in The Valkyries, nor is anything but external splendor added to the life and humor of Siegfried.

In the original poem, Brynhild delays her self-immolation on the pyre of Siegfried to read the assembled choristers a homily on the efficacy of the Love panacea. "My holiest wisdom's hoard," she says, "now I make known to the world. I believe not in property, nor money, nor godliness, nor hearth and high place, nor pomp and peerage, nor contract and custom, but in Love. Let that only prevail; and ye shall be blest in weal or woe." Here the repudiations still smack of Bakoonin; but the saviour is no longer the volition of the full-grown spirit of Man, the Free Willer of Necessity, sword in hand, but simply Love, and not even Shelleyan love, but vehement sexual passion. It is highly significant of the extent to which this uxorious commonplace lost its hold of Wagner (after disturbing his conscience, as he confesses to Roeckel, for years) that it disappears in the full score of Night Falls on The Gods, which was not completed until he was on the verge of producing Parsifal, twenty years after the publication of the poem. He cut the homily out, and composed the music of the final scene with a flagrant recklessness of the old intention. The rigorous logic with which representative musical themes are employed in the earlier dramas is here abandoned without scruple; and for the main theme at the conclusion he selects a rapturous passage sung by Sieglinda in the third act of The Valkyries . . . when Brynhild inspires her with a sense of her high destiny as the mother of the unborn hero. There is no dramatic logic whatever in the recurrence of this theme to express the transport in which Brynhild immolates herself. There is of course an excuse for it, inasmuch as both women have an impulse of self-sacrifice for the sake of Siegfried; but this is really hardly more than an excuse; since the Valhalla theme might be attached to Alberic on the no worse ground that both he and Wotan are inspired by ambition, and that the ambition has the same object, the possession of the ring. The common sense of the matter is that the only themes which had fully retained their old hold on Wagner's intellectual conscience when he composed Night Falls on The Gods are those which are mere labels of external features, such as the Dragon, the Fire, the Water and so on. This particular theme of Sieglinda's is, in truth, of no great musical merit: it might easily be the pet climax of a popular senti- mental ballad: in fact, the gushing effect which is its sole valuable quality is so cheaply attained that it is hardly going too far to call it the most trumpery phrase in the entire tetralogy. Yet, since it undoubt- edly does gush very emphatically, Wagner chose, for convenience' sake, to work up this final scene with it rather than with the more distinguished, elaborate and beautiful themes connected with the love of Brynhild and Siegfried.

He would certainly not have thought this a matter of no conse- quence had he finished the whole work ten years earlier. It must always be borne in mind that the poem of The Ring was complete and printed in 1853, and represents the sociological ideas which, after germinating in the European atmosphere for many years, had been brought home to Wagner, who was intensely susceptible to such ideas, by the crash of 1849 at Dresden. Now no man whose mind is alive and active, as Wagner's was to the day of his death, can keep his political and spiritual opinions, much less his philosophic consciousness, at a standstill for quarter of a century until he finishes an orchestral score. When Wagner first sketched Night Falls on The Gods he was 35. When he finished the score for the first Bayreuth festival in 1876 he had turned 60. No wonder he had lost his old grip of it and left it behind him.

Staging the Ring 1922†

Much water, some of it deeply stained with blood, has passed under the bridges since this book was first published twenty-four years ago. Musically Wagner is now more old-fashioned than Handel and Bach, Mozart and Beethoven, whose fashions have perished though their music remains; whilst his own fashion has been worn to rags by young composers in their first efforts to draw the bow of Ulysses. Finally, it has been discarded as Homerically impossible; and England, after two centuries of imitative negligibil- ity, has suddenly flung into the field a cohort of composers whose methods have made a technical revolution in musical composition so complete that the conductor does not dare to correct the most cacophonous errors in band parts lest the composer should have

†Published as the preface to the fourth edition of *The Perfect Wagnerite*.

intended them, and looks in vain for key signatures because young men no longer write in keys but just mark their notes flat or sharp as they come. One can imagine Wagner trying to conduct the latest British tone poem, and exclaiming in desperation, "Is this music?" just as his own contemporaries did when they were confronted with the "false relations" in the score of Tristan. It is true that most of the modern developments, as far as they are really developments and not merely experimental eccentricities, are implicit in Parsifal. Indeed, for that matter, they are implicit in Bach: still, the first man to be scandalized by a new departure is usually he that found the path for it; and I cannot feel sure that Wagner would have encouraged Messrs Bax, Ireland, Cyril Scott, Holst, Goossens, Vaughan Williams, Frank Bridge, Boughton, Holbrooke, Howells and the rest (imagine being able to remember offhand so many names of British composers turning out serious music in native styles of their own!!!) any more than Haydn encouraged Beethoven. Wagner, after his 1855 London season as conductor of the Philharmonic, would not have believed that such a thing could happen in England. Had he been told that within two years a British baby Elgar would arrive who would attain classic rank as a European composer, he would hardly have kept his temper. Yet all this has happened very much as it happened before in Shakespear's time; and the English people at large are just as unconcerned about it, and indeed unconscious of it, as they were then.

Also the English have taken, as I said in this book they might, to Wagner singing and acting; and there is now no question of going to Bayreuth or importing German singers when we wish to hear The Ring or Parsifal; for much better performances of both can be heard now from English companies in England than Wagner ever heard at Bayreuth; and even a transpontine theatre like the Old Vic. thinks no more of doing Tannhäuser than it would have thought of doing Black-Eyed Susan half a century ago.

Another change has outmoded my description of the Bayreuth Festival Playhouse as an ultra modern theatre. Bayreuth has a pictorial stage framed by a proscenium, and the framed picture stage is not now in the latest fashion. When the monarchy and the theatre were restored in England simultaneously on the accession of Charles II, the representation of Shakespear's plays as he planned them was made impossible by the introduction of pictorial scenery and of the proscenium with its two curtains, the act drop and the final green baize, to divide the plays into acts and hide the stage for intervals during which elaborate scenes were built up on it. His plays had to be chopped into fragments; divided into acts; re-written and provided with new endings to make effective "curtains", in which condition they were intolerably tedious except as mere pedestals for irresistibly attractive actors and actresses.

Thus the pictorial stage not only murdered Shakespear, and buried the old Athenian drama, but dictated the form of opera (which grew up with it) and changed the form of the spoken drama. Wagner submitted to it as inevitable; but when he conceived the performances of The Ring, and planned a theatre for them, he made a desperate effort to elaborate its machinery so as to enable complete changes of scene to be made without stopping the performance and keeping the audience staring idly for fifteen minutes at a dropped curtain, or scrambling to and from their seats to fill up the time by smoking cigarets and drinking. One of his devices was to envelop the stage in mists produced by what was called a steam curtain, which looked exactly like what it really was, and made the theatre smell like a laundry. By its aid The Rhine Gold was performed without a break instead of in three acts with long intervals between each.

One had to admit at Bayreuth that here was the utmost perfection of the pictorial stage, and that its machinery could go no further. Nevertheless, having seen it at its best, fresh from Wagner's own influence, I must also admit that my favorite way of enjoying a performance of The Ring is to sit at the back of a box, comfortable on two chairs, feet up, and listen without looking. The truth is, a man whose imagination cannot serve him better than the most costly devices of the imitative scenepainter, should not go to the theatre, and as a matter of fact does not. In planning his Bayreuth theatre, Wagner was elaborating what he had better have scrapped altogether.

But as this did not occur to him, he allowed his technical plan of The Ring to be so governed by pictorial visions that it is as unreasonable to ask Bayreuth to scrap the Wagner tradition as it would be to ask the Théâtre Français to scrap the Molière tradition. Only, I must now treat that tradition as old-fashioned, whereas when this book was first published it was the latest development. What has happened since in England is that an Englishman, Mr Harley Granville-Barker, developing certain experiments made from time to time by Mr William Poel, another Englishman, inaugurated twentieth century Shakespear by a series of performances in which the plays were given with unprecedented artistic splendor without the omission of a single decently presentable line, undivided into acts, without the old pictorial scenery, and with, as a result, a blessed revelation of Shakespear as the Prince of Entertainers instead of the most dreaded of bores, and a degree of illusion which the pictorial theatre had not only failed to attain, but had sedulously destroyed, nowhere more effectively than (save only in certain scenes of pure ritual in Parsifal) at Bayreuth.

Almost simultaneously with Mr Granville-Barker's revolutionary restoration of Shakespear, the pictorial stage triumphantly announced that at the English Bayreuth, which is the Shakespear Memorial Theatre at Stratford-on-Avon, the play of Coriolanus had been, by a climax of Procrustean adaptation, cut down to a performance lasting only one hour, in which state it was humbly hoped that the public would steel itself to bear it just once or twice for the sake of our national playwright. That was too much. Mr Bridges Adams, who had started with Mr Granville-Barker, took the new method to Stratford, where the former victims of the pictorial stage now find to their amazement that three hours of unabbreviated Shakespear fly faster than one hour of Procrusty Coriolanus. And at the Old Vic. in London, where the reform was adopted by Mr Atkins, Shakespear now draws better than would-be popular melodrama.

Thus have Englishmen left Wagner behind as to methods, and made obsolete all that part of this book which presents him as a pioneer. I must add that nobody who knows the snobbish contempt in which most Englishmen hold one another will be surprised when I mention that in England the exploits of Poel, Granville-Barker, Bridges Adams, Atkins, and the English designers and painters who have worked for them, are modestly attributed to Herr Reinhardt, their eminent German contemporary. The only Englishman who is given any credit by his countrymen is Mr Gordon Craig, a fascinating propagandist who still loves the stage picture better than the stage play, and, living in the glamor of the Continent, seldom meddles with the actual theatre except to wipe his boots on it and on all the art that grows on its boards.

As to the sociological aspect of The Ring, which is unaffected by the rapid ageing of its technical aspect as a musical composition and a theatrical spectacle, it seems to challenge the so-called Great War to invalidate it if it can. Gross as the catastrophe has been, it has not shaken Bayreuth. But post-war contemplation of The Ring must not make us forget that all the progress Wagner saw was from the revolutions of 1848, when he was with the barricaders, to the Imperialist climax of 1871, when he sang:

> Hail, hail, our Cæsar!
> Royal William!
> Rock and ward of German freedom!

What would he have said had he lived to see 1917 in Russia and 1918 in Germany, with England singing "Hang, hang that Kaiser!" and Germany sympathizing to such an extent that the grandson of Wagner's William had to seek safety in Holland? Rhine maidens walking out with British Tommies, Senegalese negroes in Goethe's house, Marx enthroned in Russia, pistolled Romanoffs, fugitive Hapsburgs, exiled Hohenzollerns marking the ruins of empires with no more chance of restoration than the Stuarts and Bourbons: such a Götterdämmerung, in short, as in its craziness can be fitted into no allegory until its upshot becomes plainer than it now is: all this has so changed the political atmosphere in which Wagner lived, and in which this book was written, that it says much for the comprehensiveness of his grasp of things that his allegory should still be valid and important. Indeed the war was more a great tearing off of masks than a change of face: the main difference is that Alberic is richer, and his slaves hungrier and harder worked when they are so lucky as to have any work to do. The Ring ends with everybody dead except three mermaids; and though the war went far enough in that conclusive direction to suggest that the next war may possibly kill even the mermaids with "depth charges", the curtain is not yet down on our drama, and we have to carry on as best we can. If we succeed, this book may have to pass into yet another edition: if not, the world itself will have to be re-edited.

· TRISTAN UND ISOLDE ·

6 August 1889 (C)

Tristan and Isolda comes off better than Parsifal by just so much as the impulse to play it is more genuine and the power to understand it more common. To enjoy Parsifal, either as a listener or an executant, one must be either a fanatic or a philosopher. To enjoy Tristan it is only necessary to have had one serious love affair; and though the number of persons possessing this qualification is popularly exaggerated, yet there are enough to keep the work alive and vigorous. In England it is not yet familiar: we contentedly lap dose after dose of such pap as the garden scene in Gounod's Faust, and think we are draining the cup of stage passion to the dregs. The truth is that all the merely romantic love scenes ever turned into music are pallid beside the second act of Tristan. It is an ocean of sentiment, immensely German, and yet universal in its appeal to human sympathy. At eight o'clock yesterday (Monday) I wondered that people fresh from such an experience did not rashly declare that all other music is leather and prunella; shrug their shoulders at the triviality of *La ci darem*; and denounce a proposal to try the effect of the fourth act of Les Huguenots as a direct incitement to crime.

The performance on Monday was an admirable one. After the scratch representations we are accustomed to in London, at which half the attention of the singers is given to the prompter, half to the conductor, and the rest to the character impersonated, the Bayreuth plays seem miracles of perfect preparedness. Nothing is forgotten; nothing is slurred; nothing on the stage contradicts its expression in the orchestra. At Covent Garden, where you cannot get an artist even to open a letter or make a sword thrust within four bars of the chord by which the band expresses his surprise or his rage, a tithe of the thought and trouble taken here would work wonders. The orchestra, too, by certain methods of treating the instruments, produce many effects of which the tradition must be handed down orally; for most of them defy such directions as a composer can write into his score with any prospect of being rightly understood. Everything that can be done by educated men thoroughly in earnest is done: the shortcomings are those which only individual gifts can overcome.

That shortcomings do exist may be inferred from the fact that, except at those supreme moments at which the Wagnerian power sweeps everything before it, it is possible for an ungrateful visitor to feel heavily bored. The reason is that the singers, in spite of their formidable physique, thick powerful voices, and intelligent and energetic declamation, are not all interesting. They lack subtlety, grace, finesse, magnetism, versatility, delicacy of attack, freedom, individuality: in a word, genius. I remember how Carl Hill sang the part of Mark when I first heard that second act: how we were made to understand the simple dignity, the quiet feeling, the noble restraint, the subdued but penetrating reproach of the old king's address to the hero whom he had loved as a son, and in whose arms he surprises his virgin wife. Herr Betz gave us hardly any of this. He turned his head away, and lifted his hands, and sang most dolefully: nobody was sorry when he had said his say and was done with it. Only a few months ago, at the Portman Rooms, I heard Mr Grove, who makes no pretension to the eminence of Herr Betz, sing this scene with much truer expression. But when Hill sang the part Wagner was conducting; so perhaps the comparison is hardly fair to Betz. In the third act again Vogl surpassed Charles II in point of being an unconscionably long time dying. Wagner's heroes have so much to say that if they have not several ways of saying it (Vogl has exactly two—a sentimental way and a vehement way) the audience is apt to get into that temper which, at English public meetings, finds vent in cries of "Time!" For the fuller a poem is, the duller is an empty recitation of it.

The honors of the occasion were carried off by the women. The men shewed that they had been heavily drilled and were under orders; but Frau Sucher and Fraulein Staudigl played as if the initiative were their own. Frau Sucher, indeed, is not a good subject for leading-strings. Her Isolda is self-assertive and even explosive from beginning to end: impetuous in love, violent in remorse, strong in despair. Frau Sucher has the singer's instinct in a degree exceptionally keen for Bayreuth: she, like Frau Materna, can fall back sometimes on methods of expression solely musical. Fraulein Staudigl's Brangaena was excellent. If I were asked to point to the page of music in which the most perfect purity of tone would produce the greatest effect I think I should select the warning of Bragaena from the tower top to the lovers in the garden. I cannot say that Fraulein Staudigl quite satisfied me in this indescribable episode; but I can praise her warmly for not having fallen much further short of perfection than she actually did.

· DIE MEISTERSINGER ·

15 July 1889 (C)

The spectacle of Mr Augustus Harris making for righteousness with a whole mob of aristocratic patrons hanging on to his coattails is one which deserves to be hailed with three times three. It is difficult to conceive a more desperate undertaking than an attempt to make Die Meistersinger a success at Covent Garden. As well try to make wild flowers spring from the upholstery by dint of engaging tremendously expensive gardeners. There are many things needed for Die Meistersinger: scenery, dresses, persons with voices of a certain strength and compass, a conductor, a band, etc., etc., etc.; but there is one pre-eminent condition, without which all the others are in vain, and that one is the true Wagner-Nuremberg atmosphere: the poetic essence of the medieval life wherein man, instead of serenading, duelling, crying "T'amo, t'amo," and finally suiciding (mostly in B flat or G), went his mortal round as apprentice, journeyman, and master; and habitually demeaned himself by doing useful work. Of this atmosphere there is hardly a breath at Covent Garden; and that is the first and last word of the higher criticism on Saturday's performance. But the practical criticism has to consider not whether the performance was perfectly satisfying, but whether it was better worth doing than letting alone; and on this point there must be a unanimous verdict in Mr Harris's favor.

The first step taken was to secure a large sale for the two-shilling librettos by substituting a colorless translation of the German poem not into English, because the audience would understand that, nor into Polish, French, or Russian, because then one or two of the singers could have declaimed it with native familiarity, but into Italian, the least congenial language in Europe for the purpose. How Johannistag sounds as "solenne di," and Wahn! Wahn! as "Si, si," may be imagined. In order to make quite sure of the librettos going off well, the usual opera bills were carefully removed from the stalls, probably not by Mr Harris's orders; for it is due to him to say that petty dodges of this stamp, characteristic as they are of fashionable entertainments in general and of opera house tradition in particular, are just those of which he has striven to rid Covent Garden. It is greatly to his credit that, in order to do as much of Die Meistersinger as possible, he dared on this occasion to begin at half-past seven, with the encouraging result that the attendance was more punctual than it usually is at eight, or even half-past eight. Yet, though the curtain did not fall until eighteen minutes past twelve on Sunday morning, chunks—absolutely whole chunks—had to be cut out of the very vitals of the work to get it over in time. The first half of Sachs's *Wahn! wahn!* Walter's denunciation of the master's pedantry in the second act, a section of the trial song, a section of the prize song, Beckmesser's scolding of Sachs in the third act, may be taken as samples of the excisions. This could have been avoided only by some such heroic measure as dispensing with the first act altogether: a fearful expedient; but then a single honest murder is better than half a dozen furtive mutilations.

So much for what was not done: now for what was. The honors of the evening went to Lassalle, whose singing was grand, especially in the third act. If he could only learn the part in German, cultivate a cobbler-like deportment about the elbows, and cure himself of his stage walk and his one perpetual gesture with the right hand, he would have very few dangerous rivals in Europe as Hans Sachs. Jean de Reszke, who wandered about the stage as if he had given Die Meistersinger up as a hopeless conundrum, but was always anxious to oblige as far as a tenor part or a spell of love-making was concerned, sang charmingly in the last two scenes. The ever condescending Montariol, as David (which he played with much spirit and evident relish), again sacrificed his dignity as *primo tenore assoluto* on the altar of devotion to the management. Abramoff gave due weight to the music of Pogner. Madame Albani is always at her sincerest— that is, her best—in playing Wagner. In the first scene of the third act she got so carried into her part that for the moment she quite looked it; and the quintet at the end was one of the happiest passages of the evening. Mdlle Bauermeister, the invaluable, whom I have heard oftener than any other living artist (I once saw her as Astriffiamante), was Magdalen.

Signor Mancinelli, who was literally dragged twice across the stage in agonies of dorsaflexion, had evidently taken great pains. With fresh impressions of Richter and Faccio rife in the house, his limitations inevitably made themselves felt, especially in the overture and first act, where the orchestra, being in a continual bustle, requires the smoothest and most sympathetic handling to prevent it getting on one's nerves. And the waltz and procession music in the last scene were much too slow: a grave fault at midnight, with watches popping in and out all over the house and the end still distant. The staging of this last scene, by the way, was excellent. The chorus, if the substitution of women for boys must be accepted without a murmur, acquitted themselves very well; but the riot in the second act would have been better if it had either been sung note for note as written, or, as usual, frankly abandoned as impossible and filled up according to the vociferative fancy of the choristers. A combination of the two plans resulted in a failure, both in accuracy and *laisser-aller*. Such misplaced nocturnal buffooneries as the emptying of vessels from the windows on the crowd, and the subsequent clowning of the nothing-if-not-stolid watchman, should be at once stopped. M. Isnardon as Beckmesser set a bad example in this way; and his chief opportunity of really funny acting—the exhibition of the miseries of acute nervousness before the public in the last scene —was entirely missed.

The audience kept together wonderfully at the end, considering the lateness of the hour; and their conduct in suppressing ill-timed applause and insisting on silence after the fall of the curtain until the very last chord was played, was quite delightful. The proceedings ended with a tremendous ovation to Mr Harris, who fished out of the wing a stout gentleman generally but erroneously supposed to be Wagner. The assembly then broke up in high good humor.

· PARSIFAL ·

7 August 1889 (C)

This Parsifal is a wonderful experience: not a doubt of it. The impression it makes is quite independent of liking the music or understanding the poem. Hardly anybody has the slightest idea of what it all means; many people are severely fatigued by it; and there must be at least some who retain enough of the old habit or regarding the theatre as an exception to the doctrine of Omni-presence, to feel some qualms concerning the propriety of an elaborate make-believe of Holy Communion, culminating in the descent of a stuffed dove through a flood of electric radiance. Yet Parsifal is the magnet that draws people to Bayreuth and disturbs their journey thence with sudden fits of desperate desire to go back again. When you leave the theatre after your first Parsifal you may not be conscious of having brought away more than a phrase or two of *leitmotif* mingled with your burden of weariness and disappointment. Yet before long the music begins to stir within you and haunt you with a growing urgency that in a few days makes another hearing seem a necessity of life. By that time, too, you will have been converted to the Church and Stage Guild's view that the theatre is as holy a place as the church and the function of the actor no less sacred than that of the priest.

The second performance given during my stay at Bayreuth was

much better than the first. It is sometimes difficult for a critic to feel
sure that an improvement of this sort is not in his own temper rather
than in what he is listening to; but as I found Klingsor decidedly
worse than before and was conscious of one or two points at which
Fraulein Malten as Kundry fell short of Frau Materna, the difference must have been objective, since, had it been merely subjective,
the apparent changes would all have been, like my mood, from
worse to better. Malten has several advantages over Materna in playing Kundry. Not only is she passably slim, but her long thin lips and
finely-turned chin, with her wild eyes, give her a certain air of *beauté
de diable*. Only an air, it is true, but enough for a willing audience.
Her voice, though a little worn, is bright; and her delivery is swift
and telling. Altogether, one may say that her individuality, though it
would not startle London, is quite magnetic in Bayreuth. Frau
Materna, the rival Kundry, is not perceptibly lighter than she was
when she sang at the Albert Hall in 1877. She is comely, but ma-
tronly. Still, as Kundry is as old as the hills no complaint need be
made on this score; indeed, the part is one which a very young
woman would play worse than a mature one, unless she were a young
woman of extraordinary genius and precocity. At moments Materna's singing is grand, and her acting powerful: at other moments she
holds up the corner of an absurd scarf as if it had descended to her
from a provincial Mrs Siddons. Fraulein Malten also clings to a scarf
rather more than is good for the sobriety of spectators with an untimely sense of fun. But nobody laughs. It is a point of honor not to
laugh in the Wagner Theatre, where the chances offered to ribalds
are innumerable: take as instances the solemn death and funeral of
the stuffed swan; the letting out of Parsifal's tucks when his mailed
shirt is taken off and his white robe pulled down; and the vagaries of
the sacred spear, which either refuses to fly at Parsifal at all or else
wraps its fixings round his ankles like an unnaturally thin boa con-
strictor. Nevertheless, nobody behaves otherwise than they would in
church. The performance is regarded on all hands as a rite. Miss
Pauline Cramer, if she had no deeper feeling than a desire to oblige
the management, like Montariol at Covent Garden, would hardly
have volunteered for the silent part of the youth whose whole duty it
is to uncover the Grail. As to Frau Materna, it is impossible to believe
that when she goes up nearly the whole depth of the Grail scene on
her knees, she is only aiming at a stage effect. As such, it is not worth
the physical exertion it costs. Van Dyck, though not so steady a singer

as Grüning, has a certain impulsive *naïveté* which, with his engaging physical exuberance, makes him the better Parsifal. The part is a unique one, full of never-to-be-forgotten situations. Impressive as the first Grail scene is, nine-tenths of its effect would be lost without the "innocent fool" gazing dumbly at it in the corner, only to be hustled out as a goose when it is over. His appearance on the rampart of Klingsor's castle, looking down in wonder at the flower maidens in the enchanted garden, is also a memorable point. And that long kiss of Kundry's from which he learns so much is one of those pregnant simplicities which stare the world in the face for centuries and yet are never pointed out except by great men.

Gounod

·FAUST·

14 April 1891 (I)

Faust on the following night was a very different affair. Miss Eames, the newest American soprano, fully justified her engagement by her performance as Margaret. The middle of her voice is exceptionally satisfactory in volume and rich in quality, enabling her to make herself heard without effort in all sorts of quiet dramatic inflections. The low notes, as might be expected, are also very good; but the upper register, though bright, does not come so easily as the rest; and it was rather by a *tour de force* that she took the final trio right through the third repetition in B natural instead of using the old Opéra Comique abridgment. However, as it was a successful *tour de force*, we were all very grateful for it; for the abridgment spoils the finest passage in the whole opera. As an actress, Miss Eames is intelligent, ladylike, and somewhat cold and colorless. The best that can be said for her playing in the last two acts is, that she was able to devise quietly pathetic business to cover her deficiency in tragic conviction. As to Mlle Guercia, the Siebel, her sex betrayed her: she was so intensely feminine in every line of her figure, every note of her voice, and every idea in her acting, that, without being at all a ridiculous or incapable artist, she presented us with quite the most comic Siebel on record. Perotti, with his *allures de danseuse* and his popular high notes, kept Goethe effectually at a distance; and the gentleman who took Devoyod's place as Valentine, though he did an admirable back-fall, was in all other respects quite as bad as anyone could be expected to be at such short notice.

Maurel's Mephistopheles cannot be dismissed with the mixture of contemptuous indulgence and conventional toleration with which one lets pass most of the acting at Covent Garden. He challenges criticism as a creative artist, not as a mere opera singer. In doing so he at once rouses antagonisms from which his brother artists are quite exempt, since his view of the characters he represents may conflict with that of his critics—a risk obviously not run by eminent baritones who have no views at all. His Mephistopheles is a distinct individual character, exhaustively premeditated, and put upon the stage with the utmost precision of execution. As to consistency, it is almost too consistent to be natural. There is no sentimental trace of the fallen son of the morning about it, much less any of the stage puerilities of the pantomime demon (for example, take his original and convincingly right play during the chorale as they break his spell with the cross-hilted swords). It is the very embodiment of that grim Gothic fancy of an obscene beast of prey with the form and intellect of a man. The artistic means by which this effect is produced—the mouse-colored costume, the ashen face and beard, the loveless tigerish voice—could not have been better chosen.

Yet I take some exception to the impersonation, especially in the last two acts, as lacking relief, both vocally and dramatically. This could be best supplied by a touch of humor, in which it is at present entirely deficient. In the scene of the serenade and duel, Maurel is cumbrous and heavy, dragging the serenade beyond all musical conscience, and taking the whole scene as tragically as Faust himself, instead of being the one person present to whom it is pure sport. In the church, too, where Gounod has provided for one of those changes of voice to which Maurel, in his Lyceum lecture, attached so much importance, he sang the pathetic, heart-searching Rammenta i lieti di, accompanied by the organ alone, in the same strident tone as the menace with which it concludes as the orchestra comes in at the words Non odi qual clamor. The only really effective passage in this scene, which Miss Eames played lachrymosely and without distinction, was his powerfully expressive play at the chorus of worshippers.

22 February 1893 (II)

Many who hear Gounod's Redemption cannot but feel somewhat scandalized by the identity in treatment and spirit of the death on the Cross with the death of Valentine in Faust.† He has to remind himself at such moments that it is in the opera and not in the oratorio that the music is out of place. Goethe's Valentine is a blunt and rather ruffianly medieval soldier, with all the indignant insistence on the need for virtue in other people which a man would naturally have

---

†This article was originally published as a review of a performance of *Redemption*.

after studying human nature in the course of helping to sack a town or two. His last words are a quaint combination of a regret that he cannot get at old Martha to blacken her eyes, with a reminder to the Almighty that a brave solider is about to exercise his right of going to heaven.

Gounod, who has no turn for this sort of realism, made Valentine a saint and a martyr; and the ideal actor for a true Gounod performance of the part is a dreamy and pathetically beautiful youth with a pure young voice. Jean de Reszke, when he sang baritone parts, and was eighteen years younger and some thirty odd pounds lighter than today, was far more moving and memorable as Valentine than Maurel is now, though Maurel acts with great power, and reconstitutes the medieval soldier in spite of Gounod's teeth, or than Lassalle, who, conscious of his merits as a singer, avoids invidious comparisons by the quick-witted expedient of not acting at all. The chief disadvantage of turning the death of Valentine into a Calvary was that when Gounod wrote Passion music he was told that it sounded operatic. To which he can only reply that if operatic means like a Gounod opera, the term is not one of reproach. This is a good answer; but Gounod should not have pressed us too hard on the point. When we have been led to associate a particular eight bars of music with the words in which the dying Valentine warns Margaret that she, too, must face her day of reckoning, it is rather disconcerting, to say the least, to hear the central figure in the Redemption transposing those very eight bars from D into B, and using them to declaim, "If my deeds have been evil, bear witness against me," etc.

And those angelic progressions which lift the voice from semitone to semitone on ineffable resolutions of diminished sevenths on to six-four chords, though beyond question most heavenly, are so welded in our minds to Gretchen's awakening from her miserable prison dreams to the consciousness of Faust's presence in her cell, that it is not easy to keep in the proper oratorio frame of mind when they begin. In fact a knowledge of Gounod's operas is a disadvantage at the Albert Hall on Redemption nights, even to the ordinary occasional opera-goer. What must it be then to the professional critic, who has to spend about ten years out of every twelve of his life listening to Faust? If Gounod's music were less seraphically soothing, it would have long ago produced an inflammatory disease—Faustitis—in my profession. Even as it is, I am far from sure that my eyesight has not been damaged by protracted contemplation of the scarlet coat and red limelight of Mephistopheles.

That is why I was so grateful to Maurel for changing the customary hue to an unexciting mouse color. However, I am wandering away from the Redemption, as to which I have no more to say generally than that if you will only take the precaution to go in long enough after it commences and to come out long enough before it is over you will not find it wearisome. Indeed some people do not find it wearisome even at full length, just as, I suppose, they would not mind going through five miles of pictures by Fra Angelico; but I am unfortunately so constituted that it I were actually in Heaven itself I should have to earn my enjoyment of it by turning out and doing a stroke of work of some sort, at the rate of at least a fortnight's hard labor for one celestial evening hour. There is nothing so insufferable as happiness, except perhaps unhappiness; and this is at the bottom of the inferiority of Gounod and Mendelssohn to Handel as oratorio writers.

Offenbach

· LES BRIGANDS ·

20 September 1889 (C)

Since Monday, when I saw Offenbach's Brigands at the Avenue Theatre, I have been trying to make up my mind whether I run any serious risk of being damned for preferring the profligacy of Offenbach, Meilhac, and Halévy to the decorum of Cellier and the dulness of Stephenson. Perhaps an item more or less in the account can make no very great difference to me personally; but I warn others solemnly that Offenbach's music is wicked. It is abandoned stuff: every accent in it is a snap of the fingers in the face of moral responsibility: every ripple and sparkle on its surface twits me for my teetotalism, and mocks at the early rising of which I fully intend to make a habit some day.

In Mr Cellier's scores, music is still the chastest of the Muses. In Offenbach's she is—what shall I say?—I am ashamed of her. I no longer wonder that the Germans came to Paris and suppressed her with fire and thunder. Here in England how respectable she is! Virtuous and rustically innocent her 6-8 measures are, even when Dorothy sings "Come, fill up your glass to the brim!" She learnt her morals from Handel, her ladylike manners from Mendelssohn, her sentiment from the Bailiff's Daughter of Islington. But listen to her in Paris, with Offenbach. Talk of 6-8 time: why, she stumbles at the second quaver, only to race off again in a wild Bacchanalian, Saturnalian, petticoat spurning, irreclaimable, shocking cancan. Nothing but the wit of a Frenchman shining through the chinks in the materialism of English comic opera artists could make such music endurable and presentable at the same time.

When Mr Gilbert translated Les Brigands for Messrs Boosey, years ago, he must have said to himself: "This Meilhac-Halévy stuff is very funny; but I could do it just as well in English; and so I would too, if only I could find an English Offenbach." In due time he did find his Offenbach in Sir Arthur Sullivan. Accordingly, when Falsacappa the brigand chief exclaims: "Marry my daughter to an honest man! NEVER!" we are not surprised to recognize in him a missing link in the ancestry of the Pirate King of Penzance. The relationship of the carbineers to the policemen is too obvious to be worth dwelling on; but there are other ties between the two phases of musical farce. The extremely funny song in the second act, *Nous avons, ce matin, tous deux,* is closely allied to When I First put this Uniform on in Patience; and the opening chorus *Deux par deux ou bien par trois* is first cousin to Carefully on Tiptoe Stealing in H.M.S. Pinafore.

I cannot, however, suppose that Mr Gilbert's objection to the use of his libretto was founded on an idiotic desire to appear "original." The people who regard the function of a writer as "creative" must surely be the most illiterate of dupes. The province of the fictionist is a common which no man has a right to enclose. I cultivate that common myself; and when someone claims to have grown a new plant there, different from all the rest, I smile sardonically, knowing that the selfsame plant grows in all our plots, and grew there before he was born. And when he discovers in my plot a plant which he has raised in his own or seen in his neighbor's, and therefore cries out "Stop thief! Stop plagiarist! Stop picker of other men's brains!" I only smile the widelier. What are brains for, if not to be picked by me and the rest of the world? In my business I know *me* and *te,* but not *meum* and *tuum.*

Mr Gilbert's book as played at the Avenue is much nearer in spirit to the original than Henry Leigh's. Leigh's lyrics sometimes flowed more smoothly than Mr Gilbert's, but his libretti were silly and raffish: the fun too often degenerated into tedious tomfoolery: his feeble and fleshy whimsicalities are inferior in grit and sparkle to even the most perfunctory paradoxes of Mr Gilbert. His Royal Horse Marines, commanded by Marshal Murphi, and his brigands Jacksheppardo, Dickturpino, and Clauduvallo, only shew how French wit of no very high order can yet be degraded by translation into English fun. The horse-collar bar-loafing buffoonery is not in the least like the genuine Meilhac and Halévy *opéra bouffe,* in which the characters, primarily persons of engaging culture, reasonableness, amiability, and address, are made irresistibly ridiculous by an exquisite folly, an impossible frivolity of motive, which exhibit them as at once miracles of wit and sensibility and monsters of moral obtuseness. Mr Gilbert has given us the English equivalent of this in his own operas; and a curiously brutalized, embittered, stolidified, middle-classical, mechanical equivalent it is; but the essential wit and incongruity are preserved. In translating Les Brigands, he naturally did not wholly miss these qualities; though, oddly enough, his version makes hardly anything of a couple of points which might have been expected to appeal specially to him: to wit, the family sentiment of Falsacappa, and the conscientious scruples of Fiorella on the subject of robbing handsome young men (just as the Pirates of Penzance drew the line at orphans).

Saint-Saëns

· SAMSON ET DALILA ·

4 October 1893 (III)

I cannot imagine why the Paris Grand Opera should fascinate English impresarios as it does. Here is Mr Farley Sinkins putting himself out of his way and charging double prices to produce a concert recital of Samson et Dalila. Who wants to hear Samson et Dalila? I respectfully suggest, Nobody. In Paris that is not a reason for not producing it, because Saint-Saëns is an illustrious French composer, and the Opera a national institution; consequently, Saint-Saëns must occasionally compose an opera, and the director produce it, for the satisfaction of the taxpayers. In the same way, we produce specially composed oratorios at our English festivals. We cannot sit them out without wishing we had never been born; but we do sit them out for all that; and though the English school does not immediately become famous over the earth, at least Messrs Novello sell a great many copies of the new work to provincial choral societies.

Now I am strongly of opinion that each nation should bear its own burden in this department of life. We do not ask the Parisians to share the weight of Job† with us; then let them not foist on to us the load of Samson. However, on reflection, this is hardly reasonable; for it is our English Mr Sinkins who has insisted on our listening to Samson; whilst the composer and the tenor, representing the French nation, have done their best to save us by bolting at the last moment. The story of their flight; of Mr Sinkins's diplomatic masterstroke of sending the soprano to win them back; and of the fugitives rising to the height of the occasion by capturing the soprano, has already been told, though not explained. The sequel, shewing how Mr Bernard Lane came to the rescue by taking the part of Samson, is, I suppose, for me to tell; but I propose to shirk that duty, out of regard for Mr Lane's feelings.

Samson with the part of Samson read at sight, is perhaps better

† Hubert Parry's oratorio; see pp. 335–39.

than Samson with the part of Samson left out: anyhow Mr Lane thought so; and no doubt in acting on that opinion he did his best under the circumstances. Miss Edith Miller, who undertook Dalila at equally short notice, was less at a disadvantage. Lyrical expression, to a musician, is much more obvious at first sight than dramatic expression, which can be planned only by careful study; and as Dalila's music is much more lyrical than Samson's, not to mention the fact that the most important number in it is already hackneyed by concert use, Miss Miller was able to make the most of her opportunity and to come off handsomely, all things considered.

The other parts, in the hands of Messrs Oudin, Barlow, Magrath, and Gawthrop, would no doubt have been well done if they had possessed any artistic substance for these gentlemen to bite on, so to speak. But the impossible Meyerbeerian Abimelech, with his brusque measures and his grim orchestral clinkings and whistlings, could have come from no place in the world but Paris, where they still regard Meyerbeer as a sort of musical Michael Angelo, and gravely offer to the wondering world commonplace imitations of the petty monstrosities and abortions of Le Prophète as sublime *hardiesses*, and pages of history read by flashes of lightning. No doubt Saint-Saëns had to copy Meyerbeer, just as poor Meyerbeer had to copy himself from the day when he made a specialty of religious fanaticism in Les Huguenots.

After the Huguenots and Catholics came the Anabaptists; and now, the Philistines and the Israelites being in question, we have Abimelech clinking and whistling as aforesaid; Samson calling his sect to arms to a trumpet motive in the best style of Raoul de Nangis at the ball given by Marguerite de Valois; stage rushes of the two factions at each other's throats, with every eye, aflame with bigotry, flashing on the conductor; and the inevitable love-duet, in which the tenor is torn by the conflicting calls of passion and party in a key with several flats in it. I did not wait for the third act of Samson; but I assume that the hero attempted to bring the house down by a drinking-song before resorting to the pillars.

If Saint-Saëns were to be commissioned to write a new "historical opera" entitled Ulster, we should have the zealous Protestants of that region devoting the Pope to perdition in a Rataplan chorus, and confining themselves to ascetic accompaniments of double bass and piccolo; whilst their opponents would pay the same compliment to King William of glorious, pious, and immortal memory, in crisp waltzes and galops, whipped along into movements of popular fury by flicks on the side-drum, *strettos*, sham *fugatos*, and *pas redoublés*, with a grand climax of all the national airs of Ireland worked in double counter-point with suitable extracts from the Church music of the rivals' creeds, played simultaneously on several military bands and a pair of organs. This is the sort of thing a French composer dreams of as the summit of operatic achievement. I feel that my own view of it cuts off my artistic sympathy with Paris at the musical main. But I cannot help that. It is not good sense to expect me to sacrifice my reputation as a serious critic for the sake of such tinpot stage history. Besides, I long ago gave up Paris as impossible from the artistic point of view. London I do not so much mind.

Your average Londoner is, no doubt, as void of feeling for the fine arts as a man can be without collapsing bodily; but then he is not at all ashamed of his condition. On the contrary, he is rather proud of it, and never feels obliged to pretend that he is an artist to the tips of his fingers. His pretences are confined to piety and politics, in both of which he is an unspeakable impostor. It is your Parisian who concentrates his ignorance and hypocrisy, not on politics and religion, but on art. He believes that Europe expects him to be, before everything, artistic. In this unwholesome state of self-consciousness he demands statues and pictures and operas in all directions, long before any appetite for beauty has set his eyes or ears aching; so that he at once becomes the prey of pedants who undertake to supply him with classical works, and swaggerers who set up in the romantic department. Hence, as the Parisian, like other people, likes to enjoy himself, and as pure pedantry is tedious and pure swaggering tiresome, what Paris chiefly loves is a genius who can make the classic voluptuous and the romantic amusing.

And so, though you cannot walk through Paris without coming at every corner upon some fountain or trophy or monument for which the only possible remedy is dynamite, you can always count upon the design including a female figure free from the defect known to photographers as under-exposure; and if you go to the Opera—which is, happily, an easily avoidable fate—you may wonder at the expensive trifling that passes as musical poetry and drama, but you will be compelled to admit that the composer has moments, carried as far as academic propriety permits, in which he rises from sham history and tragedy to genuine polka and barcarolle; whilst there is, to boot, always one happy half-hour when the opera-singers vanish, and capable, thoroughly trained, hardworking, technically skilled executants entertain you with a ballet. Of course the ballet,

like everything else in Paris, is a provincial survival, fifty years behind English time, but still it is generally complete, and well done by
people who understand ballet, whereas the opera is generally mutilated, and ill-done by people who dont understand opera.

Such being my prejudices against Paris, it is vain to expect enthusiasm from me on the subject of Samson et Dalila. Saint-Saëns
would feel sufficiently flattered, perhaps, if I were to pronounce it as
good as Les Huguenots; but I cannot do that, for a variety of reasons,
among which I may mention that if Saint-Saëns had successfully
imitated Meyerbeer's masterpiece, the effect would have been, not to
establish the merit of the imitation, but rather to destroy one of the
chief merits of the original—its uniqueness. Besides, Les Huguenots
made the Paris Opera what it is; whereas the Paris Opera has made
Samson what *it* is, unluckily for Saint-Saëns.

Some of the improvements on Meyerbeer are questionable: for
instance, in the instrumental prelude to Les Huguenots Meyerbeer
borrowed the tune and invented only the accompaniment; but
Saint-Saëns, scorning to borrow, has written a prelude consisting of
an accompaniment without any tune at all, and not a very original
accompaniment at that. I own I like Meyerbeer's plan better. I have
already confessed to a preference for Raoul over Samson; and I defy
anyone to blame me for thinking Valentine and Marcel in the Pré-
aux-Clercs worth a dozen of Dalila and the High Priest of Dagon in a
place described by the program, in the manner of a postal address, as
"The Valley of Soreck, Palestine." . . .

In conclusion, lest anything that I have said about the Parisians
should unduly strain international relations, let me add that we already have in this country a class—and a growing class—of
amateurs who have totally discarded our national hobbies of politics
and piety, and taken on the Parisian hobby of Art. As like causes
produce like effects in both countries, will these ladies and gentlemen kindly apply to themselves everything that I have said about
their neighbors across the water.

Bizet

·THE PEARL FISHERS·

20 May 1889 (C)

To lovers of poetry the pearl fisher is known as one who "held his breath, and went all naked to the hungry shark." To the patrons of the Opera he is now familiar as an expensively got-up Oriental, with an elaborate ritual conducted in temples not unlike Parisian newspaper kiosks, the precincts whereof are laid out, regardless of expense, in the manner of a Brussels tea garden. The chief ceremony is a ballet; and though here, if anywhere, we might expect to find our pearl fisher in the condition mentioned by Keats, such is by no means the case. He—or rather she—is clothed and, within operatic limits, in her right mind. As to holding his breath, he turns that accomplishment to account for the better execution of roulades and fiorituras. He keeps the hungry shark in order by the prayers of a virgin priestess, who remains veiled and secluded from all human intercourse on a rocky promontory during the oyster season.

Out of these simple and plausible conditions we get a pretty poem. Leila is the priestess. Nadir and Zenith—no: I find on looking at the libretto that the name is Zurga—fall in love with her. Nadir sacrilegiously serenades her on the promontory. She responds; and the two, amid a hideous tempest, are seized and condemned to the stake. Zurga effects a diversion, and enables them to escape by setting Ceylon on fire: an extreme measure; but then, as he doubtless reflects, you cannot have an omelette without breaking eggs. The natives then burn him; and really, under the circumstances, it is hard to blame them. That is all.

Of the choral music, the dance music, the procession music, and the melodramatic music, by all of which the dainty little poem of the two friends in love with the veiled priestess has been stuffed and padded into a big Covent Garden opera, it is needless to speak. It is effective and workmanlike enough; but a dozen composers could have done it to order as well as Bizet. The best of it is the choral unison in the first act—*Colui, che noi vogliam, per duce,* which has some-

294

thing of the swing and frankness of Donizetti's choruses. (These, by the bye, have been discovered by the Salvation Army: I heard one of their bands playing *Per te immenso giubilo* capitally one Sunday morning last year down at Merton). The leading motive which runs through the opera is very beautiful, but no more Bizet's than the chorale in Les Huguenots is Meyerbeer's: it is simply that wonderful old Dies Iræ which has fascinated generations of musicians and worshippers. Bizet is only himself—his immature self—in the love music, which has that touch of divine rapture which a young poet's love music should have, and which has the distinction and charm of the Carmen music without the firmness of its style. In the first act, the conventional amorous cavatina for the tenor is replaced by a duet in which the two rivals recall the romantic atmosphere of that evening at the gate of an eastern city when they caught their first glimpse of Leila. The duet, and all those parts of the opera which are in the same vein, are enchanting. He who has no indulgence for their want of solidity is fit for treasons, stratagems, and spoils.

· CARMEN ·

28 May 1890 (I)

Valero, the new tenor from Madrid, made his first appearance on Tuesday in Carmen with Miss de Lussan. As he is a finished exponent of the Gayarré style of singing, which I maintain to be nothing but bleating invested with artistic merit (though I admit the right of anybody to prefer it to the round pure tone and unforced production without which no singing is beautiful to my ears), I should probably have had nothing good to say of him had he not disarmed me by acting throughout with unexpected willingness, vivacity, and actually with a sense of humor. My heart retained the hardness set up by his vocal method until Carmen began singing the *seguidilla* at him, when he licked the finger and thumb with which he was putting on his glove (to shew his indifference to the siren, poor wretch!), and gave a little toss of his head and knock of his knee that there was no resisting. A man who makes me laugh by a legitimate stroke of art charms all of the criticism out of me; and I confess to having enjoyed Valero's Don José as well as any that I have seen, although he is too transparently amiable and social to seriously impersonate Mérimée's morbidly jealous and diffident dragoon.

Miss de Lussan shews remarkable cleverness as Carmen; but

Carmen is degenerating into a male Mephistopheles. Every respectable young American lady longs to put on the Spanish jacket and play at being an abandoned person, just as the harmless basso craves to mount the scarlet cock's feather and say to himself, like Barnaby Rudge's raven, "I'm a devil, I'm a devil, I'm a devil!" Miss de Lussan is no more like Carmen than her natty stockings are like those "with more than one hole in them" described by Mérimée. Perhaps, as Charles Lamb's ghost may think, stage Carmens are only delightful when and because everybody can see that they are pure make-believe. But I am not a Lambite in this matter. I miss the tragic background of ungovernable passion and superstitious fatalism to the levity and insolent waywardness which Miss de Lussan makes so much of. The truth is, she cannot act the tavern scene, nor sing the prophetic episode in the fortune-telling trio, to anything near conviction point.

30 May 1894 (III)

The difference between the old order in opera and the new suggests to my imagination such a vast period of time, that it seems odd to me that I should have witnessed Patti's latest triumph on the morrow of Calvé's appearance at Covent Garden as Carmen. It is only fair that I should warn the public against attaching too much importance to anything I may say about Madame Calvé. As I have often explained, it is one of the conditions of that high susceptibility which is my chief qualification as a critic, that good or bad art becomes a personal matter between me and the artist.

I *hate* performers who debase great works of art: I long for their annihilation: if my criticisms were flaming thunderbolts, no prudent Life or Fire Insurance Company would entertain a proposal from any singer within my range, or from the lessee of any opera-house or concert-room within my circuit. But I am necessarily no less extreme in my admiration of artists who realize the full value of great works for me, or who transfigure ordinary ones. Calvé is such an artist; and she is also a woman whose strange personal appearance recalls Titian's wonderful Virgin of the Assumption at Venice, and who has, in addition to that beauty of aspect, a beauty of action—especially of that sort of action which is the thought or conception of the artist made visible—such as one might expect from Titian's Virgin if the picture were made alive. This description will perhaps sufficiently shew the need for a little discount off such eulogies as I may presently be moved to in speaking of her performances in detail.

But I have no eulogies for her Carmen, which shocked me beyond measure. I pointed out on a previous occasion, when dealing with a very remarkable impersonation of that character by Giulia Ravogli, that the success of Bizet's opera is altogether due to the attraction, such as it is, of seeing a pretty and respectable middle-class young lady, expensively dressed, harmlessly pretending to be a wicked person, and that anything like a successful attempt to play the part realistically by a powerful actress must not only at once betray the thinness and unreality of Prosper Mérimée's romance, but must leave anything but a pleasant taste on the palate of the audience. This was proved by the fact that Giulia Ravogli's Carmen, the most powerful that had then been seen in England, was received with a good deal of grumbling, and was shelved to make way for that pretty little imposition, the Carmen of Miss De Lussan, who was, as everybody could see, a perfect young lady innocently playing at being naughty.

And yet Giulia Ravogli flattered Carmen by exhibiting her as a woman of courage and strength of character. Calvé makes no such concession. Her Carmen is a superstitious, pleasure-loving good-for-nothing, caught by the outside of anything glittering, with no power but the power of seduction, which she exercises without sense or decency. There is no suggestion of any fine quality about her, not a spark of honesty, courage, or even of the sort of honor supposed to prevail among thieves. All this is conveyed by Calvé with a positively frightful artistic power of divesting her beauty and grace of the nobility—I had almost written the sanctity—which seems inseparable from them in other parts. Nobody else dare venture on the indescribable allurements which she practices on the officers in the first act, or such touches as the attempt to get a comprehensive view of her figure in Lillas Pastia's rather small looking-glass, or her jealously critical inspection of Micaela from the same point of view in the third act.

Her death-scene, too, is horribly real. The young lady Carmen is never so effectively alive as when she falls, stage dead, beneath José's cruel knife. But to see Calvé's Carmen changing from a live creature, with properly coordinated movements, into a reeling, staggering, flopping, disorganized thing, and finally tumble down a mere heap of carrion, is to get much the same sensation as might be given by the reality of a brutal murder. It is perhaps just as well that a great artist should, once in a way, give our opera goers a glimpse of the truth about the things they play with so light-heartedly. In spite of the applause and the curtain calls, it was quite evident that the audience was by no means as comfortable after the performance as Miss de Lussan would have left them.

But nothing would induce me to go again. To me it was a desecration of a great talent. I felt furious with Calvé, as if I had been shewn some terrible caricature by Hogarth of the Titian. That, however, may have been a personal sentiment. What I am perfectly sure was a legitimate critical sentiment was my objection to Carmen carrying her abandonment to the point of being incapable of paying the smallest attention to the score. I have never seen, at Bayreuth or anywhere else, an operatic actress fit her action more perfectly and punctually to its indication in the orchestra than Giulia Ravogli did as Carmen. And I have never seen, even at Covent Garden, the same artistic duty so completely disregarded as it was by Calvé. She acted out of time the whole evening; and I do not see why artists should act out of time any more than sing out of time.

Tchaikowsky

· EUGENE ONEGIN ·

26 October 1892 (II)

Eugene Onegin . . . reminded me, I hardly know why, of The Colleen Bawn. Something in the tailoring, in the scenery, in the sound of the hero's name (pronounced O'Naygin, or, to put it in a still more Irish way, O'Neoghegan) probably combined with the Balfian musical form of the work to suggest this notion to me. There is something Irish, too, as well as Byronic, in the introduction of Eugene as an uncommonly fine fellow when there is not the smallest ground for any such estimate of him. The music suggests a vain regret that Tchaikowsky's remarkable artistic judgment, culture, imaginative vivacity, and self-respect as a musical workman, should have been unaccompanied by any original musical force. For, although I have described the form of the opera as Balfian, it must not therefore be inferred that Tchaikowsky's music is as common as Balfe's—ballads apart—generally was. Tchaikowsky composes with the seriousness of a man who knows how to value himself and his work too well to be capable of padding his opera with the childish claptrap that does duty for dramatic music in The Bohemian Girl. Balfe, whose ballads are better than Tchaikowsky's, never, as far as I know, wrote a whole scene well, whereas in Eugene Onegin there are some scenes, notably those of the letter and the duel, which are very well written, none of them being bungled or faked (factitious is the more elegant expression; but the other is right). The opera, as a whole, is a dignified composition by a man of distinguished talent whose love of music has led him to adopt the profession of composer, and who, with something of his countryman Rubinstein's disposition to make too much of cheap second-hand musical material, has nothing of his diffuseness, his occasional vulgarity, and his incapacity for seeing when to drop a worn-out theme.

The performance, as far as the principals are concerned, is by no means bad. Signor Lago was particularly fortunate in finding to his hand, in Mr Oudin, just the man for Onegin, dark, handsome, distinguished, mysterious-looking—in short, Byronic, and able to behave and to act in a manner worthy of his appearance, which is not always the case with the Don Juans and Corsairs of the stage. Miss Fanny Moody achieved a considerable dramatic success as Tatiana; and it may possibly interest her to learn, on the authority of no less critical a Russian than Stepniak, that she so exactly represented the sort of Russian woman of whom Tatiana is a type, that he is convinced that she would make a success in the part in Russia, even if she sang it in English. To my mind, however, it is a pity that Miss Moody's gifts are so exclusively dramatic. If she were only musical—if she could give that hard, penetrating voice of hers the true lyric grace of execution and beauty of sound as unerringly as she can give it convincing dramatic eloquence, she would be a prima donna in a thousand. Happily for Signor Lago, he could not have chosen a part better calculated than Tatiana to emphasize her power as an actress and cover her want of charm as a vocalist. Mr Manners scored the hit of the evening in a ballad in the last act, the audience being, to tell the truth, greatly relieved after a long spell of Mr Oudin's rather artificial style by the free, natural, sympathetic tone of Mr Manners's voice, which is as sound and powerful as ever. Mr Ivor McKay, having been shot with a terrific bang, produced by a heavy charge of anything but smokeless powder, by Mr Oudin, retired from the tenor part, which is now filled by Mr Wareham: how, I know not. Madame Swiatlowsky is good and very Russian as the nurse; and Mlle Selma fits well into the part of the mother. Miss Lily Moody, a vigorous young lady with a strong mezzo-soprano voice which has not been sweetened by her work as a dramatic contralto, is a somewhat inelegant Olga.

The stage management was, I submit, rather worse than it need have been. Granted that there is nobody capable of making the willing but helpless chorus do anything in the quarrel scene except make it ridiculous, and that the two capital dances are utterly beyond the resources of the establishment, I still think that the gentleman, whoever he was, who loaded that pistol with so fine a feeling for the stage effect of the duel, might, if promoted to the post of chief gasman, manipulate the lights so as to make the change from dark to dawn in the letter scene rather more plausible than on the first night. The dresses were quite good enough for all purposes; but the supply ran short, the dancers at Madame Larina's in Act II reappearing in the same costumes at Prince Germia's in Act III. Onegin fought the duel in a dark coat with two rows of blazing golden buttons, which made him a perfect target; and he would most certainly have been slain if he had not fired first. Years afterwards he came back, a grey-haired man, to make love in that same coat. In fact, Signor Lago might have made a "missing-word competition" out of Onegin's exclamation, "I change from one land to another, but cannot change my ——." The missing word is "heart," but would be guessed as "coat" by nine-tenths of the audience. This scrap from the book reminds me that Mr Sutherland Edwards, who knows Russian, has expiated that unnatural accomplishment by translating the libretto, the most impossible of literary tasks, but one which he has managed, with his usual tact, to accomplish without making himself at all ridiculous. Onegin is now being played three times a week; and it is to be hoped that it will pay its way for the better encouragement of Signor Lago in his policy of bringing forward novelties.

Boito

29 May 1889 (C)

Faust, no matter who writes the music to it, will remain the most popular opera story of the century until some great musician takes Henrik Ibsen's Peer Gynt as a libretto. Boito's version seems almost as popular as Gounod's, though Gounod's is a true musical creation, whereas Boito has only adapted the existing resources of orchestration and harmony very ably to his libretto. In short, Gounod has set music to Faust, and Boito has set Faust to music.

The house likes Boito's prologue, in spite of the empty stage and the two ragged holes in a cloth which realize Mr Harris's modest conception of hell and heaven. The great rolling crashes and echoes of brazen sound in the prelude transport us into illimitable space at once; and the tremendous sonority of the instrumentation at the end, with the defiant devil's whistle recklessly mocking each climax of its grandeur, literally makes us all sit up. Perhaps I am reading into the score what the composer never intended: Boito may have meant no more by the piccolo here than Beethoven meant by it in the last bars of the Egmont overture. If so, that does not invalidate my remark: it only shews how much the critic can add to the work of the composer.

There is a great deal in Mefistofele that is mere impressionism; and like impressionism in painting it is enchanting when it is successful, and nonsensically incoherent when it is the reverse. In the unrestrained colloquialism of private conversation I should not hesitate to describe a good deal of the Brocken scene and some of the rampart scene as ingenious tiddy-fol-lol. The witches' revel, with the spurious fugato at the end, is stuff for a pantomime, not for serious opera. But at innumerable points the music is full of suggestive strokes and colors in sound, happiest sometimes when they are mere inchoate instrumentation. The whole work is a curious example of what can be done in opera by an accomplished literary man without original musical gifts, but with ten times the taste and culture of a musician of only ordinary extraordinariness.

Mascagni

·CAVALLERIA RUSTICANA·

28 October 1891 (I)

If experience had not convinced me these many years that theatre managers of all kinds, and operatic impresari in particular, retain to the end the madness which first led them to their profession, I should be tempted to remonstrate with Signor Lago for getting a good thing like Cavalleria Rusticana, and tying Crispino e la Comare round its neck. As a member of a Northern race, I refuse to have patience with Crispino. Any grasshopper with a moderately good ear could write reams of such stuff after spending three months in Italy. Offenbach's lightest operetta looms in intellectual majesty above this brainless lilting, with its colorless orchestration and its exasperatingly light-hearted and empty-headed recitatives, accompanied by sickly chords on the violoncello with the third always in the bass. Perhaps Coquelin might make the farcical adventures of the shoemaker amusing; but Ciampi is not Coquelin: he is not even Ciampi in his prime. The simple-minded Italians of Soho, if they could obtain a *biglietto d'ingresso* for a shilling, would no doubt bless Signor Lago for restoring to them, in a foreign land, a sort of entertainment which gratifies their love of strumming and singing without for a moment distrubing that sunny stagnation of mind, the least disturbance of which they hate worse than cold baths. But in England the climate, the national character, and the prices of admission, are against such entertainments. When I spoke, last week, of the possibilities of a revival of the old repertory, I was thinking, as far as comic opera is concerned, of such works as Il Barbière, Don Pasquale, Les Deux Journées, Fra Diavolo, or La Grande Duchesse, and by no means of the second-hand wares of Cimarosa or Ricci. The operas which did not cross the Italian frontier when they were young, will not do so now that they are old. I also stipulated that they should be fairly well done; and, to be more particular, I may say that one of the conditions of their well-doing is that the buffo, however comic, shall sing instead of quacking, and that the tenor who revives Come gentil for us shall not have a shattering tremolo. This last remark is not, I assure you, a side-thrust at Crispino, which consists of two hours of Ciampi's buffooneries with no tenor at all, and is, indeed, so childish an affair that I really think that any party of musical boys and girls could improvise something just as clever and funny, just as one improvises a charade or a game of dumb crambo. In a very comfortable country-house (if such a thing exists), or out picnicking in the woods on a summer day, the Crispino style of entertainment would not come amiss; but in a crowded theatre, with one's mind made up to have some value for money paid at the doors, it is not good enough. In all friendliness to Signor Lago's enterprise, I recommend him to get rid of Crispino with all possible expedition, and either to give Cavalleria Rusticana by itself, without any padding, or else have it followed by a single act of one of Wagner's operas, played without cuts. Why not, for instance, the second act of Parsifal?

Of the music of Cavalleria (with the stress on the penultimate vowel, if you please: it is a mistake to suppose that the Italians call it Cavvlearea) I have already intimated that it is only what might reasonably be expected from a clever and spirited member of a generation which has Wagner, Gounod, and Verdi at its fingers' ends, and which can demand, and obtain, larger instrumental resources for a ballet than Mozart had at his disposal for his greatest operas and symphonies. Far more important than that, it has a public trained to endure, and even expect, continuous and passionate melody, instead of the lively little allegros of the old school, which were no more than classically titivated jigs and hornpipes; and to relish the most poignant discords—tonic ninths, elevenths, and thirteenths, taken unprepared in all sorts of inversions (you see, I can be as erudite as anybody else when I choose)—without making a wry face, as their fathers, coddled on the chromatic confectionery of Spohr and his contemporaries, used to do when even a dominant seventh visited their ears too harshly.

Even today you may still see here and there a big, strong, elderly man whimpering when they play the Tannhäuser overture at him, and declaring that there is no "tune" in it, and that the harmony is all discord, and the instrumentation all noise. Our young lions no longer have this infantile squeamishness and petulance to contend with, even in Italy. They may lay about them, harmonically and instrumentally, as hard as they please without rebuke: even the pedants have given up calling on them to observe "those laws of form to which the greatest masters have not disdained to submit"—which means, in effect, to keep Pop Goes the Weasel continually before them as a model of structure and modulation. Consequently, opera now offers to clever men with a turn for music and the drama an unprecedented opportunity for picturesque, brilliant, apt, novel, and yet safely familiar and popular combinations and permutations of the immense store of musical "effects" garnered up in the scores of the great modern composers, from Mozart to Wagner and Berlioz. This is the age of second-hand music. There is even growing up a school of composers who are poets and thinkers rather than musicians, but who have selected music as their means of expression out of the love of it inspired in them by the works of really original masters. It is useless to pretend that Schumann was a creative musician as Mendelssohn was one, or Boito as Verdi, or Berlioz as Gounod. Yet Schumann's setting of certain scenes from Goethe's Faust is enormously more valuable than Mendelssohn's St Paul; we could spare La Traviata better than Mefistofele; whilst Berlioz actually towers above Gounod as a French composer.

And this because, on the non-musical side of their complex art, Mendelssohn and Gounod were often trivial, genteel, or sentimental, and Verdi obvious and melodramatic, whilst Schumann was deeply serious, Berlioz extraordinarily acute in his plans and heroic in his aims, and Boito refined, subtle, and imaginative. The great composer is he who, by the rarest of chances, is at once a great musician and a great poet—who has Brahms's wonderful ear without his commonplace mind, and Molière's insight and imagination without his musical sterility. Thus it is that you get your Mozart or your Wagner—only here we must leave Molière out, as Wagner, on the extra-musical side, is comparable to nobody but himself. The honor of the second place in the hierarchy I shall not attempt to settle. Schumann, Berlioz, Boito, and Raff, borrowing music to express their ideas, have, it must be admitted, sometimes touched an even higher level of originality than Schubert, Mendelssohn, and Goetz, who had to borrow ideas for their music to express, and were unquestionably superior only in the domain of absolute music.

But nobody except the directors of the Philharmonic Society will claim any higher than fourth place for those who have borrowed both their ideas and their music, and vulgarized both in the process—your Bruchs, Rubinsteins, Moszkowskis, Benoits, Ponchiellis, and other gentlemen rather more likely to see this article and get their feelings hurt if I mentioned their names. Brahms, as a unique example of excess in one department and entire deficiency in the other, may take his place where he pleases, provided I am out of earshot of his Requiem.

I offer these illustrations to explain the difference between my critical method and that of the gentlemen who keep only one quality of margarine, which they spread impartially over all composers of established reputation; so that you shall not detect one hair's breadth of difference in their estimates of Beethoven and Meyerbeer, Wagner and Sir Arthur Sullivan, John Sebastian Bach and the President of the Royal Academy of Music. As they speak today of Mascagni, and will speak of Mozart at the forthcoming centenary celebration, they spoke yesterday of Dvorák and Villiers Stanford, four months ago of Handel, and a year ago of Moszkowski and Benoit.

The worst of it is, that the public judgment has become so pauperized by this butter bounty, that although I habitually stretch good-nature to the verge of weakness in extenuating and hushing up all manner of avoidable deficiencies in the performances I criticize, yet I find myself held up as a ruthless and malignant savage because, in spite of all my efforts to be agreeable, a little perspective will occasionally creep into my column, and will betray, for instance, the fact that I consider Ivanhoe as hardly equal in all respects to Lohengrin, and am a little loth to declare offhand that Dr Parry's oratorios are an improvement on Handel's. Some day I think I will go further, and let out the whole truth; for since I get no credit for my forbearance, it often comes into my mind that I may as well be hung for a sheep as a lamb.

All this is a mere preamble to the remark that Mascagni has set Cavalleria Rusticana to expressive and vigorous music, which music he has adapted to the business of the stage with remarkable judgment and good sense. That is the exact truth about it; and so, Mascagni being disposed of with this very considerable eulogy (implying that he is a man in a thousand, though not in a million), I go on to say that Vignas, the tenor, is completely satisfactory, both as a singer and actor, in the part of Turiddu; that there is no fault to be found with Mlle Brema and Miss Damian in the mezzo-soprano and contralto parts; that Signorina Musiani, who is not a bit older or stouter than Miss Eames, has some genuine pathos and a voice of fine natural quality to offer as a set-off to a rather serious tremolo; and that Signor Brombara is so afflicted with the same complaint that he would be better advised to resort to dumb show, since he acts with much conviction.

Puccini

23 May 1894 (III)

I have been to the Opera six times; and I still live. What is more, I am positively interested and hopeful. Hitherto I have had only one aim as regards Italian opera: not, as some have supposed, to kill it, for it was dead already, but to lay its ghost. It was a troublesome phantom enough. When one felt sure that it had been effectually squeezed out at last by French opera, or Hebraic opera, or what may be called operatic music-drama—Lohengrin, for instance—it would turn up again trying to sing Spirto gentil in the manner of Mario, raving through the mad scene in Lucia amid childish orchestral tootlings, devastating Il Trovatore with a totally obsolete style of representation, or in some way gustily rattling its unburied bones and wasting the manager's money and my patience.

The difficulty was to convince those who had been brought up to believe in it (as I was myself) that it was all over with it: they *would* go on believing that it only needed four first-rate Italian singers to bring the good old times back again and make the rum-tum rhythms, the big guitar orchestration, the florid cabalettas, the cavatinas in regular four-bar lines, the choruses in thirds and sixths, and all the rest of it swell out to their former grandeur and sweep Wagner off the boards. I have no doubt they believe it as devoutly as ever, and that if Mr Mapleson were to start again tomorrow, he would announce Lucia and Il Barbiere and Semiramide with unshaken confidence in their freshness and adequacy, perhaps adding, as a concession to the public demand for novelty, a promise of Ponchielli's La Gioconda.

But now an unlooked-for thing has happened. Italian opera has been born again. The extirpation of the Rossinian dynasty, which neither Mozart nor Wagner could effect, since what they offered in its place was too far above the heads of both the public and the artists, is now being accomplished with ease by Mascagni, Leoncavallo, Puccini, and Verdi. Nobody has ever greeted a performance of Tristan und Isolde by such a remark as "We shall never be able to go back to L'Elisire d'Amore after this," or declare that Lucrezia was impossible

307

after Brynhild. The things were too far apart to affect one another: as well might be supposed that Ibsen's plays could be accepted as a substitute for popular melodrama, or Shakespear wean people from the circus. It is only by an advance in melodrama itself or in circuses themselves that the melodrama or circus of today can become unpresentable to the audiences of ten years hence.

The same thing is true of Italian opera. The improvement of higher forms of art, or the introduction of new forms at a different level, cannot affect it at all; and that is why Tristan has no more killed L'Elisire than Brahms' symphonies have killed Jullien's British Army Quadrilles. But the moment you hear Pagliacci, you feel that it is all up with L'Elisire. It is true that Leoncavallo has shewn as yet nothing comparable to the melodic inspiration of Donizetti; but the advance in serious workmanship, in elaboration of detail, in variety of interest, and in capital expenditure on the orchestra and the stage, is enormous. There is more work in the composition of Cavalleria than in La Favorita, Lucrezia, and Lucia put together, though I cannot think—perhaps this is only my own old-fashionedness—that any part of it will live as long or move the world as much as the best half-dozen numbers in those three obsolete masterpieces.

And when you come to Puccini, the composer of the latest Manon Lescaut, then indeed the ground is so transformed that you could almost think yourself in a new country. In Cavalleria and Pagliacci I can find nothing but Donizettian opera rationalized, condensed, filled in, and thoroughly brought up to date; but in Manon Lescaut the domain of Italian opera is enlarged by an annexation of German territory. The first act, which is as gay and effective and romantic as the opening of any version of Manon need be, is also unmistakeably symphonic in its treatment. There is genuine symphonic modification, development, and occasionally combination of the thematic material, all in a dramatic way, but also in a musically homogeneous way, so that the act is really a single movement with episodes instead of being a succession of separate numbers, linked together, to conform to the modern fashion, by substituting interrupted cadences for full closes and parading a Leitmotif occasionally.

Further, the experiments in harmony and syncopation, reminding one often of the intellectual curiosities which abound in Schumann's less popular pianoforte works, shew a strong technical interest which is, in Italian music, a most refreshing symptom of mental vigor, even when it is not strictly to the real artistic point. The less studied harmonies are of the most modern and stimulating kind. When one thinks of the old school, in which a dominant seventh, or at most a minor ninth, was the extreme of permissible discord, only to be tolerated in the harsher inversions when there was a murder or a ghost on hand, one gets a rousing sense of getting along from hearing young Italy beginning its most light-hearted melodies to the chord of the thirteenth on the tonic.

Puccini is particularly fond of this chord; and it may be taken as a general technical criticism of the young Italian school that its free use of tonic discords, and its reckless prodigality of orchestral resources, give its music a robustness and variety that reduce the limited tonic and dominant harmonic technique of Donizetti and Bellini, by contrast, to mere Christy minstrelsy. No doubt this very poverty of the older masters made them so utterly dependent on the invention of tunes that they invented them better than the new men, who, with a good drama to work on, can turn out vigorous, imposing, and even enthralling operas without a bar that is their own in the sense in which Casta Diva is Bellini's own; but Puccini, at least, shews no signs of atrophy of the melodic faculty: he breaks out into catching melodies quite in the vein of Verdi: for example, Tra voi, belle, in the first act of Manon, has all the charm of the tunes beloved by the old operatic guard.

On that and other accounts, Puccini looks to me more like the heir of Verdi than any of his rivals. He has arranged his own libretto from Prevost d'Exiles' novel; and though the miserable end of poor Manon has compelled him to fall back on a rather conventional operatic death scene in which the prima donna at Covent Garden failed to make anyone believe, his third act, with the roll-call of the female convicts and the embarkation, is admirably contrived and carried out: he has served himself in this as well as Scribe ever served Meyerbeer, or Boito Verdi.

If now it is considered that this opening week at Covent Garden began with Manon, and ended with Falstaff; Cavalleria and Pagliacci coming in between, with nothing older than Faust and Carmen to fill up except the immortal Orfeo, it will be understood how I find myself with the startling new idea that Italian opera has a future as well as a past, and that perhaps Sir Augustus Harris, in keeping a house open for it, has not been acting altogether as an enemy of the human race, as I used sometimes to declare in my agony when in a moment of relenting towards that dreary past, he would let loose some stout matron to disport herself once more as Favorita, or spend untold gold in indulging Jean de Reszke with a revival of that concentrated bore and outrage, Le Prophète, when I wanted to see the prince of tenors and procrastinators as Siegfried or Tristan.

Strauss

· ELEKTRA ·

12 March 1910 (*)

Sir,—May I, as an old critic of music, and a member of the public who has not yet heard Elektra, make an appeal to Mr Ernest Newman† to give us something about that work a little less ridiculous and idiotic than his article in your last issue? I am sorry to use [such] disparaging and apparently uncivil epithets as "ridiculous and idiotic"; but what else am I to call an article which informs us, first, that Strauss does not know the difference between music and "abominable ugliness and noise"; and, second, that he is the greatest living musician of the greatest school of music the world has produced? I submit that this is ridiculous, inasmuch as it makes us laugh at Mr Newman, and idiotic because it unhesitatingly places the judgment of the writer above that of one whom he admits to be a greater authority than himself, thus assuming absolute knowledge in the matter. This is precisely what "idiotic" means.

Pray do not let me be misunderstood as objecting to Mr Newman describing how Elektra affected him. He has not, perhaps, as much right to say that it seemed ugly and nonsensical to him (noise, applied to music, can only mean nonsense, because in any other sense all music is noise) as Haydn had to say similar things of Beethoven's music, because Haydn was himself an eminent composer; still, he is perfectly in order in telling us honestly how ill Elektra pleased him, and not pretending he liked it lest his opinion should come to be regarded later on as we now regard his early opinion of Wagner. But he should by this time have been cured by experience and reflection of the trick that makes English criticism so dull and insolent—the trick, namely, of asserting that everything that does not please him is wrong, not only technically but ethically. Mr Newman, confessing that he did not enjoy and could not see the sense of a good

†On 26 February, 1910, Ernest Newman published an attack on Richard Strauss' *Elektra* in *The Nation* which elicited a response from Shaw. Newman's side of the argument is summarized by Dan H. Laurence in *How to Become a Musical Critic.*

deal of Elektra, is a respectable, if pathetic, figure; but Mr Newman treating Strauss as a moral and musical delinquent is—well, will Mr Newman himself supply the missing word, for really I cannot find one that is both adequate and considerate?

When my Candida was performed for the first time in Paris, the late Catulle Mendès was one of its critics. It affected him very much as Elektra affected Mr Newman. But he did not immediately proceed, English fashion, to demonstrate that I am a perverse and probably impotent imbecile (London criticism has not stopped short of this), and to imply that if I had submitted my play to his revision he could have shewn me how to make it perfect. He wrote to this effect: "I have seen this play. I am aware of the author's reputation, and of the fact that reputations are not to be had for nothing. I find that the play has a certain air of being a remarkable work and of having something in it which I cannot precisely seize; but I do not like it, and I cannot pretend that it gave me any sensation except one of being incommoded." Now that is what I call thoughtful and well-bred criticism, in contradistinction to ridiculous and idiotic criticism as practiced in England. Mr Newman has no right to say that Elektra is absolutely and objectionably ugly, because it is not ugly to Strauss and to his admirers. He has no right to say that it is incoherent nonsense, because such a statement implies that Strauss is mad, and that Hofmannsthal and Mr Beecham, with the artists who are executing the music, and the managers who are producing it, are insulting the public by offering them the antics of a lunatic as serious art. He has no right to imply that he knows more about Strauss's business technically than Strauss himself. These restrictions are no hardship to him; for nobody wants him to say any of these things: they are not criticism; they are not good manners nor good sense; and they take up the space that is available in The Nation for criticism proper; and criticism proper can be as severe as the critic likes to make it. There is no reason why Mr Newman should not say with all possible emphasis—if he is unlucky enough to be able to say so truly—that he finds Strauss's music disagreeable and cacophonous; that he is unable to follow its harmonic syntax; that the composer's mannerisms worry him; and that, for his taste, there is too much restless detail, and that the music is over-scored (too many notes, as the Emperor said to Mozart). He may, if he likes, go on to denounce the attractiveness of Strauss's music as a public danger, like the attraction of morphia; and to diagnose the cases of Strauss and

Hofmannstahl as psychopathic or neurasthenic, or whatever the appropriate scientific slang may be, and descant generally on the degeneracy of the age in the manner of Dr Nordau. Such diagnoses, when supported by an appeal to the symptoms made with real critical power and ingenuity, might be interesting and worth discussing. But this lazy petulance which has disgraced English journalism in the forms of anti-Wagnerism, anti-Ibsenism, and, long before that, anti-Handelism (now remembered only by Fielding's contemptuous reference to it in Tom Jones); this infatuated attempt of writers of modest local standing to talk *de haut en bas* to men of European reputation, and to dismiss them as intrusive lunatics, is an intolerable thing, an exploded thing, a foolish thing, a parochial boorish thing, a thing that should be dropped by all good critics and discouraged by all good editors as bad form, bad manners, bad sense, bad journalism, bad politics, and bad religion. Though Mr Newman is not the only offender, I purposely select his article as the occasion of a much needed protest, because his writings on music are distinguished enough to make him worth powder and shot. I can stand almost anything from Mr Newman except his posing as Strauss's governess; and I hope he has sufficient sense of humor to see the absurdity of it himself, now that he has provoked a quite friendly colleague to this yell of remonstrance.—Yours, & c.,

G. Bernard Shaw.

19 March 1910 (*)

Sir,—It is our good fortune to have produced in Professor Gilbert Murray a writer and scholar able to raise the Electra of Euripides from the dead and make it a living possession for us. Thanks to him, we know the poem as if it were an English one. But nothing Professor Murray can do ever make us feel quite as the Electra of Euripides felt about her mother's neglect to bury her father properly after murdering him. A heroine who feels that to commit murder, even husband murder, is a thing that might happen to anybody, but that to deny the victim a proper funeral is an outrage so unspeakable that it becomes her plain filial duty to murder her mother in expiation, is outside that touch of nature that makes all the ages akin: she is really too early-Victorian. To us she is more unnatural than Clytemnestra of Ægisthus; and, in the end, we pity them and secretly shrink from their slayers. What Hofmannstahl and Strauss have done is to take Clytemnestra and Ægisthus, and by identifying them with everything that is evil and cruel, with all that needs must hate the highest when it sees it, with hideous domination and coercion of the higher by the baser, with the murderous rage in which the lust for a lifetime of orgiastic pleasure turns on its slaves in the torture of its disappointment and the sleepless horror and misery of its neurasthenia, to so rouse in us an overwhelming flood of wrath against it and ruthless resolution to destroy it, that Electra's vengeance becomes holy to us; and we come to understand how even the gentlest of us could wield the axe of Orestes or twist our firm fingers in the black hair of Clytemnestra to drag back her head and leave her throat open to the stroke.

That was a task hardly possible to an ancient Greek, and not easy even to us who are face to face with the America of the Thaw case,† and the European plutocracy of which that case was only a trifling symptom. And that is the task which Hofmannstahl and Strauss have achieved. Not even in the third scene of Das Rheingold, or in the Klingsor scenes in Parsifal, is there such an atmosphere of malignant and cancerous evil as we get here. And that the power with which it is done is not the power of the evil itself, but of the passion that detests and must and finally can destroy that evil, is what makes the work great, and makes us rejoice in its horror.

Whoever understands this, however vaguely, will understand Strauss's music, and why on Saturday night the crowded house burst into frenzied shoutings, not merely of applause, but of strenuous assent and affirmation, as the curtain fell. That the power of conceiving it should occur in the same individual as the technical skill and natural faculty needed to achieve its complete and overwhelming expression in music is a stroke of the rarest good fortune that can befall a generation of men. I have often said, when asked to state the case against the fools and money changers who are trying to drive us into a war with Germany, that the case consists of the single word, Beethoven. Today I should say, with equal confidence, Strauss. That we should make war on Strauss and the heroic warfare and aspiration that he represents is treason to humanity. In this music-drama Strauss has done for us just what he has done for his own countrymen: he has said for us, with an utterly satisfying force, what all the

---

†In 1906 Henry Thaw shot the architect, Stanford White, alleging that White had seduced his wife. Several sensational trials followed.

noblest powers of life within us are clamoring to have said, in protest against and defiance of the omnipresent villainies of our civilization; and this is the highest achievement of the highest art.

It was interesting to compare our conductor, the gallant Beecham, bringing out the points in Strauss's orchestration, until sometimes the music sounded like a concerto for six drums, with Strauss himself, bringing out the meaning and achieving the purpose of his score so that we forgot that there was an orchestra there at all, and could hear nothing but the conflict and storm of passion. Human emotion is a complex thing: there are moments when our feeling is so deep and our ecstasy so exalted that the primeval monsters from whom we are evolved wake within us and utter the strange tormented cries of their ancient struggles with the Life Force. All this is in Elektra; and under the *bâton* of Strauss the voices of these epochs are kept as distinct in their unity as the parts in a Bach motet. Such colossal counterpoint is a counterpoint of all the ages; not even Beethoven in his last great Mass comprehended so much. The feat is beyond all verbal description: it must be heard and felt; and even then, it seems, you must watch and pray, lest your God should forget you, and leave you to hear only "abominable ugliness and noise," and, on remonstrance, lead you to explain handsomely that Strauss is "vulgar, and stupid, and ugly" only "sometimes," and that this art of his is so "ridiculously easy" that nothing but your own self-respect prevents you from achieving a European reputation by condescending to practice it.

So much has been said of the triumphs of our English singers in Elektra that I owe it to Germany to profess my admiration of the noble beauty and power of Frau Fassbender's Elektra. Even if Strauss's work were the wretched thing poor Mr Newman mistook it for, it would still be worth a visit to Covent Garden to see her wonderful death dance, which was the climax of one of the most perfect examples yet seen in London of how, by beautiful and eloquent gesture, movement, and bearing, a fine artist can make not only her voice, but her body, as much a part of a great music-drama as any instrument in the score. The other German artists, notably Frau Bahr-Midlenburg, shewed great power and accomplishment; but they have received fuller acknowledgment, whereas we should not have gathered from the reports that Frau Fassbender's performance was so extraordinary as it actually was. A deaf man could have listened to her. To those of us who are neither deaf nor blind nor anti-Straussian critics (which is the same thing), she was a superb Elektra.

Whatever may be the merits of the article which gave rise to the present correspondence, it is beyond question that it left the readers of The Nation without the smallest hint that the occasion was one of any special importance, or that it was at all worth their while to spend time and money in supporting Mr Beecham's splendid enterprise, and being present on what was, in fact, a historic moment in the history of art in England, such as may not occur again within our lifetime. Many persons may have been, and possibly were, prevented by that article from seizing their opportunity, not because Mr Newman does not happen to like Strauss's music, but because he belittled the situation by so miscalculating its importance that he did not think it worth even the effort of criticizing it, and dismissed it in a notice in which nothing was studied except his deliberate contemptuous insolence to the composer. It would have been an additional insult to Strauss to have waited to hear Elektra before protesting, on the plainest grounds of international courtesy and artistic good faith, against such treatment of the man who shares with Rodin the enthusiastic gratitude and admiration of the European republic, one and indivisible, of those who understand the highest art. But now that I have heard Elektra, I have a new duty to the readers of The Nation, and that is to take upon me the work Mr Newman should have done, and put them in possession of the facts.

And now, Ernest, *"Triff noch einmal"*!—Yours, & c.,

G. Bernard Shaw.

PART FOUR

English Music

Mediaeval
and Renaissance

7 February 1897 (III)

There has been a general clearing out from the hall of Barnard's Inn, the Art Workers' Guild betaking themselves to Clifford's Inn, and the whilom tenant, Mr Arnold Dolmetsch, falling back with his viols and virginals on Dowland, his own house at Dulwich. Here he opened his spring campaign on Tuesday last week with a concert of English sixteenth-century music, including a couple of pieces by Henry VIII which did more to rehabilitate that monarch in my estimation than all the arguments of Mr Froude. Sheryngam's dialogue, Ah, Gentill Jhesu, set for four voices, four viols, and organ, belongs to fifteenth-century art: it has all the naïveté, the conscientious workmanship, the deep expression, and the devout beauty of that period. The dialogue is between the Gentill Jhesu and a sinner.

From the Renascence right down to the last provincial Festival, the distinction made between two such persons would have exactly reflected the distinction between a university graduate with a handsome independent income, and a poor tradesman or other comparatively unpresentable person. The essentially medieval character of Sheryngam's work comes out in its entire freedom from this very vulgar convention. His art is as void of the gentility and intellectual ambition of the Renascence as Van Eyck's pictures are. Later on in the concert we got into the atmosphere of the sixteenth and seventeenth centuries.

The pieces by Byrd and Morley, played upon the virginals by Mr Fuller Maitland, differed, after all, only in fashion from airs by Rossini with variations by Thalberg. Some of the variations which made the greatest demands on Mr Maitland's dexterity and swiftness of hand did not contain from beginning to end as much feeling as a single progression of Schumann's. Others were pretty and lively; and the airs were tender enough. But when the corner is turned and the middle ages left behind, that charm that is akin to the charm of childhood or old age is left behind too; and thenceforth only the man of genius has any power. Once my bare historical curiosity has been satisfied, I do not value the commonplaces of *circa* 1600 a bit more than the commonplaces of *circa* 1900.

I hope, therefore, that Mr Dolmetsch will dig up plenty of genuine medieval music for us. The post-Renascence part of his scheme (which will deal mainly with great individuals like Lock, Purcell, Handel, and Bach) is unexceptionable. There will be eight concerts altogether, including some devoted to Italian and French music. The quality of the performances, which has always been surprisingly good, considering the strangeness of the instruments, continues to improve. The vocal music is still the main difficulty. The singers, with their heads full of modern "effects," shew but a feeble sense of the accuracy of intonation and tenderness of expression required by the pure vocal harmonies of the old school. Without a piano to knock their songs into them they seem at a loss; and the only vocalist whom I felt inclined to congratulate was a counter-tenor, the peculiarity of whose voice had saved him from the lot of the drawing-room songster.

Mr Dolmetsch himself seems to have increased his command of the lute, a villainously difficult instrument. None of the concerted pieces were so well executed as the two "fantazies" for treble and tenor viols which he played with Miss Helène Dolmetsch; but the three other violists, Messrs Boxall and Milne and Miss Milne, acquitted themselves creditably.

Purcell

4 March 1894 (III)

Mr Dolmetsch's concert interested me especially because it gave us a chance of hearing the chamber music of Matthew Lock, the last English musician who composed for the viols, and the founder of my school of musical criticism. His denunciation of the academic professors of his day is quite in my best manner. Lock's Macbeth used to be known to everybody: whether it is so now I cannot say; but nothing was more firmly hammered into my head when I was a child than the certainty that Macbeth would spill much more blood, and become worse to make his title good. Later on I learnt that Lock had not composed the Macbeth music, a manuscript score of it in the handwriting of Purcell (aged fourteen) having turned up.

Presently, when someone unearths the copies made of Beethoven's symphonies and posthumous quartets by Wagner in his boyhood, we shall all agree that Wagner was the real composer of these works. As a mater of fact, Lock's temperament was about as like Purcell's as Bach's was like Mozart's, or Michael Angelo's like Raphael's. If Purcell had lived to be seventy he would have been younger at that age than Lock was at twenty. If I had a good orchestra and choir at my disposal, as Mr Henschel has, I would give a concert consisting of Purcell's Yorkshire Feast and the last act of Die Meistersinger. Then the public could judge whether Purcell was really [as great a composer] as some people (including myself) assert that he was.

Mr Dolmetsch has taken up an altogether un-English position in this matter. He says, "Purcell was a great composer: let us perform some of his works." The English musicians say, "Purcell was a great composer: let us go and do Mendelssohn's Elijah over again and make the lord-lieutenant of the county chairman of the committee"—an even more intolerable conclusion than Christopher Sly's, "Tis a very excellent piece of work: would twere over," which I am afraid is exactly what most of us say to ourselves at performances of the Ninth Symphony. Mr Dolmetsch gave us the Golden Sonata, some harpsichord lessons, and several songs, one of which, Winter, created quite a burst of enthusiasm by the beauty of its harmony, which Brahms himself, in his very different way, could not have surpassed for richness, much less for eloquence.

The concert wound up with Let the dreadful engines, the finest humorous bass air I know, excepting only Madamina, and not excepting Osmin's songs from Die Entführung aus dem Serail, or even O ruddier than the cherry. It was sung with much spirit and success by Mr Albert Fairbairn, who only needs a somewhat lighter and freer vocal touch to make him a valuable bass singer. So good a voice as his does not need to be ground out as he is apt to grind it. The first part of the program was perhaps the more important, as the quality of Purcell's genius is so much better known than that of Lock's. Lock came at a time when musicians had neither given up counterpoint nor taken to the endless repetitions, sequences, and rosalias, the crescendos, doubles and redoubles, of the operatic instrumental style, the absurdity of which culminated in that immortal composition, the overture to Zampa.

In the pieces selected by Mr Dolmetsch, Lock steers equally clear of the hackneyed imitative entries of the old school and the overdoing of the rosalias of the new. He had not, it seems to me, the delicate poetic sense or dramatic vivacity of Purcell and Mozart, nor the deep feeling of Bach: indeed, I rather doubt whether he was much more "passion's slave" than the elegant Ferdinand Hiller; but he had a depth of musical sense, and a certain force of intelligence and character which enabled him to compose in a genuinely masterly way. The organ fugue which Mr Dolmetsch played had not the gigantic energy and mass of a Bach fugue; but its inferiority was much more one of dimension only than one would have expected: its difference, as distinguished from its inferiority, lay in its intention, which was less exalted than Bach's, but also more captivating to people in search of musical pastime. Its decorative passages were fresh, ingenious, original, and, to my ear, very pretty.

I should perhaps apologize for having devoted so much space to a concert of English music given by a foreigner, when I have on hand plenty of concerts of foreign music given by Englishmen. But if anyone, however unpatriotic, will face the fact that up to the time of Purcell nobody ever supposed that the English were less musical than other people, and that since then they have been blotted out of the music-map of Europe, he cannot but feel curious as to whether any change occurred in the construction of the English ear at the end of the seventeenth century. But that was not what happened; for there were a few later Englishmen—Pearsall, for instance—who took the old school for their starting-point, and shewed that the musical powers of the nation were still as robust as ever.

What broke up English music was opera. The Englishman is musical, but he is not operatic; and since during the last two centuries music has been so confounded with opera that even instrumental music has been either opera without words or else the expression in tone of a sort of poetry which the English express with great mastery in spoken verse, our composers have been able to do nothing but abjectly imitate foreign models: for instance, Sterndale Bennett and Mendelssohn, Bishop and Mozart, Crotch and Handel. It seemed on the point of ending in our being able to compose nothing but analytic programs of foreign masterpieces, when opera, providentially, began to die of its own absurdity, and music at once shewed signs of reviving. Now I am convinced that in this revival the old music must serve as a startingpoint, just as thirteenth-century work has served, and is serving, in modern revivals of the other arts. That is why I attach such importance to these concerts of Mr Dolmetsch, which are, besides, highly enjoyable both to experts in music and to the ordinary Englishman who, with every respect for "classical music," has deep down in his breast a rooted belief (which I rather share) that three-quarters of an hour is too long for any one instrumental composition to last.

In this connection let me hail with three times three the proposal of Mr Fuller Maitland and Mr Barclay Squire to republish in modern notation, but otherwise without addition or omission, that treasure of the Fitzwilliam Museum at Cambridge, Queen Elizabeth's Virginal Book, so called because, as it contains several pieces which were not composed until after Queen Elizabeth's death, it could not possibly have belonged to her. The editors, who are, as far as I know, the two most competent men in England for the work, will issue it as The Fitzwilliam Virginal Book. It contains nearly three hundred pieces, many of them of great beauty, and all, at this time of day, of some interest. The publication, through Messrs Breitkopf & Härtel, will be by thirty-six monthly parts, costing, by subscription, thirty shillings a year, or, separately, three shillings apiece. As the enterprise is one of enthusiasm and not of commerce, and the editors will probably wish they had never been born before it is completed, I recommend it confidently to the support, not only of musicians, but of those who are in the habit of buying three new waltzes every month, and are consequently beginning to feel the want of some music that they have never heard before.

· DIDO AND ÆNEAS ·

21 February 1889 (C)

Dido and Eneas is 200 years old, and not a bit the worse for wear. I daresay many of the Bowegians† thought that the unintentional quaintnesses of the amateurs in the orchestra were Purcellian antiquities. If so, they were never more mistaken in their lives. Henry Purcell was a great composer: a very great composer indeed; and even this little boarding-school opera is full of his spirit, his freshness, his dramatic expression, and his unapproached art of setting English speech to music. The Handel Society did not do him full justice: the work in fact is by no means easy; but the choir made up bravely for the distracting dances of the string quartet. Eneas should not have called Dido Deedo, any more than Juliet should call Romeo Ro-*may*-oh, or Othello call his wife Days-*day*-mona. If Purcell chose to pronounce Dido English fashion, it is not for a Bow-Bromley tenor to presume to correct him. Belinda, too, was careless in the matter of time. She not only arrived after her part had been half finished by volunteers from the choir, but in Oft She Visits she lost her place somewhat conspicuously. An unnamed singer took Come away, fellow sailors, come away: that salt sea air that makes you wonder how anyone has ever had the face to compose another sailor's song after it. I quote the concluding lines, and wish I could quote the incomparably jolly and humorous setting:—

> Take a bowsy short leave of your nymphs on the shore;
> > And silence their mourning
> > With vows of returning,
> Though never intending to visit them more.

SAILORS (*greatly tickled*). Though never—!
OTHER SAILORS (*ready to burst with laughter*). Though never—!
ALL (*uproariously*). Inte-en-ding to vi-isit them more.

---

†Shaw's humorous name for the inhabitants of Bow, in East London.

I am sorry to have to add that the Handel choir, feeling that they were nothing if not solemn, contrived to subdue this rousing strain to the decorum of a Sunday school hymn; and it missed fire accordingly. Of Alexander's Feast I need only say that I enjoyed it thoroughly, even though I was sitting on a cane-bottomed chair (Thackeray overrated this description of furniture) without adequate room for my knees. The band, reinforced by wind and organ, got through with a healthy roughness that refreshed me; and the choruses were capital. Mr Bantock Pierpoint, the bass, covered himself with merited glory, and Mr John Probert would have been satisfactory had he been more consistently careful of his intonation. Miss Fresselle acquitted herself fairly; but her singing is like that of the society generally: it lacks point and color. Mr Docker must cure his singers of the notion that choral singing is merely a habit caught in church, and that it is profane and indecorous to sing Handel's music as if it meant anything. That, however, is the worst I have to say of them. I am, in the whole, surprised and delighted with the East end, and shall soon venture there without my revolver. At the end of the concert, a gentleman, to my entire stupefaction, came forward and moved a vote of thanks to the performers. It was passed by acclamation, but without musical honors.

Sullivan

The Scots Observer, 6 September 1890 (*)

If a boy wishes to waste his life by taking himself too seriously, he cannot do better than get educated in a cathedral choir with a view to winning the Mendelssohn Scholarship and devoting himself thenceforth to the cultivation of high-class music. Once fortified with a degree of Mus. Bac. and a calm confidence in his power to write a Magnificat in eight real parts, to "analyze" the last movement of the Jupiter Symphony, and to mention at any moment the birthday of Orlandus Lassus, he enters life as a gentleman and a scholar, with a frightful contempt for Offenbach and a deep sense of belonging to the same artistic caste as Handel. Not that he thinks himself as good a man as Handel; but his modesty is of the *anch'io son pittore* kind—for he, too, can write a fugue. Presently he finds that nobody wants fugues—that they are never asked for, nor properly relished when offered gratuitously. Publishers issue them at the composer's expense only: a rule which applies also to Magnificats, Tantum Ergos, and other fearful wild-fowl. He begins to feel the force of that old professorial "wheeze": "Learn to write a fugue; and then dont do it." Hereupon he asks himself, How is a man to live? Well, there are still young people who have not yet realized the situation; and these want to be taught to write fugues. Accordingly, the Mus. Bac. takes pupils and a church organ, which is a highly serious instrument, lending itself to counterpoint by its construction, and reserved for music of the exclusive kind—Jackson in B flat, Goss in F, Handel's anthems, and the like. Then, there is the prospect of promotion to a church with an important musical service, perhaps to a cathedral. The provincial festivals may commission an oratorio once in twenty years or so; and the Philharmonic might even rise—(such things have been!)—at an overture. An occasional Christmas carol (or even anthem) to keep one's hand in is sure, on attaining a hearing in his own choir, to create that acceptable awe with which an impressionable public regards the man who understands the "theory of music."

This is no bad life for one whose turn for music does not include inventiveness, nor grace of workmanship, nor humor (creative originality is here left out of account, as it must always fight and conquer as best it can). But if he has these three gifts, his proper sphere is the theatre—not the "Royal Italian Opera," but the Savoy, the Prince of Wales, and the Lyric. Now the pedigree of such houses will not bear investigation: in vain do they imply that they are first cousins to the Opéra Comique: their common and all-too immediate ancestor was the Bouffes Parisiennes; and he who composes for them must risk being cut by the decorous and eminently gentlemanly remnant of the Sterndale Bennett set, and must mix with that of the profane and scandalous Offenbach. Anyone who knows the number of foot-pounds of respectability under which an organist lies flattened can imagine the superhuman courage required for such an act of self-declassation. Not even the present writer, though shrouded in anonymity and wholly independent of the organ, dares positively assert that Offenbach was a much greater composer than Sterndale Bennett, although he submits that the fact is obvious. Grove's Dictionary of Music gives nine columns of eulogy, tombstone-like in its fervor and solemnity, to Bennett; whilst Offenbach has one shamefaced column, recalling by its tone an unspeakable passage in Robertson's history of Queen Mary, in which apology is made for the deplorable necessity of mentioning one so far beneath the dignity of history as Rizzio. Grove—the institution, not the individual Sir George—owes it to society not to mention that La Grande Duchesse, as an original complete work of art, places its composer heavens high above the superfine academician who won rest and self-complacency as a superior person by doing for Mendelssohn what Pasteur has done for the hydrophobia virus, and who by example and precept urged his pupils never to strive after effect. This counsel, worthy of the best form of Mrs General, was not only, as Wagner remarked, "all very well, but rather negative": it was also a rebuke to Offenbach, who was always striving after effect, as every artist who is not ashamed of his calling must unceasingly strive from his cradle to his grave.

The reader is now in a position to understand the tragedy of Sir Arthur Sullivan. He was a Mendelssohn Scholar. He was an organist (St Somebody's, Chester-square). He wrote a symphony. He composed overtures, cantatas, oratorios. His masters were Goss and Sterndale Bennett himself. Of Magnificats he is guiltless; but two Te Deums and about a dozen anthems are among the fruits of his efforts to avoid the achievement of an effect. He has shewn his reverence for the classics in the usual way by writing "additional accompaniments" to Handel's Jephtha; and now he has five columns in Grove and is a knight. What more could a serious musician desire? Alas! the same question might have been put to Tannhäuser at the singing-bee in the Wartburg, before he broke out with his unholy longing for Venus. Offenbach was Sullivan's Venus as Mendelssohn was his St Elizabeth. He furtively set Box and Cox† to music in 1869, and then, overcome with remorse, produced Onward, Christian Soldiers and over three dozen hymns besides. As the remorse mellowed, he composed a group of songs—Let Me Dream Again, Thou'rt Passing Hence, Sweethearts, and My Dearest Heart—all of the very best in their *genre*, such as it is. And yet in the very thick of them he perpetrated Trial by Jury, in which he outdid Offenbach in wickedness, and that too without any prompting from the celebrated cynic, Mr W. S. Gilbert. When Offenbach wrote Orphée aux Enfers he certainly burlesqued *le classique*; but he spared Gluck: it is no parody of *Che faro* that he introduces in the Olympus scene, but the veritable air itself; and when some goddess—Diana?—says an affectionate word of recognition, one feels that for the moment *opéra bouffe* has softened—has taken off its hat to the saintly days of yore. But Sullivan wantonly burlesqued *D' un pensiero* in the quintet with chorus beginning A nice dilemma. Had it been *Chi mi frena* or *Un di si ben* one might have laughed; but the innocent, tender, touching, beloved-from-of-old *D' un pensiero*! Nobody but an irreclaimable ribald would have selected that for his gibes. Sullivan murdered his better nature with this crime. He rose to eloquence again for a moment in setting certain words—

> I have sought, but I seek it vainly,
> That one lost chord divine.

No wonder. This was in 1877, when he was thirtyfive. But no retreat was possible after A Nice Dilemma: not even a visit from the ghost of Sterndale Bennett could have waved him back from the Venusberg then. The Sorcerer belongs to 1877 as well as The Lost Chord; and everybody knows Pinafore and The Gondoliers and all that between them is; so that now the first of the Mendelssohn Scholars stands convicted of ten godless mockeries of everything sacred to Goss and Bennett. They trained him to make Europe yawn; and he took ad-

---

†A highly popular farce by John Morton (1847).

vantage of their teaching to make London and New York laugh and whistle.

A critic with no sense of decency might say out loud that in following Offenbach Sir Arthur has chosen the better part. The Mendelssohn school—with all its superficiality of conception, its miserable failure to comprehend Beethoven or even Weber, and the gentlemanlike vapidity which it deliberately inculcated as taste, discretion, reticence, chastity, refinement, finish, and what not—did undoubtedly give its capable pupils good mechanical skill. Their workmanship is plausible and elegant—just what it should be in comic opera. And the workmanship of our comic operas is often abominable. The technical work of Planquette, for instance, compared to that of Sullivan and Cellier, is crude, illiterate, hopelessly inept. Auber himself could not have written the concerted music in Patience or Pinafore without more effort than it is worth. The question remains, would the skill that produced these two works have been more worthily employed upon another oratorio, another cantata? When all our musicians are brought to their last account, will Sullivan dissemble the score of the Pirates with a blush and call on the mountains to cover him, whilst Villiers Stanford and Hubert Parry table The Revenge, Prometheus Unbound, and Judith with pride? With which note of interrogation let us pass.

· GILBERT AND SULLIVAN ·

13 December 1889 (C)

The past week has, I believe, been a busy one for the musical critics. It has certainly been a busy one for me, but not musically: I have not even been to the Savoy opera. The first night I have to spare, I shall—but stop! I have not seen the Dead Heart yet, nor La Tosca, nor A Man's Shadow. So let us fix the fourth night I have to spare for The Gondoliers. It will probably come about Easter, or if not then, towards the end of August.

Do not be disappointed at this, eager reader. A new Savoy opera is an event of no greater artistic significance than—to take the most flattering comparison—a new oratorio by Gounod. We know the exact limits of Mr Gilbert's and Sir Arthur Sullivan's talents by this time, as well as we know the width of the Thames at Waterloo Bridge; and I am just as likely to find Somerset House under water next Easter or autumn, as to find The Gondoliers one hair's-breadth better than The Mikado, or Gounod's promised Mass a step in advance of Mors et Vita. The Savoy has a certain artistic position, like the German Reed entertainment; but it is not a movable position. The Red Hussar might have been a new departure at the Lyric; Gretna Green might have been anything; but I am already as absolutely certain of what The Gondoliers is as I shall be when I have witnessed the performance.

One result of this is that I have no real curiosity on the subject. Indeed, I may as well confess that I have no real conviction that I shall ever fulfil my promise to go. Would you be surprised to learn that I have never seen The Sorcerer, Iolanthe, Princess Ida, and Ruddigore at all, nor even Patience, except from behind the scenes at an amateur performance. I have a sorrowfully minute acquaintance with the music of them all; but it has been imposed upon me by circumstances over which I have no control. And as I have seen Trial by Jury only as an afterpiece by a provincial company when it first appeared ever so many years ago; as I saw the Pirates at the Opera Comique, and H.M.S. Pinafore by the secessionists at the Imperial, I begin to realize the fact that I have been only once inside the Savoy Theatre. On that occasion I was haled thither forcibly by a friend who had a spare stall for a Mikado matinée. The conclusion is irresistible that the attraction of Gilbert-Sullivan opera is not sufficient to overcome my inertia. The reason is not far to seek. Mr Gilbert's paradoxical wit, astonishing to the ordinary Englishman, is nothing to me. Nature has cursed me with a facility for the same trick; and I could paradox Mr Gilbert's head off were I not convinced that such trifling is morally unjustifiable. As to Sir Arthur's scores, they form an easy introduction to dramatic music and picturesque or topical orchestration for perfect novices; but as I had learned it all from Meyerbeer (not to profane the great name of Mozart in such a connection), and was pretty well tired of Offenbach before Trial by Jury was born, there was no musical novelty in the affair for me. Besides, Sir Arthur's school is an exploded one. Neatly and cleverly as he exploits it, he cannot get a progression or a melody out of it that is not the worse for wear. It smells mustily of Dr Day and his sham science of harmony, beloved of the Royal Academy of Music. Give me unaffected melodies consisting chiefly of augmented intervals, a natural harmony progressing by consecutive fifths and sevenths, plenty of healthy unprepared tonic discords and major ninths, elevenths, and thirteenths, without any pedantic dread of "false relations"; and then I will listen with some interest. But no more of Dr Day for me.

· UTOPIA LIMITED ·

11 October 1893 (III)

Pleasant it is to see Mr Gilbert and Sir Arthur Sullivan working together again full brotherly. They should be on the best of terms; for henceforth Sir Arthur can always say, "Any other librettist would do just as well: look at Haddon Hall"; whilst Mr Gilbert can retort, "Any other musician would do just as well: look at the Mountebanks." Thus have the years of divorce cemented the happy reunion at which we all assisted last Saturday. The twain still excite the expectations of the public as much as ever. How Trial by Jury and The Sorcerer surprised the public, and how Pinafore, The Pirates, and Patience kept the sensation fresh, can be guessed by the youngest man from the fact that the announcement of a new Savoy opera always throws the middle-aged playgoer into the attitude of expecting a surprise. As for me, I avoid this attitude, if only because it is a middle-aged one. Still, I expect a good deal that I could not have hoped for when I first made the acquaintance of comic opera.

Those who are old enough to compare the Savoy performances with those of the dark ages, taking into account the pictorial treatment of the fabrics and colors on the stage, the cultivation and intelligence of the choristers, the quality of the orchestra, and the degree of artistic good breeding, so to speak, expected from the principals, best know how great an advance has been made by Mr D'Oyly Carte in organizing and harmonizing that complex cooperation of artists of all kinds which goes to make up a satisfactory operatic performance. Long before the run of a successful Savoy opera is over Sir Arthur's melodies are dinned into our ears by every promenade band and street piano, and Mr Gilbert's sallies are quoted threadbare by conversationalists and journalists; but the whole work as presented to eye and ear on the Savoy stage remains unhackneyed.

Further, no theatre in London is more independent of those executants whose personal popularity enables them to demand ruinous salaries; and this is not the least advantageous of the differences between opera as the work of a combination of manager, poet, and musician, all three making the most of one another in their concerted striving for the common object of a completely successful representation, and opera as the result of a speculator picking up a libretto, getting somebody with a name to set it to music, ordering a few tradesmen to "mount" it, and then, with a stage manager hired here, an acting manager hired there, and a popular prima donna, comedian, and serpentine dancer stuck in at reckless salaries like almonds into an underdone dumpling, engaging some empty theatre on the chance of the affair "catching on."

If any capitalist wants to succeed with comic opera, I can assure him that he can do so with tolerable security if he only possesses the requisite managerial ability. There is no lack of artistic material for him to set to work on: London is overstocked with artistic talent ready to the hand of anyone who can recognize it and select from it. The difficulty is to find the man with this power of recognition and selection. The effect of the finer artistic temperaments and talents on the ordinary speculator is not merely nil (for in that case he might give them an engagement by accident), but antipathetic. People sometimes complain of the indifference of the public and the managers to the highest elements in fine art. There never was a greater mistake. The Philistine is not indifferent to fine art: he *hates* it.

The relevance of these observations will be apparent when I say that, though I enjoyed the score of Utopia more than that of any of the previous Savoy operas, I am quite prepared to hear that it is not as palatable to the majority of the human race—otherwise the mob—as it was to me. It is written with an artistic absorption and enjoyment of which Sir Arthur Sullivan always had moments, but which seem to have become constant with him only since he was knighted, though I do not suggest that the two things stand in the relation of cause and effect. The orchestral work is charmingly humorous; and as I happen to mean by this only what I say, perhaps I had better warn my readers not to infer that Utopia is full of buffooneries with the bassoon and piccolo, or of patter and tumtum.

Whoever can listen to such caressing wind parts—zephyr parts, in fact—as those in the trio for the King and the two Judges in the first act, without being coaxed to feel pleased and amused, is not fit even for treasons, stratagems, and spoils; whilst anyone whose ears are capable of taking in more than one thing at a time must be tickled by the sudden busyness of the orchestra as the city man takes up the parable. I also confidently recommend those who go into solemn academic raptures over themes "in diminution" to go and hear how prettily the chorus of the Christy Minstrel song (borrowed from the plantation dance Johnnie, get a gun) is used, very much in diminution, to make an exquisite mock-banjo accompaniment. In these examples we are on the plane, not of the bones and tambourine, but of Mozart's accompaniments to Soave sia il vento in Cosi fan tutte and the entry of the gardener in Le Nozze di Figaro. Of course these things are as much thrown away on people who are not musicians as a copy of Fliegende Blätter on people who do not read German, whereas anyone can understand mere horseplay with the instruments. . . .

The book has Mr Gilbert's lighter qualities without his faults. Its main idea, the Anglicization of Utopia by a people boundlessly credulous as to the superiority of the English race, is as certain of popularity as that reference to England by the Gravedigger in Hamlet, which never yet failed to make the house laugh. There is, happily, no plot; and the stage business is fresh and well invented—for instance, the lecture already alluded to, the adoration of the troopers by the female Utopians, the Cabinet Council "as held at the Court of St James's Hall," and the quadrille, are capital strokes. As to the "Drawing Room," with *débutantes*, cards, trains, and presentations all complete, and the little innovation of a cup of tea and a plate of cheap biscuits, I cannot vouch for its verisimilitude, as I have never, strange as it may appear, been present at a Drawing Room; but that is exactly why I enjoyed it, and why the majority of the Savoyards will share my appreciation of it.

Parry

·JUDITH·

12 December 1888 (C)

London has now had two opportunities of tasting Mr Hubert Parry's Judith, the oratorio which he composed for this year's Birmingham festival. It was performed on the 6th of this month at St James's Hall, and again on Saturday last at the Crystal Palace, with Dr Mackenzie in the seat of Mr Manns (gone to Scotland), and the Palace choir replaced by that of Novello's oratorio concerts. The truth about the oratorio is one of those matters which a critic is sorely tempted to mince. Mr Parry is a gentleman of culture and independent means, pursuing his beloved art with a devotion and disinterestedness which is not possible to musicians who have to live by their profession. He is guiltless of potboilers and catchpennies, and both in his compositions and in his excellent literary essays on music he has proved the constant elevation of his musical ideal. Never was there a musician easier and pleasanter to praise, painfuller and more ungracious to disparage. But—! yes, there is a serious but in the case on the present occasion; and its significance is that when a man takes it upon himself to write an oratorio—perhaps the most gratuitous exploit open to a nineteenth century Englishman—he must take the consequences.

Judith, then, consists of a sort of musical fabric that any gentleman of Mr Parry's general culture, with a turn for music and the requisite technical training, can turn out to any extent needful for the purposes of a Festival Committee. There is not a rhythm in it, not a progression, not a modulation that brings a breath of freshness with it. The pretentious choruses are made up of phrases mechanically repeated on ascending degrees of the scale, or of hackneyed scraps of fugato and pedal point. The unpretentious choruses, smooth and sometimes pretty hymnings about nothing in particular, would pass muster in a mild cantata: in an oratorio they are flavorless. It is impossible to work up any interest in emasculated Handel and watered Mendelssohn, even with all the modern adulterations.

The instrumentation is conventional to the sleepiest degree: tromboned solemnities, sentimentalities for solo horn with tremolo accompaniment, nervous excitement fiddled *in excelsis*, drum points as invented by Beethoven, and the rest of the worn-out novelties of modern scoring.

Of the music assigned to the principal singers, that of Judith is the hardest to judge, as Miss Anna Williams labored through its difficulties without eloquence or appropriate expression, and hardly ever got quite safely and reassuringly into tune. Mdme. Patey as Meshullemeth discoursed in lugubrious dramatic recitative about desolate courts and profaned altars. She was repaid for her thankless exertions by one popular number in the form of a ballad which consisted of the first line of The Minstrel Boy, followed by the second line of Tom Bowling, connected by an "augmentation" of a passage from the finale of the second act of Lucrezia Borgia, with an ingenious blend of The Girl I Left Behind Me and We be Three Poor Mariners. It will be understood, of course, that the intervals—except in the Lucrezia Borgia case—are altered, and that the source of Mr Parry's unconscious inspiration is betrayed by the accent and measure only. Manasseh, a paltry creature who sings Sunday music for the drawing-room whilst his two sons are cremated alive before his eyes, was impersonated by Mr Barton McGuckin, who roused a bored audience by his delivery of a Handelian song, which has the fault of not being by Handel, but is otherwise an agreeable composition, and a great relief to the music which precedes it. Indeed matters generally grow livelier towards the end.

The Israelites become comparatively bright and vigorous when Judith cuts Holofernes' head off. The ballad is gratefully remembered; the enchanting singing of Manasseh's son is dwelt upon; the Handelian song is quoted as a fine thing; and so Judith passes muster for the time.

· JOB ·

3 May 1893 (II)

For some time past I have been carefully dodging Dr Hubert Parry's Job. I had presentiments about it from the first. I foresaw that all the other critics would cleverly imply that they thought it the greatest oratorio of ancient or modern times—that Handel is rebuked, Mendelssohn eclipsed, and the rest nowhere. And I was right: they did. The future historian of music, studying the English papers of 1892–3, will learn that these years produced two entire and perfect chrysolites, Job and Falstaff, especially Job. I was so afraid of being unable to concur unreservedly in the verdict that I lay low and stopped my ears. The first step was to avoid the Gloucester Festival. That gave me no trouble: nothing is easier than not to go to Gloucester. . . .

Such being my sentiments, it will be understood that I forewent Gloucester and Job last autumn without regret. I have explained the matter at some length, not because I have not said all the above before, but solely to put off for awhile the moment when I must at last say what I think of Dr Parry's masterpiece. For I unluckily went last Wednesday to the concert of the Middlesex Choral Union, where the first thing that happened was the appearance of Dr Parry amid the burst of affectionate applause which always greets him. That made me uneasy; and I was not reassured when he mounted the conductor's rostrum, and led the band into a prelude which struck me as being a serious set of footnotes to the bridal march from Lohengrin. Presently up got Mr Bantock Pierpoint, and sang, without a word of warning, There was a man in the land of Uz whose name was Job. Then I knew I was in for it; and now I must do my duty.

I take Job to be, on the whole, the most utter failure ever achieved by a thoroughly respectworthy musician. There is not one bar in it that comes within fifty thousand miles of the tamest line in the poem. This is the naked, unexaggerated truth. Is anybody surprised at it? Here, on the one hand, is an ancient poem which has lived from civilization to civilization, and has been translated into an English version of haunting beauty and nobility of style, offering to the musician a subject which would have taxed to the utmost the highest powers of Bach, Handel, Mozart, Beethoven, or Wagner. Here on the other is, not Bach nor Handel nor Mozart nor Beethoven nor Wagner, not even Mendelssohn or Schumann, but Dr Parry, an enthusiastic and popular professor, forty-five years old, and therefore of ascertained powers.

Now, will any reasonable person pretend that it lies within the limits of those powers to let us hear the morning stars singing together and the sons of God shouting for joy? True, it is impossible to say what a man can do until he tries. I may before the end of this year write a tragedy on the subject of King Lear that will efface Shakespear's; but if I do it will be a surprise, not perhaps to myself, but to the public. It is certain that if I took the work in hand I should be able to turn out five acts about King Lear that would be, at least, grammatical, superficially coherent, and arranged in lines that would scan. And I doubt not at all that some friendly and ingenious critic would say of it, "Lear is, from beginning to end, a remarkable work, and one which nobody but an English author could have written. Every page bears the stamp of G. B. S.'s genius; and no higher praise can be awarded to it than to say that it is fully worthy of his reputation." What critic would need to be so unfriendly as to face the plain question, "Has the author been able for his subject?"

I might easily shirk that question in the case of Job: there are no end of nice little things I could point out about the workmanship shewn in the score, its fine feeling, its scrupulous moderation, its entire freedom from any base element of art or character, and so on through a whole epitaph of pleasant and perfectly true irrelevancies. I might even say that Dr Parry's setting of Job placed him infinitely above the gentleman who set to music The Man that broke the Bank. But would that alter the fact that Dr Parry has left his subject practically untouched, whilst his music-hall rival has most exhaustively succeeded in covering his? It is the great glory of Job that he shamed the devil. Let me imitate him by telling the truth about the work as it appeared to me. Of course I may be wrong: even I am not infallible, at least not always.

And it must be remembered that I am violently prejudiced against the professorial school of which Dr Parry is a distinguished member. I always said, and say still, that his much-admired oratorio Judith has absolutely no merit whatever. I allowed a certain vigor and geniality in his L' Allegro ed il Pensieroso, and a certain youthful inspiration in his Prometheus. But even these admissions I regarded as concessions to the academic faction which he leans to; and I was so afraid of being further disarmed that I lived in fear of meeting him and making his acquaintance; for I had noticed that the critics to whom this happens become hopelessly corrupt, and say anything to please him without the least regard to public duty. Let Job then have the benefit of whatever suspicion may be cast on my verdict by my prepossessions against the composer's school.

The first conspicuous failure in the work is Satan, who, after a feeble attempt to give himself an infernal air by getting the bassoon to announce him with a few frog-like croaks, gives up the pretence, and, though a tenor and a fiend, models himself on Mendelssohn's St Paul. He has no tact as an orator. For example, when he says "Put forth thine hand now and touch all that he hath, and he will curse thee to thy face," there is not a shade of scepticism or irony in him; and he ineptly tries to drive his point home by a melodramatic shriek on the word "curse." When one thinks—I will not say of Loki or Klingsor, but of Verdi's Iago and Boito's Mefistofele, and even of Gounod's stage devil, it is impossible to accept this pale shadow of an excitable curate as one of the poles of the great world magnet.

As to Job, there is no sort of grit in him: he is abject from first to last, and is only genuinely touching when he longs to lie still and be quiet where the wicked cease from troubling and the weary are at rest. That is the one tolerable moment in the work; and Job passes from it to relapse into dullness, not to rise into greater strength of spirit. He is much distracted by fragments of themes from the best composers coming into his head from time to time, and sometimes cutting off the thread of his discourse altogether. When he talks of mountains being removed, he flourishes on the flute in an absurdly inadequate manner; and his challenge to God, Shew me wherefore Thou contendest with me, is too poor to be described.

Not until he has given in completely, and is saying his last word, does it suddenly occur to him to make a hit; and then, in announcing that he repents in dust and ashes, he explodes in the most unlooked-for way on the final word "ashes," which produces the effect of a sneeze. The expostulation of God with Job is given to the chorus: the voice that sometimes speaks through the mouths of babes and sucklings here speaks through the mouths of Brixton and Bayswater, and the effect is precisely what might have been expected. It is hard to come down thus from the "heil'gen Hallen" of Sarastro to the suburbs.

There is one stroke of humor in the work. When Job says, The Lord gave, and the Lord taketh away: blessed be the name of the Lord, a long and rueful interval after the words "taketh away" elapses before poor Job can resign himself to utter the last clause. That is the sole trace of real dramatic treatment in this dreary ramble of Dr Parry's through the wastes of artistic error. It is the old academic story—an attempt to bedizen a dramatic poem with scraps of sonata music.

Dr Parry reads, The walls are broken down: destroyed are the pleasant places; and it sounds beautifully to him. So it associates itself with something else that sounds beautifully—Mendelssohn's violin concerto, as it happens in this case—and straightway he rambles off into a rhythm suggested by the first movement of the concerto, and produces a tedious combination which has none of the charm or propriety of either poem or concerto. For the sake of relief he drags in by the ears a piece of martial tumult—See! upon the distant plain, a white cloud of dust, the ravagers come—compounded from the same academic prescription as the business of the dragon's teeth coming up armed men in Mackenzie's Jason; and the two pieces of music are consequently indistinguishable in my memory—in fact, I do not remember a note of either of them.

I have no wish to linger over a barbarous task. In time I may forgive Dr Parry, especially if he will write a few more essays on the great composers, and confine himself to the composition of "absolute music," with not more than three pedal points to the page. But at this moment I feel sore. He might have let Job alone, and let me alone; for, patient as we both are, there are limits to human endurance. I hope he will burn the score, and throw Judith in when the blaze begins to flag.

Stanford

14 October 1891 (I)

It is not easy to fit Villiers Stanford's Eden with a critical formula which will satisfy all parties. If I call it brilliant balderdash, I shall not only be convicted of having used an "ungenteel" expression, but I shall grievously offend those friends of his whose motto is *Floreat Stanford: ruat caelum!* If, on the other hand, I call it a masterpiece of scholarship and genius, and expatiate on its erudite modal harmonies and its brilliant instrumentation, I shall hardly feel that I have expressed my own inmost mind. Not that I am prejudiced against modal harmonies. I can harmonize themes in keys other than that of C, and leave out all the sharps and flats against any man alive; and though for the life of me I never can remember which of the scales produced in this manner is the mixophrygian mode, and which the hypoionian, or Dorian, or what not, yet I am content to be able to perpetrate the harmonies and to leave more learned men to fit them with their proper names. But what I cannot do is to persuade myself that if I write in this fashion my music will sound angelic, and that if I use the ordinary major and minor scales the result will be comparatively diabolic. I find it works out rather the other way.

I know, of course, that several modern composers, from Handel to Beethoven, and from Beethoven to Bourgault-Ducoudray, have done very pretty things in the modal manner. But when Professor Stanford asks me to admit that his choristers are angels merely because they persistently sing B flat instead of B natural in the key of C major (as the Siamese band used to do when they played our national anthem, to our great alarm, on stone dulcimers), I feel that he is becoming exorbitant. I see no reason why heaven should be behind earth in the use of the leading note in the scale. Perhaps this is not serious criticism; but I really cannot take Eden seriously. From the mixolydian motet at the beginning to the striking up of Three Blind Mice to the words Sleep, Adam, Sleep by the Archangel Michael at

340

the end, I caught not a single definite purpose or idea at all commensurate with the huge pretension of the musical design. That pretension is the ruin of Eden. There is one interlude which I should applaud if it were a piece of hurdy-gurdy music for a new setting of Linda di Chamounix; and there are plenty of other passages which would be acceptable on similar terms.

But in a work which stands or falls as a great musical epic, they only made me wonder what Mr Stanford would think of me if I took advantage of my literary craftsmanship to write inane imitations of Milton's Paradise Lost with all the latest graces of style, and got my friends to go into raptures over its grammar and its correct scansion. However, who am I that I should be believed, to the disparagement of eminent musicians? If you doubt that Eden is a masterpiece, ask Dr Parry and Dr Mackenzie, and they will applaud it to the skies. Surely Dr Mackenzie's opinion is conclusive; for is he not the composer of Veni Creator, guaranteed as excellent music by Professor Stanford and Dr Parry? You want to know who Dr Parry is? Why, the composer of Blest Pair of Sirens, as to the merits of which you have only to consult Dr Mackenzie and Professor Stanford. Nevertheless, I remain unshaken in my opinion that these gentlemen are wasting their talent and industry. The sham classics which they are producing are worth no more than the forgotten pictures of Hilton and epics of Hoole.

· IRISH SYMPHONY ·

10 May 1893 (II)

The success of Professor Stanford's Irish Symphony last Thursday was, from the Philharmonic point of view, somewhat scandalous. The spectacle of a university professor "going Fantee" is indecorous, though to me personally it is delightful. When Professor Stanford is genteel, cultured, classic, pious, and experimentally mixolydian, he is dull beyond belief. His dullness is all the harder to bear because it is the restless, ingenious, trifling, flippant dullness of the Irishman, instead of the stupid, bovine, sleepable-through dullness of the Englishman, or even the aggressive, ambitious, sentimental dullness of the Scot. But Mr Villiers Stanford cannot be dismissed as merely the Irish variety of the professorial species.

Take any of the British oratorios and cantatas which have been produced recently for the Festivals, and your single comment on any of them will be—if you know anything about music—"Oh! anybody with a bachelor's degree could have written that." But you cannot say this of Stanford's Eden. It is as insufferable a composition as any Festival committee could desire; but it is ingenious and peculiar; and although in it you see the Irish professor trifling in a world of ideas, in marked contrast to the English professor conscientiously wrestling in a vacuum, yet over and above this national difference, which would assert itself equally in the case of any other Irishman, you find certain traces of a talent for composition, which is precisely what the ordinary professor, with all his grammatical and historical accomplishments, utterly lacks. But the conditions of making this talent serviceable are not supplied by Festival commissions. Far from being a respectable oratorio-manufacturing talent, it is, when it gets loose, eccentric, violent, romantic, patriotic, and held in check only by a mortal fear of being found deficient in what are called "the manners and tone of good society." This fear, too, is Irish: it is, possibly, the racial consciousness of having missed that four hundred years of Roman civilization which gave England a sort of university education when Ireland was in the hedge school.

In those periods when nobody questions the superiority of the university to the hedge school, the Irishman, lamed by a sense of inferiority, blusters most intolerably, and not unfrequently goes the length of alleging that Balfe was a great composer. Then the fashion changes; Ruskin leads young Oxford out into the hedge school to dig roads; there is a general disparagement in advanced circles of civilization, the university, respectability, law and order; and a heroic renunciation of worldly and artificial things is insisted upon by those who, having had their fling, are tired of them, a demand powerfully reinforced by the multitude, who want to have their fling but cannot get it under existing circumstances, and are driven to console themselves by crying sour grapes.

This reaction is the opportunity of the Irishman in England to rehabilitate his self-respect, since it gives him a standpoint from which he can value himself as a hedge-school man, patronize the university product, and escape from the dreary and abortive task of branding himself all over as an Irish snob under the impression that he is hallmarking himself as an English gentleman. If he seizes the opportunity, he may end in founding a race of cultivated Irishmen whose mission in England will be to teach Englishmen to play with their brains as well as with their bodies; for it is all work and no play in the brain department that makes John Bull such an uncommonly dull boy.

The beginning of this "return to nature" in music has been effected, not by a sudden repudiation of the whole academic system, but by the smuggling into academic music of ancient folk-music under various pretences as to its archæological importance; its real recommendation, of course, being that the musicians like the tunes, and the critics and programists find it much easier to write about "national characteristics" and "the interval of the augmented second" than to write to the point. First we had Mendelssohn's "Scotch" Symphony, and then came a deluge of pseudo-Hungarian, gipsy, and other folk-music—Liszt, Bruch, Dvořák, and Brahms all trying their hands—with, in due course, "pibrochs" by Dr Mackenzie, Land of the Mountain and the Flood overture from Mr Hamish Mac-Cunn, and Villiers Stanford's Irish Symphony. No general criticism of the works produced in this movement is possible.

The poorer composers, unable to invent interesting themes for their works in sonata form, gladly availed themselves of the licence to steal popular airs, with results that left them as far as ever behind the geniuses who assimilated what served their turn in folk-music as in every other store of music. But, at all events, the new fashion produced music quite different in kind from the Turkish music devised by the German Mozart for Il Seraglio, the Arabian music copied by his countryman Weber for Oberon, or the African and Scotch music invented by Mendelssohn and Meyerbeer (both Jews) for L'Africaine and the Scotch Symphony. This sort of "national" music takes the artificial operatic or sonata forms quite easily, submitting to be soaped and washed and toiletted for its visit to Covent Garden or St James's Hall without the least awkwardness.

But in the recent cases where the so-called folk-music is written by a composer born of the fold himself, and especially of the Celtic folk, with its intense national sentiment, there is the most violent repugnance between the popular music and the sonata form. The Irish Symphony, composed by an Irishman, is a record of fearful conflict between the aboriginal Celt and the Professor. The scherzo is not a scherzo at all, but a shindy, expending its force in riotous dancing. However hopelessly an English orchestra may fail to catch the wild nuances of the Irish fiddler, it cannot altogether drown the "hurroosh" with which Stanford the Celt drags Stanford the Professor into the orgy. Again, in the slow movement the emotional development is such as would not be possible in an English or German symphony. At first it is slow, plaintive, passionately sad about nothing.

According to all classic precedent, it should end in hopeless gloom, in healing resignation, or in pathetic sentiment. What it does end in is blue murder, the Professor this time aiding and abetting the transition with all his contrapuntal might. In the last movement the rival Stanfords agree to a compromise which does not work. The essence of the sonata form is the development of themes; and even in a rondo a theme that will not develop will not fit the form. Now the greatest folk-songs are final developments themselves: they cannot be carried any further. You cannot develop God Save the Queen, though you may, like Beethoven, write some interesting but retrograde variations on it. Neither can you develop Let Erin remember. You might, of course, develop it inversely, debasing it touch by touch until you had The Marseillaise in all its vulgarity; and the doing of this might be instructive, though it would not be symphony writing. But no forward development is possible.

Yet in the last movement of the Irish Symphony, Stanford the Celt, wishing to rejoin in Molly Macalpine (Remember the glories) and The Red Fox (Let Erin remember), insisted that if Stanford the Professor wanted to develop themes, he should develop these two. The Professor succumbed to the shillelagh of his double, but, finding development impossible, got out of the difficulty by breaking Molly up into fragments, exhibiting these fantastically, and then putting them together again. This process is not in the least like the true sonata development. It would not work at all with The Red Fox, which comes in as a flagrant patch upon the rondo—for the perfect tune that is one moment a war song, and the next, without the alteration of a single note, the saddest of patriotic reveries "on Lough Neagh's bank where the fisherman strays in the clear cold eve's declining," flatly refuses to merge itself into any sonata movement, and loftily asserts itself in right of ancient descent as entitled to walk before any symphony that ever professor penned.

It is only in the second subject of this movement, an original theme of the composer's own minting, that the form and the material really combine chemically into sonata. And this satisfactory result is presently upset by the digression to the utterly incompatible aim of the composer to display the charms of his native folk-music.

In the first movement the sonata writer keeps to his point better: there are no national airs lifted bodily into it. Nevertheless the first movement does not convince me that Professor Stanford's talent is a symphonic talent any more than Meyerbeer's was. In mentioning Meyerbeer I know I run the risk of having the implied comparison interpreted in the light of the Wagnerian criticism—that is, as a deliberate disparagement. I do not mean it so. The Wagnerian criticism of Meyerbeer is valid only as a page in the history of the development of opera into Wagnerian music-drama. Taken out of this connection it will not stand verification for a moment.

· BECKET ·

11 April 1894 (III)

The audience at the Crystal Palace Saturday Concerts lately had a much better opportunity of judging Professor Villiers Stanford's Becket music than ever Mr Irving enjoyed. Technically, it is a very good piece of work—it has qualities that may almost be described as moral excellences. For instance, the handling of the orchestra is first rate: by which I do not mean, if you please, that there are sensational tremolandos, or voluptuous murmurs for the wind, or delicate embroideries for the flute, or solos for the English horn, or scintillations for the triangle, or, generally speaking, any of that rouging of the cheeks of the music and underlining of its eyes which is so cheap nowadays: I mean that the composer knows how and where to get his tone of the right shade and of the best quality, how to balance it, how to vary it otherwise than by crudely obvious contrasts, and how to get from the full band that clear, smooth, solid effect for which one has to go to Brahms, or even back to Cherubini, for satisfactory examples.

Add to this a complete intellectual mastery of harmony, and you have an equipment which enables the composer to do anything he wants to do within the known limits of musical composition. As to what he wants, I approach that subject with less than my usual confidence. Something is happening to my attitude towards absolute music. Perhaps I am fossilizing, perhaps I am merely beginning to acquire at last some elementary knowledge of my business as a critic: I cannot say. I am not sure that I did not think at one time that absolute music was dead: that Mozart had been faithless to it; that

Beethoven had definitely deserted it; and that Wagner had finally knocked it on the head and buried it at the bottom of the Red Sea. And certainly, whenever an attempt was made to galvanize it by attaching it to an oratorio libretto, or festival cantata, or mayhap to the Requiem Mass, its appearance was sufficiently ghastly and ridiculous to make me regard it as a product, not of composition, but of decomposition; so I reviled its professors for not burying it decently, and devoting themselves with frank singleness of purpose to tone poems and music-dramas.

For example, it seemed to me that Professor Stanford would have done better to follow up his Cavalier Romances and write for the stage than to hammer away at absolute music. Unfortunately, he did neither the one nor the other: he tried to combine the two in such hybrid works as Eden and The Revenge, concerning which I remain impenitent, more convinced than ever that they are hopeless mistakes. The only opening for critical error concerning them lay in the doubt as to whether the case was one of an absolute musician hampered by a libretto, or a dramatic musician hampered by the traditions of absolute music.

Naturally I was sure to decide in the latter sense when once I had assumed beforehand that absolute music was dead. This decision of mine proves—what it concerns every reader of these columns to bear constantly in mind—that I can be incredibly prejudiced and stupid on occasion, considering that I am in many ways rather an intelligent man. For could anything have been more obvious than that the disturbing element in all these oratorios and contatas is the libretto—that it is in his efforts to be a poet and dramatist that the composer is an ineffectual amateur, while in his counterpoint he often shews ten times the skill and knowledge of an opera composer? The man who roused me into common sense on this subject was no other than our friend Brahms.

The truth in his case was too clear to be overlooked. The moment he tried to use music for the purpose of expressing or describing anything in the least degree extraneous to itself he became commonplace and tedious, there being nothing distinguished either in his own or in his view of other men's ideas. On the other hand, when he made music purely for the sake of music, designing sound patterns without any reference to literary subjects or specific emotions, he became one of the wonders of the world: I found myself able to sit listening to him for forty-five minutes at a stretch without being bored. Absolute music was in him abundant, fresh, hopeful, joyous, powerful, and characterized by a certain virile seriousness and loftiness of taste which gave great relief after the Byzantine corruption of the latest developments of operatic music. It was only when he touched a literary subject of any dimensions that he became, by overpowering contrast with his other self, a positive blockhead. Even his songs are remarkably deficient in vividness after those of Gounod or Schubert.

In other men the ascendant movement of absolute music was less apparent; but the *dégringolade* of dramatic music was obvious. Test it by the operas of European popularity—Don Juan a century ago, Carmen today. Or take program music, with Beethoven's Pastoral Symphony to begin with, and Moszkowski's Joan of Arc and Benoit's Charlotte Corday to finish with. Or compare Mozart's Requiem and Rossini's Stabat Mater with Dvořák's. Surely we have along these lines the most frightful degeneration, which has only been masked from us by the irresistible power with which Wagner drew our attention to himself alone while he was crowning the dramatic movement by his combination of all the arts into the Bayreuth music-drama, just as Bach crowned the contrapuntal movement at the moment when it was worn out and tumbling to pieces in all directions.

Even with Wagner the wearing out of the purely musical material is patent to all unsympathetic critics. If you take Parsifal, and set aside that large part of the score (the best part) which is senseless apart from the poem, and consider the rest from the point of view of absolute music, you find that a good deal of it will not bear comparison for a moment with the musical material of the Leonora overture or the Ninth Symphony.

Music, in fact, is now in revolt against the union of all the arts, since it has meant to her a ruthless exploitation not only by the poet and higher dramatist, but by the sensation-monger and pander. She is now, like our revolting daughters and Doll's House Noras, insisting on being once more considered as an end in herself; and so the union of all the arts falls to pieces before Wagner's cement is dry, and his Art Work of the Future is already the art work of the past.

Of late this view has been pressed home on me in another way. One of the unsolved problems which all critics have been conscious of for a long time has been the collapse of English music in the eighteenth century. So long as our knowledge of the old music was confined to the madrigals and other vocal pieces—that is, to the least absolutely musical specimens—the problem remained inert at the back of our minds.

Some of us, of course, had a paper knowledge of the old instrumental music; but I am so deeply sceptical as to the value of such paper knowledge that whenever a musician tells me that reading a score is to him the same as hearing it performed, I either give him credit for deceiving himself, or else accept the statement exactly as I would accept it from a deaf man. Those who make it usually contradict themselves, whenever they get the chance, by taking the trouble to attend performances of the very scores which are on the shelves of their libraries.

Now, for some time past Mr Arnold Dolmetsch has been bringing the old instrumental music to actual performance under conditions as closely as possible resembling those contemplated by the composers; and under this stimulus the unsolved problem has suddenly become active and begun to struggle after its solution as a discord struggles after its resolution. And the explanation appears to be the very simple one that the English gained their great musical reputation up to the eighteenth century in absolute music. In the eighteenth century the world left off writing absolute music and took to operatic music, for which the English—to the great credit of their national character—had no sort of aptitude. And if they wish to regain their old fame, they must begin where they left off.

While I was still in my teens, the verbal horrors of "opera in English," by the Carl Rosa and other companies, convinced me that if the English language is to be musically treated at all it must be done in the style of Purcell, and not in that of Verdi. This was my first superficial formulation of the solution which completed itself quite lately in my mind at the viol concerts at Mr Dolmetsch's house at Dulwich. Here the music, completely free from all operatic and literary aims, ought, one might have supposed, to have sounded quaintly archaic.

But not a bit of it. It made operatic music sound positively wizened in comparison. Its richness of detail, especially in the beauty and interest of the harmony, made one think of modern "English" music of the Bohemian-Girl school as one thinks of a jerry-built suburban square after walking through a medieval quadrangle at Oxford. The operatic charms that were once irresistible—the freedom of melody, the determinateness of form and harmonic movement, the intelligibility of treatment gained by the establishment of a single popular scale and its relative minor as the mode for all music—these seemed for the moment almost as contemptible as the cheapness of workmanship and the theatrical vulgarity and superficiality of aim which they had brought with them.

But the most significant feature of the old English music was its identity in kind with the best music of Brahms, and with all that is hopeful and vital in the efforts of Parry, Stanford, and our latest composers. So that I had no sooner reached the conviction that English music must come to life again by resuming its old exclusive aims, than I began to see that this was what it was actually doing. Consequently the whole problem for the critics at present is how to make Professor Stanford and the rest see their own destiny clearly, and save themselves from the fate of Lot's wife, which will most assuredly overtake them if they look back to the librettos, operatic and "sacred" (save the mark!), which are superstitions from the age of England's musical impotence. Let them leave the theatrical exploitation of music to Kistler, Mascagni, and the rest of the brood of young lions: they themselves, the absolute musicians, will only succeed by sticking to absolute music, wherein their strength lies.

Having thus, I hope, made my critical position clear, I may say of Professor Stanford's Becket music that, together with those excellences which I have already indicated, it marks an advance in the only direction along which he now can advance, and that is the intensification of his grip of his thematic material. He no longer resorts to clever technical trifling to conceal his want of interest in his own work: he now keeps to the point; only the grip is not yet so earnest or the vision so penetrating as—shall I say Beethoven's, since he has reminded me of that mighty man by unconsciously transferring one of the most striking phrases in the finale of the Eighth Symphony to the Becket overture. The mills of the gods have not yet ground his cleverness small enough nor his inner purpose fine enough to make it wise to claim for him the place among European composers which he is probably capable of reaching, for he is in some ways a tough, incorrigible subject; but I confess I am more than commonly curious to hear what his next symphony will be like.

Elgar

Music and Letters, January 1920 (*)

Edward Elgar, the figurehead of music in England, is a composer whose rank it is neither prudent nor indeed possible to determine. Either it is one so high that only time and posterity can confer it, or else he is one of the Seven Humbugs of Christendom. Comtemporary judgments are sound enough on Second Bests; but when it comes to Bests they acclaim ephemerals as immortals, and simultaneously denounce immortals as pestilent charlatans.

Elgar has not left us any room to hedge. From the beginning, quite naturally and as a matter of course, he has played the great game and professed the Best. He has taken up the work of a great man so spontaneously that it is impossible to believe that he ever gave any consideration to the enormity of the assumption, or was even conscious of it. But there it is, unmistakeable. To the north countryman who, on hearing of Wordsworth's death, said, "I suppose his son will carry on the business," it would be plain today that Elgar is carrying on Beethoven's business. The names are up on the shop front for everyone to read. ELGAR, late BEETHOVEN & CO., Classics and Italian & German Warehousemen. Symphonies, Overtures, Chamber Music, Oratorios, Bagatelles.

This, it will be seen, is a very different challenge from that of, say, Debussy and Stravinsky. You can rave about Stravinsky without the slightest risk of being classed as a lunatic by the next generation. You can declare the Après-midi d'un Faune the most delightful and enchanting orchestral piece ever written without really compromising yourself. But, if you say that Elgar's Cockaigne overture combines every classic quality of the overture to Die Meistersinger, you are either uttering a platitude as safe as a compliment to Handel on the majesty of the Hallelujah chorus, or else damning yourself to all critical posterity by a *gaffe* that will make your grandson blush for you.

Personally, I am prepared to take the risk. What do I care about my grandson? Give me Cockaigne. But my recklessness cannot settle the question. It would be so much easier if Cockaigne were *genre* music, with the Westminster chimes, snatches of Yip-i-addy, and a march of the costermongers to Covent Garden. Then we should know where we are: the case would be as simple as Gilbert and Sullivan.

But there is nothing of the kind: the material of the Cockaigne overture is purely classical. You may hear all sorts of footsteps in it, and it may tell you all sorts of stories; but it is classical music as Beethoven's Les Adieux sonata is classical music: it tells you no story external to itself and yourself. Therefore, who knows whether it appeals to the temporal or the eternal in us; in other words, whether it will be alive or dead in the twentyfirst century?

Certain things one can say without hestitation. For example, that Elgar could turn out Debussy and Stravinsky music by the thousand bars for fun in his spare time. That to him such standbys as the whole-tone-scale of Debussy, the Helmholtzian chords of Scriabin, the exciting modulations of the operatic school, the zylophone and celesta orchestration by which country dances steal into classical concerts, are what farthings are to a millionaire. That his range is so Handelian that he can give the people a universal melody or march with as sure a hand as he can give the Philharmonic Society a symphonic adagio, such as has not been given since Beethoven died. That, to come down to technical things, his knowledge of the orchestra is almost uncanny.

When Gerontius made Elgar widely known, there was a good deal of fine writing about it; but what every genuine connoisseur in orchestration must have said at the first hearing (among other things) was, "What a devil of a *fortissimo!*" Here was no literary paper instrumentation, no muddle and noise, but an absolutely new energy given to the band by a consummate knowledge of exactly what it could do and how it could do it.

We were fed up to the throats at that time with mere piquancies of orchestration: every scorer of ballets could scatter pearls from the *pavillon chinois* (alias Jingling Johnny) over the plush and cotton velvet of his harmonies; but Elgar is no mere effect monger: he takes the whole orchestra in his hand and raises every separate instrument in it to its highest efficiency until its strength is as the strength of ten. One was not surprised to learn that he could play them all, and was actually something of a *virtuoso* on instruments as different as the violin and trombone.

The enormous command of existing resources, which this orchestral skill of his exemplifies, extends over the whole musical field, and explains the fact that, though he has a most active and curious mind, he does not appear in music as an experimenter and explorer, like Scriabin and Schönberg. He took music where Beethoven left it, and where Schumann and Brahms found it. Naturally he did not pick up and put on the shackles that Wagner had knocked off, any more than he [wrote] his trumpet parts in tonic and dominant *clichés* in the eighteenth-century manner, as some of his contemporaries made a point of honor of doing, for the sake of being in the classical fashion. But his musical mind was formed before Wagner reached him; and his natural power over the material then available was so great that he was never driven outside it by lack of means for expressing himself.

He was no keyboard composer: music wrote itself on the skies for him, and wrote itself in the language perfected by Beethoven and his great predecessors. With the same inheritance, Schumann, who had less faculty and less knowledge, devotedly tried to be another Beethoven, and failed. Brahms, with a facility as convenient as Elgar's, was a musical sensualist with intellectual affectations, and succeeded only as an incoherent voluptuary, too fundamentally addleheaded to make anything great out of the delicious musical luxuries he wallowed in. Mendelssohn was never really in the running: he was, in his own light, impetuous, and often lovely style, *sui generis*, superficial if you like, but always his own unique self, composing in an idiom invented by himself, not following a school and not founding one.

Elgar, neither an imitator nor a voluptuary, went his own way without bothering to invent a new language, and by sheer personal originality produced symphonies that are really symphonies in the Beethovenian sense, a feat in which neither Schumann, Mendelssohn, nor Brahms, often as they tried, ever succeeded convincingly. If I were king, or Minister of Fine Arts, I would give Elgar an annuity of five thousand dollars a year on condition that he produce a symphony every eighteen months.

It will be noted, I hope, that this way of Elgar's, of accepting the language and forms of his art in his time as quite sufficient for anyone with plenty of courage and a masterly natural command of them, is the way of Shakespear, of Bach, of all the greatest artists. The notion that Wagner was a great technical innovator is now seen to be a delusion that had already done duty for Mozart and Handel: it meant nothing more than that the born-great composer always has the courage and common sense not to be a pedant.

Elgar has certainly never let any pedantry stand in his way. He has indeed not been aware of its academic stumbling blocks; for, like Bach, he has never been taught harmony and counter-point. A perso who had been corrupted by Day's treatise on harmony once tried to describe a phrase of Wagner's to him by a reference to the chord of the supertonic. Elgar opened his eyes wide, and, with an awe which was at least very well acted, asked, "What on earth is the chord of the supertonic?" And then, after a pause, "What *is* the supertonic? I never heard of it."

This little incident may help to explain the effect produced at first by Elgar on the little clique of devoted musicians who, with the late Hubert Parry as its centre, stood for British music thirty-five years ago. This clique was the London section of the Clara Schumann-Joachim-Brahms clique in Germany, and the relations between the two were almost sacred. Of that international clique the present generation knows nothing, I am afraid, except that when Madame Schumann found that Wagner's Walküre fire music was to be played at a concert for which she was engaged, she declined to appear in such disgraceful company, and only with great difficulty was induced, after anxious consultation with the clique, to make a supreme effort of condescension and compromise herself rather than disappoint the people who had bought tickets to hear her.

This is too good a joke against the clique to be forgotten; and the result is that poor Clara and Joachim and company are now regarded as a ridiculous little mutual-admiration gang of snobs. I entreat our snorting young lions to reconsider that harsh judgment. If they had heard Clara Schumann at her best, they could not think of her in that way. She and her clique were snobs, no doubt; but so are we all, more or less. There are many virtues mixed up with snobbery; and the clique was entirely sincere in its snobbery, and thought it was holding up a noble ideal on the art it loved. Wagner was about as eligible for it as a 450 h.p. aeroplane engine for a perambulator.

It was much the same at first with Elgar and the London branch of the clique. A young man from the west country without a musical degree, proceeding calmly and sweetly on the unconscious assumption that he was by nature and destiny one of the great composers, when, as a matter of fact, he had never heard of the supertonic, shocked and irritated the clique very painfully. It was not, of course, Elgar's fault. He pitied them, and was quite willing to shew them how a really handy man (they were the unhandiest of mortals) should write for the trombones, tune the organ, flyfish, or groom and harness and drive a horse. He could talk about every unmusical subject on earth, from pigs to Elizabethan literature.

A certain unmistakeably royal pride and temper was getatable on occasion; but normally a less pretentious person than Elgar could not be found. To this day you may meet him and talk to him for a week without suspecting that he is anything more than a very typical English country gentleman who does not know a fugue from a *fandango*. The landlady in Pickwick whose complaint of her husband was that "Raddle aint like a man" would have said, if destiny had led her to the altar with the composer of the great symphony in A flat, "Elgar aint like a musician." The clique took Mrs Raddle's view. And certainly Elgar's music acted very differently from theirs. His Enigma Variations took away your breath. The respiration induced by their compositions was perfectly regular, and occasionally perfectly audible.

That attitude towards him was speedily reduced to absurdity by the mere sound of his music. But some initial incredulity as to his genius may be excused when we recollect that England had waited two hundred years for a great English composer, and waited in vain. The phenomenon of greatness in music had vanished from England with Purcell. Musical facility had survived abundantly. England had maintained a fair supply of amazingly dexterous and resourceful orchestral players, brassbandsmen, organists, glee singers, and the like. But they lacked culture, and could not produce a really musical atmosphere for the local conductors who tried to organize them. And the only alternatives were the university musicians who made up the metropolitan cliques, gentlemen amateurs to a man, infatuated with classical music, and earnestly striving to compose it exactly as the great composers did. And that, of course, was no use at all. Elgar had all the dexterities of the bandsmen; sucked libraries dry as a child sucks its mother's breasts; and gathered inspiration from the skies. Is it any wonder that we were skeptical of such a miracle? For my part, I expected nothing from any English composer; and when the excitement about Gerontius began, I said wearily, "Another Wardour-street festival oratorio!" But when I heard the Variations (which had not attracted me to the concert) I sat up and said, "Whew!" I knew we had got it at last.

Since then English and American composers have sprung up like mushrooms: that is, not very plentifully, but conspicuously. The clique is, if not dead, toothless; and our Cyril Scotts and Percy

Graingers, our Rutland Boughtons and Granville Bantocks and the rest pay not the smallest attention to its standard. The British Musical Society offers to name forty British composers of merit without falling back on Elgar or any member of his generation. But, so far, Elgar alone is for Westminster Abbey.

As I said to begin with, neither I nor any living man can say with certainty whether these odds and ends which I have been able to relate about Elgar are the stigmata of what we call immortality. But they look to me very like it; and I give them accordingly for what they may prove to be worth.

The Future of
British Music

The Outlook, 19 and 26 July 1919 (*)

It has never been possible for modern British composers to live by the practice of the higher forms of their art in their own country; but until 1914 Germany provided a market which enabled them to produce a symphony with at least some hope of having it performed and even published. That is now at an end. Performances of British music in Germany have ceased; and remittances are cut off. Thus British composers who have obtained a hearing in that country are suffering seriously from a closing of the most important source of their incomes from classic work; and the economic inducement to our younger composers to keep British music in the front rank of culture no longer exists.

This situation is not creditable to us as a nation. And it has arisen at a moment when the introduction of compulsory military service and the waging of a long war has dealt a heavy blow to the fine arts. To realize the weight of that blow it is necessary to consider what the state of music would have been if Sebastian Bach had been engaged in the Thirty Years War, and Mozart, Beethoven, and Wagner sent to the trenches for the few years (no longer than the duration of the present war) during which they produced, respectively, Don Giovanni, Figaro, the Jupiter Symphony and its successors in G minor and E flat, the Eroica Symphony and the Emperor Concerto, and the Ring Poem and the scores of Das Rheingold and Die Walküre. Such a sacrifice to militarism would have left the world three centuries behindhand in musical development. Yet an instalment of that sacrifice befell British music during the war. We were so little conscious of it that attempts to persuade tribunals that the composition of serious music is work of national importance were received with derision. Almost in the same week we saw one energetic young composer and organizer of musical festivals sneered at and sent into the army by the tribunal in a leading English city, and another

356

exempted elsewhere with something like awe because he had once composed a popular waltz.

Such a state of public opinion is inexcusable in a civilized country once famous throughout Europe for the quality of its music. Yet it has lasted for two centuries, which may be reckoned as the dark ages of British music. During that time musicians have supported themselves by giving piano lessons to young ladies without serious musical intentions, or by composing drawing-room ballads, or as church organists by accompanying hymns and "sacred music" which seldom rose above the level of Jackson's Te Deum. Sterndale Bennett, for example, with a promise as bright and a character as high as Mendelssohn's, was sterilized by a lifetime of drudgery as a piano teacher.

The notion that musical genius is independent of the substantial encouragements which attract men towards other careers is strikingly contradicted by the history of music in England. It is true that British composers of a sort survived when the overwhelming pecuniary temptations of the industrial revolution turned the genius of England to commerce in the eighteenth century; but the outstanding fact about them is that they wrote no British music except trivial drawing-room music or vulgar dance music with less national character than their knives and forks. In the higher departments they produced shoddy Handel, a little Mozart and water, and, finally, a great deal of secondhand Mendelssohn and Spohr. They expressed nothing of the British character or the British imagination: all that their scores convey to us is their love of foreign music and their vain ambition to become great composers by imitating it. With the exception of a few sturdily unfashionable Britons like Pearsall, who kept up the old tradition in his motets and madrigals, our composers posed as Germans as ridiculously as our singers posed as Italians. And the main reason clearly was that it is not in the British character, if indeed it be in any sound character, to accept success in art at the cost of poverty and contempt in the common life of the nation. Under such circumstances art will be practiced only by those who are infatuated with their love of music (the character of the amateur), or who are good for nothing else—and it is a disastrous mistake to suppose that the great artists are good for nothing else. Yet it is a very common mistake: it is even considered a mark of soulful enlightenment in artistic matters to believe that if Phidias had been born an Andaman Islander and Beethoven a Patagonian, they would have produced the Parthenon and the Ninth Symphony by inspiration. Genius, it is supposed, will bridge all chasms and vanquish all difficulties, the inevitable result being that England tends towards the condition of Patagonia or the Andaman Islands as far as the higher forms of music are concerned. Under this false, mean, lazy, and stupid assumption that it is sordid and Philistine to regard music as a product of national respect for it, and national practical encouragement of and inducement to it, classical music is left to "irresistible vocation," and perishes accordingly. Even the really irresistible vocations, such as Mozart's or Elgar's, are dependent on the quite easily resistible ones. Mozart could not have occurred except in a Europe in which there had been many generations of thousands of commonplace musicians whose vocation was by no means irresistible, and many of whom had been driven to the first study of their art by blows. Michael Angelo could not have occurred in the England of his day, and did not. He was the product of a great craft of masonry, and of a magnificent patronage of its artistic application. There is not a single case in the whole history of art in which artists have produced the greatest work of which art is capable except as a final step in an elaborate civilization built up and maintained by a multitude of citizens, mostly amateurs employing professional artists of whom not one-tenth [of one] per cent. were original geniuses, but all accepting fine art as an indispensable element in the greatness of States and the glory of God.

Public opinion must be roused to the need for providing in England the conditions in which it will be possible for Englishmen, after a lapse of two centuries, once more to express themselves in genuinely British music with a weight and depth possible only in the higher forms of music. Here there is no question of the sort of "national music" that is produced by forcing music into local dance forms, or into the pseudo-modes which can be imitated by omitting those intervals of our scale which could not be played on primitive forms of the bag-pipe or the harp. All such *bric-à-brac* already receives more than enough encouragement. The language and instrumentation of music are now international; and what is meant by British music is music in which British musicians express their British character in that international language. When Elgar startled us by suddenly reasserting the British character in music he did it in an idiom which was no more distinctively English than the idiom of

Schumann; but Schumann could not, or rather would not, have written ten bars of an Elgar symphony.

The needs of the situation may be roughly summed up as more performances, more publication, and more advertisement. Taking the [last], how many people are aware of the fact that the British Isles can put into the field about forty living composers of serious music without counting those nineteenth-century composers whose names are well known to the public, such as Elgar, Stanford, Parry, Cowen, Bantock, Delius, and others? It is not only possible to find enthusiastic musical amateurs who do not know this, but positively difficult to find any who do know it. Our resources must be advertized.

The most effective advertisements of the fine arts are the performances and exhibitions attended by the critics who deal with them in the press. Mere commerce is never up to date in this matter. The pioneering must be done by societies of enthusiasts. If our critics of the drama know something more of modern dramatic literature than can be picked up by attending commercial performances, they owe their knowledge to the efforts of private societies such as the Stage Society and the Pioneer Players. If there were no other picture exhibitions than those of the Royal Academy, the modern developments of painting would not exist either for the critics or for the public. If the commercial concert-givers are ever to insist on their conductors undertaking the labor of studying new works by troublesome young men, they must be sharply criticized for their neglect, and made to feel that programs without a single novelty, whether British or foreign, are ridiculous. Before the critics can be expected to do that, societies like the British Music Society must bring the new work to their knowledge.

And the performances cannot be followed up unless the music is published at reasonable prices in vocal score or in transcription for the piano in two-handed and four-handed arrangements or in pianola rolls; for it remains as true now as when Wagner said it that music is kept alive on the cottage pianos of the amateurs, and not by commercial performances.

What the British Music Society may be able to do in these directions will depend on the support it receives. It is impossible to feel very sanguine in the face of such facts as the influentially launched Shakespear Memorial National Theatre scheme with, as a result of years of expensive agitation, a single subscription of £70,000 from a

German gentleman, or the ruthless seizure during the war of the public picture galleries throughout the country for the commonest office purposes, culminating in a shameless attempt, which fortunately collapsed through some accident at the last moment, to crown the sacrifice by the seizure of the British Museum. These things, be it noted, happened at a moment when we were claiming to be the champions of European civilization against Hunnish barbarism. When at last the Armistice came, what was it that sprang to the front to demand restoration and reconstruction as the first relief and recreation brought by our victory? Racing, hunting, football, cricket. Not a word about music, though perhaps the most ridiculous incident that relieved the tragedy of the war had been the demand for the instant exclusion of German music from the programs of the Promenade Concerts, which, being at once effected amid patriotic cheers, resulted in empty concert rooms for a week, at the end of which an unparalleled outburst of Beethoven and Wagner crowded them again. It need not be said harshly and uppishly that all this is disgraceful to us. But it will be said, and indeed must be said, that it makes our pretensions to be a cultured nation (not, to be quite just, that we often make such pretensions, or seem to be the least bit ashamed of ourselves) so absurd that we ourselves have to laugh heartily at them like the cheerful savages we are on that plane.

During the war we borrowed our music not only from Germany but from Russia. This is a sort of borrowing for which an honest nation should pay in kind. If we have to borrow tea from China and pay for it in hardware, we can at least plead that our soil will not produce tea. Now music it *can* produce. It has done it before and can do it again. The stuff is there waiting for a market to make it worth mining. It is kept waiting because we are a people of low pleasures. And we are a people of low pleasures because we are brought up to them: the British workman finds the public-house and the football field offering themselves to him insistently at every turn; and the British gentleman is actually forced to spend his boyish leisure at cricket and football before he enters an adult society in which he cannot escape hunting, shooting, bridge, and billiards, though he can go through life as a complete gentleman without hearing a Beethoven sonata in any other form than that of a disagreeable noise which he forbids his daughters to make in the schoolroom except during the hours when he is usually out of doors. If you eliminate smoking and the element of gambling, you will be amazed to find that almost all an Englishman's pleasures can be, and mostly are, shared by his dog.

Why is this state of things described always as "healthy"? Simply because there are worse pleasures in ambush for human leisure in our civilization. Compulsory perpetual athletics at school are to send the boy to bed too tired for mischief. The meet in the hunting field is better than the meet in Picadilly Circus. But what is the worth of a society which has to resort to such barbarous shifts? Are not the Muses always there to give our leisure the most delightful entertainment, and to refine our tastes and strengthen our intellects at the same time? We banish them, and then find that we must resort to the occupations of greyhounds and ferrets, and the migrations of birds, to rescue us from the snares of the pestilential rivals of the Muses.

It is a pitiful state of things; and I, for one, wish the British Music Society luck in its resolve to educate, agitate, and organize against it in the sacred names of Euterpe and Polyhymnia, Thalia and Terpsichore. I am tired of being suspected of being no gentleman because I am more interested in these goddesses than in the mares in the stables of those of my friends who represent the culture of the Empire.

Index of Names and Compositions

This index provides brief identifications of some of the composers, performers, and authors who were relatively well known in Shaw's day but are now obscure.